THE
SKY PIRATES

THE
SKY PIRATES

JAMES A. AREY

CHARLES SCRIBNER'S SONS / NEW YORK

5
—
90

3 3759 00071 3125

For,
   Elizabeth Ann . . .

CONTENTS

1/THE SKYJACK TAPES:
  ANATOMY OF A HIJACKING   1

2/TAKE ME TO HAVANA   49

3/FLY THE FRIENDLY SKIES OF THE PFLP   75

4/LOSERS: SQUARE PEGS AND OTHER MISFITS   97

5/EMOTIONAL DISASTER CASES:
  THE SICK AT HEART AND SUICIDAL   127

6/CRIMINALS: FUGITIVES FROM THE LAW   146

7/POLITICS IN THE SKY   182

8/THE WORLD FIGHTS BACK   215

9/NO HAVEN ANYWHERE   248

10/WE'VE COME A LONG WAY, BUT . . .   268

11/TOMORROW THE WORLD?   284

EPILOGUE: AND THE WAR GOES ON   307

ACKNOWLEDGMENTS   312

APPENDICES   315

THE
SKY PIRATES

1 / THE SKYJACK TAPES: ANATOMY OF A HIGHJACKING

Will Gerken is a cool, composed, unflappable man. He has to be. As a schedule control manager for Pan American World Airways, he keeps tabs on some 172 jetliners operating daily over 85,000 miles of route structure around the world. Gerken is one of an elite corps of men who work concentrated eight-hour shifts in a "war room" type of office in a Pan American hangar at John F. Kennedy International Airport. These men are like master puppeteers guiding huge airplanes between New York and London . . . Rome and Beirut . . . Hong Kong and Bangkok . . . Caracas and Buenos Aires. . . .

On September 6, 1970, the string broke on Flight 93.

Gerken leaned over a closed-circuit teletype machine linking his office with the Pan Am dispatcher at London's Heathrow Airport 3,456 miles away. A message rattled out on the machine:

AFTER DEPARTURE AMSTERDAM FLIGHT 93/06SEP SUFFERED 9052 REPEAT 9052 AND PROCEEDING MIDEAST STOP FINAL DESTINATION NOT KNOWN BUT LAST WORD REPORT CAPTAIN FILED FLIGHT PLAN FOR BEIRUT STOP WILL KEEP YOU ADVISED STOP.

9052—the code for aircraft hijacking.

A shock wave went through the control center. The Middle East? This one looked bad. But Gerken was not altogether surprised. The hijacking of Pan Am Flight 93 made a sort of sense to him. He had even half-suspected that something like this might happen—because only minutes before, London dispatch had passed along word that an El Al 707 had been commandeered . . . as had a Swissair DC-8. Later, word was to be received that a TWA 707 was under the guns of hijackers also.

There was a uniqueness about the takeover of Pan Am Flight 93 in the midst of this series of hijackings. Flight 93 was a Boeing 747, the giant of the airways—all 712,000 pounds of it—two and a half times bigger than anything else in the air.

Details of the hijackings began to unfold.

Sunday, September 6, 1970.
Pan American Schedule Control Center log:

FINAL DESTINATION FLIGHT 93 STILL NOT KNOWN BUT LAST REPORT AIRCRAFT DIVERTED BEIRUT AND NOW HOLDING OVERHEAD BEIRUT AWAITING WORD FROM HIJACKERS AS TO DESTINATION.

Monitored radio transmission between PAA Clipper *Fortune*, Flight 93, and Pan American flight operations, Beirut Airport:

CAPTAIN CALLING PANOP: Have somebody there to translate a message.
DISPATCH [PANOP]: Go ahead with your message.
HIJACKER IN COCKPIT: Panop Beirut—I want a responsible official from the Popular Front to be in your office so that I can talk to him.
DISPATCH: Do you have a telephone number?
HIJACKER: No, I do not have a telephone number.
DISPATCH: Thanks. Please wait a little.

This was the seventh hijacking in Pan American history and the first since August 2 of that year. Not a bad score. But for the world it was only one of four skyjackings committed in one day. In New York time, this was the schedule:

7:17 A.M. A Trans World Airlines Boeing 707, attempting to fly from Frankfurt, West Germany, to New York, is hijacked near Zagreb, Yugoslavia, and diverted to some country presumably sympathetic to the Arab cause.

7:30 A.M. An El Al Boeing 707, en route from Tel Aviv to New York via Amsterdam, is hijacked somewhere over or near the North Sea in an attempt to divert it to—probably—Amman.

8:14 A.M. A Swissair DC-8, flying from Zurich to New York, is hijacked near Luxeuil, France, and forcibly turned toward a desert landing strip in the Middle East.

10:00 A.M. A Pan American Boeing 747 is commandeered on its way out of Amsterdam.

It was rumored, and then quickly confirmed, that the Arab guerrilla group calling itself the Popular Front for the Liberation of Palestine was claiming credit for all these attempts.

Pan American Clipper 93 took off from Amsterdam on September 6, 1970, shortly before 10 o'clock in the morning, New York time. It was late, having been late in from Brussels, but nobody seemed particularly concerned by that. (Its lateness should have helped it to avoid disaster, but unfortunately the warning message that came just before takeoff was not explicit enough to be of value.) The jumbo jet was bound for New York after its Amsterdam stop, and carried a load of 152 passengers and 17 crew. Captain John Priddy commanded. Among the passengers were Captain Priddy's wife, Valerie, four members of a deadheading crew captained by Paul La Chapelle, and two young men, purportedly students, who had been declined passage by El Al.

To anyone who had never before seen a 747, Clipper *Fortune* (Flight 93) looked awesomely enormous and somehow invulnerable. Invulnerable it was not, but enormous it certainly was: a big, beautiful piece of high-precision equipment worth about $24 million and capable of carrying 210 more passengers than it had aboard. The relatively light booking turned out to be a fortunate circumstance when it came to debarkation time. If there had been more people aboard, evacuation would necessarily have been slower and perhaps less orderly.

The flight from Brussels to Amsterdam had been routine. The rest of the trip was not. Only a few minutes after a more or less uneventful departure from Amsterdam's Schiphol Airport, any resemblance to a routine flight suddenly disintegrated. Flight schedule controllers at Pan Am's schedule control center in New York, logging Pan Am's operations all over the world, found themselves setting down on their log sheets one of the most mind-bending stories in aviation history. In their terse and cryptic way—"AFTER DEPT AMS SUFFERED 9052"—they took routine note of a happening that was to reverberate around the world. Their notes, translated slightly from professional jargon to layman's English, form the outline of the story that follows.

Most of the details of the story are provided by an on-the-ball ham radio enthusiast who monitored and recorded all radio conversations that took place between PAA Flight 93 and persons at Beirut Airport. Speaking from the cockpit were Captain John Priddy and the hijackers; speaking from the ground were Pan American flight control/operations personnel, Lebanese government and army officials, and representatives of the Popular Front for the Liberation of Palestine (PFLP). The radio communications, extraordinary though they may seem, are unquestionably authentic. They have necessarily been edited down to manageable length, and—for the most part—translated from colloquial Arabic to literal English, with perhaps some loss of flavor, but they are nonetheless the genuine article.

The ham in question prefers not to be publicly identified because he was monitoring and taping the air-to-ground-to-air transmissions without official government permission, but he is known to the author by name, address, profession, and reputation. Fellow hams may be interested to know that he used, in conducting the recording, a Pye Bantam, Gonset Communicator, Xtal Converter with Collins KWM-2, TEAC 20, and Sony TC-120 and TC-350 tape recorders.

On-the-spot observations were offered later by Captain John Priddy in person.

The radio communications continue:

AIRCRAFT CALLING PANOP: Put the Arabic-speaking man back on.
DISPATCH: Go ahead.
HIJACKER: Brother—have you made contact with any of the responsible officials?
DISPATCH: We are now in contact with a responsible official, and shall communicate with you on this same frequency when he comes to the office.
HIJACKER: Thanks. Who do you have in the office with you? Is there a Lebanese responsible official or a policeman with you?
DISPATCH: Only Pan American personnel are here. . . . Do you want one of the officials to talk to you?
HIJACKER: Yes.
DISPATCH: Okay, wait a second.

Schedule Control Center log entries:

	SUMMARY—AIRCRAFT STILL HOLDING OVERHEAD BEIRUT. (Log notes all Greenwich Mean Time.)
1835Z	NEH [Najeeb E. Halaby, President of Pan American] ADVISED HE HAS JCL [a high-ranking Pan Am official, expert in international law] WORKING THROUGH HIS CONTACTS.
1840	CALLED SEELEY STATE DEPARTMENT DUTY OFFICER ADVISED HIM GENERAL CONTENT OF 061840

[telegram, datelined 1840 Greenwich Time of the 06 September, representing official notification of the hijacking].

1845 KONIĞ [Hans A. M. Koniğ, Airport Services Manager for Pan American in Amsterdam] SAID THAT 2 PASSENGERS RECEIVED FROM EL AL BY ENDORSE-MENT DUE EL AL CLAIMED THEY OVERSOLD FIRST CLASS. NAMES OF PAXS LISTED AS (1) DIOP (2) GUEYE, SENEGALESE. BOOKED AMSTERDAM/JFK, THEN SANTIAGO CHILE. TICKETS PURCHASED AND CONFIRMED FROM EL AL.

1855 ISRAELI DESK STATE DEPARTMENT CALLED TO ADVISE THAT EL AL HAD REFUSED PASSAGE TO 2 PAXS BELIEVED NOW ON PAA.

1918 ADVISED SEELEY STATE DEPARTMENT THAT AIR-CRAFT ARRIVED BEY [Beirut] AWAITING ARRIVAL NLF [National Liberation Front] REPRESENTATIVE. CAPTAIN IN CONTACT PANOP [Pan American Flight Control/Operations in Beirut]. HIJACKER IN CON-TACT BEY VIA TOWER FREQUENCY 118.1.

The prologue of the story now begins to reveal itself as in a series of flashbacks. El Al had taken a long second look at two of its own previously ticketed passengers due to board at Amsterdam for JFK, decided that they did not like what they were seeing, and regretfully informed the two young gentlemen that first class was oversold. However, El Al said helpfully, some other carrier would surely be able to accommodate them. Among the possibilities was a Pan American flight leaving for New York on the day of their desired departure, and they would check at once to see if there was space available on Pan Am or any other flight leaving for the U.S.A. The tickets of the two passengers were then given an "open endorsement," which meant they could present themselves at any ticket counter at any time of any day and, if there was space available, be admitted passage.

As it happened, there was space available on Pan Am's jumbo jet—Flight 93—and they took it.

Flight 93 duly taxied away from the ramp with the two rejects from El Al comfortably aboard, somewhat overawed by the size of the 747 but nevertheless prepared to cope.

But Pan Am ticket-counter agents had by this time become suspicious of the "open endorsement" ticket coupons and realized the possibility that a pair of undesirable passengers might be aboard Flight 93. The Schiphol Airport police were notified immediately. The police did not attach a great deal of importance to the matter, although the attempt on El Al's Flight 219 had already taken place. Since Flight 93 had left the departure gate, they informed the control tower that two passengers onboard the Pan Am 747 had been refused passage by El Al. They did not mention any concrete reason for suspicion, nor did they tie in this alert with the El Al seizure. The Amsterdam control tower thus could forward only a very vague warning to Captain Priddy.

As Captain Priddy afterward described it: "They had already cleared us and told us to hold our position for landing traffic, and we were sitting there waiting for an airplane to land before we could take off when the guy on takeoff frequency said, 'Change over to ground control for a minute—they have a message for you.' I called ground control, and they said, 'We have just been informed that there are two passengers on your flight that were refused passage by El Al.' So we said, 'For what reason?' They said, 'We have no idea.'

"Anyway, we got the names of the two passengers—Diop and Gueye. I called the flight director up and asked if he knew these guys, and he said, 'No, I don't.' So the first officer said he'd try to find out something on the radio, and I said, 'Well, let's go down and talk to them.' And we went downstairs and paged these guys. We went through first class, and we walked all the way through to the back of the airplane and across and back up the other aisle, and nobody said anything, so we paged them again. When we got back into first class, these two guys said, 'Hey, that's us.' They were sitting in the last row of seats in first class in the middle.

"So I talked to them for a while. I figured I didn't have any right to search them. I didn't know what I was looking for, anyway. They were pretty well dressed and they spoke pretty good English. We talked for a few minutes. I said, 'Well, there's been some sort of misunderstanding, but I'll either have to take you back or give you the option of being searched.' So they said,

'Well, if you want to search us, go ahead.' So I did. I searched them, and they had two little Samsonite briefcases with just some papers in, and that was all. So I apologized and said we were very sorry, that apparently there was some mistake, and then we went back up front and took off. And then—!

"Some of the passengers later said that the two guys had been sitting in the third row of the first class seats on the starboard side, and after we started paging them they moved back to the last row of seats. So whether they left the stuff up front I don't know, or whether they had crotch holsters I don't know—I'd never heard of a crotch holster until the FBI told me about it. But when we saw them later, they each had a revolver and they each had a hand grenade."

At the time, and for a while afterward, it seemed that Diop and Gueye had made a last-minute transfer from El Al to Pan Am. But when the details began to emerge, it became apparent that they had originally booked their tickets with El Al some ten days earlier. El Al security officers had been dubious of them and had arranged to have them watched.

Captain Priddy: "Apparently El Al had their reasons to be suspicious. These men were on Senegalese passports, which were probably phonies, and they were going to South America via New York when it would have been a hell of a lot cheaper to go direct. They bought first-class tickets and paid in cash, which was unusual for guys claiming to be students. And they were one-way tickets. So I guess there were a lot of things that set El Al to thinking. They had reason to be suspicious—Israel was at war with the Arabs. So they took their reservations but said they couldn't confirm them. Then some time later they called them and said they were very sorry—all their flights were full. So El Al put an open endorsement on the tickets, and these guys made their reservation with Pan Am about three days before the flight."

This gave them sufficient time to plan the hijacking of Flight 93. As professional hijackers, they had contingency instructions on what to do in case of the failure of Plan A. Unfortunately for the two hijackers who did manage to slip through the El Al security net, there was no time to find replacements for Diop and Gueye on El Al Flight 219.

It was only when the El Al plane was seized, following the

TWA hijacking, that El Al security officers suddenly realized the possible implications of Diop and Gueye's presence on the Pan Am flight. And the warning, when it finally came through the Amsterdam airport police, was too little and too late.

Captain Priddy was communicating with PANOP, London, explaining how he had searched the two passengers without finding anything when the two men burst into the cockpit. For the rest of the trip either one or both of the hijackers remained in the observer's seat behind the captain.

Captain Priddy: "They had the pin pulled on a grenade, whichever one was in there at the time—it was mostly Gueye— and they sat there like that through the whole flight. That was the one big deterring factor to anything we might have tried to do. There's a machete sitting in back of the cockpit. . . . It would have been very simple to split him wide open—but what would have happened six seconds after his muscles relaxed? The idea of those things going off—that kind of got to you, you know. In fact, he was flipping the pin around his finger there once and he dropped it on the floor—Jesus! The engineer has a flashlight in there, and he's down on the floor looking for this bloody thing, you know. . . . I heard this commotion and looked around, and I said, 'What the hell's going on?' And he says, 'Never mind, keep flyin', I'll find it.' " (And Captain Priddy laughs in retrospect.)

Soon after the takeover, the hijackers told Priddy that they wanted him to head for Beirut. "Are we going to land there?" asked Priddy. "I don't know," said Gueye. "I'll tell you when we get there. I have to talk to my people on the ground."

Captain Priddy was perfectly happy to go to Beirut, so long as he was under hijack and had no hope of heading for New York. He felt that once they were on the ground the hijackers would let the people go.

Captain Priddy: "Of course, I didn't realize the whole plot. I didn't know that they had hijacked the other airplanes, or why, or anything like that. So actually I *wanted* to land at Beirut, and when we got there I tried to force them into a landing, because I thought I could talk them into turning everybody loose."

So they went to Beirut and held overhead for over two hours. The Lebanese government did not want Clipper 93 to land; they wanted no part of this affair.

Radio communication between Clipper 93 and PANOP, Beirut:

DISPATCH CALLING CLIPPER 93: Clipper 93 from PANOP BEY—I have a message to relay to the gentleman talking in Arabic on the radio.

HIJACKER: Okay, go ahead.

DISPATCH: I have a telegram from Mr. Najeeb Halaby, Chairman of Pan American World Airways from the United States of America, which reads as follows: "Mr. Najeeb Halaby requests hijackers permit his flight to land Beirut for safety of passengers and for cause of freedom and that there are no provisions in any other location this area to deplane passengers safely and comfortably."

(At this point, down on the ground, A. Bedran, deputy manager of the Beirut International Airport, and Colonel Salloum of the Lebanese army enter the operations office and request Pan Am operations personnel to tell the aircraft *not* to land at Beirut. PANOP has no chance to relay this message.)

HIJACKER: We are going to land it at Beirut. However, before landing, we want you to comply with the condition that no one is to approach the aircraft excepting for a responsible official from the Popular Front. Inform the authorities in Beirut, Lebanon, that we shall land at Beirut, but if any attempt is made to approach the aircraft we will destroy it. I repeat, inform the Lebanese authorities that we shall land at Beirut Airport and that if any attempt is made to approach the aircraft we will destroy it.

DEPUTY AIRPORT MANAGER BEDRAN TALKING TO HIJACKER: For your information, the main runway at Beirut Airport is closed at the present time due to work in progress. The other runway cannot tolerate the weight of the Boeing 747. We suggest that the aircraft be directed to Damascus Airport, which airport is presently ready to receive this type of aircraft.

HIJACKER: We will not land at Damascus Airport, but will land at Beirut Airport. Did you hear? I will not land at Damascus, but will land at Beirut Airport. Answer, answer! We will land at Beirut Airport and will not land at any other airport unless contact is established with a responsible official from the Popular Front. I want an answer.

DEPUTY AIRPORT MANAGER: We are in contact—attempting to contact—the Popular Front to send a representative to the airport.

Therefore, please fly overhead Beirut until contact is established and agreement reached to head to another airport as Beirut Airport is not technically ready to receive this aircraft.

(Deputy Airport Manager Bedran and Colonel Salloum leave the operations office to contact a representative of the PFLP.)

DISPATCH CALLING CLIPPER 93: The airport authorities are now trying to contact a representative from the party of these men aboard, and until then please hold overhead.

CAPTAIN: Okay, we will hold overhead Beirut and will be standing by on this frequency for the arrival of the party involved.

DISPATCH: Okay, thank you.

HIJACKER: I want to give you a message—do you hear me?

DISPATCH: Yes.

HIJACKER: In case this aircraft lands at Beirut Airport, I repeat for the third time, if any attempt is made by any person, policeman, or military to approach the aircraft we will blast it. We have sufficient quantity of dynamite to totally destroy the aircraft.

DISPATCH: Contact has been established with a representative from the Popular Front, and in ten minutes' time he will be at the airport to talk to you.

HIJACKER: The Popular Front for the Liberation of Palestine. The party of George Habash.

DISPATCH: We confirm—and in ten minutes' time he will be at the airport.

HIJACKER: May I know his name?

DISPATCH: Please wait a second. We are inquiring about his name. Will contact you over the radio when I get his name.

HIJACKER: Didn't you obtain his name *yet?*

DISPATCH: We are still waiting. An airport official has gone to get the name of the person or representative who is coming over to talk to you, so we are still awaiting his return to the office. Our information is that in a matter of minutes the representative will be here and will communicate with you on this radio then.

(They all wait. The deputy airport manager returns to the operations office and transmits a request to the aircraft to switch frequency in order to communicate with the airport authorities and the Popular Front representative.)

CAPTAIN: Clipper 93 to PANOP—did you copy? What is the progress in contacting the responsible party?

DISPATCH: I have the airport authorities office . . . [garbled] . . . and they said that the representative is on the way . . . [garbled] . . . and that they moved up to the control tower room in order to run the conversation with the party on board your flight on frequency 118.9.

CAPTAIN: Understand.

DISPATCH: Everybody is still standing by.

CAPTAIN: Many thanks.

(Another pause. Then the deputy airport manager advises the hijacker from the tower that the PFLP representatives are coming down from Bhamdoun, a summer resort to the north of Beirut on the mountain road leading to Damascus. The distance is about a half-hour's driving time from the airport. Some of those listening in begin to suspect that the local PFLP representatives might not have been completely prepared for the arrival of the hijacker at this time and place and with such a gigantic trophy.)

TOWER: . . . From Bhamdoun to Beirut takes some time, therefore we are obliged to make you wait for some time.

HIJACKER: Okay, thanks.

(In the cockpit, Captain Priddy comments on the delay. He says to Gueye: It's taking them a long time to get those people." Gueye, not yet anxious, answers: "Well, you know the traffic in Beirut on a Sunday night . . .")

TOWER: For information, as we have stated earlier, the only one main runway is completely closed for over a month, and of the second runway the first 700 meters are unserviceable. It is extremely difficult for the 747 to land at the airport here.

HIJACKER: We will look into this matter.

TOWER: We have contacted Damascus Airport and they informed us that all their runways are in good condition and can receive this type of aircraft.

HIJACKER (agitated): Who contacted Damascus Airport? Who contacted Damascus Airport?

TOWER: The local authorities in Beirut have direct contact with Damascus Airport.

HIJACKER (now sounding extremely nervous and excited): Has this contact been made under the supervision of a representative from the Popular Front?

TOWER: No—because he has not arrived yet. We inquired from them for information only.

HIJACKER: Therefore we will not abide by anything pending the arrival of a responsible representative.

TOWER: We are awaiting.

HIJACKER: Is it possible for me to know the name of the person talking to me at the present time on this line?

TOWER: Deputy airport manager Beirut on duty is the person talking to you now.

HIJACKER: Can I ask you some questions?

TOWER: Go ahead.

HIJACKER: An El Al aircraft was hijacked today from . . . [garbled] . . . en route to London—where did it land?

TOWER: It looks like it has landed at London.

HIJACKER: Who is responsible for its hijacking?

TOWER: Oh . . . by God, we don't know, excepting that it has landed at London at the present time.

HIJACKER: Thanks.

(Over the PANOP frequency the captain discusses with Dispatch the possibility and practicability of a landing in Baghdad. The chances there do not look good. Neither Baghdad Airport nor the handling airline, Iraqi Airways, is equipped to handle the 747.)

CAPTAIN TO PANOP: Advise Iraqi Airways here in Beirut that we may require assistance when we get there—if we go there—from their company.

DISPATCH: Okay. I have all concerned here in the office, and as soon as we know of the decision we will rush for immediate action.

HIJACKER TO TOWER: We are still awaiting the arrival of the representative.

TOWER TO HIJACKER: We are still awaiting their arrival.

HIJACKER: Is there not a telephone to contact them?

TOWER: We have contacted the responsible authorities and they in turn contacted them. They advised they were coming over from Bhamdoun to Beirut and we are still awaiting their arrival.

HIJACKER (impatient now): How long ago has this been done?—ten minutes, half an hour ago, how long ago?

TOWER: I again repeat that the airport here is not technically ready to receive the aircraft.

HIJACKER: I repeat too—I will not enter into any discussion about this point unless a responsible representative from the Popular Front comes over.

TOWER: We are in accord concerning this and are still awaiting. . . . We have attempted to make contact again and were informed that he is on his way to the airport.

(The waiting and the holding continue. The hijacker makes a tentative inquiry as to the technical capability of Cairo Airport to receive the 747. Then, about an hour and a half after the initial contact, a car drives into the airport grounds. A man gets out and heads for the tower.)

TOWER: To American aircraft—for your information a member from the Liberation Front has arrived and in a few minutes will start communicating with you. . . . A responsible official from the Popular Front will talk to you now and his name is Abou-Khaled.

PARTY REPRESENTATIVE ABOU-KHALED FROM TOWER: Hello, hello!

HIJACKER: Yes, go ahead.

ABOU-KHALED: Hello, hello, this is Abou-Khaled speaking—do you hear me?

HIJACKER: Who?

ABOU-KHALED: Walid Kaddoura speaking—do you hear me? Hello, who is talking to me? Do you hear me, brother? Who is talking?

HIJACKER: Samir.

ABOU-KHALED: Samir?

HIJACKER: Yes.

(One of the occupational hazards of hijacking is the need to conceal your identity from your victims and the law while revealing it to your comrades. Ordinarily the professional hijacker stocks his vocabulary with code names and code words for use in an air-to-ground meeting with his "people," but due to a quirk of fate this has not been possible for the hijackers of Flight 93. The conversation here is thus a little awkward at times; neither party knows exactly whom he is talking to, and neither wants to use his real name. Yet real names are slipping into the conversation: One of the hijackers, probably Gueye, is actually Samir Abdel Maguid.)

ABOU-KHALED: We have news from Amman that you could not land at the airport there.

HIJACKER: Of course we cannot land there.

ABOU-KHALED: Who is talking, brother? What squad?

HIJACKER: Well . . . do you want to disclose names?

ABOU-KHALED: No, the name of the squad, the name of the squad! You originated from Amsterdam, is that right?

HIJACKER: Yes, from Amsterdam.

ABOU-KHALED: What happened?

HIJACKER: What happened when we entered Amsterdam Airport is that those responsible on the aircraft were suspicious and started to search us but could not find the weapons. When the aircraft took off, its destination was diverted in accordance with instructions we received.

ABOU-KHALED: Can you go to any other place? Can you go to any other place?

HIJACKER: Where do you want us to take it?

ABOU-KHALED: Is there enough fuel?

HIJACKER: Is there enough fuel? I will ask the captain. . . . Hello, hello—he informed us that he has fuel enough for forty minutes.

ABOU-KHALED: Can you go to Amman? Is the fuel sufficient to reach the destined place?

HIJACKER: Yes, it is—but landing is impossible. We can reach the destined place, but landing there is impossible.

Captain Priddy did not know it until much later, but there were already two hijacked planes on the Amman strip, which was "the destined place." The 707 and the DC-8 had barely managed to make safe landings on the desert field. Gueye and Diop, or whatever their names were, knew a great deal about aircraft operation—instrumentation, communication, maps and charts, and the characteristics of a 707 or DC-8 as opposed to those of a larger plane—but there were some things that they did not know.

Captain Priddy: "My only ace in the hole was knowing how much fuel I had aboard. The hijackers didn't really know how much fuel we had, because they couldn't read *all* the instruments. Gueye, by the way, told me this was his third hijacking. . . . Anyway, I was still trying to force a landing at Beirut, so I tried to give them the idea we were running low and would have to land pretty soon. We had a lot more fuel than we told the hijackers we had. Now when they said on the ground that the main runway was closed, this was true. If we had been a 707, we'd have been in Dawson's Field in Amman right now—none of this circling around overhead Beirut. But Gueye was afraid we'd break through the desert crust, so he wanted to talk it over.

"Then we got a message from the company saying they wanted us to go to Amman. Well, Jesus Christ, I don't know what they've got for an airport in Amman, but the last time I went in there was on an Arab Airline DC-9 and they had about a 3,000-foot strip. . . ! And I wasn't about to go through the hills of Amman at night in a 747."

Radio communication between Clipper 93 and Beirut tower:

ABOU-KHALED: Brother, if anything happens to the aircraft there, it does not matter—is this possible?

HIJACKER: It doesn't matter if anything happens to the aircraft there?

ABOU-KHALED: It does not matter if anything happens to the aircraft. It did happen to the TWA's Amman landing to a certain extent but it did not matter.

HIJACKER: Does this mean that we can land there at the destined place . . . ? What I want you to understand is that this is a 747 aircraft and it weighs many times the weight of a 707 aircraft. It is impossible to land at the destined place under any circumstance whatsoever . . . the destined airport definitely cannot stand it, and if it lands there it will be a wreck. . . .

ABOU-KHALED: Do not at all land at Damascus.

HIJACKER: I will certainly not land at Damascus. However, is it possible for me—uh, shall I land at either Cairo Airport or Baghdad

Airport for refueling and then receive new instructions to any destination you want?

ABOU-KHALED: Hold it, brother—hold on the line a little.

(In the tower, Abou-Khaled turns away to listen to Bill Hamad and J. N. Vasquez, respectively Pan Am's deputy airport manager and airport service manager in Beirut. They are attempting to convince him to permit the 747's passengers, or at least the women and children, to disembark.)

HIJACKER: Did you understand what I told you?

ABOU-KHALED: Yes, I heard you, brother. Stay on the line with me, brother—stay on the line.

HIJACKER: I am with you on the line all the time. We want a quick answer in order not to run out of fuel. Time is tight—think quickly!

ABOU-KHALED: I heard you, brother.

HIJACKER: The Captain advises you have to find an answer within twenty minutes because, supposing he wants to go to Baghdad, the fuel will not suffice if he is delayed more than that. So in twenty minutes he would want an answer in order to be able to go to Baghdad Airport and have enough fuel to land there or at any other airport. So I beg of you to give an answer in less than fifteen minutes.

ABOU-KHALED: Within five minutes we will give you an answer, brother.

(Abou-Khaled now directs himself to a Colonel Hamdan and the airport manager, who have joined the group in the tower, and tells them that if they do not give him a decision in minutes, he will issue instructions to the hijacker to blow up the aircraft. The Lebanese officials are extremely reluctant to receive the craft, and the PFLP representative still seems unsure as to how to handle the situation.)

HIJACKER: We are awaiting the instructions from Amman . . . we are ready. . . . We are awaiting instructions only.

ABOU-KHALED TO HIJACKER: The instructions are to refuel and to safeguard the aircraft passengers and within five minutes I will inform you as to where from you can refuel. Only the safeguarding of the aircraft passengers during this period pending receipt of instructions for you.

HIJACKER: I am safeguarding the passengers with utmost care and all are being treated excellently well, and there are no obstacles or problems.

ABOU-KHALED: Well done [garbling] . . .

HIJACKER: Are you ready to talk to me? I want to ask a few questions.

ABOU-KHALED: Go ahead, brother.

HIJACKER: How can I know or what is the proof that you are a member of the Popular Front?

ABOU-KHALED: Abou-Khaled is talking, brother . . . [garbled] . . . Walid Kaddoura. . . .

HIJACKER: Are you alone?

ABOU-KHALED: I am with Abou-Ahmad—"Younes Njeim."

HIJACKER: Who is Abou-Ahmad?

ABOU-KHALED: Younes Njeim, brother. . . . Do you hear me, brother? Ashraf, brother, Ashraf. . . .

HIJACKER: Yeah . . . I know. . . .

ABOU-AHMAD: Hello! Abou-Ahmad talking to you, brother—hold it a moment, he is talking on the phone.

HIJACKER: Okay, I am waiting.

(Colonel Hamdan is on the tower phone talking to Pierre Gemayel, Lebanese Minister of Public Works and Transportation, telling him that the hijackers will blow up the aircraft in the air if they are not allowed to land at Beirut. He asks for permission to let the aircraft land.)

ABOU-KHALED TO HIJACKER: Talk to Abou-Ahmad.

HIJACKER: Hello, Abou-Ahmad—what shall we do? Have you received an answer, or not yet?

ABOU-AHMAD: Abou-Ahmad talking to you. I will give you an answer in three minutes.

HIJACKER: Okay, I am listening to you. . . . [fades out]. Didn't you expect us here, or what? Is that why you cannot give us a quick answer? Four minutes are over, and we are still waiting.

ABOU-AHMAD: They will allow you to land at the airport to refuel, and in forty-five minutes will give you instructions . . . [garbling] . . . aircraft.

HIJACKER: Land at what airport?

ABOU-AHMAD: Instructions will be given to land at Beirut Airport to refuel, which will take forty-five minutes, after which we will give you instructions as to where to go.

HIJACKER: Does this mean that the Lebanese authorities agreed to our landing at Beirut? They said technically the airport was not fit for landing. Did you hear me? I said the Lebanese authorities stated that the airport was not technically fit to receive the aircraft. Shall we land, or is it just . . . ? [fades out].

ABOU-AHMAD: Technically you can land—you can land. The authorities have approved landing at the airport for refueling.

HIJACKER: Please inform them of the following message: "If any attempt is made to approach the aircraft, we will destroy the aircraft completely."

ABOU-AHMAD: Brother—is it possible for me, Abou-Ahmad, and Abou-Khaled to come to the aircraft and reach an agreement with you?

HIJACKER: Please, let us establish some kind of a code between us so that we can identify you. You know it is dark and difficult to identify any person approaching the aircraft. I will not permit any ordinary person to come aboard the aircraft without first being able to identify him.

ABOU-AHMAD: Brother—I am wearing a blue sweater with short sleeves. Abou-Khaled is wearing a gray sweater with long sleeves.

HIJACKER: Okay, agreed. But—the two of you only. I will fire at any other person coming with you.

ABOU-AHMAD: Okay, brother. Only the two of us will come.

HIJACKER: A remark—concerning us on the aircraft, do you have any idea as to how many we are?

ABOU-AHMAD: No, I do not have any idea.

HIJACKER: Do you know who is talking to you?

ABOU-AHMAD: No—who?

HIJACKER: I am astounded that you do not know who is talking to you as long as you know that I originated in Amsterdam.

ABOU-AHMAD: Brother—! It was not planned for you to land at Beirut. Ashraf and Abou-Hani (party leaders in Amman) did not tell you to land at Beirut. This is an emergency—I am not supposed to know. . . .

HIJACKER: I know it is an emergency. We also did not expect it to be a 747.

ABOU-AHMAD: Therefore—it *is* an emergency, and we do not know. . . . [garbling and fadeout].

(It seems to be a case of the left hand not knowing what the other left hand is doing. No one has been prepared for this landing attempt, not even the hijackers themselves. When "Gueye" and "Diop" had their tickets validated over to Pan Am, it did not occur to them that they might find themselves aboard a 747. Now they don't quite know what to do with it, and neither do their comrades on the ground. At this point the chief hijacker is further alarmed by news from Abou-Khaled in the tower that the refueling operation requires "attendance by some workers," who will therefore naturally have to approach the plane. He hotly insists that the two PFLP representatives with whom he has been talking first board the aircraft for a discussion before anyone else approaches the plane or any refueling gets under way. He warns that any attempt to invade the aircraft is bound to result in dire consequences. "You," he tells the tower, "will be responsible." "Understood," replies the tower.)

TOWER: Now, please let me talk to the captain to give him the frequency of contact for radar landing.

HIJACKER: Okay, will pass the captain on to talk to you.

CAPTAIN: Beirut—this is Clipper 93.

TOWER: Okay, Clipper 93—calling for landing—you have to be very smooth on landing and you have to choose either 03 which is landing from over the sea or runway 21 from over the sea. The full length will be available—I mean runway 03. On runway 21 the first 600 meters are to be avoided, and anyhow on runway 03 and 21 there will be a VASI [visual approach slope indicator] which will guide you in for landing.

CAPTAIN: What is the field elevation?

TOWER: The field elevation is eighty-seven feet, sir.

CAPTAIN: Eighty-seven feet okay. What is the wind direction and velocity . . . ?

(Captain Priddy is not particularly concerned about any purported difficulties in landing. Even though main runway 18 really is closed due to work in progress, he knows from his continuing conversation with the tower that available runway length is 3,180 meters, which he regards as plenty. He has also been getting basic navigation data from the Pan Am facility in Frankfurt, so he is not unduly disturbed by the fact that he has no approach plates for Beirut. John Priddy, too, is an unflappable man; in his view, the Lebanese have exaggerated the technical incapacity of the airfield because they do not want the hijacked plane to land on their soil.

While captain and tower discuss landing technicalities, others discuss how the plane is to be received once it lands. Pan Am's airport services manager, J. N. Vasquez, leaves the tower and goes to the operations office to join Harold L. Williams (Pan American's director for Lebanon), representatives of the United States embassy, and the station emergency staff. They are deeply concerned about the passengers and the eventual destination of the plane. There is a semblance of normalcy for a few short moments. Then the party members in the tower, who have now been joined by at least one other brother, suddenly get extremely excited.)

> ABOU-AHMAD FROM TOWER: Do not land pending further instructions! There are army vehicles at the airport—do *not* land now. Hello, hello!
>
> HIJACKER: Go ahead. Hello! Go ahead. . . . Hello—who is talking? Speak in Arabic.
>
> ABOU-AHMAD: There is an aircraft—now army vehicles moving toward it. As for us here, if any attempt is made to approach the aircraft, we will create a problem from our side. We definitely will not permit this to happen. For the time being, postpone the aircraft landing to see this problem with them.

(It seems that an Olympic Airways Boeing 727 on the center taxiway has been mistaken for the hijacked plane and is being surrounded by army trucks, half-tracks, jeeps, and troops. Either that, or the trucks and troops are massing to prevent the landing of the 747, in spite of the permission already given, and the Olympic 727 just happens to be in their path. In either case, the PFLP people become very agitated and tell Colonel Hamdan of the Lebanese army to get those troops and vehicles out of there at once. If they do not pull out, and if they attempt to surround the Pan Am 747 in the same way, the hijackers will be instructed to blow up the aircraft in the air. Furthermore, there are armed commandos ranged in front of the terminal who can be expected to "create a problem" if provoked by army interference. None of this is known to those aboard the aircraft. At 27,000 feet and several miles away they obviously cannot see what is happening at the airport; and for some reason the hijacker does not immediately grasp what his colleague in the tower is trying to tell him.)

HIJACKER [bewildered] : Delay the aircraft landing? Why?

PARTY MEMBER FROM TOWER: In case an attempt is made to approach the aircraft, they are not going to be happy at all.

HIJACKER: Who is attempting to approach the aircraft? Answer! Who is attempting to approach the aircraft? Answer!

PARTY MEMBER FROM TOWER: Can you postpone landing for the time being, brother?

HIJACKER: Why? Give me convincing reasons.

PARTY MEMBER ABOU-AHMAD FROM TOWER: Brother, brother—! Abou-Ahmad is talking to you. We now see on the ramp army vehicles moving here and there. Therefore, any attempt to approach the aircraft from the army will not be tolerated by us at all. So please postpone the landing a few minutes to enable us to agree with them to pull out all army vehicles.

HIJACKER: Okay—I will inform the captain of this. I want to tell you something which you must accept and understand quickly, in that, if any obstacles develop and we could not land at Beirut, in about ten or fifteen minutes we will not be able to go to any other airport as the fuel would not suffice.

ABOU-AHMAD: Okay, I heard you—you will definitely land at Beirut Airport for refueling, but we beg you to postpone landing for a few minutes in order for us to come to an agreement with the army to withdraw all his vehicles.

HIJACKER: Fifteen minutes enough?

ABOU-AHMAD: Fifteen minutes in order.

HIJACKER: Okay—will postpone landing for fifteen minutes.

CAPTAIN: Clipper 93 calling Tower.

TOWER: Go ahead.

CAPTAIN: Okay—this is the captain speaking. How about clearing that runway so that we can get down, huh? Do not cause us any more trouble. These folks are serious and are willing to destroy the airplane.

TOWER: Okay, sir. We are going to give—the military here are going to give orders to clear all the military around the runway so as to give way for landing safely.

CAPTAIN: Okay, as fast as you can, huh?

TOWER: Okay, as fast as we can . . . [some garbling] . . . .

CAPTAIN: We just want to land in Beirut.

TOWER: Do you prefer to land on runway 03 or runway 21?

CAPTAIN: We'd rather land on 03.

TOWER: Roger. Stand by, please.

CAPTAIN: We need descent plans.

TOWER: Say again, please?

CAPTAIN: Clipper 93 needs descent plans.

TOWER: What is your altitude now?

CAPTAIN: Twenty-seven thousand. . . .

(There is an interruption here while the hijacker hits the ceiling and once again demands that his colleague on the ground identify himself and his location. He wants to be absolutely sure that when the plane lands it will be landing at Beirut Airport and not some other place. What has prompted this explosion is explained by Captain Priddy.)

Captain Priddy: "The Israelis called us on the radio and tried to talk us into going to Tel Aviv. Gueye went right up through the goddamned ceiling, because he was listening to all of this— he went wild. They called us while were were still circling. It's only fifty-six miles to the border. They knew we were hijacked—because maybe they routinely monitor the Beirut frequencies. They called us and said, 'Hey, Clipper 93, come on down! We've got two beautiful, long, lighted runways—we got emergency equipment standing by—we'll give you fighter escort—you just make a dash for it.' Well, Gueye went right up the wall . . . he was going to pull the pin. We kept telling Tel Aviv to shut up, and they finally got the message and left us alone."

CAPTAIN TO BEIRUT TOWER: From Clipper 93—they say they know the airport and if there are any tricks they will blow up the airplane. So cut out the horsing around down there and get the runway cleared and get us down, huh?

TOWER: Okay, that is what we are doing now. . . . Request your endurance, please.

CAPTAIN: We are stuck to stay here now. We are below our fuel to go to Baghdad.

TOWER: You are not going to Baghdad. You are landing in Beirut definitely, but it takes some ten minutes more. I request your endurance on board, please.

CAPTAIN: Okay, will hold here ten more minutes.

TOWER: What is your endurance, what is your fuel on board, please? . . . [fadeout].

CAPTAIN TO DISPATCH ON PANOP FREQUENCY: Try to impress on these people down there that these guys are serious. They got guns, they got grenades and the whole works. They say if there is any trickery or anything they are going to blow up the airplane— plus they claim they have ground troops and support who will bomb the aircraft.

DISPATCH TO CAPTAIN: Understand. . . . For your information, I personally saw some groups of forces, policemen and army groups, pulling out of the airport in order to avoid a clash with the men on board. I would say that it is about to be cleared.

(At this time, Pan Am's Vasquez and Hamad are briefing the maintenance group down on the ramp, telling them not to approach the aircraft on the ramp and designating one maintenance man to drive the passenger stand to the aircraft when directed to do so.

The captain gets impatient and tells the tower that their ten minutes are up. The tower gives the go ahead for Clipper 93 to start descent. Captain Priddy switches over to radar frequency, and Clipper 93 begins its descent from the darkness at 27,000 feet to the brightness far below.

On the ramp, Vasquez and Hamad are appealing to the three PFLP representatives now down there with them to allow passengers to disembark at Beirut, or at least release women and children. The first plea is summarily rejected; to the second, their answer is that they will see what conditions are after landing.

The captain continues his approach. People gathered at Beirut Airport on PFLP or legitimate business have become aware of the drama in the sky. They have heard that the landing is going to be tricky, and they are on the watch for it. Dark as it is, they want to see whatever there is to be seen.

Minister of Public Works and Transportation Pierre Gemayel arrives at the airport and inquires into the adequacy of the runways and the safety of the aircraft and its passengers. He, too, requests the PFLP to release women and children. Their reply, now, is an unequivocal No.)

RADAR TO AIRCRAFT: Clipper 93—eight miles from touchdown.

CAPTAIN: Okay, we will stay with you for the moment. . . . Now we have the runway in sight.

RADAR: Understand you have the runway in sight. Take over visually to runway 03—call Tower frequency 118.9.

CAPTAIN: Okay.

TOWER TO CAPTAIN: Clipper 93, Beirut Tower—your height, please.

CAPTAIN: Okay . . . we are about eight miles out and we have the runway in sight.

TOWER: Roger—we have the VASI on now. Cleared to land on runway 03, wind east 05 knots.

CAPTAIN: Okay, understand the wind is east 05 knots and cleared to land on runway 03.

TOWER: Okay, and I suggest you try to stop as soon as possible, please . . . we will take you to the parking.

CAPTAIN: Okay, I will try to run short if we can. I will stay on your frequency for taxi and instructions—do you understand?

TOWER: It is correct—remain on this frequency.

CAPTAIN: Okay.

TOWER: East section cleared to parking. Use the first left intersection and pick up the follow-me jeep.

CAPTAIN: Okay, we understand that. . . .

TOWER: Clipper 93, this is Beirut tower.

CAPTAIN: Okay, go ahead.

TOWER: After you stop, call the frequency 121.9, please, and let somebody of the people who are with you talk with us.

CAPTAIN: Okay.

Schedule Control Center log:

2040Z	AIRCRAFT TOUCHING DOWN ON RUNWAY 03. BEY [Beirut] REPORTS HIJACKERS ARE ARMED WITH HAND GRENADES, PISTOLS, AND HIGH-POWERED RIFLES.

(Watchers at Beirut Airport break into applause as the 747 touches down safely. To Captain Priddy, the landing is a little rougher than usual, but pretty much routine.)

2045   N752 [Clipper 93] ARRIVED TERMINAL. TURNED TO FACE TAXIWAY. STOPPED AND SHUT DOWN ENGINES.

Radio:

HIJACKER: I want the two persons we agreed for them to come near the door, to come over, and any attempt . . . [garbling and interruptions while the hijacker and the PFLP representative try to talk at once] . . . will not be in their interest.

PARTY MEMBER FROM TOWER [a different voice]: Going over to you one named Abou-Khaled who is slim and short, and the second named Abou-Ahmad who is husky and bald.

HIJACKER: Anyway, if I do not recognize him, I will not permit him to come up.

PARTY MEMBER FROM TOWER: Contact Salah—*Salah*—at the control tower if you want anything . . . [garbled] . . . .

Log:

2046Z   JEEP MOVING FORWARD WITH PFLP MEMBERS ABOARD.

2047   JEEP NOW MOVING RAPIDLY TOWARD TERMINAL.

Radio:

HIJACKER: Come closer—I see you—come closer.

PARTY MEMBER FROM JEEP: Aren't you going to open the aircraft door?

HIJACKER: First draw in the jeep. . . . I tell you, draw in the jeep and then disembark from the jeep so that I can see you from the aircraft window and then I will open the door for you.

PARTY MEMBER FROM JEEP: Can't you see me from the cabin?

HIJACKER: I see you—I can see you from the cabin and I am watching everything. . . . Now stop the jeep—stop the jeep, stop it.

PARTY MEMBER FROM JEEP: And then?

HIJACKER: Disembark from the jeep with the person accompanying you. . . . Get moving—hurry up.

Log:

2048Z	TWO PEOPLE APPROACHING AIRCRAFT. NO ACTIVITY FROM INSIDE OF AIRCRAFT.
2049	LEFT HAND FORWARD MAIN ENTRANCE DOOR OPENED. CONVERSATION BETWEEN TWO PEOPLE ON THE GROUND AND TWO PEOPLE ON THE AIRCRAFT.

Radio:

PARTY MEMBER FROM TOWER: Inform Abou-Khaled and Abou-Ahmad that we have contacted Amman and they will call us back in half an hour's time.

CAPTAIN TO TOWER: Beirut, this is 93—the people aboard would like you to take the jeep with one person *only* and bring up some steps.

TOWER: Okay, you want some steps with one person only—that is correct?

CAPTAIN: Okay.

Log:

2052Z	AIRCRAFT REQUESTS PASSENGER LADDER WITH ONE PERSON ONLY.
2053	TWO PEOPLE IN AIRCRAFT DOORWAY TALKING TO COMMANDOES ON THE GROUND.

Radio:

PARTY MEMBER SALAH FROM TOWER: Keep us informed of whatever happens at your end. Call Salah at the control tower. For whatever you want, call Salah at the control tower.

HIJACKER: Okay, but. . . . [The sound becomes completely garbled, but the tone of the hijacker's voice indicates that he is very much on edge.]

SALAH: I only asked you if you needed any help. Please talk quietly . . . relax. I told you that the two chaps down there are the ones we sent from here, and they are Abou-Ahmad and Abou-Khaled. You can trust them and discuss with them anything you want. It will also be very good if you will give them details concerning the El Al's problem, because the El Al's, as you may possibly have heard, has failed. . . .

Log:

2058Z	ADVISED THAT PFLP IS STILL AWAITING INSTRUC- TIONS AMMAN.
2100	LADDER POSITIONED AT FORWARD MAIN ENTRANCE DOOR. TWO PFLP PEOPLE BOARD AIRCRAFT.
2104	FWD MAIN ENTRANCE DOOR CLOSED AND LADDER BACKING AWAY FROM AIRCRAFT.

The "El Al's problem" referred to by party member Salah was not so much El Al's as the PFLP's. The tables had been turned on the El Al flight from Amsterdam, and Britain now had a hostage that the Israelis would dearly have loved to get their own hands on ... someone who was very important to the PFLP. No doubt one reason for the failure of the attempted El Al hijacking was the presence of hijacker "Gueye" and his accomplice on Pan Am Flight 93 instead of on the El Al flight that they had originally planned to take. When PFLP hijackers attempt seizures of "enemy" craft such as El Al planes, they usually work in teams of four. Without the help of the two men now aboard the 747, female hijacker Leila Khaled and her companion were unable to bring off their coup.

Due, then, to the reduced forces of the PFLP hijackers on El Al Flight 219 and the combined efforts of Israeli security guards, male passengers and crew, the attempt that had begun about thirty minutes out of Amsterdam ended a very few minutes later. Patrick Arguello (occupation: revolutionary) suddenly let out a wild scream—"like a subhuman animal sound," as his startled seatmate subsequently described it—and ran into the first class section waving a pistol. Leila Khaled ran too, pulling a pair of hand grenades out of her bra and war-whooping down the aisle with one grenade in each hand. There was a short but furious scuffle—hand-to-hand grappling, shots, screams—and when it was over a steward lay badly wounded and Patrick Arguello was dead. Leila was subdued and securely bound. The pilot, in spite of radioed pleas from Israel to turn around and head at once for Tel Aviv with the captured lady sky pirate, took it upon himself to land in London as scheduled so that he could get the wounded man to hospital without delay.

The Israelis were not happy about this because it kept Leila out of their custody, but that is another story.

Leila had actually pulled the pin from one of the hand grenades during the battle up there in the sky somewhere over the North Sea. The grenade was old, the spring was weak . . . and many lives were spared.

The "El Al's problem" was something of a miracle.

(But Gueye-Samir knows none of these details. All he knows is that he and his helper were eased out of the El Al flight and now are stuck with a 747.)

Monitored radio communication between Beirut tower and Pan American aircraft now at terminal:

PARTY MEMBER SALAH FROM TOWER TO HIJACKER: Give us one of the two persons—Abou-Ahmad or Abou-Khaled—who came aboard your aircraft to give them Amman instructions.

HIJACKER: All right—talk to Abou-Khaled.

ABOU-KHALED FROM AIRCRAFT: Hello—Salah?

SALAH: Who is talking?

ABOU-KHALED: Abou-Khaled is talking to you.

SALAH: Take the following instructions: News received from Amman to the effect that you first refuel. This means that the first thing you do is refuel, and if they refuse refueling here, we will blow up the aircraft at Beirut Airport, of course after you disembark. Also, of course, we have notified the airport manager of this, and he is making the necessary arrangements for you to refuel. After you refuel, the same chaps who are commanding the aircraft now will head on it to Cairo. In Cairo they will precisely act in like manner as Abou-Doummar and Leila Khaled have acted. Clearly, they will act the way Abou-Doummar and Leila Khaled have acted—but they have to avoid all the mistakes that occurred in the operation of Leila Khaled and Abou-Doummar at Damascus Airport. You remember what happened at Damascus Airport?—the way Abou-Doummar and Leila Khaled acted—but they have to avoid the mistakes that occurred. This means that the operation must be accomplished in a perfect manner—the front and the rear, that is, the nose and the tail.

Heroine of the Palestine Liberation movement though she may be, Leila Khaled does make her mistakes . . . several of them. The reference here is not to the unsuccessful El Al escapade but to the incident of August 29, 1969, in which Leila Khaled and a young male companion hijacked a TWA 707 while on its way from Rome to Tel Aviv via Athens and forced it to Damascus. Minutes after landing at Damascus Airport, the jet-liner's captain was obliged to warn his passengers that a time bomb was about to explode in the craft. The exodus was hasty but successful. Then, with passengers and crew just barely clear, an explosion rocked the aircraft and shattered the nose to the tune of $3 million.

Leila's error: The damage, though costly and time-consuming, was not irreparable. She was supposed to have blown up the plane front *and* rear, "the nose and the tail." The aircraft eventually—forty-five days later—took off in one piece.

The point of this adventure? "Hijacking is one of the operational aspects of our war against Zionism," Leila explained, "and all those who support it, including the United States." She and her accomplice had hijacked the TWA craft "because it brought visitors and tourists to our enemies who are occupying our land by force of arms. . . . It was a perfectly normal thing to do, the sort of thing all freedom fighters have to tackle." That the plane was not a total write-off was just one of those things, a mistake to be avoided in the future.

(Now, on the Beirut strip, the door is closed on the 747. Aboard with the hijackers, passengers and crew are the two local PFLP representatives known as Abou-Khaled and Abou-Ahmad . . . grimly determined to see that the job, this time, is accomplished "in a perfect manner.")

Radio:

ABOU-KHALED FROM AIRCRAFT TO TOWER: We have heard Amman's instructions, we have heard Amman's instructions. We have heard Amman's instructions! Over. Did you hear me?

SALAH: Yes, I heard you. If you have something new, inform us about it.

ABOU-KHALED: Okay, will do.

Log:

2125Z   INTERCEPTED MESSAGE FROM JORDAN: "FUEL AIR-CRAFT AND CONTINUE TO CAIRO WHERE THE AIR-CRAFT IS TO BE BLOWN UP LIKE TWA IN DAMASCUS."

2130   1) FURTHER, "BEFORE BLOWING UP AIRCRAFT, DUMP FUEL ON AIRCRAFT."

2) MINISTER OF PUBLIC WORKS GEMAYEL WILL ATTEMPT TO DELIVER PRESIDENT HALABY'S MESSAGE TO PFLP GROUP ASSEMBLED IN TERMINAL AREA. THE PFLP CROWD IS IRATE AND HAL DOUBTS THEY WILL RECEIVE MR. GEMAYEL. ["Hal" is Harold L. Williams, Pan Am's director for Lebanon.]

3) LEBANESE GOVERNMENT RELUCTANT TO COMMIT ANY POSITIVE ACTION TO DISABLE AIRCRAFT.

(The normal crowd at Beirut Airport has been swelled by a good many PFLP members, most of them armed commandos. Their presence in force is adding immeasurably to the tension.)

Radio:

ABOU-KHALED FROM AIRCRAFT TO TOWER: Salah—secure for us all the items that must travel to Cairo. The chaps only got the items necessary for the accomplishment of the hijacking mission only. Did you hear me, Salah? Salah, did you hear me?

SALAH [puzzled] : Abou-Khaled, per our contact with Amman—we have contacted Amman, and their instructions were as relayed to you by me. I do not have any idea about any other requirements the friends aboard the aircraft have. Answer?

ABOU-KHALED: We are supposed to secure all the items required by the friends here because . . . did you hear me, Salah? . . . they are going to travel immediately they refuel. . . . Salah!—secure all the items required for the chaps to travel to Cairo regardless of the consequences. Did you hear?

SALAH: I have relayed to you instructions received from Amman, in that the chaps should travel to Cairo and land the aircraft at the airport there.

ABOU-KHALED: I heard you and am aware of the instructions, but the instructions from here are that there are items required by the chaps—uh, the items are required—well, does it suit you that they leave without them?

SALAH: Possibly Abou-Ahmad may have a better idea about the proposal contained in the plan of Leila and Salim. Anyway, Abou-Amad [another party member now in the tower] is in contact with Amman now, so hold it to see if there is anything new. . . . Abou-Amad ascertains validity of the same instructions and considers that the plan originally made with the friends is canceled. He ascertains the plan we have mentioned, in that they are to deal with the aircraft after it lands at the airport within any possible means to destroy it completely—burn it with fuel, blow it up if they have explosive devices, to act within any possible means—these are the final instructions. See if it is possible for you to help in any manner. Try to work it out with them . . . [pause] . . . Salah calling Abou-Khaled, calling Abou-Khaled at the aircraft—answer!

ABOU-KHALED: Go ahead—this is Abou-Khaled talking.

SALAH: The proposal now is for Captain Ali [a member of the PFLP] to supervise the refueling process as this may take an hour to an hour and a half. During this period you would have fixed yourselves up with the friends aboard the aircraft.

(A lengthy and involved discussion in regard to refueling gets under way. Captain Ali and another member of the PFLP are to supervise the five men who will be refueling the craft.)

ABOU-KHALED: During this period, kindly secure the items required by the chaps here for travel to Cairo. . . . There is a possibility that one of us would travel with the chaps to Cairo. Did you hear me, Salah?

SALAH: I heard you, Abou-Khaled, and have arranged everything. All the items will be available quickly. Samir El-Saheb and Captain Ali are going to supervise five other elements to refuel the aircraft. And sandwiches will be sent to you so that the comrades may have dinner.

(There is plenty of food on the plane; no need for the comrades to send out for it. "Sandwiches" is the cloak-and-dagger term for *dynamite*. Another and more pressing problem to be considered is how much fuel this aircraft should take to get to Cairo or some alternative destination in case Egyptian authorities refuse to let it land. They may do just that; the main reason for choosing a Cairo landing is to embarrass Nasser because he had agreed to peace negotiations that did not include the Palestinian refugees. The voice of Dispatch sensibly suggests that they take on as much fuel as they can, but adds plaintively that "this is the first time I personally see this airplane," and suggests that the hijackers take this question up with the captain. They do so, and the captain defines his requirements. Salah comments that direct instructions have been received from the President of the Republic to give the aircraft all the fuel it needs for takeoff to Cairo. While waiting for the fueling to get started, Salah talks revolutionary shop.)

SALAH: Of course, the other information is very good. The activities are constantly increasing. The military information relative to the ratio of activities undertaken by the Popular Front has greatly increased over that of the previous month. There are developments in the Jordan of which you are possibly aware. Problems developed during the last three-four days between the reactionary regime [of King Hussein] and the Palestinian Resistance there, and this resulted in some casualties. Do you hear me? Stay with us. We ordered sandwiches for you in accordance with Abou-Khaled's request. The brothers inform us that the sandwiches arrived half an hour ago but they have not been received by us yet—so we want to see what happened to it.

HIJACKER: Okay—continue brother. Tell us, brother, about the good news that developed today. With regard to the aircraft hijacking—how many aircraft were hijacked today?

(The transmission becomes garbled as the two brothers talk to each other at the same time.)

Log:

2150Z   FUELING COMMENCING WITH FOUR LOCAL FUELERS, ONE PAN AM SUPERVISOR AND TWO MEMBERS PFLP. APU [Auxiliary Power Unit] OPERATIVE.

Radio:

HIJACKER: Salah—I want you to know one thing . . . [garbling and interruption] . . . .

SALAH: The sandwiches which we have sent to get for you from downtown will be here in ten minutes—

HIJACKER: No, no—there is something else I would like you to know—do you hear me?

SALAH: . . . [garbling] . . . Anything you want from us, just ask for it and we will prepare it for you. Also we would like to know how the morals of your comrades are. [This is doubtful; he is surely less interested in morals than morale.]

HIJACKER: Salah—do you hear me?

SALAH: I hear you. Go ahead.

HIJACKER: With regards to the passengers—shall we release them at Cairo Airport?

SALAH: You will release all passengers at Cairo Airport. After you release them—

HIJACKER: —We will execute the plan of Abou-Doummar and Leila—

SALAH: —You will execute the plan you will now work out at your end—that is to say that you, Abou-Khaled, the comrades you have, and Abou-Ahmad will work out a plan as to how you should act there. With regards to the passengers, deplane them quietly and smoothly. After the passengers deplane, determine the distribution of your responsibilities as to who in the front and who in the rear. The quantity of the sandwiches which we will give to you—you will amuse yourselves with them on the way—arrange them properly in order for your plan to be a complete success. This means that you will work out all the details with Abou-Ahmad and Abou-Khaled. Tell them this for me. You have received the instructions. Make out the arrangements, work out a detailed plan, this is your mission. Consider all plans previously made as canceled. All of you aboard the aircraft work out a complete plan as to how you should act there. Secure the passengers deplaning. Of course, it is important for us that the passengers deplane safely.

(Of course it is: he wouldn't want to give hijacking a bad name nor the PFLP an unsavory reputation. Odd, though, that the flight deck crew keeps getting the feeling that their captors are prepared to blow up the plane *with or without* the passengers.)

HIJACKER: ... [garbled] ....

SALAH: Are there any Jews amongst them? If there are Jews amongst them of other nationalities, ascertain their nationalities and collect their passports and take them all and keep them with you after you get down.

HIJACKER: We have collected all the passports, but there is France's representative to the United Nations or a French diplomat, as well as other diplomats. We regarded them with respect and returned their passports to them and have treated them excellently.

(This is true. Before the landing, all passengers were strictly admonished to stay in their seats and sit absolutely still. But now that they are on the ground they have a certain amount of freedom, and are being treated to cocktails and courtesy. The hijackers have been through the plane in turns, inquiring into the nationalities of the various people aboard and asking if anyone has any questions. Few people care to engage in conversation with their hosts, except for "a couple of hippie-type passengers who get pretty cheeky." The rest of the passengers appreciate the calmness and courtesy of the man who chats with them so congenially, but they do not care for the pistol that he holds in one hand and the grenade held so uncomfortably close to his mouth. Though most of them know little about weaponry, they have heard that the man who throws grenades often yanks the pin out with his teeth. And even though they can now move around a little, they are being very closely watched.)

Captain Priddy elaborates: "They got all the people downstairs; they moved everybody aft from economy first, while we were still in the air, and then they picked up passports from all the passengers and went through them. Then they segregated the military personnel, diplomatic personnel—anybody they figured could give them trouble—and moved them up to first class. I guess the deadhead crew was up there with them. There was a French diplomat and his wife and baby, I think, and some other people. . . . Then the old Jewish fellow they didn't bother—he was Dutch, I guess, or Belgian—he must have been in his early seventies. They didn't bother him. But the old man kept wanting to put on that little skullcap and pray, and he was going to go up to the hijackers and try to bargain with them. He wanted to tell them to kill him; he'd spent five years in a concentration camp and it didn't matter to him what they did with him. But Paul La Chapelle wasn't about to let him. The old man put on this little cap, and Paul yanked it off his head and stuck it in his pocket. Said, 'God knows you want to wear it, but God knows you're smart enough not to!' "

Radio:

SALAH: The important thing for you is to act and behave in a manner appertaining to the Popular Front.

HIJACKER: Concerning the other passports, like Americans, military men, lieutenants, pilots, and a mechanic in El Al—we have taken the passports of all of these.

SALAH [suspiciously]: A mechanic in the El Al?

HIJACKER: Yes, but American.

SALAH: You have to watch him—we fear he may be a Jew from those Jews who have American citizenship. This should not escape your thoughts.

HIJACKER: No—immediately we take off, I am going to isolate him. There are also another two Englishmen whom I suspected, and isolated them.

SALAH: The important thing for you is to be careful and to take all necessary measures—I mean, to be extremely cautious.

HIJACKER: Don't worry. Give my regards to all the chaps.

SALAH: All the chaps here are on the alert, and send you their regards and wish you success, and await your news from Cairo.

HIJACKER: With the help of God . . . !

SALAH: We just want to continue informing you of our latest news and accomplishments. The Secretary General—the doctor [George Habash]—has gone to North Korea with a delegate. We wish he was here to supervise the heroic acts accomplished by his fighting children of the Popular Front. No doubt he will hear the news about these activities, and this will strengthen and make more clear his standing in front of the Korean people.

HIJACKER: May God bless him and come to the aid of all! Now I am going to go down and will leave the captain for a little while in the cabin, in order to make the arrangements for the Cairo trip. This means that I will be away from the cabin for fifteen minutes in order for him to get ready and also to send the crew to him.

(Salah gives him another brief pep talk and passes on regards and all good wishes for luck and success from all the brothers in the Armed Struggle in Lebanon.)

HIJACKER: God save them, and we are very grateful. This is just an obligation, and I hope that we have fulfilled the obligation. Thanks to God that the mission has been successful, and this is a great victory for us and for all the Arabs, and so God wish. . . . I am going down now, leaving my friend here if you want to talk to him.

(Exit hijacker. Here ends the radio transmission.)

Log:

2235Z	1) FUELING STILL IN PROGRESS. AIRCRAFT HAS REQUESTED OIL AND WATER. 2) COMMANDOES HAVE TAKEN "FOOD" TO AIRCRAFT FOR THEIR COMRADES BUT HAL FEELS COULD BE EXPLOSIVES.
2240	MAINTENANCE LADDER POSITIONED AT FORWARD ENTRY DOOR AND SEVERAL COMMANDOES INCLUDING A FEMALE BOARD AIRCRAFT. ALSO CARRIED ON LARGE SEAMAN'S BAG [packed with "sandwiches"?] WHICH APPEARED HEAVY. GROUP EMBRACED EACH OTHER IN AIRCRAFT AT DOORWAY, THEN DOOR WAS CLOSED AND LADDER REMOVED.

(The boarding party seems to be some sort of propaganda unit. Either that, or its members want to experience the thrill of being in on the hijacking of a 747. In any event, only one of the visiting group makes other than a verbal contribution to the proceedings. That one is the explosives expert, who now has to assist the hijackers in planning out the distribution and wiring of the devices brought aboard. The others stroll through the plane, admiring its spaciousness and talking to the passengers. The hijackers have already read a political statement to the passengers and tried to "do a selling job for the Palestinian refugees." Now their friends develop the theme.

They encourage questions; they ask for every opportunity to justify themselves. Why do they hijack planes? Because they have lost their homes, their land, their security, and therefore the most desperate measures are called for. But why an American plane? Because Nixon is sending planes to Israel. But isn't Russia similarly helping the Arabs? Heavens, no! Certainly not; where did you ever get that idea? Next question, please. Well, what do they hope to gain by this particular hijacking? To put Nasser in an awkward position and, hopefully, scuttle the forthcoming peace talks. Also, to obtain the release of the three Arabs being held in Switzerland, the freedom fighters who had attempted to take the life of Moshe Dayan's son. And what if those men were not released? Supposing—comes the answer—". . . supposing you all get killed . . . ?")

Captain Priddy: "I didn't stay in the cockpit the whole time—not after he got us all downstairs. I saw these people come aboard, nine of them. Christ! they brought on a whole bunch of forty-fives and about eighty pounds of dynamite . . . you know, the 'sandwiches' they were referring to. They held their conference in first class. . . . I asked them if I could go back and talk to the passengers, so I went back and talked to everybody for a while. Then Gueye got us up to the cockpit about forty-five minutes before we left Beirut because we had to figure out fuel and oil and get the inertial setup and the whole thing. . . . Of course I asked Gueye—I tried to talk him into turning everybody loose and letting the crew fly him to Cairo, and he said, 'No, you don't understand.' So I said, 'What will happen when we get to Cairo?' And he said, 'Everybody will get off the airplane, I promise you.' He didn't tell me they were going to blow it up. There were a lot of things he didn't tell me but he never told us a lie. So I figured that, if everybody's going to get off in Cairo—I interpreted that to mean he was going to let us loose. I guess all this was decided in their conference on the ground, but all their conversation was in Arabic so we didn't know what they were planning."

Log:

2252Z	CABIN DOOR REOPENED. FUELING COMPLETED AND FUEL TRUCKS REMOVED FROM AIRCRAFT. SEVERAL PEOPLE (PFLP) APPROACHING AIRCRAFT FROM GROUND AND TALKING TO PEOPLE IN DOORWAY OF AIRCRAFT.
2300	THE PEOPLE WHO BOARDED ARE TOLD TO DIS- EMBARK. ETD IS IN TEN MINUTES. LARGE SMOKE- SCREEN FROM RIGHT-HAND SIDE OF AIRCRAFT.

(The maintenance ladder again approaches the aircraft. Several people disembark: All but one of the visiting commandos, and—according to the log but unconfirmed by Captain Priddy—a pregnant woman with her husband.)

2320	CABIN DOOR CLOSED. COMMANDOES ON GROUND LEAVING VICINITY AIRCRAFT. STARTING ENGINES.
2323	AMMAN TOWER NOW ADVISES THAT AIRCRAFT IS TO

	PROCEED AMMAN AND WHEN OVERHEAD AMMAN DECISION WILL BE MADE TO EITHER LAND AMMAN OR PROCEED TO CAIRO.
2330	AIRPORT SERVICE MANAGER VASQUEZ REQUESTS WE CONTACT JORDANIAN EMBASSY WASHINGTON D.C. AND PREVAIL UPON THEM TO PRESS FOR AN AMMAN LANDING. COMMANDOES FEEL THEY WILL BE BETTER RECEIVED IN AMMAN AND IF THEY CONTINUED TO CAIRO THEY WILL BE ARRESTED AND HAVE NO CHOICE BUT TO BLOW UP THE AIRCRAFT. VICE PRESIDENT [of Pan Am Airport Services] RICE CONTACTING U.S. STATE DEPARTMENT. AIRCRAFT TAXIING TO RUNWAY.

(There is a misunderstanding here. The commandos in the aircraft do not wish to go to Amman because of the landing difficulties there, and have every intention of going to Cairo. Both Captain Priddy and the hijackers tell the tower that they want clearance to Cairo, and the tower reads back a clearance for Amman. Captain Priddy is not "about to go through the hills of Amman at night in a 747," because he has many lives to consider, and refuses the clearance to Amman. The message comes back from the tower: "Well, you're cleared for takeoff—for wherever you want to go!" A few minutes later they are cleared all the way to Cairo.)

2333	BEIRUT TOWER [still in the hands of PFLP commandos] ADVISED COMMANDO IN COCKPIT NOT TO INFORM ANYONE OF DESTINATION OUT OF BEIRUT. TAKE OFF WITHOUT COMMUNICATIONS [that is, without official permission].
2336	TAKEOFF ROLL STARTED.
2337	AIRBORNE.
2340	COMMANDO IN TOWER TOLD COMMANDO IN AIRCRAFT TO LAND IN A COUNTRY "FRIENDLY TO THE COMMANDOES."
2350	AIRCRAFT RECEIVED INSTRUCTIONS TO PROCEED DIRECT TO CAIRO. BEIRUT ATTEMPTING TO ESTABLISH COMMUNICATION VIA HIGH FREQUENCY WITH

CAIRO. CAPTAIN MAXWELL [Vice President-Flight Operations, head of Schedule Control] ARRANGED FOR TWA TO GROUND-HANDLE IN CAIRO.

(TWA serves Cairo, which Pan American does not. Pan Am, therefore, not having the necessary airport services at Cairo, has had to ask TWA for help.)

Captain Priddy: "From Beirut to Cairo we had three hijackers on board. The third one was in his early twenties—maybe twenty-one. He was the demolitions expert who had brought the dynamite aboard. All the way from Beirut this kid that go on was cutting fuses and putting bundles of dynamite all over the place . . . in the closets, lavs, and scattered all around the airplane. I didn't personally see him do this, but the flight service did and told me later."

0030Z [of the next Greenwich day]	AT 070015 AIRCRAFT WAS RELEASED BY NICOSIA AIR TRAFFIC CONTROL TO CAIRO FIR [flight information region]. ETA CAIRO 070108Z.
0050	1) ON FINAL TO CAIRO 2) BEYOAPA [Pan Am's Beirut Airport Operations Manager Hal Williams] CONFIRMS DIPLOMATIC CHANNELS IN CAIRO HAVE BEEN CONTACTED. ATTEMPTING TO NOTIFY PRESIDENT NASSER.
0100	BEYOAPA ADVISES UNABLE TO ESTABLISH VOICE CONTACT WITH CAIRO. USING SWISSAIR TELEX BEY/CAIRO.

(At 0115 there is indirect confirmation that the aircraft has been on "final" for twenty-five minutes. For some reason, known to no one outside the aircraft, it is taking its time to descend into Cairo.)

0123	NICOSIA AIR TRAFFIC CONTROL ADVISES BEYOAPA THAT AS OF 070121Z AIRCRAFT HAD NOT—REPEAT—NOT LANDED CAIRO.
0135	NICOSIA ATC CONFIRMS AIRCRAFT LANDED CAIRO 070124Z, SAFELY.
0140	NO RESPONSE FROM SWISSAIR, CAIRO.

(Arrangements are already under way for Pan Am maintenance men to fly to Cairo and for a relief aircraft to be sent from London to pick up the presumably stranded passengers and crew. But it is impossible to establish direct contact with the aircraft, or even—for a while—with Cairo, and the 747 seems lost in silence.

It is, in fact, beyond communication.)

0215Z	UNCONFIRMED REPORTS VIA PARIS RADIO ADVISE AIRCRAFT OUT OF SERVICE AND ALL PAXS AND CREW SAFE.
0220	SET UP B707 RELIEF LONDON HEATHROW/CAIRO TO PICK UP THE STRANDED PASSENGERS. AIRCRAFT WILL BE IN CHARTER CONFIG. BEYOAPA ADVISED OF THESE PLANS VIA FONE.
0305	BEYOAPA CONFIRMS BBC RADIO BROADCAST STATES "AIRCRAFT IS DESTROYED AND CAIRO AIRPORT IS CLOSED." THEY HAVE ALSO RECEIVED A TELEX FROM SWISSAIR IN CAIRO STATING AIRCRAFT IS DESTROYED.
0330	PRESIDENT HALABY SPOKE TO BEYOAPA AND THEN COMMUNICATIONS BETWEEN NYC/BEY.

Monday, September 7, 1970.

A new day begins in New York; a new controller is on the job at JFK. Much of the action is over by now, and the summary of his log entries is succinct.

LATEST REPORT FROM CAIRO INDICATES 5 TO 6 PAX HOSPITALIZED WITH MINOR INJURIES, REMAINDER OF PAX AT AIRPORT HOTEL. UAR AUTHORITIES APPREHENDED 3 SABOTEURS (HIJACKERS) AND SEARCHING FOR FOURTH WHO ESCAPED. [The report is in error. There is no fourth man.] U.S. EMBASSY OFFICER CONFIRMS AIRCRAFT COMPLETELY DESTROYED WITH ONLY PART OF TAIL REMAINING. LONOW [London Flight Dispatch] CONFIRMED AT 0530Z THAT CAIRO AIRPORT OPEN AND COBUS [relief plane] LEAVING BLOCKS LONDON HEATHROW. . . . NOW DELAYED DUE VHF TROUBLE. FONE BILL FOR CALL TO BEY WAS $1023.75 PLUS TAX. . . .

LONOW HAD FONE CONTACT WITH CAPTAIN PRIDDY: CONFIRMED ALL PAX AND CREW SAFE, AIRCRAFT TOTAL LOSS. SEVEN PAX INJURED AND HOSPITALIZED AND MAY NOT BE ABLE TO TRAVEL ON COBUS N405PA. AIRCRAFT WAS EVACUATED THROUGH EMERGENCY CHUTES.

All efforts now are concentrated on ensuring the safety and comfort of passengers and crew. The relief plane picks up all those who are in condition to travel, and arrangements are made for those who are not. The Pan Am plot line of the multiple-hijack story seems to be over, though the parallel plots are still developing on the Amman desert airstrip.

But what really happened in the last few minutes of the life of Clipper 93?

The demolitions expert who had joined the two-man hijack team in Beirut was very busy on the flight to Cairo, wiring the plane and supervising the distribution of the dynamite. The job was so coolly done—so professionally and unobtrusively—that few people realized what was happening: that explosives were carefully being spread throughout the plane, with emphasis on the front section. Among those who did notice were two or three passengers who had been invited to go up front for "isolation" or further inspection, the deadheading crew, first class purser Augusta Schneider, and inflight service director John Ferruggio.

John Ferruggio: "When we were about forty-five minutes from Cairo, I asked one of the two original hijackers exactly what was going to happen. All he would tell me was that they would give us eight minutes. 'Eight minutes for what?' I wanted to know. He wouldn't say.

"I asked him about the explosives. 'What about this stuff?' I said, and pointed at some of it. And he said, 'What do you care about this imperialistic piece of equipment?' I told him I thought it was a beautiful piece of equipment, imperialistic or not, and that I did care. He told me it was going to be blown up.

"He was serious. He said we would have eight minutes to get out. I asked that he allow me to tell the crew and passengers how to get off the plane. I called all the crew, including the deadheading crew, into first class, and completely briefed them.

"We divided up the passengers. I stationed the deadheading crew members at the doors, and told each to take a baby and slide out first. The mothers were to go next, take the babies from the crew, and the crew members would then help people off and away from the evacuation chutes."

And now, of course, the passengers had to be briefed as thoroughly and yet diplomatically as possible. Surprisingly, they showed not a trace of fear or anxiety, and the flight felt almost normal.

A passenger: "Food was served, children ran up and down the aisles, no one panicked. I think maybe we were all too stunned to be frightened. Also, the hijackers weren't particularly frightening. Actually, they behaved like perfect gentlemen— even though they were planning to blow up the plane. Emergency procedures were first-rate. We knew exactly what to do and when to do it. The stewardesses spoke to all the passengers in small groups and advised us that we were to evacuate the plane in Cairo immediately upon landing. Any valuables we wanted to take with us, we had to wear. Shoes had to come off. These we would dump in blankets and, hopefully, get back later. (Some got lost.) Only small, soft handbags with straps were to be taken with us. I don't know what the men did with their briefcases. Left them, I guess. But probably didn't mind— we were only too glad to get out."

But they weren't out yet. The plane was nearing Cairo . . . was over Cairo . . . and then circling . . . and circling.

Captain Priddy: "With the other guy on board, coming into Cairo there were two of them up there in the cockpit. And they made us circle Cairo down low to make sure it *was* Cairo. They were doing a lot of jabbering . . . of course, everything was in Arabic, and it was kind of awkward because you didn't have a clue to what they were talking about. Apparently they were looking. . . . And finally Gueye says, 'Okay, it's Cairo—go ahead and land.' We were just circling over the river, downtown Cairo, so he must have seen something he recognized."

Satisfied, the hijackers let him make his *final* final approach.

Augusta Schneider: "Meanwhile, this demolitions expert of theirs was looking for a light. We'd seen him going around planting the dynamite and we knew pretty much what was going to happen. But—! Just before we were ready to land, this guy came over to me and asked me for a match . . . and I gave it to him. What else could I do?"

The explosive fuse was burning even before the aircraft landed.

It was going to be a very short eight minutes.

The aircraft touched down on the dark runway and rolled to a stop. The evacuation began immediately.

A passenger: "The chutes were lowered to the ground and we were told we had eight minutes to evacuate the plane—but if we could do it faster, so much the better. The crew was incredible. Really cool. Efficient. No panic. They had us briefed and ready long before we landed. When we hit ground, they told us, we were to run as fast as possible in any direction, so long as it was away from the plane, without waiting or looking back. We went out carrying only what we stood up in, and we hit the ground and ran. Seems to me it took about a minute and a half to empty that plane—and a good thing, too, because it blew up in another couple of minutes."

Time and action telescoped for this passenger and many of the others. It all seemed to happen even more quickly than it did. But for other passengers there was a complication: the plane began to move again even as they were getting out.

Captain Priddy had not yet been warned that the plane was going to be blown up.

Captain Priddy: "When we landed in Cairo, Gueye and the tower both said, 'Go all the way to the end of the runway.' And I thought to myself, Well, that's stupid—if I go all the way to the end of the runway, I don't know what the taxi strip is like, and I might not be able to turn this thing around. Now apparently Gueye must have told the control tower that they were going to blow up the airplane, so they wanted the plane at the end of the runway so it wouldn't block the whole runway. But I didn't have a clue about this. I knew they didn't have any tugs or anything to handle it, and I said, 'I want to stop short enough that I have room to turn around.' So I stopped. And that's when the trouble began—as soon as we stopped. Of course I didn't know it, but the guys downstairs had told flight service to bail 'em out . . . and so as soon as I stopped, Gueye and the tower began screaming to go all the way to the end. So I started up again, and John Ferruggio came part way up the stairs with a microphone and said, 'For God sake, stop—we're evacuating!' and I slammed on the brakes and cut the engines."

John Ferruggio: "He couldn't believe it when I told him the evacuation had already begun! By the time I got back downstairs the plane was empty. I scooped up two blankets full of shoes, threw them down a chute, and then went out myself. As I ran from the plane I heard rapid-fire pistol shots and I thought for sure that the men had shot the cockpit crew. I was about 130 yards away from the plane when I saw it start to disintegrate.''

Captain Priddy: "Gueye told Zuby [Julius Dzuiba, the flight engineer] to go, and Pat Levix the first officer started to stand up, and Gueye said, 'No, you two guys stay.' And we just sat there and he watched his watch, and pretty soon he said, 'Okay—go—and good luck.' So we went down the stairs, leaving Gueye still in the cockpit. He was the last to get off the plane. Downstairs, I checked the right aisle and Pat checked the left. There was just one stewardess, Augie Schneider, still in the back of the airplane trying to pick up shoes. There was nobody else on the airplane. We told her to beat it . . . and she went out, took off in the darkness in the opposite direction from us. Pat and I went out and Gueye came right down behind us. Then there was a lot of shooting . . . I don't know what that was all about. We made it somewhere in the vicinity of the outboard engine—and up she went, in the cockpit area first, then a tremendous explosion in the tail area. Then the whole top of the airplane went up. . . . Pretty sad, really was . . . pretty sad.''

Passengers, crew, hijackers and explosives expert scrambled and stumbled away across the desert sand.

Egyptian officialdom received passengers and crew with kindness but was distinctly cool in its attitude toward the hijackers. The UAR did not—as a rule, with an exception or two—believe that the cause of the Palestinian struggle was well served by attacks on international civil aviation, and least of all when a hijacked plane ended up on Egyptian soil. The semi-official Cairo newspaper, *Al Ahram*, commented shortly after the Pan Am hijackers had been taken into custody that the rash of seizures would tend to turn the world against the Palestinian cause. "One of the main goals of the battle (with Israel)," this paper proclaimed, "is to gain world opinion on the side of the Palestinian struggle and not to lose it." In *Al Ahram*'s view, the flurry of guerrilla hijackings would incite "a feeling of criticism in the ordinary man."

As for Leila Khaled, she was no less dangerous in British custody than on the loose.

One of the closing entries in the Pan Am operations control center log for September 7, 1970, reads as follows:

```
1756Z        LONDON FLIGHT DISPATCH CALLED TO ADVISE
             THAT U.S. EMBASSY LONDON RECEIVED CALL
             STATING THAT "UNLESS GIRL IS RELEASED, NO U.S.
             AIRCRAFT WILL BE SAFE."
```

This was not the last of the threatening phone calls, nor was it the end of the action. There was a slight change of plan, though: the next plane to be compromised was not a U.S. aircraft but a BOAC VC-10, hijacked September 9 while en route from Bombay to London. The guerrillas already had as hostages the passengers of two planes force-landed on the Amman strip, but to them it was only poetic justice to grab a British plane in order to pressure the British government into releasing Leila Khaled.

Thus three planes baked in the Amman desert, and three sets of hostages faced the prospect of extinction by explosion if a package of PFLP demands was not swiftly met.

When the dust finally settled—if it has settled yet—there were three more wrecked planes lying scattered in the sand, and a massive exchange of hostages and captive terrorists had taken place. The beautiful Leila, all smiles, was safe in the arms of her comrades, and there was much celebration throughout the ranks of the PFLP and their friends in other countries.

The final score for the PFLP:

TWA 707 en route from Tel Aviv to New York—taken over by PFLP guerrillas on September 6, 1970, after its stop at Frankfurt; diverted to a landing at Dawson Field in Jordan. Passengers held hostage, but evacuated from plane before its demolition on September 12.

Swissair DC-8 en route from Zurich to New York—hijacked by PFLP guerrillas on September 6 near Paris and forced to land virtually on the tail of the TWA craft. Passengers held hostage, but evacuated from plane before it is blown up on September 12.

PAA 747 en route from Amsterdam to London—diverted to Beirut by PFLP guerrillas on September 6 and subsequently taken to Cairo where it is precipitately emptied of passengers (who are thus freed from hostage) and blown up on September 7.

El Al 707 en route from Tel Aviv to New York—almost commandeered after departure from Amsterdam on September 6 by Leila Khaled and Patrick Arguello. Hijack attempt fails and plane lands in London with wounded steward, captive Khaled, and dead Arguello.

BOAC VC-10 en route from Bombay to London—captured on September 9 by PFLP guerrillas who force it to refuel at Beirut and then fly to Dawson Field in Amman. Passengers held hostage but evacuated from plane before it is blown up on September 12. Leila Khaled is later released by British government.

Later, enormously pleased with themselves, the PFLP issued commemorative "tickets" marking the five-part event; one ticket for each of the airlines involved. On the back of the BOAC commemorative they added a little mockery; borrowing BOAC's slogan, they changed it to read, "All over the world PFLP takes good care of you."

Apparently some members of the PFLP are not lacking in a sly sense of humor . . . but the laughter of the victims was hollow indeed. The joke was, at best, in very poor taste, and only the guerrillas chuckled warmly over their own cleverness.

The implications of the ugly, five-pronged episode shook the establishment world to its foundations. In Beirut on September 10, while concern over the passenger-hostages was running high, a spokesman for the Arab guerrillas struck an ominous note when he declared that the hijackings were part of a revolution and that "revolutions have no rules." He went on to say: "With a handful of hijackings under our belts, we know a lot about jetliners, their pilots, and the control towers they deal with." Unsaid, but underlying the words, was this: We have found an effective revolutionary tactic, and we are going to keep on using it.

While it may be true that the hijackings in themselves did not gain public sympathy, it is equally true that they did call worldwide attention to the plight of homeless Arab refugees from Palestine. Many passengers, after the event, commented:

"I can't approve of what they did, but what they said made a lot of sense." "They didn't try to hurt us—they just wanted us to listen and ask questions." "Now I *do* understand their problems. I see a lot of things I never saw before." The Western press, too, learned a whole lot more about the Middle East, its people, and its complex problems than it had ever known.

Through the news media, the world at large was shaken into recognizing the existence of a "Palestinian problem," and into feeling sympathy for people if not for their tactics. There was even talk about getting down to the root cause of the conflict, and trying to do something about it. In this, at least, the PFLP succeeded in what they set out to do. (Also, they freed a lot of their fellow "freedom fighters" from the jails of various countries.)

There were other ramifications. While the underground radical press in the United States was by no means unanimous in supporting the action, the Berkeley *Tribe* offered the editorial comment that "We are all the new barbarians. We are closer to the Palestinians than some like to admit. We are the people without power in the world. Maybe soon, planes carrying very prominent international pigs like (Reagan) will be hijacked from the U.S. to parts unknown. By, say, freaks." (And "freaks," of course, is not a term of contempt. Freaks are the psychedelic-revolutionary underground good guys.)

Uneasily, we became aware that if it could happen there it could happen here.

This luridly dramatic episode, almost incomprehensible in its scope, introduced a new dimension to the hijacking saga—a saga already infinitely more complex than most people realized, and one that had begun long before Castro's takeover of Cuba. We in the United States had been jolted a time or two before by spectacular hijackings, but never so badly as now. Many of us had felt a kind of admiration for the hijacker, particularly if he was escaping from an iron curtain country to seek refuge in the West or if he seemed to be a baffled but bold young man trying to fly his way out of his problems. We even felt a certain sympathy for people disenchanted with our own establishment, and for the misfit who thought he would find paradise at the far end of the flight. Innocently, blindly, we attached little deep significance to the routine skyjackings we were witnessing so often, and made jokes about "Coffee, tea or rum?" and "What time do we get to Havana?"

Suddenly, the time of innocence was over and the laughter stopped. We had a new breed of hijacker on our hands: not a homesick Cuban or a crybaby with a popgun and an aerosol can, but a cool professional who knew his airplanes and his weapons. We had a new kind of hijacking to cope with: not an individual or family effort but a slick operation carried out by a group with a cause, an organized unit with ground support, whose objective was to propagandize, terrorize, and engage in international blackmail at the expense of helpless hostages under the threat of death.

2/TAKE ME TO HAVANA

Hijacking is an old American story. It is, in fact, a story much older than America, and we can trace it right back to the times of Julius Caesar. It used to be called kidnapping for ransom, or piracy, or highway robbery, or holdup, depending on the circumstances, but the effect was always pretty much the same. A vehicle got held up, either on land or out on the high seas. People were put on the spot and threatened with injury or death: "Your money or your life!" Always the "—or else." The end result was theft; theft of cash, valuables, time, spirit, company revenue, and a slice of people's lives. The perpetrators were all pirates of one kind or another.

In modern times we have the truck hijacker and the aircraft skyjacker. These people are pirates, too. But while the truck hijacker is only a common thief, the sky pirate is a slightly different proposition. His primary objective is not the loot, and his threat is not so much "Your money or your life!" as *My freedom or your lives!* Mere cash payoff will not appease him.

It may be a series of long steps from the marauding expeditions of Blackbeard, Drake, and the Barbary pirates to the seizure of ships for political purposes and the destruction of four airliners by a guerrilla group. But all such incidents have one thing in common: You do thus and so, or else. One word for this is *blackmail.*

The events of September 6-12, 1970, were the ultimate in piracy—to date. Yet they were only the high point of a long series of airborne seizures, most of which had been regarded by casual observers as the actions of "some nut."

The first recorded skyjacking took place in 1930, and it was not the work of some nut. It was pulled off by a group of political activists in Peru, which had been rocked by revolution for many years. This particular revolution wasn't even a very big one. It amounted to little more than a bitter exchange of viewpoints. Yet it was big enough for a group of rebels to commandeer an F-7 piloted by an American, Byron D. Richards, and use it to shower Peru with propaganda pamphlets. As a first, it made so little impact on the record books that some hijack buffs think it may have occurred even before, in

1928, but Peru's history and the recollections of the pilot suggest the 1930 date.

This small occurrence got lost in the shuffle of major events. The thirties, forties, and fifties were torn by invasion, threat of war, preparation for war, and war itself . . . and then the aftermath of war. The first skyjacking seemed the last; an isolated incident. During the war years there must have been more than a few hijackings of military aircraft, as there have been since, but these were so much a part of battle that they were never sifted from the rest of battle to stand alone as hijackings. The only one that made a worldwide splash was the sudden, strange flight of Rudolf Hess to Scotland in 1941. Hess made news because he had been Hitler's deputy Führer, a man of great power in Nazi Germany but one who apparently saw, long before his fellow Nazis, the writing in the sky.

There were thirty-two skyjacking attempts, nearly all of them successful, between the Peruvian event of 1930 and the American skyjacking of May 1, 1961, which is almost invariably referred to as *the* first skyjacking ever. None of the thirty-two incidents involved American aircraft, and none of them involved American hijackers. It seems strange, in a way, that we did not invent the phenomenon: there has been a tendency in some parts of the globe to regard hijacking as something basically American, like baseball, Hollywood movies, rock festivals, Al Capone, high-powered cars, and student riots; just another of those rather violent and flashy things for which we have become notorious and managed to foist off on a guileless world. We ourselves tend to forget that skyjacking is not just something that goes on between the United States and Cuba—or did forget until the PFLP came along and stole our thunder.

After the Hess hijacking, the next recorded seizure occurred in July, 1947. Little is known about it, largely because it originated in a Communist country and partly because we were not paying attention, but it seems to have involved a private plane on a domestic Rumanian run. A group of Rumanians seized it and forced it to land in Turkey. One crew member was rumored to have been killed because he was not cooperative.

In 1948 there were seven acts of aerial piracy. The first two—those of April and May—involved groups of Czechoslovakians who preferred to take their chances in the U.S. Zone of Germany to remaining in a homeland in which the Communists had seized power in February. In June there were three aerial escapes: One from Yugoslavia to Italy, one from Rumania to Austria, and one from Bulgaria to Turkey. All involved large groups of refugees.

The skyjacking from Bulgaria to Turkey marked the first occasion on which any injuries are positively known to have been caused during a skyjacking. The intruders in the cockpit managed to wound both pilot and copilot before the plane limped to a landing in Istanbul. There was a message in this if we had only read it: All hijackings, no matter what the motivation, infringe upon the basic human rights of other people and carry with them the seeds of injury or death.

A skimpily reported skyjacking occurred in July of 1948 on a flight between Macao and Hong Kong. Though proof is lacking, it seems to have been an old-fashioned hijacking attempt by skyway robbers to relieve the passengers of their cash and valuables. It was the sort of job that might just as well have been pulled on stagecoach, train, or truck—but wasn't.

In mid-September of that year a group of armed Greeks came up with an innovation of their own and skyjacked a Greek commercial airliner to Yugoslavia. It was the first break, by air, into a country on the wrong side of the iron curtain, and it did not receive much applause in the Western world.

In 1949, Rumania was hit twice, Poland once. All attempts were successful. The seizure of the Polish airliner was achieved by more than a dozen Poles who had decided that they would rather live in Denmark. The Danes granted them political asylum.

It was Czechoslovakia's turn again in 1950. On March 24 three planes were headed for Prague: one from Brno, one from Ostrava, and one from Bratislava. They left as scheduled, and all landed not in Prague but in the U.S. Zone of Germany. The hijackers were Czechs who had been crewmen in the British Royal Air Force and knew a thing or two about aircraft themselves. Again, there is little official information on this triple hijacking, but it is believed that the airmen had been faced with trial and imprisonment even before they made their illegal flight to freedom. Their only crime, before the hijackings, was that they had been members of a Western armed service. This, in the Stalinist atmosphere of the early fifties, was enough to have the men branded as spies. They left barely before the ax fell, and they used the only way they knew. We in the West were of course pleased by their safe arrival in Denmark, and we accepted without question their right to political asylum. The moral question of methods versus aspirations did not occur to us.

In 1952 there was an abortive hijacking attempt on a flight between the Philippines and Red China, and in 1953 another Czechoslovakian refugee chose a landing in West Germany.

There were no recorded skyjackings for the next few years; but 1958 marked the return of the phenomenon. In February there was a successful nonscheduled flight from South Korea to North Korea, and in April there was an unsuccessful trip in the same direction. Also in 1958, the Cuban hijackings began. The first and third are scarcely more than footnotes in hijacking history. They occurred on Cuban domestic flights, and no details are available. The suspicion is that they may have been accomplished by Fidelistas on their way to power, but this is only a suspicion. It was the second of the three Cuban-involved hijackings that made more than historical footnotes. It did so because it was (in retrospect) a mindless, clumsy, almost pointless sort of adventure; and because it was the first hijacking known to have resulted in the death of passengers who had nothing to do with the affair but just sit there in the plane and be skyjacked. To that date, hijackings had been almost bloodless. No hijackers had been killed. Possibly one crew member had died. Two pilots had been injured. That was all.

This time, seventeen people were killed.

It happened on November 1, 1958, on a Cubana Airlines Viscount bound from Miami to Varadero Airport in Cuba. There were only three survivors, and it is through one of them, Osiris Martinez, that we know the story. (He told it to the Associated Press years later. His nightmares and his fear are with him still.)

Batista was coming to the end of the road in Cuba. Martinez may not have known this at the time, but had decided to return to Cuba with his wife and family after an absence in the United States for several years. Tennessee was not a bad place to live and work, but he missed the country of his birth. And so, with a new job already lined up, he was taking his loved ones back home.

"Suddenly a man jumped up from his seat and pointed a gun at us. Four other men did the same thing. Nobody knew what was happening until the five men opened a small luggage compartment on the floor and pulled out fatigue-type uniforms and machine guns." Then, says Martinez, the five men changed into the uniforms, which were marked with the red and black armbands worn by Castro's 26th-of-July movement. They were talking about landing in Cuba at a place of their own choice, getting off there with their guns and "a bundle of money," and then letting the plane proceed with the rest of its passengers.

"Some of the hijackers went into the cockpit. Later we were told that the pilot had refused to change the course of the aircraft and had been hit over the head."

A hijacker then took the controls and turned the aircraft toward a landing area in Oriente Province, near Castro's guerrilla stronghold in the mountains. But darkness fell as they approached and the passenger-pilot was unable to guide the plane to a landing on the small, unlighted strips.

"The plane repeatedly juggled up and down as time after time we couldn't land. It was like a madhouse. Everybody was screaming and vomiting. The luggage tumbled over our heads. Suddenly one of the hijackers rushed out of the cockpit and jumped into a seat, bracing himself for a crash.

"Then we hit. It was indescribable. Everything went blank and I don't recall what happened until I found myself under water, struggling to surface. I was bleeding profusely from the mouth, gashes on my head. I had several cracked ribs and my feet were torn. I couldn't move.

"I frantically shouted for my family, but they had all gone down amid the debris. I hung onto something, an object floating on the water. I heard shouts from the other two survivors. Then all was silent."

It was the silence of seventeen dead. Imagine the silence if this were to happen to a fully loaded 747.

The series for 1959 opened with a run-of-the-mill skyjacking from Cuba to the United States. This was followed by a trip from Haiti to Cuba. The series ended with another jaunt from Cuba to the U.S.A. By this time Batista was out and Castro was in. There was no sign, yet, of any possible stampede from Cuba to the U.S.A. or from the U.S.A. to Cuba. Three trips in one year do not suggest an approaching-epidemic.

But early in 1960 the stolen—that is, hijacked—fishing boats began to leave Cuba for Miami, and on April 12 the four-man crew of a Cubana Airlines Viscount diverted their domestic flight to Miami and landed in a blaze of applause from the American public. The men asked for political asylum, and we welcomed them with open arms. Furthermore, we kept the plane. We also kept the fishing boats that continued to arrive. After all, Castro had taken over American property, businesses, and investments in Cuba without offering to pay, so there was no reason why we should return an airplane and some fishing boats—especially since they had been used as escape vehicles by refugees from a Communist country.

There was a little activity on Cubana Airlines during the following months, but nothing really notable until late in October. In the meantime Trans-Australia had suffered an abortive attempt, and the USSR admitted to foiling an attempt on one of their aircraft. We of the Western world were quite interested in what little we heard of this: clearly a country that was stingy about its exit permits was bound to suffer such attempts sooner or later. It was very unlikely that anything of the sort should happen to us. People escape to freedom, not from it.

We were bolstered in our smugness, and in our sympathy for the underdog, on October 29, 1960. We may also have been a little impressed by the size of the operation. Nine disenchanted Cubans commandeered a Cubana DC-3 flying from Havana to the Isle of Pines and tried to divert it painlessly to the United States. But the diversion was not painless. The refugees were armed and ready for battle. A Cuban guard aboard the plane countered the seizure with gunfire, and a fight broke out in cockpit and in cabin. Four people were wounded, including the pilot, and the Cuban guard was killed. The DC-3 made an emergency landing at Key West, and we hailed the conquering heroes even though they had killed a man. These hijackers, too, were granted political asylum, and we gave little if any thought to the murder they had committed in their bold bid for escape.

Yet we were deeply concerned, those of us who were even aware of the event, with the result of an attempted hijacking of another Cubana plane on December 8. All five would-be hijackers were seized and swiftly executed by the Castro government. Their flight for freedom captured our imagination, and the results of failure horrified us.

Then the totally unexpected happened. On May 1, 1961, shortly after the Bay of Pigs fiasco, a National Airlines Convair 440 took off from Marathon in the Florida Keys on its way from Miami to Key West and was hijacked to Cuba. The man, who was armed with knife and pistol, told Captain Francis X. Riley that his intention was to warn Castro of an assassination attempt. The crew described the hijacker as a psychopath, which perhaps he was; but on the other hand the man may have got wind of a murder plot.

The plane, with its crew of three and handful of astonished passengers, was briefly detained and then permitted to return to Florida that same night. The hijacker remained, and has not been heard from since. To those who scan records in search of clues, it may be of interest to know that the hijacker, when purchasing his ticket, had first given his name as Elpir Cofrisi and then asked the ticket agent to add the letters "ata" to his Christian name. This spelled out "Elpirata" Cofrisi. *El Pirata* Cofrisi is said to have been a Spanish pirate of the eighteenth century. The twentieth-century Pirata was the first man in history to hijack an American commercial airliner to Cuba.

It shocked us, but not deeply. On the scoreboard of U.S. versus Cuba hijackings, we were still way ahead of the game. The fishing boats kept coming in, and a Cubana DC-3 arrived in Miami on July 3 with fourteen hijacker-refugees aboard, so we relaxed and assumed that *our* hijacking was just a one-shot deal.

We were wrong. On July 24 an armed passenger, who later proved to be an American citizen of Cuban birth, took over an Eastern Airlines Electra with thirty-eight aboard and diverted it from its Tampa destination to Havana. Crew and passengers were fed, entertained, and sent back to Miami after a brief but pleasant visit to Cuba. But the Electra was not released. It stayed behind as a pawn in a game that Castro was just beginning to learn. The United States was in possession of a hijacked Cuban naval vessel, a number of small boats, and several Cuban airplanes. Castro did suggest that now was as good a time as any to discuss the whole question of exchanging captured craft and returning skyjackers to their country of origin. But we in the United States did not want to talk and we did not want to return Cuban vessels.

So there were no discussions about the arrest and extradition of skyjackers or the return of Cuban craft.

An apparent attempt to divert a Pacific Airlines DC-3 to Cuba on July 31 failed in a blaze of gunfire. The culprit, Bruce Britt, boarded the plane in California without a ticket but with "intent to hijack the airliner and fly to Arkansas to see his estranged wife." Some of those aboard got the impression that his actual destination was Cuba. Told to deplane, he shot the passenger agent and ordered the pilot to take off. The pilot refused. Britt shot the pilot. Copilot and passengers then converged upon him and disarmed him. The pilot was blinded and the agent critically wounded.

The public was puzzled. Surely one did not hijack planes to get to Arkansas . . . ? And shoot two people on the way? This must have been an attempt to get to Cuba. But it was not. Britt really *had* wanted to get to Arkansas. Then it was probably just a freak case that we didn't have to worry about. It was unlikely that we would see any more of such ugly affairs.

This sanguine attitude was dissipated at least in part by the events of August 3.

Early in the morning of that hot summer day a gun-toting father-and-son team named Bearden commandeered a Continental Air Lines Boeing 707 jet—the first jet to be thus compromised—and demanded to be taken to Cuba. Bearden the elder seemed to have some sort of grudge against the United States. So did Cuba. What more natural, then, for a man to run to a country that shared his hostility? Bearden the younger was less embittered, but did what his father told him.

Captain B. D. Richards, veteran hijackee of the Peruvian revolution that had spawned the first known skyjacking, coolly landed in El Paso to refuel and did not take off again. The Beardens held him and several hostages imprisoned aboard the plane for nine terrifying hours on the El Paso runway until at last they were tricked into surrender by border patrolmen working with the FBI. This was a fairly satisfactory ending to a story that could have ended in the loss of a nice jet to Cuba . . . or the destruction of every human being aboard. National relief at the foiling of the attempt was muted by our realization of what could have happened; and by the growing, uncomfortable feeling that American planes were beginning to look like sitting ducks for the privateer. Sooner or later we were going to have to do something about this menace.

A sidelight to hijacking history is the ultimate fate of the Continental 707 rescued from the Beardens: As Flight 11, it was en route from Chicago to Los Angeles on May 23, 1962, skimming toward the southern fringe of Iowa, when it was suddenly rocked by a bomb exploding in the aft lavatory. The explosion caused the tail assembly to separate from the aircraft and the after portion of the fuselage to disintegrate. Out of control, the plane plunged onward and downward, and eight passengers plummeted to their deaths from the shattered after section. Shortly afterward the plane crashed near Unionville, Missouri. Thirty-six people died on impact and one, horribly injured, survived only long enough to gasp out the grim, fragmental details of the story. Not one life was spared. The FBI investigated this apparent sabotage case thoroughly and long, but failed to come to a definitive conclusion. The question still arises after all these years: Could the bomb-carrier have been a would-be hijacker? Experience with saboteurs and insurance bombers answers: Probably not. But . . . .

On August 9, 1961, six days after the El Paso siege, the third successful hijacking of a U.S.-flag carrier took place aboard a Pan American World Airways DC-8 jetliner flying from Mexico City to Guatemala. The pirate was a French national named Albert Cadon, who expressed himself as embittered by U.S. policy on Algerian independence. In what was to become *the* classic maneuver, he pulled out a .38, jammed it against the neck of a stewardess, and demanded to be taken to the cockpit.

The stewardess didn't know the rules of the hijacking game. She paused and stared at him, startled, wondering if she really ought to permit this kind of thing. Cadon was in no mood to wait while she made up her mind. Impatiently, he kicked in the cockpit door, trained the .38 on the pilot, and said, "Take me to Havana." He seemed very tense and nervous, and the crew saw no sense in arguing with him.

The Cubans were delighted to see the plane and greet the Americano tourists. Cadon was escorted quietly away by the Cuban police, but all the others aboard were treated to a generous dose of Cuban hospitality. Castro himself appeared at the airport to greet a Latin American diplomat aboard the Pan Am flight, and while the rest of the passengers did not see the premier, they did have a wonderful time. The women shopped for souvenirs and the men bought cigars and rum. (U.S. Customs later showed displeasure at these purchases.) Drinks and flowers were provided for all.

Plane, passengers, and crew were released after a stopover of several hours, and a large sigh of relief was breathed in Washington. At least Castro hadn't kept our jet, and at least the passengers had been treated well.

But relief soon gave way to anger. We had not liked the May 1 affair of the Convair, minor though it had been. The Electra still had not been returned. We had been scared by Britt and Bearden. Now we were outraged. If the newspapers had failed to make much of the previous hijackings, they made up for it now. The Pan Am plane was the third of our planes to be commandeered, the first jet transport ever to be successfully hijacked. It carried seventy-two passengers and eight crew members, a complement which added up to the largest number of persons ever to be taken out of their way—virtually kidnapped—by any single hijack attempt. Worst of all was the fact that it had been taken to Cuba; no doubt Castro was splitting his sides with laughter. One of our overseas flag carriers had been snatched with ease and carelessly returned, and we were wounded to the core of our national pride.

More important, and more appropriately, we were for the first time seriously alarmed. President Kennedy asked for special anti-hijack legislation. Some airlines, with the encouragement and cooperation of Federal Aviation Administration Chief Najeeb E. Halaby (later head of Pan Am), put security guards or sky marshals aboard many of their flights. At the same time, the FAA issued a regulation requiring airline crews to keep cockpit doors locked except during takeoffs and landings. The man in the street became suddenly and dramatically aware that there were new dangers in the air.

Congress met the presidential and public outcry by passing a law making it a federal crime for unauthorized persons to carry concealed deadly weapons aboard airliners. The law also made it a federal offense to attempt to assault, intimidate, or threaten crew members in any way that would interfere with their duties or compromise the safety of the flight. Sky piracy was to be punishable by a prison term of up to twenty years, or even by death in some cases if so determined by the jury.

Albert Cadon, even though he was not returned to us, did get his knuckles rapped with some severity. Castro may have been pleased and even flattered by Cadon's visit, but he had little use for the man himself. Cadon was extradited to Mexico, where he was tried and sentenced to eight years and nine months in prison.

As for the hijackers of his own airplanes, Castro continued to be tough, not only after the event but before and during it. At this time, Cuban guards, usually soldiers, traveled aboard many if not all Cubana flights. On the very same day that the Pan Am jet was diverted to Cuba, a dramatic illustration of the pros and cons of onboard guards was acted out in the Caribbean skies. A group of anti-Castro Cubans tried to coerce a Cubana DC-3 into going to Miami. The Cuban soldier-guards aboard went into swift and violent action, and a wild gun-battle ensued. One of the first casualties was the pilot. The copilot barely managed to bring the spinning plane under control and guide it—riddled with bullet holes—to an emergency landing in a canefield on the Isle of Pines. The embattled flight ended with three men killed, including the pilot, six wounded, and the surviving hijackers under arrest.

The Eastern Electra hijacked on July 24 was released on

August 15 and Castro got his naval vessel back. But no effort was made to come to terms on the question of the extradition or punishment of U.S. or Cuban hijackers.

There were no hijackings of American planes in the remaining months of 1961, and only one in 1962. During that time three men attempted, and failed, to hijack a private YAK-13 out of Russia. Five men took over a Venezuelan plane, landed it in Curaçao, and were extradited. Six pamphlet-dropping revolutionaries forced a Portuguese Transportes Aeros craft to Morocco and eventually to Brazil. Next, France nipped an attempt in the bud; and then it was our turn for another.

On April 13, 1962, David Healy and Leonard Oeth chartered a private Cessna 170 and hijacked it to Cuba. The victimized pilot was permitted to return to Miami with his plane, and the hijackers were subsequently returned to the United States in a roundabout way and prosecuted. Their sentence: twenty years.

There was little activity on the hijacking scene for the next three years, so little that we were almost justified in thinking that sky piracy would never become a major problem. Yet the sparks that glowed briefly and then died out were interesting because of where they glowed. KLM of the Netherlands suffered its first seizure, which was unsuccessful, and AVENSA of Venezuela suffered its second. The latter event was of more than passing interest. Six terrorists, including a young woman, menaced crew and passengers with submachine guns and forced the pilot to fly over Ciudad Bolivar so that they might drop leaflets instructing the Venezuelan voters not to vote in the forthcoming elections.

A pair of embezzlers hijacked a private plane from Miami to Cuba, an irritating but insignificant event that marked the only American seizure of 1964. Of much more interest to anyone who happened to notice the brief news items from the USSR were two attempted hijackings that originated in Russia. These were foiled, even though in one case the pilot was wounded. There had now been three attempts on Russian craft, and all of them had failed. Perhaps there had been others, unreported but successful. We could only speculate.

At home, all was calm.

And then, on October 26, 1965, the first American commercial airliner to be threatened by the hijack menace in over four years was commandeered by a young Cuban exile named Luis Medina Perez. He chose a National Airlines Electra en route from Miami to Key West, and he used a Luger-shaped toy pistol to persuade a stewardess to escort him to the cockpit so that he might order the pilot to take him to Havana. "But it's against regulations for you to talk to the captain," the stewardess explained. "Never mind that," Perez said, and gestured meaningfully with his pellet gun. The stewardess did not know it was a toy, but nevertheless coolly informed him that she would have to tell the captain they were coming. On their way to the cockpit she paused to murmur a warning message into the intercom.

Captain K. I. Carlile gave terse instructions to his copilot and flight engineer, then left the cockpit to talk to Perez in the cabin. Perez was a little taken aback by this turn of events, but insisted that he be taken to Cuba because his relatives were there and he wanted to get them out. He had tried all kinds of other ways to get there, but nothing had worked and this was the only way left. When he got to Cuba he was going to present himself to Fidel Castro and remind him of his recently proclaimed "open door" policy for Cubans opposed to his regime. Then he would ask Castro to let his relatives leave. On what? There was no air service from Cuba to the United States. Well, he would tackle that problem when he came to it.

Carlile talked to him in English and Spanish, hoping to dissuade him in one language or the other, but found the young man determined to go to Cuba. "He said unless we took him to Havana, he would kill the crew and blow up the airplane. I tried to reason with him in the cabin. He said if we landed in Key West, he would go off the deep end."

So much for reason. Carlile then asked Perez to accompany him to the cockpit, where—a point which he failed to mention to the skyjacker—Flight Engineer Wiedemann was waiting behind the door with a fire ax taken from the cockpit wall.

Perez sat down in the jump seat behind the pilot's seat without so much as a glance over his shoulder. Wiedemann moved in silently from behind and brought the fire ax down past the skyjacker's head and shoulders and clamped it, bar-like, against his chest to pin him to the seat. Perez gave up and surrendered the gun. "He was willing to cooperate and behave after he realized we held all the chips," the captain said, and emphasized that the ax had only been used to pin the man down and not batter him to pieces.

For an unsuccessful skyjacking, the story made big news. It was, as noted, the first American attempt in several years, but what really gave it headline value was the nature of the hijacker. His wistful tale of trying to free his relatives tugged at American hearts. The gun he had brandished was only a pellet gun, unloaded at that. He was only twenty-one years old, a lonely exile. As a veteran of the Bay of Pigs, he had been taking his life into his hands by trying to return to Cuba.

The public and the jury loved him. Nice young Perez went free.

What happened next may have been inspired by the Perez episode itself or by the surge of anti-Castro feeling that followed. Certainly it was an echo of some sort and not an unrelated incident. On November 17, 1965, a sixteen-year-old boy—"brilliant youth," "teen-aged honor student," "straight-A student, just the kind of boy you'd want your son to be," trumpeted the press—tried to hijack a National Airlines DC-8 bound from New Orleans to Melbourne, Florida.

Young Thomas Robinson had never missed a day of school until the day he boarded the plane. His favorite hobby was keeping up with current events. He read the papers avidly, clipped editorials, and once in a while wrote letters to the editor. He described himself as an anti-Communist and spoke proudly of his patriotism. Apathy toward a dictatorship was something that he could not understand, and apparently he felt that the Cuban people were exploited, uninformed, and unaware of their own plight, or else they would not tolerate Fidel Castro.

He got up from his seat in the tourist cabin of the plane about twenty minutes after takeoff from New Orleans, entered the first class compartment, walked up the aisle until he found an empty seat not far from the cockpit, and sat down across the aisle from Christopher (Chris) Kraft. On board with Kraft, Project Gemini Mission director, were twelve other key space agency officials including Public Affairs officer Paul Haney. There was also a Houston businessman named Edward T. Haake, with quick reflexes, among the ninety passengers.

For a few moments the boy just sat and fiddled with a newspaper on his lap. Chris Kraft watched him from across the aisle, and it seemed to him that the kid was hiding something underneath the paper.

"What have you got under that newspaper?" he asked.

Robinson answered by whipping out a .22-caliber target pistol and shoving it into Kraft's face—*and pulling back the hammer.* There was a click but no discharge.

Kraft turned pale and Robinson tried again, fanning the hammer in the manner but not with the skill of a western gunfighter. When the gun failed to go off the boy turned away from Kraft and tried to open the cockpit door. Stewardess Nancy Taylor told him that the cockpit was off limits and that he could not go in. He accepted that, turned and faced the passengers, and launched into a diatribe about the dangers of Castroism. It was not a bad speech at first. He told his captive audience that it was time somebody went to the aid of people who wanted to get out of Cuba. He said he hoped somebody would wake up. He complained that the U.S. government was not militant enough about Castroism. And then he drew a second gun from his pocket and started walking down the aisle yelling about the evils of communism and how he wanted to go to Cuba to free the prisoners.

Miss Taylor kept the cockpit informed over the intercom. Captain Dean Cooper radioed New Orleans Airport that he was returning. "There is a guy aboard who is waving guns."

At this stage, 20,000 feet above the Gulf Coast, he was waving a .32-caliber pistol and shouting about going to Havana to shoot somebody or get shot. Suddenly he started to punctuate his points by firing into the cabin floor. Nine bullets later he lowered his gun to reload it, and businessman Edward Haake sprang at him and grabbed both pistols.

The boy deflated like a pricked balloon. He looked for the holes in the cabin floor and couldn't see the sky through them. But the holes were there, small but real . . . and the plane landed safely.

Robinson was held under $50,000 bond and indicted on three counts by a federal grand jury: piracy; assaulting, intimidating and threatening the stewardess; intimidating and interfering with the pilot. The judge granted a government request for a sanity test, and federal authorities said they planned to prosecute the boy as an adult because of the seriousness of the charges.

He was subsequently declared a juvenile delinquent and confined to a correctional institution.

The year 1966 added little to the skyjack records, though it offered a couple of new twists.

Shortly after sunset on the evening of March 27, a Cubana Airlines Russian-built Ilyushin 18 took off from Santiago on a routine domestic run to Havana. The flight engineer was a man named Angel Betancourt Cueto, who was nursing a plan to escape from Cuba. He made his move when the craft was about seventy miles west of Havana. After casually locking the cockpit door, he pulled a gun, slugged the armed guard who was standing behind the pilot, and shot him dead. Then he ordered the pilot to fly to Miami. The pilot nodded, made a turn, and contacted Cuban flight control. Defensive strategy was worked out virtually under Betancourt's nose. The pilot was to fly for some distance and then start communicating in English, as if he were in contact with Miami, after which he was to circle slowly over the sea until darkness fell.

As radar screens showed the plane nearing Key West, four U.S. Navy F-102s scrambled to meet it and take a closer look. But by the time they were aloft the Cuban plane had already doubled back in a slow, graceful curve and was diminishing in the distance. Strange that the flight engineer did not catch on; but he did not. It was well after dark when the plane touched down on the runway at Havana's José Martí Airport and Betancourt finally realized how he had been tricked. Furiously, he ordered the pilot to take off again. The pilot refused. Betancourt killed him with one shot, wounded the copilot, and tried desperately to wrestle the plane off the ground himself. It would not rise; it plowed into a field at the end of the runway and skidded to a stop. Betancourt fled into the darkness. Armed militiamen immediately swarmed through the area and a massive manhunt got under way.

It went on for many days.

Betancourt was captured two weeks later in a Franciscan monastery in Havana. Three Franciscans were reportedly arrested with him. Relations between the Roman Catholic Church and the Castro government were already strained. Now they were worse.

On July 7 another Cubana Ilyushin was hijacked out of Santiago. This time the pilot himself was one of the nine hijackers. The destination was Jamaica, and the landing was a success from the point of view of the refugees. And this time the copilot was severely wounded.

In that year there were two more attempts, one in spring and one in summer, on Soviet airliners. Again the attempts failed, and again there was gunfire and injury. Skyjacking was getting to be quite a bloody affair. Certainly when the pilots were armed or trained soldier-guards were aboard, some injury almost always occurred.

September 28 marked the last hijacking of the year. It was perfect for a finale: almost a score of people were on stage, including the beautiful blonde star. An Argentine nationalist group, consisting of eighteen not very terrifying terrorists led by the lovely Maria Christina Varrier, boarded an Argentine Airlines DC-4 bound from Buenos Aires to Rio Gallegos and forced it to fly instead to the Falkland Islands, a diminutive British colony in the south Atlantic. That there was no airfield to accommodate the DC-4 bothered no one, not even the pilot; he managed a neat landing on a fairly level area that the islanders sometimes use as a race track. Around the emergency airstrip were sheep meadows and a scattering of farmhouses. Not far away was the capital, Stanley (population 1,250, half the total of the island). A crowd soon gathered. Sheepherders get up very early in the morning, especially those who have never seen a plane before. Maria and her band announced themselves as members of El Condor, a group dedicated—on this occasion, anyway—to the proposition that the Falklands belong to the Argentine and should be returned by Britain to their rightful owners.

They planted flags and made rousing speeches in Spanish reasserting Argentina's claim to the tiny, windswept islands, and the islanders listened in polite astonishment because they themselves do not speak Spanish. Miss Varrier and her associates, their speeches made, withdrew into the plane and held it as if it were their captured castle. All they had really wanted to do was draw attention to their country's long-standing claim to the British-ruled Falklands, and in this they succeeded admirably.

The whole thing blew over quickly but the little Falklands actually made headlines while it was going on. A certain awkwardness complicated the end of the story. The DC-4 did not have enough room to take off again and was out of fuel anyway; there were no hotel accommodations on the islands, so that the crew and twenty-five passengers who were not part of the hijacking team had to find shelter in the homes of hospitable islanders; in view of the nonexistent airport facilities there was no prospect of a rescue plane, and the monthly mail ship was not due in for another week and might not even have room for so many passengers; and no one knew exactly what to do with the Condor group, including the Condor group. After a couple of days they crept out of the plane and sheltered in a church, and then they surrendered and waited for someone to pick them up. Eventually they were expatriated and everyone got home safely though quite late.

The events of 1967 were more ominous. The first skyjacking of the year featured the seizure of a Russian-built Egyptian plane by a man named Riyad Hajjaj who wanted to go to Jordan, and did, taking forty-one passengers with him. It was a small incident, and Hajjaj was described by the Egyptian police as a common criminal; but the hijacking picture had now widened to include a new arena—one that was already beginning to crackle with tension.

Two and a half months later five men took a free ride on a Nigerian plane, and no one seemed to mind too much. It was only a local trip.

And then, on June 30, 1967, a private plane on its way from Spain to Majorca was diverted to Algiers. Seizures of private planes are seldom accorded much attention. They are a nuisance to the pilots and owners of the craft, and sometimes an expense, but as a rule they have nothing like the shock value or significance involved in the commandeering of a big commercial jet with many lives aboard and thousands of dollars at stake.

This seizure was different, because Moise Tshombe was aboard. The former premier of the Congo had gone abroad ostensibly for medical treatment, which he undoubtedly needed, but he had also found it expedient to absent himself from Africa and particularly the Congo because of the countless bitter enmities he had made during his years of power.

So hated was Tshombe that there was a death sentence waiting for him in the Congo. It looked very much as though he had been kidnapped by some or other of his enemies so that he might be returned to the Congo to face execution or be quietly murdered in Algeria. The strongest possibility was that he would be formally extradited and legally disposed of by the Congolese.

None of these things happened. Nobody really wanted Tshombe dead and nobody really wanted him alive. Especially, nobody seemed to want him on the loose. He was kept in Algiers under house arrest until he died of a heart attack, which was certified by a team of medical experts called in by his Algerian hosts, two years later almost to the day.

It was the first plainly political kidnap-skyjacking on record. With it, a tiny little seed was sown; an ominous little seed that grew slowly, unobtrusively, into an enormous, ugly parasitic growth.

The episode was significant for another reason. Tshombe's fellow passengers on the plane were promptly released, but the plane and its two pilots were not. When ten weeks had passed and the pilots were still under detention, the International Federation of Air Line Pilots Association began to toy loudly and publicly with the idea of boycotting Algerian airports. The pilots were freed soon afterward. Another little germ of an idea had been sown, and this one eventually grew into the suggestion that any country that harbored hijackers should be totally boycotted by the airlines.

On August 6, 1967, five armed men described as "pro-Castro guerrillas" hijacked a Colombian Aerocondor DC-4 and forced it to land in Havana. A month later, three heavily armed men diverted a Colombian Avianca DC-3 to Santiago. In November, another private plane left Florida for Cuba. In February of 1968, a young Marine tried unsuccessfully to hijack a Pan Am

DC-6 at Danang, South Vietnam. Eight days later a man named Thomas Boynton forced the pilot of a private plane to drop him off in Cuba. Three days after that, on February 21, 1968, Lawrence Rhodes, Jr., who was wanted for a payroll robbery, jammed an automatic pistol against a stewardess's head and forced a Delta Airlines DC-8 to take him to Cuba.

More or less run-of-the-mill cases, nearly all of them. The major significance of the Rhodes skyjacking was that it was the first successful seizure of an American commercial airliner since 1961. One major skyjacking in seven years is no cause for hysteria.

What we did not notice at first was how the momentum, worldwide, had started to build. In March of '68 there were four skyjackings, in June there were two, in July there were six (two of which failed); and that was only the beginning. By the end of the year, twenty commercial airliners had been successfully commandeered to Cuba and another three to other countries. Unsuccessful ventures and diversions of private planes, once quite interesting news, got lost in the shuffle. It should have been clear to every aviation authority and every government in the world that hijacking was starting to catch on in a big way; we should have suspected that an epidemic was in the wind. But we did not. Most of us did not even place much significance on the hijacking by three Arab nationalists of an El Al 707 to Algiers on July 23. It made headlines because the crew and some of the passengers were held hostage for some time while pressure was exerted on Israel by the Palestine Liberation Front for the release of a number of Arab guerrillas held captive by the Israelis. The incident was ugly and dragged on for many days, but it seemed to be an isolated one.

Trend-spotters could only spot a trend toward Cuba, which was natural in view of the amount of traffic in that direction. They also noted that most of the hijackers of the year had been Cubans wanting to return to Cuba without going through regular channels, or criminals seeking a haven in a country unfriendly to the United States, or people mentally unbalanced. Almost reluctantly they conceded that there was no evidence available to show that the Castro regime had sponsored or even encouraged air piracy activities.

They further observed that Castro was treating his visitors from the North with elaborate courtesy and possibly exaggerated concern. He would not permit jetliner passengers to depart on the plane which had brought them to Cuba because, as his spokesmen solicitously explained, the runways at Havana's José Martí Airport were too short to permit safe takeoff with a load of passengers. The pilots disagreed, but Cuban authorities paid no attention to them.

A pattern was established for the treatment of the victims of hijackers: American crews rested briefly and then flew their planes back home without their passengers. The passengers would be dined, wined, given books, cigars, and photographs of Che Guevara. Then they would be taken on a sightseeing tour and driven by bus to Varadero ninety miles away. The route to Varadero offered fine views of modern buildings and unpolluted countryside, and the passengers generally enjoyed the experience. Sometimes they would be put up overnight in one of the finer hotels. From Varadero Airport they would be flown back home in a special plane sent from the United States. The reasons for this runaround were not completely clear, because the José Martí runways were and always had been more than adequate to cope with all kinds of air traffic, but the suspicion grew that Castro welcomed the opportunity of showing off socialist Cuba and showering hospitality upon his uninvited guests.

Nor was the hospitality exactly free. Castro let himself get stuck with part of the tab a time or two and then started sending bills. For every plane hijacked to Havana he would collect at least $2,500 to $3,000. This charge covered landing fees, fuel, food for passengers, accommodations as needed, and incidentals. The airlines soon got into the habit of paying promptly rather than take the risk of having their planes impounded in Cuba. They were losing enough money as it was in out-of-service time, which, for a commercial jet, is likely to mean $45,000 or more per day in lost revenue.

By the middle of 1968 the jokes about the Cuban joyride were coming thick and fast. There were so many of them that airline personnel began to lose their sense of humor and react very sternly to facetious queries about how long it took to get to Cuba, or the weather in Havana. Even the Cuban news services began to get funny. "Relax and enjoy it!" was the advice in one newspaper. So long as you were going to be hijacked, you might just as well—according to the Cuban newsman—turn a friendly smile upon the hijacker and lean back to think cheering thoughts about cigars and rum.

Suggestions about how to prevent skyjackings were as numerous as the jokes, and some of them were almost as funny. "Strip every boarding passenger bare," one wag suggested; then you wouldn't have to worry about concealed weapons. Another, also dwelling on nudity, suggested that the stewardess do a striptease to distract the hijacker. The government, the Federal Aviation Administration, and other agencies were not amused. Suggestions being mulled over in official quarters were much more serious. One of them attempted to tackle head-on the question of the Cuban exiles in the United States who sought to return to their native land via skyjacked airliners. Back in December, 1965, the United States government had set into operation the so-called Freedom Airlift, which consisted of daily flights from the United States to Cuba to airlift Cuban refugees to Miami. Castro had by this time announced his open-door policy, which was that any Cubans wishing to leave Cuba would be more than welcome to do so, and good riddance. Legitimate means of departure were few, and so the United States was providing the transportation.

Now, on July 11, 1968, the State Department announced that it would permit Cuban exiles wishing to return home to ride free aboard the planes that otherwise flew empty to Cuba for the pickups. It seemed an excellent way to prevent dis-enchanted Cubans from grabbing their own free rides on planes that were supposed to be going somewhere else. But Castro turned down the idea.

Skyjackings to Cuba continued unhindered, and indeed escalated from August throughout the rest of the year.

It seemed that only the United States and Cuba were at all concerned by the phenomenon. Other governments, and their airlines, were not taking the skyjack threat seriously. That it occasionally happened in other countries was nothing to worry about—so they thought.

But the International Air Transport Association was deeply concerned. Members of this body, and primarily its director general, Knut Hammarskjöld, were disturbed not only by the skyjackings but by the apathy of governments and airlines. From the very beginning, when the skyjack menace was only a tiny black cloud on the horizon, they felt that it was something that could happen to anyone, anywhere, any time, and that no country was exempt. They said this loud and clear; but their audience was deaf. Hammarskjöld himself was particularly concerned that the prominence given by all the media to the audacious El Al hijacking of July 23, coupled with the escalation of hijackings to Cuba, would offer examples to people worldwide and inspire those anywhere, anytime hijackings that had worried him so long.

With this in mind, IATA initiated discussions with the U.S. State Department. State was also worried. They had only one channel of communications with the Cuban government, and that was through the Swiss embassy in Havana. Hammarskjöld felt that IATA, as a completely neutral body and one devoted solely to the interests of international air transport, might be able to make more direct contact with the Cubans. After long talks, Hammarskjöld told the State Department that he would be prepared to go to Cuba and see what might be done. At least he would be able to establish one more line of communication in regard to aviation affairs. Cubana Airlines was a member of IATA, and there was every good reason in the world for IATA's director general to visit their home base.

Hammarskjöld went to Cuba with the State Department's blessing. He had already received an invitation from his Cuban colleagues, in response to his expressed desire to discuss a variety of air transport matters, and he knew that they would welcome him. He arrived in Havana on January 18, 1969, having left from a neutral country in a Canadian-registered plane piloted by one Canadian and one Jamaican. "Neutrality" and "objectivity" were the key words for his trip.

The meeting was little noted in the press and the main purpose of it was kept under wraps until much later. In fact, it is only now, in these pages, that it is being made public. Present were six high-echelon Cuban aviation authorities, including Commander C. Rey Morina, general director of IACC (Instituto de Aviación Civil de Cuba), as well as Knut Hammarskjöld and Dr. J. G. Thomka-Gazdik, general counsel for IATA.

It was an historic conference, in its quiet way, and we do not yet know all the fruits of it. But it was immediately established that the Cuban government, and Cuban aviation authorities, were extremely disturbed by the hijackings in both directions and fully agreed with Hammarskjöld that they presented a severe problem for aviation in general. At the same time Mr. Hammarskjöld told his Cuban colleagues in all frankness that, so long as Cuba did not actively try to discourage the incidents, Cuba would be increasingly regarded by the general public as being in part responsible for them.

The director general brought up a number of points for discussion, mainly the following:

1. That some of the people who had hijacked planes to Cuba had been welcomed as friends, but that most hijackers were criminals or abnormal individuals not wanted in Cuba. Possibly a way could be found to establish whether the person was a bona fide political refugee or somebody who had robbed the Bank of Texas.

2. That the hijackings were contagious, like the Hong Kong flu, and abnormal people reading about them might be tempted to try the same thing themselves. It would have psychological impact, therefore, if the Cubans were to make it known that their friends were welcome but that criminals would be dealt with as criminals.

3. That it might be helpful if normal means of air transport could be somehow provided for bona fide travelers wishing to come to Cuba from, for example, the United States and Colombia.

4. That it should be possible, in the event of a hijacking, to facilitate procedures at the receiving end in order to reduce as much as possible the inconvenience suffered by people who had been diverted from their normal destination. (Here, Mr. Hammarskjöld remarked that it would be a great advantage from many points of view if the hijacked plane could be allowed to leave as soon as possible *with* its passengers, and

observed that the runway at Cuba's international airport was in all respects suitable for takeoff by fully loaded jetliners.)

5. That Cuba and Cubana Airlines were highly respected in the field of aviation, and that it would have an enormous impact of good will if some sort of initiative could be taken by the Cuban government or other Cuban authorities in relation to hijacking.

6. That it was particularly important that their good influences be used, and the sooner the better, in the light of the strange and ugly developments that had recently occurred in Beirut and Athens—such as killing people and blowing up aircraft.

Mr. Hammarskjöld's Cuban hosts responded freely and fully to his comments and made a number of cogent points of their own. Of particular interest to us was their reply to Hammarskjöld's remarks about the swift return of passengers and crew in the aircraft on which they had arrived.

Commander C. Rey Morina explained the Cuban position as follows:

"A commander of a flight which has been deviated to Cuba is very upset and nervous. We have spoken several times to the captains of the aircrafts which had been brought to Cuba and they are emotionally upset. It shows in their faces and in their general behavior. We do not think that in these conditions they can assume the responsibility of taking the passengers back to the point of origin. . . . For ourselves, we think human life is the most important thing. . . . We have the highest respect and interest and concern for the lives of the passengers and the safety of the flight. . . . We have had certain cases in which the planes have been delayed here for some hours because we have noticed that the condition of the pilot was not good at all and we did not want to have an accident happen to the plane."

Of equal interest and more potential significance was the Cuban reaction to the idea of introducing, or reintroducing, normal means of air transport to Cuba from such countries as Colombia and the United States: ". . . We have not told them not to fly to Cuba. . . . We have never prohibited the airlines from these countries to fly to Cuba—they have done so on their own decision, and they have discontinued their flights to Cuba.

. . . The problem is not on our side but on the other side. . . . If they make a request to recognize their flights, then we would consider their request. . . . We do not think there will be any problem if they make such a request."

The suggestion here is that if Pan American or Delta, for example, were to decide that they would like to fly to Cuba, they would be welcome there; the implication is that, since discussions regarding such flights would have to be conducted on a diplomatic level, the Cuban government was looking for official recognition. (It still is.) Initial negotiations between the United States and Cuba would have to be taken up through the Swiss, and if an interest in an agreement were to be shown by the Cubans—which it almost certainly would be—the two countries could go into direct negotiation to bring about reasonably normal air traffic. Any bilateral agreement relating to traffic rights and routes would also include extradition provisions and other anti-hijacking articles.

We have already seen at least one of the results of Mr. Hammarskjöld's quick and quiet trip to Cuba, and one of these days we will be seeing more.

But even while IATA's top man was trying earnestly to come to grips with it, the problem was multiplying and becoming increasingly slippery.

By no means all skyjackings of this period originated in the United States, nor did all of them end up in Cuba. One began and ended in the Philippines; the hijacker was electrocuted. One began and ended in Greece; the hijacker was sent to prison for eight months. Others ended successfully wherever the hijackers wanted to go. The failures were vastly outnumbered by the successes. Skyjacking was turning out to be as easy as thumbing a ride.

3 / FLY THE FRIENDLY SKIES OF THE PFLP

The skyjack epidemic hit the world in 1969.

In that year, fifty-eight airliners were diverted to Cuba from the United States and other countries. Thirteen others were skyjacked to other lands.

For some time the United States had been wrestling with the problem almost alone. Now, if it was any consolation—which it was not—we had plenty of company in our worries. The countries in which the skyjacked flights originated in that bonanza year of 1969 included Greece, Colombia, Peru, Ecuador, Mexico, Venezuela, Portuguese Angola, Nicaragua, Ethiopia, the United Arab Republic, Honduras, Turkey, Brazil, Argentina, Poland, Chile, South Korea, Costa Rica, and, of course, the United States. Many of these countries were afflicted more than once, and some of them several times. The United States was still well in the lead, but the field of operations was widening to envelop more and more nations.

The influence of the press in, as the Russians might phrase it, "putting ideas into people's heads and stimulating further such acts of violence" is a question that will be argued from now to doomsday without being satisfactorily answered. No good purpose is ever served by buttoning up the press. In the case of such newsworthy stories as skyjackings, the press can do much to tell the world—including would-be skyjackers—about the horrors of skyjacking and its consequences.

But somehow the word had got around that the thing to do these days was skyjack. It worked in the United States, so why not here?

The hijackers for the most part consisted of the usual assortment of homesick Cubans, jobless misfits, criminals on the run, and lost souls suffering from various degrees of mental illness. And, considering the great number of successes and attempts, there were relatively few casualties. But there were some new elements in the picture, or at least new developments on earlier themes, and they were ugly ones.

One was the increasing ease with which all kinds of hijackers, from trembling little failures to powerful-looking Black

Nationalists, were taking over planes. True, loaded guns and long-bladed knives were often used, but so were toy pistols and such things as cans of mosquito spray, bottles of shaving lotion, and candles concealed in newspapers or handkerchiefs and described by the hijackers as grenades and bombs and sticks of dynamite. Who was to guess the true nature of the hidden weapon? A stewardess could hardly ask the hijacker if his gun was real, and if so, loaded; a pilot would not dare to take the chance of discovering, in one last, hideously explosive moment, that the package did contain a bomb. Airline directives made it very clear that "the most important consideration under the act of aircraft piracy is the safety of the lives of passengers and crew." Crews were urged to comply, in the face of an armed or apparent armed attempt, with the demands of the skyjacker, and not make any attempt to "disarm, shoot out, or otherwise jeopardize the safety of the flight." The wording of the directive varied from airline to airline, but the gist was always the same: Do not take chances.

The problem was further aggravated by the fact that the detection devices coming into use could scarcely pinpoint every hairbrush, aerosol can, or cosmetic bottle as a potentially dangerous weapon.

Another nasty note was the resurgence of the purely political hijacking. (The idea of a "purely" political act of such violent nature is arguable. Many people, the author included, believe that under no circumstances is skyjacking the act of a well-balanced individual or group mentality. Yet for the sake of convenience and clarity, some skyjackings must be described as essentially political in nature.) The most outstanding seizure of 1969 was that of a Trans World Airlines 707 bound from Los Angeles to Tel Aviv.

It was August 29. The jet had stopped over in New York and Rome and was scheduled to land in Athens before concluding its flight to Tel Aviv. It carried twelve crew members and 101 passengers, two of whom were hijackers. The craft was over the Adriatic Sea, not long after its departure from Rome, when two persons got up from their first-class seats and threaded their way down the aisle. One was an attractive (or, according to some, "strikingly beautiful") brunette who was flourishing a pistol and grenade, and the other was a male confederate with a gun in his hand and a time bomb in his pocket. Their names were Leila Khaled and Salim Isawi or Essawai, and they described themselves as members of the Popular Front for the Liberation of Palestine. They marched into the cockpit with their weapons and announced that they were now in command. Captain Dean Carter, looking down the barrel of a pistol, was obliged to agree.

The ninety-nine passengers still in their seats now heard an announcement from the cockpit:

"Ladies and gentlemen, please kindly fasten your seat belts. This is your new captain speaking. The Che Guevara Commando Unit of PFLP, which has taken command of TWA Flight 840, requests all passengers to adhere to the following instructions: Remain seated and be calm. For your own safety, place your hands behind your heads."

Captain Dean Carter radioed the control tower in Athens. "I am overflying Athens," he said, and overflew it. Requests from the ground for further information went unanswered. TWA in Athens alerted their company's headquarters: Flight 840 had been hijacked.

Certain now that they were on their way to wherever they wanted to go, the hijackers had another talk to Flight 840's passengers.

"Make no move that would endanger the life of other passengers. We will consider all your demands—within the safe limits of our plans.

"Among you is a passenger responsible for death and misery of a number of Palestinian children, women, and men, on behalf of whom we are carrying out this operation. This assassin will be brought before a Palestinian revolutionary court. The rest of you will be honorable guests in a hospitable and friendly country.

"Every one of you, regardless of religion or citizenship, is guaranteed freedom to go wherever he pleases as soon as the plane has safely landed. Thank you for your cooperation, and we wish you a happy journey."

Having thus stolen a line or two customarily spoken by the legitimate captain of the ship, the skyjackers proceeded to steal another. Captain Carter, in radio contact with a ground control center below, started to identify himself as "TWA Flight—" when the woman interrupted him. "This is Popular Front Number One. We are the flight of the Palestine liberation forces." Carter could scarcely argue. There was, after all, a bomb in the cockpit and a gun against his head.

Later, the woman's voice again crackled over the radio, this time for the benefit of the Israeli air controller at Lydda Airport near Tel Aviv. "We have kidnapped this American plane because Israel is a colony of America and the Americans are giving the Israelis Phantom planes. . . . Tel Aviv! We are from the Popular Front for the Liberation of Palestine. What can you do about it?"

Obviously, nothing.

The plane started heading for a Damascus landing. Syrian jet fighters zoomed aloft to escort it to the landing strip.

Somehow the passengers did not get the impression that they were landing in a particularly friendly and hospitable country. The jets looked ominous. Nor was the debarkation to be orderly and easy. A bomb, the captain informed them, was about to explode, and all aboard had better follow the instructions of the crew and move out quickly. They leapt out without waiting for the gangway and began scurrying to safety.

Moments later, the plane rocked with an explosion and the cockpit blew apart. (This was a mistake: The plane was supposed to have been destroyed, but some of the explosives were faulty and only the cockpit blew up.)

There was no "assassin" aboard the plane, except perhaps Miss Khaled or her companion, nor was anyone taken before a Palestinian revolutionary court. This had been revolutionary raving. The line about freedom of movement for all the honorable guests also turned out to be hot air. Most of the passengers were questioned at length and taken, hours after landing, to temporary accommodations. Soon afterward they were permitted to leave Syria. Six Israelis, however, were kept and subjected to intensive interrogation by Syrian authorities. The four women in the group were released after two days of this, but the two Israeli men (both civilians) were held until December 5—that is, for three months and more after their forced landing in that friendly, hospitable country. The price of their freedom was the release of thirteen Syrians kept prisoner by Israel.

The loudest outcry during this affair, apart from that raised by Israel, came from airline pilots. They were appalled by the detention of passengers, and furiously denounced the lack of action by international organizations in affairs such as this one and the El Al hijacking to Algeria of July 1968. The International Federation of Airline Pilots Association (IFALPA) held an emergency meeting at which they threatened to call a twenty-four-hour worldwide strike unless the United Nations took immediate action. They also sent a furious cable to the Syrian government, protesting the fact that no punitive action had been taken against the hijackers.

In the end there was no strike, but the pilots' voices had been clear. Some observers thought that they had come up with one of the best anti-hijacking propositions thus far. Perhaps a worldwide strike would not be the answer, but how about an airline boycott of countries harboring hijackers? It was something to think about.

So we thought . . . and thought and thought.

This type of skyjacking activity was not confined to the Middle East. Nor, though the shameful Damascus episode was the most newsworthy of the year, was it the first of its kind. The others were not so "purely" political, but they certainly had revolutionary overtones.

On January 19 an Ecuadorian prop-jet en route from Guayaquil to Quito had been overrun by fifteen hijackers, all apparently Ecuadorians. Three of them were armed with machine guns and some of the rest with pistols, knives, and other weapons. One of them produced a homemade bomb as another persuasive reason why Captain Dean Ricker should change his route and go to Cuba. Typically, they threatened the captain with death; typically, the captain was forced to comply in order to avoid tragic consequences for all.

When the plane landed at José Martí Airport the hijackers burst out of it like young delinquents who had succeeded in closing down a school and were now abandoning it to its fate. "Viva Fidel!" they yelled, waving their guns and knives. "Long live Fidel Castro!" They ranged in age from about fifteen to twenty-five, and there were three young women among them. Airport guards promptly took them into custody.

One of the hijackers, a teen-ager, told stewardess Maria Flores that he wanted to go to Cuba so that he could see freedom. "Cuba is a paradise," he said. "I want equality." There were other groups in Ecuador, he and his companions told her, who wanted to hijack a plane to Cuba.

True enough, there were several such attempts in the months that followed.

On September 6, 1969, something new in the history of air piracy happened—a double hijacking. In retrospect it seems a crudely simple, unimaginative, and even puny affair, but it was a first.

Twelve men and a woman, armed with machine guns and pistols, hijacked two Ecuadorian Air Force C-47 transport planes and attempted to force them both to Cuba. Both planes had been on domestic flights from Quito to Guayaquil when they were commandeered, and did not have the fuel capacity for a Cuban flight. With seven hijackers on one plane and six on the other, both aircraft flew to Tumaco, Colombia, for refueling. There were no incidents aboard one of the planes during this first of its several refueling stops, but for reasons that we will never know things got out of hand aboard the other. The copilot was shot and killed and another crewman was severely wounded. The hijackers abandoned the bloodied plane and left fourteen passengers to their own devices in Tumaco, then joined their comrades on the second plane. Thus thirteen hijackers, seven crew members, and thirty-four passengers took off for Cuba, but still with insufficient fuel to get there.

A second refueling stop was made at Panama, and then another at Jamaica. It was late in the evening of a very long day that the plane arrived at Santiago de Cuba to disgorge its weary load. By this time the passengers of the abandoned plane had had a chance to tell their story. They said that the hijackers had referred to their mission as "Operation Ho Chi Minh," and that the dual seizure was in retaliation for the deaths, in May, of several students during anti-government riots at the University of Guayaquil in Ecuador.

Meanwhile, in another part of the widening arena, Eritrean

guerrillas were preparing an encore to one of their performances. In August, they had diverted a plane to Khartoum; on September 14, 1969, three of them diverted an Ethiopian flight bound from Addis Ababa to Djibouti and forced the pilot to land in Aden. None of the sixty-six passengers were hurt and the crew also went unscathed, but one of the youthful hijackers was shot repeatedly by an Ethiopian secret police official who was listed as a passenger on the flight. The youth, he said, had tried to escape after the plane landed, and had had to be stopped by six bullets pumped into his arms and stomach.

In Damascus, a spokesman for the Eritrean Liberation Front claimed credit for the hijacking and said that it "was not the first blow to be aimed against Ethiopian economic interests abroad, nor will it be the last." One aim of the operation was to dramatize the campaign for Eritrean independence from Ethiopia, which has ruled Eritrea since 1952. Another was to retaliate "for the mass and brutal annihilation campaign waged by the cowardly occupation forces in Eritrea." Other methods employed by the ELF, according to their own statements, include the assassination of Ethiopian officials in Eritrea and repeated acts of sabotage in Ethiopia. What next?—the kidnapping for blackmail-and-ransom of Ethiopian diplomats? That would not shatter any precedents.

The Eritrean Liberation Front is no fly-by-night organization, in spite of its penchant for skyjacking. It is based in Damascus, Syria, where it maintains a large office, and has the official backing of the Syrian government which supplies it with weapons and permits it to train its guerrillas on Syrian soil. It claims to have recruited an army of 10,000 to 15,000 men to fight for independence.

Postscript: Addis Ababa, Ethiopia, December 13. An Ethiopian airliner arrived here today from Athens with the bodies of two would-be hijackers aboard. The two men, armed with pistol and a knife, were killed by the plane's security guards when they tried to hijack the Ethiopian Airlines Boeing 727 jet shortly after it left Madrid Friday (December 12) for Addis Ababa. They were carrying bombs, a pistol, and a knife. The plane's guards killed them both in simultaneous gun battles in economy and first-class cabins before screaming and cowering passengers. The incident marked the first time hijackers were slain aboard an airborne jet. In Syria, the hijackers were identified as members of the Eritrean Liberation Front, a movement seeking the independence of Moslem Eritrea from predominantly Christian Ethiopia. A spokesman in Syria demanded the arrest of the "Ethiopian murderers."

Skyjackings were getting increasingly bloody—and frequent. Also well-organized and expensive.

A Chilean Airlines Boeing 727 was seized on December 19, 1969, after taking off for Asunción, Paraguay, and its pilot ordered to Cuba. The lone hijacker was a man named Patricio Alarcon Rojas, a member of Chile's Leftist Revolutionary Movement, a pro-Peking organization. His revolutionary affiliations may not be particularly significant, nor did his action spearhead an influx to Cuba of Chilean planes. And a good thing that was, too; what really hit the Chilean government below the belt was the bill sent to them by Havana authorities to cover provisions, fuel, and landing rights—$20,000! But they paid.

Throughout the year American planes continued to fly to Cuba on a more or less regular basis. At the first word of a hijacking in progress the air traffic control center in Miami would make a hot-line call to the air traffic control center in Havana to inform the Cubans that company was on the way. This was no mere courtesy; this was a move to ensure that the arriving plane would not be shot down by Cuban air defenses. At the same time the U.S. State Department's man in Miami would be calling the State Department's Cuba desk in Washington, after which the State Department's coordinator of Cuban affairs would put in a swift call to the hijacking specialist at the Swiss embassy. The hijacking specialist would then send a message to the Swiss embassy in Havana, preparing them for the arrival of the aircraft and asking them to take all appropriate steps for the safe return of plane and passengers. Sometimes the Czech hijacking specialist, rather than the Swiss, would act as intermediary. But the result was the same. By the time a hijacked plane arrived in Cuba, all Havana was ready for it.

But a few details had begun to change. The restaurant and gift shop at the Havana airport had expanded facilities to take care of the land-office business brought in by the unscheduled landings and were making more money than ever. The landing fees had gone up. Runways and electronic landing aids had been further improved, not only for the sake of hijacked planes but because Cuban aviation authorities did not want to run the risk of wrapping up a runway with a disabled airplane when they had other traffic coming in. Also, Castro seemed to have lost interest in exploiting the propaganda possibilities offered by the hijackings. On February 10, 1969, Cuban authorities omitted the usual scenic tour and bus trip to Varadero and allowed a hijacked Eastern Air Lines DC-8 to take off with its full load of passengers and return with them to the United States. This became the pattern: no more long nights in Cuban hotels; no more uneasy takeoffs without the passengers; no more special flights flown in to remove the guests. A new understanding had been reached between the U.S. and Cuban governments for the prompt return of hijacked passengers—possibly as a result of Knut Hammarskjöld's January trip to Cuba. The move did not decrease the incidence of hijackings, but at least it made things a little less burdensome for the hundreds of innocent people involved.

If there had been any hope that the year 1970 would see a significant dip on the hijacking chart, that hope was promptly shattered. There were six attempted hijackings in January alone, and from then on the graph continued to climb upward. By the end of the year, eighty-four skyjacking attempts appeared on the record books. Fifty-five were successful. Most of these involved commercial airliners carrying hundreds of passengers. The total loss of time and revenue for the airlines is incalculable, though statisticians will someday probably come up with the approximate financial cost to the industry. But no one will ever be able to figure out the cost to the non-industry people caught up in the skyjacking experience—not just the money loss, if any, but the over-all cost.

There is the fear, for one thing: The fear of the Cuban exile on a domestic flight who suddenly realizes that he is being returned against his will to a land from which he once escaped and which will now offer him God alone knows what kind of welcome. The fear of the Israeli citizen or American Jew who finds himself sweltering in an airless plane parked on a desert strip in an alien land, not daring to think that what might happen to him next. The fear of the ordinary passenger who sees a gunman forcing his way into the cockpit and can only imagine what is going on inside, until perhaps he hears a shot and feels a terrible shuddering go through the plane. The fear of a man coming out of a washroom and finding himself staring into the barrel of a gun. The fear of a hundred people sitting aloft at 20,000 feet with nothing to do but wait. . . .

Then there is the time loss, the hours of life snatched away, hours that should have been spent on the firmness of earth in the ordinary course of daily living. How many vital appointments have been postponed, or altogether missed? What business deals have gone down the drain, what opportunities irretrievably lost? What weddings have been delayed, what deathbed scenes left unattended, what reunions missed, what family occasions ruined by the absence of some and the anxiety of others? How many people have followed the course of any single hijacking and waited fearfully, hour after hour, for news of its happy or unhappy ending? For each of the thousands of passengers involved in a hijacking, there have been one or two or several or many other people down on the ground who have been affected one way or another by what happens to the one aloft. If there are one hundred passengers on one hijacked plane, the ripple effect of the incident must reach many hundreds of people.

The total effect is truly incalculable.

Though the threat of a major disaster still hangs in the air, some of the events of 1970 are going to be hard to top. In that year, the skyjacking pattern got increasingly outlandish and bizarre.

The first seizure of the year occurred on New Year's Day. That is to say, it *began* on the first day of the year, but was afflicted by so many mishaps and dragged on for so long that some records log it as a January 2 occurrence. Not that any distance records were set; the trip consumed far more time than mileage.

The craft chosen for the flight was a Brazilian Cruzeiro Do Sul Caravelle en route between Montevideo, Uruguay, and Rio de

Janeiro. The hijackers struck shortly after takeoff and forced the pilot, at gunpoint, to divert to Buenos Aires. There, they told him he was to take on additional fuel and pick up navigation maps with routes to Cuba. This was done.

There were five hijackers—four young men and a woman (described as "pretty"), who admitted to being revolutionaries and said that their mission was to escort to Havana the wife and two small daughters of a revolutionary comrade who was in jail and being tortured in Brazil. Fine, they were on their way.

The Caravelle jet left the Buenos Aires airport for Antofagasta, Chile, where the plane refueled again and once more took off. Next stop was to be Lima, Peru, for another infusion of gas. (This plane seems to have had an extraordinarily thirsty tank. Or could the pilot have been stalling?) Refueling in Lima proceeded as scheduled. But when the pilot tried to take off again he found that one of the two jet engines would not start because of a dead battery. That was only the beginning. Problem followed problem, and one mechanical difficulty after another kept the plane grounded on the tarmac for twenty-seven hours.

No one was allowed to leave the plane. The five hijackers kept the twenty-one passengers and crew of seven under guard with pistols. Meals were sent aboard. The heat inside was suffocating; there was no air conditioning because of the mechanical failure. It was suggested to the hijackers that they transfer to another airliner, but this did not appeal to them. They were Brazilian revolutionaries, at odds with their own government, and they wanted to hijack a Brazilian plane. If the plane they were aboard would not start, then they wanted another airliner sent from Brazil. Peruvian riot police ringed the plane but they could think of nothing to do. There wasn't a great deal to do inside, either. At one point the girl hijacker, bored with just sitting there holding a pistol on the cockpit crew, tossed a letter out of the window identifying the group as members of the Valpamares Revolutionary Command and protesting the torture of political prisoners in Brazilian jails. The mother of the little girls, the message added, would return to "fight in Brazil" after leaving her children in Cuba.

It got hotter and stuffier and drearier. Finally, the Caravelle managed to take off and, after only one more stop (in Panama) for fuel and a maintenance check that took no more than a few hours, it landed in Cuba. The trip had taken forty-eight hours. For several days after arrival the plane remained parked at Havana Airport, and there was much speculation as to why the Cubans were holding it. Perhaps they weren't; they were probably at their wits' end trying to find out how to get that thing to leave the ground.

The revolutionaries should really have known better. It was not the first time, nor was it to be the last, that the balky Caravelle caused problems for the otherwise well-organized hijacker. Only two months before, a jet malfunction on a Caravelle had prevented a takeoff after a refueling stop, necessitated a change to another plane (again a Caravelle), and indirectly resulted in the capture of two youthful Chilean skyjackers.

Skyjack buffs were amused. They didn't have much else to laugh about. At least there was something grimly funny about the aircraft fighting back. It would develop engine trouble, run out of gas unexpectedly soon, suffer from a variety of jet or electrical malfunctions, have to be landed for repairs, and then refuse to go aloft again. This plane, at least, was on the side of the anti-hijack forces.

But of course a plane that doesn't want to fly is no solution to the skyjacking problem. That was something we still had to find.

February was an unusually ugly month, even for the ugly business of hijacking. On the tenth of that month an El Al 707 was parked on a Munich ramp waiting to be boarded by its London-bound passengers. Three Arab terrorists, armed with grenades, entered the terminal and apparently lost their heads. The original idea, according to written instructions that were turned up later in a search, had been for them to skyjack the craft on its way to London. There was also a strong suggestion that the main target of the attack was Israeli Defense Minister Moshe Dayan's son Assaf, who was among the passengers at the Munich terminal. But something went wrong. Instead of permitting the normal boarding procedures and then giving the standard instructions to obey or die, the three terrorists suddenly let loose their grenades in and around the transit lounge where the passengers were getting themselves ready to board an airport bus that was to take them to the plane. Explosions, a loud crash, searing smoke, dust, screams, and the sound of falling objects filled the lounge. When the air cleared and the shouting died, eleven people were found wounded and one Israeli was dead.

It was an appalling event, but it was not something new. The Popular Front for the Liberation of Palestine had rehearsed this type of action before, once at Athens Airport in 1968 and then again in Zurich in 1969.

There were two other particularly obscene occurrences in February that cannot be classed as hijackings but are nevertheless related because of their motivation, their targets, and their perpetrators. Both were acts of sabotage, which is just one more tactic in the guerrilla-terrorist-kidnapper handbook. One was the airborne explosion of February 21, which caused an Austrian airliner flying at 14,000 feet on its way from Frankfurt to Vienna to convulse violently as if struck by lightning. The plane limped back from Frankfurt with part of its fuselage missing and the torn edges obviously ripped by a bomb. It had been carrying mail meant to be transferred to an Israeli flight later in the day, and the bomb had been in one of the mailbags. Luckily—incredibly luckily—the cargo had been loaded in such a way that the lethal mailbag was packed firmly between layer upon layer of tightly wadded newspapers, which absorbed the main force of the blast.

The next occurrence of that same day had a disastrous ending. Swissair Flight 330 was fifteen minutes out of Zurich with fourteen Israelis aboard when its pilot messaged Zurich control tower: "We are on fire!" Then the plane was gone from radar, wiped off the screens and out of the sky.

It had exploded in midair, killing all forty-seven persons aboard. The fragments were so small and widely scattered that putting them together again to form a meaningful picture was an almost impossible task. When it was done, as it had to be done, the finished picture told the story: A bomb had gone off in the cargo compartment, and this time it had torn the plane apart.

Flight 330 had been on its way to Israel. That was enough reason for it to be blasted out of the sky.

The General Command of the Popular Front for the Liberation of Palestine claimed "credit" for this savagery. A little later, when they became aware that they were not receiving any congratulatory telegrams and had, in fact, earned worldwide revulsion and condemnation, they changed their minds and said they hadn't done it after all. This time no one believed them.

It must be said that Israel was not altogether blameless in this skyjack-bombing war. Israel had taken extremely severe reprisal action after an armed PFLP attack on an El Al 707 warming up at Athens International Airport in which several people had been injured, one Israeli had been shot to death, and one engine had caught fire and almost ignited the wing tanks. Israel's reaction had been to wipe out virtually all Arab aircraft parked at Beirut International Airport. Thirteen, altogether, were destroyed, including practically every airplane in Lebanon's Middle East Airlines. Beirut had been chosen for the attack because it was from that city that the Arab terrorists had left for Athens International. It was the Israeli position that acts of anti-Israeli terrorism were condoned if not actively encouraged by the Lebanese.

World reaction to the Israeli reprisal was so vociferously critical that Israel engaged in no more such counterattacks. But not for a moment did the PFLP moderate their bomb-and-grenade attacks on airplanes and even El Al offices in cities such as Brussels and Athens.

For years the FAA has steadfastly held that the hijacker and the saboteur are usually distinctly different types of people. Events were beginning to shake this theory. To be sure, there are still many hijackers, particularly among the ranks of those who skyjack for personal reasons, who have not the slightest interest in sabotage and even abhor such action. There are also saboteurs who would not for the life of them want to hijack an airplane. But there is now a gray area, constantly widening, in which hijacking and sabotage become one. If it is not convenient for the hijacker to take over the plane, then let the time bomb do it. Or, "If you don't land this plane in Damascus, we'll blow it up with everybody aboard." Or, "Better hit the ground fast when we land in Cairo—the plane is going to explode." Which it promptly does.

Increasingly, the hijacker is employing sabotage or the threat of sabotage; increasingly, the guerrilla-infiltrator-fighter-saboteur is adding hijacking to his list of skills. We are thus faced now with a two-fisted menace: the hijacker-saboteur.

On March 9, 1970, the world noted another type of hijacking attempt and was saddened by it. It is the author's position that every skyjacking is a crime and that every sky pirate, no matter what his motive or what kind of "curtain" he is breaking through, is a criminal. Yet it is impossible to be unmoved by private desperation. A young married couple aboard an East German Interflug airliner tried to hijack the plane shortly after its takeoff from East Berlin to Leipzig. Drawing guns, they attempted to enter the cockpit, but the door was locked and they could not manage to force their way in. The pilot, realizing what was happening, turned back to land at East Berlin. The man and his wife, both about twenty, turned their guns on themselves and committed suicide.

The hijackings to Cuba continued, but on a lesser scale than before (although on May 25 there were three in one day). Of all hijackings originating in the United States, two of the most spectacular featured attempts that were suicidal. One was the work of Arthur Barkley, who had a grudge against the United States worth $100 million. At no time did he attempt or threaten suicide, but such was his behavior on the plane that at times it seemed frighteningly clear that unless he got what he wanted he was prepared to take himself and all aboard into limbo. The suicidal motif was even clearer in the case of John Di Vivo, who commandeered a Boston-bound Eastern Air Lines shuttle with no destination in mind but the open, endless sea.

On other fronts, Aeroflot of the USSR was struck twice; and the various guerrilla skyjack wars were waged with greater heat than ever.

Enter Aristotle Onassis.

On July 22, six Arab commandos, including a woman, commandeered an Olympic Airways jetliner while it was flying over the island of Rhodes on its way from Beirut to Athens. According to an American passenger, it began like this: "We had just had breakfast and I was looking at a young Arab and a pretty girl who looked like newlyweds. They suddenly got up and the man, holding a gun, stuck it into the ribs of the stewardess. The girl held a grenade. The man said, 'Don't get excited and you won't get hurt.' " Then four more heavily armed Arabs got up. One of them, holding a submachine gun, confided to the passengers: "We have a plan. We will land in Athens and no one will get hurt."

Here was a twist. The plane was going to Athens anyway—but now it was in the hands of six guerrillas with a plan. That plan, it turned out, was to hold the crew members and passengers as hostages against the release of seven Arab guerrillas held in jails by the Greek government. Two of the seven were about to face trial, having been charged with the murder of a Greek child during a grenade attack on the Athens office of El Al Airlines eight months earlier.

The plane landed and sat on the ground at the Athens Airport with its six hijackers, fifty-three passengers, and five crew members for nearly eight hours while the guerrillas negotiated over the radio for the release of their comrades. Aristotle Onassis himself, owner of Olympic Airways, went to the airport, and spent half an hour in radio contact with the hijackers, asking for the release of the passengers and offering himself as a substitute hostage. Onassis is a man of much influence and many interests, including oil, but his argument was not sufficiently persuasive and his offer was rejected. Again he tried; again he was rejected. (Following the episode there was a rumor to the effect that the hijackers would have settled for Jackie Onassis, but this may be just one of those apocryphal things.)

Finally, the Greek government was forced into a deal. With the help of the International Red Cross, they arranged for the release of the passengers in exchange for their own solemn promise that all seven imprisoned terrorists would be freed in one month's time, after the trial of the two accused murderers. The trial would be held anyway, but no matter what its result the two suspects would be released.

Something interesting was happening here, something that we had not seen before. For one thing, Arab guerrillas were conducting a successful blackmailing deal on the soil of a country that, unlike Algeria and Syria, has never been known to be friendly to the Palestinian cause. For another, the Red Cross negotiators were so proficient that they were not only able to reason with the Greek government but—reportedly—knew all the right code words for talking to the hijackers aboard the plane. We see here a dress rehearsal for what later happened in Amman, although of course we did not know it at the time.

The passengers were permitted to debark, but the crew remained and a Red Cross official was taken aboard as a guarantor of the agreement between the guerrillas and the government. The plane then left for Cairo, to permit the hijackers to take their chances in a more friendly and hospitable country. With them they took the solemn assurance of the Greek government, and of Mr. Onassis, that their pact with the Greeks would be honored.

Protests arose from various quarters. The Greek government (and the Greek aviation system) was, after all, internationally bound in relation to all other governments to deal with hijackers in a certain way. Surely they would not put their promise to gangsters ahead of their promise to all other countries. Why should they feel it necessary to go through with an agreement made under duress and blackmail, particularly when that agreement involved the release of criminals?

The Greek government was adamant. A deal was a deal.

Eventually the Red Cross official returned home safely, and so did the Arab terrorists who had been briefly imprisoned in Greece and so successfully sprung by coercion. As for the two who had been charged with murder, convicted for premeditated manslaughter and then freed, a funny thing happened to them on their way out of court. The kindly prosecutor told them that he hoped to see them back in Greece at some future date, as tourists.

Such was the rousing success of this blackmail scheme that it was bound to encourage similar efforts. And thus was the precedent set for the Amman hijackings that took place shortly afterward.

All through the year the fear had been building that someday one of the new Boeing 747 colossi would be hijacked with possibly disastrous results. There were madmen in the sky, and there was no one associated with the airline industry who did not look with horror to the day when a false move, a wrong word, a hasty judgment or a short-fused bomb would blow one of the jumbo jets out of the sky. In the United States, as in other countries, anti-hijack measures had already been put into effect.

The main thrust of the American system involved a two-pronged safeguard consisting of a "behavioral characteristics" check of ticket buyers and a magnetometer inspection of boarding travelers. Since its inception the system seemed to be working pretty well.

And then, on August 2, 1970, Rudolfo Rivera Rios, of Puerto Rico out of the Bronx, made history by achieving the first skyjacking of a 747. The Pan Am jet had left Kennedy International Airport in New York late on the night of August 1 bound for San Juan, Puerto Rico. There were 360 passengers aboard, just two short of capacity, and nineteen crew members. At about 200 miles and twenty-six minutes from San Juan the hijacker got out of his first-class seat and forced a stewardess to take him to the cockpit. There, armed with a pistol, a switchblade knife, and a bottle of something he claimed was nitroglycerin, the hijacker told the captain that he wished to be taken to Cuba.

Captain Augustus Watkins changed course and notified New York. When the plane landed in Cuba, Prime Minister Fidel Castro himself hurried to José Martí Airport to admire it. The hijacker got off the plane and disappeared; Captain Watkins got out and talked to Castro. Castro was fascinated with the gigantic craft. He asked a lot of questions. What was the plane's capacity and speed? Watkins told him. Would the plane be able to take off from the Cuban airfield? Watkins assured him that it would not be a problem. (Castro knew that already; the main José Martí runway had been lengthened months before to meet this very contingency.) How much cargo would it carry? Watkins spelled it out. Could the hijacker get his luggage off the plane? Sorry, no: the 747 required special baggage-handling equipment which was not available in Havana; the man's luggage would be shipped back to Havana on another flight. Then Captain Watkins asked a question. Would Premier Castro like to board the plane to see how it looked inside? Castro graciously declined. "I would probably scare the passengers," he said.

After less than an hour on Cuban soil, the plane took off without difficulty and completed its flight to San Juan. Then another question arose: How had the hijacker managed to elude the detection net?

Well, you see . . . it had been a very busy night at Kennedy Airport; flights were backed up because of foul weather, and the agents who were checking tickets scarcely had a chance to glance at passengers. The plane was scheduled to depart at 11 P.M. but was delayed by mechanical problems, and the U.S. marshal who was supposed to go off duty at midnight did so and was not relieved because traffic is usually slow after that hour and marshals ordinarily are not needed. The magnetometer, which is supposed to detect such metallic objects as pistols and knives, had been in operation but there was not enough manpower on hand to monitor it.

Afterward it was said that the hijacker fitted the "psychological profile of behavioral characteristics" to the proverbial T, and if the detection system had been in operation he would have been spotted immediately. Never mind the metal detector; the fabled profile alone should have done the trick if it had been referred to.

Question from the public: Apart from the fact that you *always* say the system was not in use when a hijacker manages to slip through, how can you be so sure that the use of the profile would have caught him?

Answer: Well, as a matter of fact, he wore a fatigue jacket, khaki pants, a black beret emblazoned with a Cuban flag, and a goatee. Actually, he looked a lot like Che Guevara.

The red faces over this episode paled during the Labor Day weekend of 1970 and the grim days that followed. The Popular Front for the Liberation of Palestine outdid itself: four hijackings in one day, three of them successful, and another successful hijacking three days later.

All five planes commandeered were major flag airliners on long-range international flights. Four of them were destroyed at a cost to the airlines of about $52 million. Four hundred and thirty passengers and crewmen were held hostage, some under shameful conditions and for an unforgivably long time. A total of 769 men, women, and children, none of whom had anything to do with the matter at issue, were played with like cheap, throwaway toys, as if each body did not represent a life but a pawn in someone else's war game.

In return for the release of these civilians, the game-players demanded freedom for 2,000 Palestinian guerrillas, including several responsible for previous hijackings and terrorist attacks. It makes little difference whether their prime motive was to dramatize their cause, disrupt pending negotiations for peace in the Middle East, weaken the fabric of international aviation, or free their fellow commandos. What they did was turn their People's War into a very strange thing indeed—a war against people. In this war, the ordinary citizens of many countries of the world were thrust into the middle of the battlefield to become its chief victims.

What you thought of the whole thing depended on where you sat.

If you sat in one of the heat-drenched, stinking, lifeless planes or crouched in the corridor of the guerrilla-besieged hotel into which you had been herded, you would probably not have agreed with the Lebanese observer who said: "We feel about hijackers the way the American Jews feel about the sabras of Israel. Here's somebody of our own kind who has shown the whole world that, dammit, we know how to fight."

United Nations Secretary General U Thant' condemned the action as "savage and inhuman."

A Palestinian lecturer in economics at the American University in Beirut said: "The only way to get the world to notice us is to speak and act as Palestinians."

King Hussein of Jordan described the episode as "the shame of the Arab nation."

George Habash, founder of the Marxist-Maoist Popular Front for the Liberation of Palestine, rejoiced in the nightmarish mass kidnappings and scoffed at the idea of ever coming to peace with Israel or the more conservative Arab governments. "We do not want peace! Peace would be the end of all our hopes. We shall sabotage any peace negotiations in the future." And if World War III were to be precipitated by further crisis in the Middle East, Habash would not shed any tears. "If this should be the only possibility to destroy Israel, Zionism, and Arab reactionism, then we wish for it. The entire world except us has something to lose."

That seems to be the key. Anything goes for "us," and the hell with you.

This is the voice of desperation, of a people surrounded by

enemies and for whom all means are justified by the hoped-for end. And it is not a sane voice.

There were other hijackings in the closing months of 1970. Somebody wanted to go to North Korea via TWA and was wounded by a Brinks guard who just happened to be on the plane. Someone else chose Allegheny for a flight to Cairo, settled for Havana instead, and held a gun at the throat of a stewardess while a professional wrestler wrestled with himself to keep from trying to overpower the hijacker. And, oh yes, there was that Aeroflot business with the father and son escaping from Russia; and some sort of guerrilla episode in Costa Rica; and then a whole series of nickel-and-dime hijackings to wrap up the year and continue into the early months of 1971. But these were anticlimatic. We had been cushioned against shock. The warning rumbles of years past had culminated in four world-shaking explosions. Skyjacking had mutated into a monster, and nothing could surprise us any more. We had seen it all.

But we hadn't.

On May 28, 1971, ex-policeman James E. Bennett commandeered a New York-to-Miami Eastern 727 flight and ordered it flown to Nassau, where he allegedly demanded a $500,000 ransom—for donation, he said, to the Irish Republican Army—to let the plane go. He was overpowered upon landing at Nassau. This episode had barely left the front pages when, on May 29, a Venezuelan hijacker "with political motives" seized a Miami-bound Pan Am 707 and directed it to Cuba, holding a knife at the throat of a thirteen-year-old girl to make sure that his orders were followed. Jetliner and passengers were kept in Havana, for unspecified reasons possibly relating to the seizure of eight Cuban fishermen by the United States Coast Guard, for an unprecedented four days before being released.

Less than two weeks later, on June 11, the first passenger fatality aboard a U.S. aircraft was recorded with the death of Howard L. Franks, who was shot by a hijacker shortly after the latter had seized a TWA 727 at the boarding gate in Chicago and threatened a stewardess. After a bullet-punctuated flight to New York, Gregory White was arrested on charges of murder and aerial piracy. He had wanted to be supplied with $75,000, a machine gun, and a free ride to North Vietnam.

A cliff-hanger of a skyjack attempt began on July 2 and ended forty-four hours later and 7,500 miles away from point of origin to establish a new record for lengthy hijackings. Robert Lee Jackson and Ligia Lucrecia Sanchez Archilla took over a Braniff 707 on a Mexico City-San Antonio flight and ordered the plane flown to Buenos Aires—by way of Monterrey, Lima, and Rio de Janeiro. While in Monterrey they demanded, and received, $100,000 in ransom money for the release of a passenger-hostage. Argentine police took the cash away from them when they arrested the pair.

On July 23, an FBI marksman armed with a high-powered rifle took aim at Richard Obergfell, hijacker of a TWA jetliner, on a Kennedy Airport runway where Obergfell expected to board a plane for Italy. After forcing Chicago-bound Flight 335 to return to La Guardia Airport, he had demanded ground transportation to Kennedy and had taken a stewardess-hostage along with him. The FBI agent's aim was accurate; the stewardess was uninjured, but the suspect was severely wounded in the stomach and shoulder and died about twenty-five minutes after he was shot. This was another first—the first time that the American hijacker of an American aircraft had been slain on U.S. soil in the course of a hijacking.

The next day brought more bloodshed. In the year's seventh skyjacking to Cuba, a man armed with a small-caliber pistol and a stick of dynamite took over a National DC-8 jetliner. On the way to Havana he opened fire and wounded a male passenger and a stewardess.

Had the skyjack monster mutated again? It was too soon to tell. One thing we were sure of was that, though skyjackings appeared to be on the decline, they were still far from over. We did not know what to expect of the monster—how much bigger it would grow, or what its final form might be.

4/LOSERS: SQUARE PEGS AND OTHER MISFITS

As practically everybody seems to agree, you cannot stop the hijacker unless you recognize him. Perhaps you cannot stop him even then, but recognition is a necessary beginning. In different countries different skyjack parlor games are played by official agencies, the public, the news media, and the psychiatrists. It used to be the custom in iron curtain countries to poke fun at hijackers, to sneer at them in print if they were mentioned at all and make fools of them so that they would not be admired and emulated but snickered at. Of more recent months the heavy scorn has turned to outrage against "criminal defectors," and we have been made to see the red bloc hijacker or would-be hijacker as a "diabolical schemer," "arch-fiend" and "venomous traitor."

In the United States, too, the definition or stereotype of the aircraft hijacker has changed throughout the years. Our skyjacker image has begun to dissolve from bold adventurer to ineffectual misfit. Once in a while we note an exception and we offer him our admiration, our compassion or our fear; but our current conditioning makes us regard the sky pirate generally as timid, cringing, weak, and sexually inadequate. We don't know exactly how to fit guerrilla groups into this picture, but we are trying hard.

Today's sky pirate is not the pirate of old nor the truck hijacker of today. Yet he does come close to both. He holds people for ransom, and he is a thief of time and services. Although the skyjacker's motive may not be material gain in the sense of pockets full of loot, he does rob others for his own gain. Sky piracy, or aerial hijacking, is a violent means of getting a free ride and gratifying some sort of need at the *expense* of other people. The need, usually, is to escape from something, not necessarily a genuine enemy or inimical situation, but from a kind of trap that the skyjacker feels he must get himself out of. He is seldom a thief *per se* but a square peg in a round society—or a round peg in a square society. He is a dropout from everyday life, a malcontent, a political fanatic, a rebel with or without a cause, or an emotional disaster. He is much more difficult to define or deter than the common thief. He may be as young as fourteen or as old as seventy-four. He may be illiterate or he may be college-educated. He may have long hair or a crewcut. He may carry an expensive-looking attaché case or a paper bag. He may be a cool professional or he may be a whimpering coward. He may have dreams of glory or a vision of a bright new homeland or a hope for a spectacular death. He just does not fit neatly into any single package.

Much as we would like to, we can see no single definite pattern to skyjackings or skyjackers. Some hijack cases bear clear and close relationships to others. Some hijack cases are virtually unique. Either we are looking at several patterns, linked by that one thing called an airplane; or we are looking at one extremely complex pattern that is getting more complex all the time. The basic problem—what is a hijacker and why does he hijack?—is a slippery one, not easily solved by definitions and pet theories. Yet we need our definitions. We must try to understand what makes all these people tick.

In the United States, Federal Aviation Administration psychologists have been trying to do this for years. It was they who first conducted interviews with what we might call deactivated skyjackers—those who failed and those who returned home after discovering that there was no haven for them at the other end of the line—and with the families of skyjackers who did not return. It was on the basis of this extensive research that the "behavioral profile" of the skyjacker was devised. This profile has been criticized for a number of reasons, among them that it is much too broad and that it is based on American skyjackers and cannot have universal application. The latter objection rather contradicts the former, but in fact the profile has proved to be extremely useful as part of a passenger screening system and is constantly being revised in the light of changing conditions. FAA psychologists recognize as readily as anyone that the system is not perfect and that the behavioral characteristics of hijackers—here and there, today and tomorrow—are not constant.

The details of the present profile, few as they are, are a closely guarded secret. Yet Dr. John T. Dailey, chief psycholo-

gist of the Federal Aviation Administration and the man responsible for the development of the profile, is not hush-hush about
hijackings and the nature of the men and women who commit
them. In an interview with the author he discussed the famous
profile. He declined to fill in the specific features, but he would
say this:

"On the positive side is that the typical air traveler is a very
successful businessman going somewhere in a hurry—either he,
or his dependents. These people are quite different from the
general population of hijacker . . . that is, the American amateur
hijackers. We have found in our studies that they *are* amateurs.
They weren't organized, they weren't very resourceful, they
weren't very determined. They were a real bunch of losers.
Many of our hijacking attempts have been very inept, undertaken by people who break down in the middle and quit trying,
who can be talked out of what they may have started, or are so
incompetent that the crew is able to disarm them without
endangering the passengers.

"One common denominator among them is that they are
losers, unsuccessful people. They've never done anything very
well. They're failure-prone. They tend to give up when they run
up against an obstacle. And they're not very clever. This is the
reason we thought, at first, that we would be able to scare them
off—some of them, at least—by making them believe that hijacking is a very difficult thing to do. The thing that we faced when
we started to fight the epidemic was this public image of
hijacking being the simplest thing in the world to do, that
anybody could do it without risk of failure. This was a sort of
backwash of the public idea that there was an airline policy of
nonresistance. We know from interviews with some hijackers
that they were acutely aware of this policy. They were expecting no resistance and no obstacles. The headlines told them that
there was nothing that could be done to stop hijacking, so
people were hijacking with very little weaponry or no weaponry
at all. They had the idea there was no risk, that you had
guaranteed success. . . . We thought that there were people who
could be discouraged very easily and whose motivation could be
undercut. And that again is part of what we were able to

capitalize on in differentiating between the usual travelers and these people, the skyjackers."

The question arises again and again: *Why hijack?* Why, of all things, grab an airplane? Many psychologists have offered reasons: there is a symbolism about flight and about airplanes, and to commandeer a plane and jab a gun into a stewardess fulfills a certain need . . . for an uncertain type of person. But to a layman it seems there may be another reason: *Because the plane is there.* Skyjacking is a form of protest, and it happens to be one of the current forms, because the modern jetliner is the very essence of our current technology. You don't hitch an illegal ride on a fishing boat if there is a small private plane ready to hand, and you don't commandeer that small plane if you can just as easily climb aboard a jet. Viking ships, galleons, stagecoaches, and horses are out; the vast modern jet is in. It is today. We produce airplanes, and we produce air pirates. Furthermore, as a means of transportation as well as twentieth-century protest, you cannot beat a jet . . . unless you do it with a supersonic transport.

But that is just a layman's passing thought. The layman also wonders why some hijackers don't simply buy tickets to get to wherever they want to go. Obviously this isn't always possible, but often it is. Do some people hijack airplanes just for the sake of hijacking airplanes or to get a cut-rate ride? And *does* the size of today's jets have any appeal for the hijacker?

Dr. Dailey answers: "I think hardly anybody ever hijacks an airplane just to get transportation. That's not the ball game— there are all kinds of other factors involved. They might hijack to get transportation if that's the only way to get out of a country, let's say Russia, for example. With Russia, that *is* the only way for some. If they were free to leave Russia and could just buy a ticket and go somewhere, I don't think there would be hijackings from there. . . . Sure, the size of the airplane has something to do with hijacking. It definitely does. To start with, there were quite a few hijackings of small civilian planes to Cuba. But after it became epidemic, and was obvious that just anybody could hijack a big airliner to Cuba, then the hijackings of small planes virtually ceased. Since then we've had perhaps one or two—very few. People will want to hijack the big airplanes.''

What kinds of people do hijack airplanes?

"Several kinds. Some do it for out-and-out political demonstration, for propaganda purposes. In some cases they've gone somewhere to drop political leaflets, to make political statements, and so on. In other cases that are not political in that sense—and I'm talking about Americans now—those people were fully aware that Castro was Communist and we were not. They were making a deliverate choice of going to a Communist country to live. There are very few exceptions . . . one or two of them were going over apparently to try to assassinate Castro.

"Others have been simply common criminals escaping. There was one case in particular where it looked as though some people the United States authorities caught before they boarded were going to hijack a plane, people who had done a lot of robberies the night before and were going to flee with the loot. This happened in Atlanta. A Negro and a Cuban together were arrested and found to be armed. They had with them the loot from the robberies of the night before, and they had tickets for San Juan. I'm truly convinced that they were on their way to Cuba.

"Then there have been several cases recently where the apparent motive was suicide. The Boston case was one; the Dulles case another. There have been a couple of other obscure attempts where suicide might have been a motivation.

"Also, you have the so-called homesick Cuban. This isn't just a matter of homesickness. These people are not allowed to go back if they want to. If they were, we'd give them free transportation back to Cuba. Everybody says, 'Why don't you give them a free ride home?' Well, we have a standing offer to Castro to do that, but he won't accept it, he won't do it. And still, some of them for one reason and another want to get back so bad that they hijack an airplane. And when they do, they are punished. Not so badly, I expect, as if they had gone back by boat. But, at any rate, they seem to think they can put up with the consequences if they can hijack an airplane to get home. We've had statements from some hijackers that they don't mind going to jail for a few months and then going out into the cane fields. They're willing to do that to get home. Most of the hijackings to Cuba since 1969 have been done by Cubans going home."

These hijackers are people who cannot settle down satisfactorily in the United States, either because this country does not live up to their expectations or because it simply is not home. Their motivation is not political. Essentially they go for family reasons, and a yearning to be with their own people. They leave because they are not happy in exile, and they hijack because they know no other way of getting back.

"Then there was quite a flurry of black militant hijackings back in late 1968 and early 1969 coincident with Eldridge Cleaver being over there. They started about the time Cleaver went over to Cuba and ended about the time he left. There were reports from some of those hijackers that they were mistreated by Castro; they said he didn't treat Negroes well. . . .I guess this was why some of these people were disappointed and left.

"There have also been a few cases of disenchanted white Americans going to Cuba, and maybe being a little better received. These people don't usually take the whole family along. In a few cases they have taken some of their children, and there was one case where a guy took his girl friend along. Typically, the American white hijacker is in the disenchanted category. He is disenchanted with our country, and he wants to leave it to go to a Communist country under conditions that he thinks will hurt the prestige of America and enhance the prestige of Cuba, or whatever country he's going to. It's a very dramatic way of defecting to another country.

"More recently, of course, we have had a different type of hijacking, like the hijackings of the PFLP. Most of the Cuba-bound hijackers are amateurs, but not these people. The amateurs know very little about airplanes. They haven't flown very much. But when you get among the professional, organized groups, you'll find that they know where the controls and gauges are, they know how much gas is aboard. They've really made a study ot it . . . like the Popular Front, and the ones who took the Japanese airliner to Korea. So now we have the political professionals."

Back to the layman:

In writing this book, I do not set myself up as a psychologist or a political analyst. But as a concerned citizen and a member of the aviation fraternity, I have been observing the hijacking scene and gathering data since 1961. It is my opinion that skyjackers fall into five (sometimes overlapping) categories:

1. Losers and misfits
2. Emotional disaster cases
3. Criminals on the run
4. Individuals with personal-political reasons
5. People or groups with organized-political motivations.

Based on these groupings, let us take a closer look at the men and women who are skyjackers. To do this we will occasionally return to ground already touched upon, but only so that we may more thoroughly explore the territory and develop patterns that were suggested earlier.

The following case studies are based on personal files and interviews, press reports, and highly authoritative official records. In certain instances the various sources offer slightly conflicting accounts, which should come as no surprise to anyone who has ever heard or read the several eyewitness reports of any single incident. But the discrepancies are only in the minor details, and every effort has been made to marshal the facts as accurately as possible.

LOSERS AND MISFITS

The losers and misfits of our list are people with whom nearly all of us can identify, even if they do go out and hijack planes whereas we do not. They are Everyman—not Everyman at his best, but Everyman nevertheless. They are just plain people with a problem compounded by their own weaknesses, or perhaps rooted in those weaknesses. They do not have a deep and tragic flaw but a lack of some sort. Something is missing from them and their lives, and they know it. They have a sense of failure, of not belonging, of not being with it, of not making it.

We would be less than human ourselves if we did not feel

sympathy for many of these people. They are like the rest of us in many ways. The difference between them and other have-nots or nonentities is that they lose harder; they give up totally; they try to wipe out altogether what is past; they choose skyjacking as the one way out of their difficulties.

But, really, they are quite ordinary people.

Take, for example, Thomas Wáshington.

The Case of the Jobless American

On the morning of December 19, 1968, Thomas George Washington of Philadelphia, a twenty-nine-year-old unemployed chemist, appeared unexpectedly at his former wife's apartment and asked permission to take his three-year-old daughter Jennifer for a walk. His former wife, Joanne, from whom he had been divorced in March of that year, gathered the impression that father and daughter were to spend the day in town together, probably shopping. Since the weather was seasonably chilly, she bundled the child up in a snowsuit before waving her good-bye.

Mr. Washington did not go shopping with the child—or if he did, it was not to buy Christmas presents but a cap pistol. Not long after leaving Joanne's apartment, Washington and his little girl boarded an Eastern Air Lines DC-8 bound from Philadelphia to Miami. Flight 47 was scheduled as a nonstop flight, but Washington changed the schedule, and a stop was made . . . in Cuba.

Twenty-three-year-old German-born stewardess Uta Risse was in the galley when Washington made his move. Flight 47 was flying over the Atlantic down the Florida coast. Washington got up from his seat in the last row, went up to the stewardess, and asked her what time they would get to Miami. Then, says Miss Risse, "He threw down a note and said, 'Tell the captain we won't get there. Tell him we're going some place else.' "

The note received by Captain Orris Firth read: "Dear captain, this flight is going to Havana. I have a gun and nitroglycerin. I've studied chemistry."

To the captain, it was a bit of a jolt but not much of a surprise. For the fifth consecutive week, an airliner was being hijacked to Cuba, and this time it was his. During the previous four weeks six commercial planes had already gone the southern route, bringing the year's tally—rather suddenly—up to twenty. Flight 47's predicament wasn't a novelty. As the flight was overpassing Jacksonville, Captain Firth radioed a familiar message to the ground controllers. "Looks like we're going to have to go to Havana." He said later that he had no hesitancy about flying to Cuba when he got word to divert the plane. "The threat was enough for me," he said, after returning to Miami with his crew of seven. "I had 142 other people on board."

During the hour or so it took to reach José Martí Airport, Miss Risse sat in the last row with the hijacker and the child. Washington did not seem particularly menacing. Miss Risse said she was worried but not scared, and the hijacker was very nervous. "A very tall and slender black man, six-four or five, and he was shaking, and once he cried and said he was doing it for his daughter. The little girl was crying, and I cried, and she used some tissue I had given her to wipe *my* tears."

Miss Risse listened while Washington talked. Bitterness spilled out of him. Why shouldn't he be able to get a job? He was a chemist; he was qualified. Why should his wife have custody of the child—their child, his child? Yes, she was employed as a saleswoman in Philadelphia, but why should that give her the sole right to their baby? What was the point of going on living in a country that had no use for him? "He said he was getting out of this country because of the hatred and prejudice," Miss Risse said afterward. "I felt sorry for him. He said he had tried to get a job every place in America, but couldn't."

When the plane landed in Havana, Washington apologized to the passengers and the captain. "I'm sorry," he said. "I wouldn't have hurt anybody." And, with the little girl in his arms, he left the aircraft escorted by six Cuban soldiers.

Probably he would not have hurt anybody. We have no evidence that he was actually armed. The note given to the pilot referred to nitroglycerin, but no nitroglycerin was seen. He may have had something in a paper bag that he held in his hand as he sat with the stewardess, but he said at one point that it was a cap pistol, and at no time did he show it.

As was customary in those days, the hijacked craft was not

permitted to take off fully loaded from José Martí. Captain and crew returned to Miami with the plane. The 142 legitimate passengers went by bus from Havana to Varadero and subsequently returned to Miami aboard two Electra prop-jets flown to Cuba by Eastern. Washington and his daughter stayed behind.

Washington's case is typical of more than a few Cuba-bound hijackings that occurred during the epidemic of 1968-1969; hijackings perpetrated by men who decided to make their break for Cuba because of joblessness, marriage problems, and disaffection with life in America. But Washington, typically again, did not like Cuba either. Less than a year after arriving in Cuba, he was reported by the Associated Press as saying he would like to return to the United States, but not if it meant going to the electric chair or spending twenty years in prison. He said he wanted to return to Philadelphia to see his family, and that he would feel more at home in the United States. In the space of about eight months, he had become a homesick American.

"I am not a Communist and I could never be a Communist. My reasons were personal. I wanted to save my daughter from some of the hatred and viciousness that is perpetuated today in the U.S."

Eventually, Thomas Washington did return to the United States with his daughter. Apparently, like the five other men who returned with him, he had chosen Cuba as a sanctuary simply because it was *not* the United States, was not amicably disposed toward the United States, and seemed to be a popular haven for unhappy Americans. He found a job in Cuba, but he did not find paradise.

One psychiatrist interviewed by the author suggested that Washington was looking for a mother (mother-country) substitute. Maybe so. But he did not find one. He found a cruel stepmother, and he is back in the United States . . . in jail. Mother America put him there.

Let it be noted that he claimed—and somehow we believe him—that he was unarmed when he hijacked the plane. He said he put his hand in a paper sack and let people think it was a weapon.

To Cuba with Love: Homesickness, Family-Style

While Thomas Washington was having second thoughts about the style of life in Cuba, a man who has since been identified as Medrand Esquivel was regretting his earlier decision to settle in the United States and deciding to do something about it. Like so many other people who find themselves obliged to make a sudden trip, he had urgent family reasons for his flight.

There were three of them in the immediate family, and they purchased tickets in Newark, New Jersey, under the name of "Perez." The man appeared to be in his early fifties. His face was deeply lined, he wore a neat dark suit, and he spoke only Spanish. His wife, about the same age, said very little during the boarding process. Although she was on the plump side, she looked pale and ill. Their fifteen-year-old daughter was the most self-assured and composed of the three. She was small, pretty, with shoulder-length black hair and brown eyes, nice legs, and a mini-skirt. At least, so say the male passengers who were aboard Flight 7 that day.

The Perezes did not appear to be seasoned travelers. Either that, or they simply had not had the time, money, or inclination to provide themselves with store-bought luggage for the trip. They were conspicuous at the airport terminal because each of them was carrying four or five paper shopping bags. As one passenger later noted, "It looked like everything they owned was stuffed into those shopping bags."

The date was June 22, 1969, and the Eastern Air Lines jet was about to take off from Newark to Miami with eighty-one passengers and a crew of eight. The Perez family seated themselves in the rear section of the plane, fumbling clumsily with their paper bags. Mrs. Perez seemed to be extremely nervous and uncomfortable. She spoke only to her husband, who muttered back in monosyllables. The daughter, however, fell into casual conversation with a fellow passenger, a young man in his twenties and easy to talk to. Even before Flight 7 left Newark she was telling him that her mother was very ill and needed an operation. The young man, looking at the trembling Mrs. Perez and her bleak-faced husband, could well believe it. The woman seemed on the verge of collapse. "She's afraid she won't live through the operation," the girl told him. "She says she wants to see her family before she dies."

The girl did not add that her mother's family lived in Cuba.

The big DC-8 took off from Newark at 9:13 A.M., due to land in Miami at 11:25. When it reached a point approximately 100 miles north of Wilmington, North Carolina, Mr. Perez suddenly stood up in the aisle and started talking in Spanish to stewardess Rosemary Evans. She did not, at first, understand what he was saying, but she quickly got the idea when he pulled out a butcher knife and said, "Havana, Havana!"

With the aid of the knife he persuaded her to unlock the cockpit door.

"We were just south of Norfolk, Virginia," says the pilot, Captain Bernard L. Hautain, "when Rosemary let this Cuban in with a knife in his hand. He couldn't speak English, except to say, 'Havana, Havana,' so his daughter came in and translated." And so, at 9:55 A.M., Hautain radioed that he was proceeding to Cuba.

Few of the passengers noticed anything amiss. Most did not even see the hijacker and his family until they left the plane. Of all the people in the passengers' cabin, only the stewardesses knew more or less what was happening. They knew they were headed for Cuba, but they were very much concerned about what might be going on in the cockpit. Also, it was obvious to them that Mrs. Perez was ill. She sat, now, in a first class seat, fidgeting nervously, looking wan and distraught. Once she got up to go to the rest room. Her stomach, she managed to tell a stewardess, was upset, and she asked for medicine. Several times she seemed to be about to faint.

In the cockpit, the mini-skirted teen-ager was interpreting for her father. Perez, in the jump seat behind the pilot, was very nervous by this time. According to Second Officer David Savage, he was not only brandishing a knife but had a bottle labeled DANGER: EXPLOSIVES tied to his wrist with a string. "It looked like pink sugar," says Savage, "and inside this was a test tube of what looked like methiolate with wax on top of it. It probably was just a diversion, but you don't *know* what it is, of course. . ."

Perez made no move to demonstrate the properties of the

mystery bottle. Nor was any attempt made to overpower him. According to Hautain, "It's Eastern's policy not to resist if they are armed." And no matter what the bottle contained, there was no doubt that the knife was real.

The girl was calm and spoke little more than necessary, though she did volunteer the information that they were from Newark, that she herself was fifteen and a high school student, and that her mother was sick. Perez spoke even less and was extremely jumpy. Hautain was acutely aware of the man's nervousness and had no wish to exacerbate it. Quietly and reasonably he explained, through the girl, that he would have to open bags to get out maps and that Perez must not be alarmed when he did so. Eastern would be cooperative, he said reassuringly; if Perez wanted to go to Cuba, then by all means they would go to Cuba.

Perez watched him. Gradually, very gradually, he relaxed a little.

Perez talked occasionally during the next hour and a half. His daughter translated. He and his wife had not been happy in the United States. He was uncomfortable with the language problem. Cuba was their country and they wanted to go back. It had been very difficult for him, even impossible (so the pilot gathered), to adjust to the cultural differences between Cuba and the United States. He yearned for the solid familiarity of his homeland. He could not feel at home in Newark, New Jersey, or anywhere else in the United States. He also said that his sick wife wanted to see her family in Cuba before she died.

When the plane was over Miami, Hautain told the man it was his last chance to change his mind, but all he got in reply was "Havana!" and another flicker of the knife blade.

Havana it was. At 11:55 A.M., half an hour after Flight 7 should have touched down in Miami, it landed at José Martí Airport.

Hijacker, wife, and daughter disembarked. There was no sign of an enthusiastic reception committee, although Cuban militiamen were on hand to perform their usual welcoming duties. The mother's knees buckled when she got off the plane, and she almost fell. One of the militiamen grabbed her and kept her on her feet.

And thus did the Perez-Esquivel family come home.

These family-style hijackings, particularly those originating in the United States, have been quite common. They happen in other countries, too, but not as often, perhaps because the chances of success are considerably slimmer. Red bloc pilots, for example, almost invariably flip the plane into a controlled but sudden spin while the copilot whips out his gun and shoots. But time and time again we read of family groups diverting planes to Cuba, particularly in 1968, 1969, and early 1970. They usually landed there successfully. There would be "Three armed men, accompanied by a woman and her infant son . . ." "Four men, two women and three small children . . ." "A young man, a woman and a little girl . . ." "A gunman with his wife and two sons . . ." "A man and a pregnant woman . . ." "A hijacker with his wife and four children . . ." "A mother and son team . . ." "Three men, two women and a baby . . ." These were the stories we heard over and over again.

But even more common is the type of hijacking committed by one man acting alone; one man who is essentially a loner even though he may have acquaintances, friends, or even a wife somewhere in his muddled background. Sometimes he does it for no apparent reason, and he does it so haphazardly that it seems almost accidental. Always beneath the bluster or the cool façade there is some kind of reason, but often it is one that only a psychiatrist can determine. For the man in the street there is a type of hijacker whose motives are difficult to comprehend. This hijacker is a man who isn't really going any place, has no apparent need to escape, is too old for the draft, has no political affiliations or interests, feels no bitterness toward the United States—but nevertheless goes out and hijacks a plane. This is the real loser, the fellow whose most spectacular act in life is the act of skyjacking.

The Credit-Card Caper

A federal judge in Baltimore described Raymond L. Anthony as a drunk, and referred to the Anthony episode as "the tragic case of an alcoholic whose life is a failure at the age of fifty-six."

On June 28, 1969, Raymond Anthony, at that time an unemployed automobile salesman in Baltimore, commandeered a jet on its flight from Baltimore to Miami. Once again Eastern Air Lines was the target; the plane was a Boeing 727. Anthony was casually dressed in shorts and sandals (appropriate for the time of year but not exactly *de rigueur* for the well-dressed air traveler), and was said afterward to have been drunk during the hijacking.

He must have looked like the world's least likely hijacker as he weaved his way onto the plane on that hot Saturday in June—that is, if anybody bothered to look at him at all. Perhaps if they had they would have seen something incongruous about him. Harmless, of course, but, well, a little odd.

What was particularly odd was that he, this seedy little man in the inappropriate clothes and the liquor on his breath, had bought his ticket with a *credit card.*

Unemployed and reportedly alcoholic, Raymond Anthony was destitute when, according to the lawyer who later spoke for him, he received an unsolicited credit card in the mail, went out and used it to have a few too many drinks, then bumbled his way to the airport and onto the Miami-bound Eastern Air Lines jet. The 727 was carrying ninety-six passengers and a crew of seven, and among the passengers if not among the crew there was probably some half-serious joking about the possibility of winding up in Cuba. It was the season for this kind of talk. Maybe Anthony heard it, or maybe he had already made his fuzzy plans while drinking. What he did was to pull out his pocket penknife while the plane was flying over Daytona Beach, force a stewardess to take him to the cockpit at knife point, and order the crew to fly him to Havana.

Which they did.

Why in the world would Anthony want to go to Havana? Well, why anywhere? And if anywhere, where else? That's where practically everyone was going in those days, everyone who was any kind of hijacker. In Anthony's muddled mind there must have been some sort of picture of a haven for a man like himself, and some sort of memory of the hijacking stories he had read in the newspapers. Before he diverted the 727 that day, there had already been forty hijack attempts from the start of 1969, all but two of them to Cuba and all but seven of them successful.

Plane, crew, and passengers—minus Anthony—returned briefly to the United States after a brief stopover at José Martí. Back in Baltimore, a federal warrant was issued charging Anthony with hijacking the airliner, but of course Anthony was not available to be taken into custody. On August 5 he was indicted on the hijacking charge by a Baltimore grand jury. Toward the end of October he wrote to his sister in Baltimore, telling her that he had asked Cuban officials to let him go back home.

Anthony was eventually tried and sentenced in his homeland. It was then that Judge Alexander Harvey 2d commented about "the tragic case of an alcoholic." He could not understand why the plane's crew had obeyed "the drunken orders of a little man holding a penknife."

One sympathizes with the judge's puzzlement and, to a degree, shares it, but the fact is that Anthony *was* armed, even if only with a penknife, and the crew was under orders not to take any action that might conceivably endanger the passengers. Even if their orders had given them any latitude, they could not have predicted how the little man might have behaved if they had tried to resist him. Yet the judge's comment points up the nature of this hijacker: a bemused, befuddled little man, virtually without identity, weak yet unpredictable, copping out via airplane and heading for he knew not what. A real loser.

Hijacking Vendetta Style: The Man Who Hated the IRS

Everybody talks about the Internal Revenue Service but hardly anybody does anything about it. Those who do are seldom inspired to take anything like such bizarre and drastic measures as those adopted by Arthur G. Barkley of Phoenix, Arizona.

Before his fantastic exploits made the headlines and socked home once again the point that hijacking is not merely a safe if time-wasting side trip to Cuba but a criminally dangerous and potentially disastrous escapade, Arthur Barkley showed most of the surface evidence of a man who was winning his tussle with life. True, he had his gripes, and when he felt his rights were being trampled on he reacted with the tenacity of a bulldog, but on the American scene there is nothing unusual about that. When he started out for the Phoenix Airport on the morning of June 4, 1970, "to settle his tax case in Washington," he left behind him a modest but pleasant home (described in the newspapers as a $25,000 ranch house) and two late-model Cadillacs. Though he himself had not worked for some time his wife was employed, and the Barkleys were not in any apparent financial difficulty. Nor were there any family problems. His wife was, and is, extremely loyal to him, and no fault could be found with their two sons. One was already married and the other was a student at Phoenix College.

Barkley is a big, well-built man, who at least until the weird culmination of his tax case was fond of sports and comfortable in sports clothes. His co-workers in the Continental Baking Company, where he worked as driver-salesman from 1955 to 1963, regarded hin as a serious, purposeful man, an effective salesman along his route, and a devoted supporter of the Teamsters local to which he belonged. Reportedly, he used to go to the Church of God every Sunday with his two sons and was quick to lend money to his colleagues whenever they needed it. By 1963, when his troubles began, he was earning $9,500 a year and had bought his north Phoenix home. At forty-two he was certainly not rich, but he was reasonably well off.

Yet a sour note must have started to creep in during those years. Interviewed after the events that made Barkley infamous, his former boss at Continental said of him that he was "unpredictable," and that "he lied a lot." Said Edward Bennett: "He was real conscientious, but he was kind of a screwball. You never knew what was coming next."

What came next in Barkley's employment history was his dismissal from the Continental Baking Company. Eight years with the firm went down the drain and Barkley was jobless and resentful. William McCord, the bakery supervisor, said that Barkley had been dismissed "for failure to perform his work properly," but other people told other stories. One version of the Barkley firing is that Barkley got into a fist fight with a competitor in a Phoenix grocery one morning and was let go because of it. Vern Case, secretary-treasurer of Local 272 of the

International Brotherhood of Teamsters, said that Barkley lost his job because of his insistence that "he was the only one who knew how to run the company." And according to a spokesman for Continental, Barkley himself contended that he was dismissed without good reason over an issue of nineteen days sick leave that he had taken and was unable to verify with medical reports.

The question of the nineteen days sick leave began to loom large in Barkley's life. His claim was that an auto accident had affected his hearing and that the company had refused to pay him for the nineteen days sick leave because he had not thought it necessary to obtain a statement from a physician that he actually suffered pressures, bordering on deafness, in his right ear. Barkley, now forty-nine and jobless, filed suit both against the company and against the Teamsters, the latter because the union would not support him in his dispute with the company. The union, he charged, had not only failed to back his claim but had interfered with his efforts to find another job. Every day for a month Barkley picketed the Teamsters office in Phoenix. He also took his grievance to the National Labor Relations Board. The Board took no action. Neither did the Wage and Hour Division, to which he next applied. According to Vern Case, he next tried to get help from the governor's office and a justice of the peace.

No help was forthcoming. Interestingly, Barkley continued to pay his union dues. "After all these years," Case added, the day Barkley went berserk. "If he can't come in, he sends them by registered mail."

In 1964 he dropped his suits against both union and company because he thought he had found a way to get his money. Nineteen days' unpaid sick leave, he reasoned, was worth exactly $471.78. Therefore he would simply withhold that sum from his federal income tax payment for the year.

The Internal Revenue Bureau did not see things his way. They demanded payment of the unpaid taxes, and when he refused to pay they sued him for the sum plus a penalty fee. Barkley persisted in his refusal to pay, and the longer he refused the higher rose the penalty fee. Still, it was the $471.78 that became his symbol of injustice, the measure of his fury. In the meantime Barkley was far from idle. Suits, countersuits, and appeals became his way of life. His suit against Internal Revenue, in which he asked damages of $100 million, was thrown out in federal court, but still Barkley wasn't through. His next move was to appeal his tax case to the United States Supreme Court.

Opening his appeal to the high court with the statement that he was "being held a slave by the United States," Barkley contended that his constitutional rights had been violated and that he had been blacklisted in connection with the loss of his bakery job. In his brief, he alleged that it was not he who owed the government money, it was the government that owed *him* money . . . namely, $100 million. The Supreme Court refused, without comment, to hear Barkley's appeal. "They gave him the runaround and wouldn't even listen to him," said his wife, Sue; and Barkley became increasingly embittered.

Though he had been turned down, Barkley continued to bombard various Washington offices with letters and legal documents. In some of the letters he indicated that he had been studying law for the purpose of better equipping himself to proceed with his case. When not pursuing his legal career he was engaging in abrasive encounters with neighbors, which got him into further brushes with the law. According to Phoenix police, Barkley often complained about his neighbors, and neighbors often complained about Barkley. In 1969 Barkley got into a dispute with a neighbor after apparently driving his car over her property. The lady took him to court, and it seemed at first that Barkley was going to lose out on this one too because he was convicted in city court and sentenced to sixteen days in jail or a $50 fine. Happily, Barkley's appeal in this small case was successful and the conviction was overturned.

His big case was getting nowhere, however. For all the letters and documents he had sent to Washington, and for all the trips he had made there to seek redress in person, Barkley was still being dunned for $471.78 (plus fine), and he was still no closer to the $100 million goal. Therefore he decided to make one more trip to Washington, D.C. "I'm going to settle the tax case today," he told his wife, and shortly afterward boarded TWA Flight 486 to Washington. . . .

Within about forty-five minutes the chronology becomes confused, as it often does when the unexpected happens. The
situation develops into a tangle of desperate messages winging
back and forth. But, as we piece it together, this is more or less
what happened:

10:30 A.M. (approximately): Trans World Airlines 727 jet,
Flight 486 bound for Washington, D.C., departs Phoenix airport
with fifty-eight aboard.

11:00 A.M.: Arthur G. Barkley, in sports jacket and gold
shirt, his face as ruddy as usual, emerges from a rest room and
tells stewardess Robin Urrea, who is on her next-to-last flight
and would prefer it to be an uneventful one, that he wants to
see the captain. By way of persuasion, he shows her his gun. She
says, "Oh . . . okay," and knocks on the cockpit door. Barkley
enters, carrying the gun, a straight-edge razor, and what the
crew takes to be a can of gasoline. He orders Captain Dale C.
Hupe to bypass the scheduled stop at St. Louis and go directly
to Washington. Captain Hupe signals ahead with news of the
hijacking. Few of the passengers realize that the plane has been
commandeered, even when the scheduled stop at St. Louis is
skipped. Bad weather is used as an excuse.

Barkley now sends his own message. It is directed to the
United States Supreme Court, the new object of Barkley's ire.
In his radioed message Arthur Barkley demands that the Supreme Court have $100 million in small bills delivered to the
plane upon its landing in Washington.

There is now a hiatus while the 727 heads for Washington and
ground officials in Washington scurry frantically, trying to figure out what to do and how to raise any part of the money. The
atmosphere in the passenger cabin is relaxed. It is more tense in
the cockpit. Barkley has not said where he wants to go or what
he intends to do after the plane lands in Washington.

The suspicion on the ground is that Barkley might be planning
to leave the country. Captain Billy Williams, TWA's senior
international pilot, volunteers to meet the 727 upon its landing
and, if necessary, take over the controls in case Barkley does
decide he wants to fly abroad. Neither of the two pilots presently aboard the plane is qualified for international flight. Furthermore, Williams is a man who knows how to talk to hijackers. It

was he who, on October 31, 1969, volunteered to take command of a Boeing 707 at Kennedy International Airport after AWOL Marine Raffaele Minichiello had hijacked it over California, and who then flew the plane to Rome.

3:40 P.M.: The plane lands at Dulles Airport in Washington. TWA has managed to raise ransom money to the amount of $100,750, all that could be provided by two nearby banks. In accordance with the hijacker's demands, a fuel truck is waiting near the outer perimeter of the airport. The plane stops at the end of a runway. During the fifty-four minutes that it remains on the ground it takes on 47,000 gallons of kerosene jet fuel while FBI agents watch from a quarter of a mile away. The passengers are not permitted to disembark and are now made aware of the fact that the plane has been commandeered. Oddly enough, they do not all grasp what they are being told. Captain Billy Williams boards the plane with the money in a brown canvas bag.

4:30 P.M.: Williams, in the cockpit, tries to calm the grudge-infuriated Barkley. Barkley declines to be soothed by talk and swiftly cuts open the money bag. Unfortunately, the first package he pulls out of the satchel is made up of one-dollar bills. He has asked for small bills, but not *that* small. With mounting rage he pulls out more packages, glances at them, tosses them aside; he realizes at once that he has been given nothing like $100 million. Williams observes that Barkley is very, very upset. The money is all over the cockpit floor, like a carpet—he is wading in it.

Outraged, Barkley abruptly orders the aircraft back into the air. Captain Hupe, still at the controls, is obliged to take off without informing the Dulles tower. It is now 4:34. Barkley commands the pilot to fly south. Hupe obeys. He has no choice. Barkley gets on the radio again, this time with a message apparently intended for President Nixon: "To the President and the State Department: You don't know the rules of law. You don't even know how to count money."

Word of the hijacking is now getting around among the passengers who did not catch on at first. They keep calm. It is probably just another routine side trip to the south.

4:40 P.M.: Captain Hupe radios that he has been ordered to

turn around and is now flying northeast. Barkley does not seem to know where he wants to go. He tells the pilot to fly "zero heading," which means north, and once he asks what country lies to the north. Now he is apparently becoming increasingly disturbed. It is clear to all in the cockpit that this is no ordinary hijacking. Not only does Barkley have no fixed destination, but he is now referring to the passengers as his hostages.

4:45 P.M.: The hijacker radios another message: "Send a message to the President. Tell him his orders failed. They were not carried out." Barkley is still burning over being short-changed. He seems to be groping around to the idea that somehow he may be able to obtain more ransom money, but at the same time his manner is increasingly irrational and his occasionally rambling talk takes on an ominous tone. Several times he tells the men in the cockpit, "It's a shame to go by yourself. When you go you shouldn't go alone. You ought to take a lot of money and people with you. You ought to take as much money and as many people as possible. You should never go alone." Williams, listening, feels that Barkley means to destroy the money, the aircraft, and all the people aboard. To him, Barkley is cold, deliberate; he sends cold chills down the spine. Yet it is warm in the cockpit, and at one point Williams asks if he might take his jacket off. Barkley replies, "Sure, might as well be comfortable when we go down."

A subdued party-like atmosphere prevails among the passengers. Because of Barkley's inability to decide upon a destination and his consequent conflicting orders to the pilot, there is much speculation in the cabin as to where they might be going. The passengers make a bit of a game of it. "We headed north and we all said it's got to be Russia. We headed south and we said it's got to be Cuba. We headed north again and we were all confused. We were all betting on it. Nobody won." Nobody is winning in the cockpit either. The mood of the crew is grim. They are almost sure that Barkley intends to kill himself and everybody aboard.

5:00 P.M.: Barkley demands that yet another message be sent. "We're going to give them one more chance to come across with the money," he tells the cockpit crew. The message goes out: "Is the President ready to fulfill my request? That request was for $100 million." It occurs to Williams that Barkley may be thinking seriously about going back for the rest of the money, even though he has said nothing about turning back. He wonders where the money will come from, if at all, or just what the ground authorities are planning to do. Unfortunately, there is no effective radio communication between ground control and the plane, no system of coded messages that might escape the attention of Barkley. The hijacker is the only one who is able to use the radio freely and say what he chooses, but what he is saying is no help whatsoever to crew, airline officials, or FAA. All they have to go on is the growing suspicion, based on his rambling, incoherent messages—which are a compound of dire warning and demand—that Barkley has no rational plan. They realize that the hijack situation is more than usually dangerous because of this.

The passengers are still playing the game of where-will-we-end-up? because of the continuing wigwag course. Barkley is ordering course changes but at no time does he tell the crew where he ultimately wants the aircraft to land. Instead, he is telling Hupe to fly by compass headings. Now he again orders the craft to turn south. The passengers go on with their party—drinks are flowing freely although the atmosphere is scarcely that of a bacchanal—and jokes are being made about, "See you in Havana tonight!" and "How about Montreal?" There are a lot of children aboard. Those who are old enough to understand what is happening accept it calmly. But their presence is an additional worry to Captain Hupe, copilot Donald Salmonson, and Williams. The thought of so many young people being involved in this potentially disastrous situation is an ugly one. Among the load of hostages is a six-day-old baby, an elderly woman with a heart condition, a number of college students, several young married couples, and the children. But what difference does it make who and what the passengers are? Nobody wants to die. Except perhaps Arthur Barkley.

Barkley is by turns mercenary and menacing. At one point he toys with the idea of pouring gasoline all over the scattered money and setting fire to it. At another he repeats his ransom demands. But what is he going to do with the money if he gets it? Nobody asks him, though they try to humor him and listen patiently to his tirades against the federal government, the Internal Revenue Service, the White House, and the Supreme Court. They don't *want* to ask him, because Barkley keeps repeating, "No man should die alone. He should take a lot of people and a lot of money with him."

5:35 P.M.: The pilot radios: "In all probability we will return to Dulles if all conditions are met." The conditions are that the remainder of the $100 million is to be awaiting Barkley's return to Dulles Airport, and that the money is to be "in hundred-dollar bills and nothing less." Barkley then orders the airplane to turn back to Dulles.

6:00 P.M.: Barkley reinforces his demands. Gun at all times firmly in hand, razor at the ready, he has total control over the situation in the air. He seems sure that the money can be raised if ground authorities will only try—never mind whether it comes from the Supreme Court or anywhere else. He has the pilot radio another message that the cash is to be in a hundred sacks full of bills of not less than hundred-dollar denominations, and that the sacks should be placed along the end of the runway upon which they are to touch down.

In the cockpit, Williams can do nothing but try to keep the hijacker as calm as possible and let Hupe go about his business of flying the plane. It is now Williams's absolute conviction that Barkley is murderously dangerous and unbalanced, and that he is more than likely to "do away with the airplane and all of us," whether or not he gets the money. The likelihood that any international flying will be done is now just about zero. Indeed, the likelihood of continued flight of any sort is rapidly diminishing.

The mood on the ground is barely less tense. TWA President Forwood C. Wiser is in constant contact with the Federal Aviation Administration and the FBI. His overriding concern at all times is for the safety of his passengers. He knows the danger of taking action against this apparently crazed hijacker, but he dreads the catastrophe that seems inevitable if no action is taken. This hijacker has been humored long enough; he cannot be permitted to go on with this. To Dulles Airport manager Dan Mahaney he says: "Don't let that plane get off the ground again. You stop them." Mahaney asks for suggestions as to how this might be accomplished. Wiser replies: "That's up to you."

But he does not leave it entirely in Mahaney's hands. While the plane approaches Washington, there is a conference between TWA's top officials, FAA's Mahaney, FAA administrator John H. Shaffer, director of National Capital Airports Arvan H. Saunders, and the FBI. It is unthinkable to let the plane take off again with the hijacker still in command. But first of all they must make sure that Barkley will not change his mind about landing. A plan is decided upon. Money sacks are prepared. Barkley must be able to see them or he will not be lured down. Then, as Mahaney puts it, "We have to go in and get him."

6:40 P.M.: Barkley radios that he wants more fuel. This seems to indicate that he is not contemplating the immediate destruction of the plane and all aboard, but intends to take off again for . . . somewhere. This is positively not to be permitted. The FAA proposes that two people be permitted to refuel and two to hand up the money. Barkley refuses, saying that he will permit only one individual to refuel and one to hand up the money.

The jetliner maintains a holding pattern in the gray skies over the capital while officials at Dulles stuff the mail sacks with the "ransom money" and line them up along the runway.

7:02 P.M.: The jetliner touches down on runway 1-R, about two miles from the main terminal. The pilot advises that he wants no one on the runway. He wheels toward the money bags; the jet rolls to a stop. Three fire trucks come into position on the north, middle, and south side of the runway. This is a normal procedure at Dulles Airport, but Barkley does not like it. He yells out over the radio, "Get those vehicles off the runway!" The trucks drive off. But another, smaller truck has been following the jetliner and has not been noticed by the hijacker from his position in the cockpit. Two FAA policemen inside the truck open fire with .30-caliber rifles. They are aiming at the wheels. The first shots miss, but the second volley flattens out the four huge tires on the main landing gear. Sounds from outside cannot be heard within the plane; Barkley does not realize what has happened. Hupe and Williams do, though they have not been expecting this. Obviously it has not been possible for ground authorities to warn them without also tipping off Barkley. They brace themselves for an ugly showdown. What crisis will be precipitated by the flattening of the tires? How will this unstable man react when it dawns on him that the tires have been shot out and the plane immobilized?

But it does not dawn on Barkley; he has no inkling of it. Nor does he know that the money bags are stuffed with shredded newspaper (what Dan Mahaney calls play money)—something he is intended never to find out under any circumstances. All Barkley does comprehend is that fire trucks, police cars, and other vehicles are actually surrounding the plane.

7:18 P.M.: Barkley angrily orders the pilot to get rid of the vehicular barricade—or else. The pilot radios the Dulles tower. "He wants you to get the vehicles off the runway. He says he's going to kill us if you don't get them off right now." Now Barkley comes on the radio himself. "You're stalling. Get the vehicles off the runway." The tower operator replies: "Negative. We are not stalling. We are trying to contact the people in the vehicles to get them off."

For the moment Barkley appears to be satisfied by this, and turns his attention to the more urgent questions of fuel and money. Prodded by him, the pilot radios, "Get that gas truck here." Dulles tower replies: "We're working on that." Barkley orders Captain Williams and the flight engineer to go through the cabin to open the rear door preparatory to picking up the money bags. When they step out of the cockpit it immediately becomes apparent that something else is going on of which those on the flight deck have not been apprised. Williams and the engineer pause briefly, then go on through the cabin according to orders. Barkley, sticking his head out of the cockpit door at an unexpected sound, suddenly realizes that his "hostages" are fleeing the plane. Some of them are already out. They have run about a hundred yards back of the plane and are lying flat down on the ground in expectation of gunfire. Others, similarly disregarding the advice of the crew, are still spilling rapidly out of the emergency exists, which they have opened themselves, and are making for the tall grass or any other available cover. Barkley is completely taken aback. He does not know how to react. It is as if he cannot believe the evidence of his own eyes. Now, if he goes anywhere, he will not be taking "a lot of people with him." The crew is also disturbed by this turn of events. They have not initiated any attempt to evacuate the passengers because of their fear that Barkley might start shooting indiscriminately. However, the passengers have taken this part of the operation into their own hands. A passenger named Richard Gillen later tells this story: "When we finally came back after that ridiculous ride, I looked out and saw the gasoline truck lined up for another refueling, and I said to myself, the heck with that. I asked the senior captain if it would endanger the crew to pop the door, and he said, yes, it would. I told him it might endanger us all the more to stay. So I turned the big handle on the door, flopped open the chute, and told my wife, 'Honey, out you go!' "

Nineteen-year-old Louis Laspata is among several passengers who open emergency doors and run from the plane. He races out over a wing and jumps off it. Some FBI men catch him. Laspata and a few others run into the grass to hide, or duck behind the fire trucks which have served to transport a number of FBI agents and various other officials to the immediate vicinity of the plane.

Williams has reached the rear door of the aircraft. Mahaney, from the ground below, tosses a .38 up through the now-open door and Williams catches it. Barkley, peering out of the cockpit door, eyes going back and forth across the cabin, does not see this move. All he sees is that his hostages are rapidly disappearing. "Stop them!" he yells to Williams. "Shut the doors!" Williams stalls, by the simple expedient of doing nothing. Barkley's attention swings to one of the departing passengers, who is only a few feet away from him. "You stay where you are!" he snarls, and brandishes his pistol. The passenger looks him right in the eye and says, "I'm leaving"—and leaves. Barkley makes little further attempt to stop the exodus. With one eye on the flight-deck crew in the cockpit and the other on the emptying cabin with Williams down at the end, doing nothing to hold back the passengers or pick up the money, he must be aware that a crisis is approaching. He will have to make a decisive move.

In the cockpit, Captain Dale Hupe and his copilot Don Salmonson are exchanging silent signals. They, too, are acutely aware that the time is *now*, and are ready for a hand-to-hand tussle. Barkley is going to have to be jumped, preferably when his attention is distracted. But Barkley seems to have eyes everywhere. He is watching Williams coming slowly back up the aisle toward him; he is watching the passengers spilling out of the doors; but he is also watching Hupe and Salmonson. Also, it has now dawned upon him that the tires have been blown out and that the plane cannot be moved.

This touches off his final round of threats. "I am going to kill you," he tells the pilots calmly. They receive this threat with equal calm. They do not know that Williams is armed and ready to shoot the hijacker as soon as the cabin is clear. They only know that they are close to Barkley and in a position—though obviously not a safe one—to wrestle him down. But because there are still some passengers aboard, they are hoping against hope for a few more moments of grace or a diversion that will permit them to tackle Barkley without risking a hail of gunfire in the cabin.

And now, suddenly, Barkley *is* distracted.

7:30 P.M.: Armed FBI agents wearing bulletproof jackets have gathered under the nose of the plane. One is boosted on the shoulders of the others and thrust up into the plane through the door nearest the cockpit. He bounces in virtually under the muzzle of the hijacker's gun.

Barkley fires. Two, three, four shots blast into the cabin.

The thought that sears through Hupe's mind is that Barkley is firing at the passengers. Hupe actually sees two passengers in the cabin as he hurls himself at Barkley. All he wants to do at this moment is grab the man and stop him from firing at those people.

Or perhaps they are FBI agents, for by now at least two agents and possibly more are on the plane and shooting back at Barkley. But whoever and whatever Barkley's targets are, there is shooting in the cabin; and the captain has dived in low to slam into the hijacker. Copilot Salmonson lunges at the same time, hitting high. Barkley, off balance and almost down, twists around.

In the tussle Hupe is knocked over backward and the hijacker's gun goes off. A bullet tears into the captain's abdomen. Oddly, Hupe is relieved. Barkley's fire has been drawn away from the cabin and he is swaying punchily; Hupe himself is still alive, and he feels that "now we have him stopped."

Salmonson wrenches the gun away from Barkley. The cockpit fills with FBI men. They seize the hijacker and swiftly clamp handcuffs on him. Barkley, disheveled, has been wounded in the left thumb, and blood—either from the thumb or from Hupe's wound—speckles his sports shirt. He is otherwise unhurt and fairly calm. The agents escort him off the plane. Only a few moments have passed since the first agent went in under Barkley's nose.

7:42 P.M.: The copilot's voice, slightly shaky, is heard over the radio. He says he wishes to advise the families of other crew members that no one but the pilot has been hurt, and that the injury does not appear to be serious.

The story of the flight ends here, more than eight hours after it began. Those who watched Barkley being led off the plane saw him as a big man, about six feet tall and weighing 210 pounds, with sandy hair, a slightly bloodied nose, and a contented expression on his face. With a friendly smile he greeted onlookers, including airport policemen, with, "Hi. Hello there. Hi."

Late that Thursday night, when Barkley was taken before a federal magistrate in Alexandria, Virginia, he announced that he was not guilty and confided to newsmen: "It's all pending in the Supreme Court of the United States Tax Court."

He was arraigned and ordered jailed without bond on a charge of air piracy.

There are several sequels to Barkley's story. The first is his wife's indignant reaction—directed against all the anti-Barkley forces. "He's a man who believes in his country," she said of her husband. "He believed in what he was fighting for in World War II. And now look what they've done to him." As far as she is concerned, Barkley's difficulties began when he lost his job. Nobody would listen to him. "We've been having this court battle for years. It went all the way to the Supreme Court and they gave him a runaround and wouldn't even listen to him." According to her, he did the hijacking to draw attention to his cause, his cause being his tax troubles and his inability to get a job. "They are letting us sit here and starve to death," she said. Apparently Mrs. Barkley is completely on her husband's side, or at least believes in presenting a united front. She does not seem to regard him as unreasonable or unbalanced.

On June 15, eleven days after the Phoenix-to-Washington-to-Washington flight, a federal judge ordered that Barkley be sent to a mental institution to determine whether he was sane on the day he made his hijack and ransom attempt, and whether he is competent to stand trail.

A further sequel is that Captain Dale Hupe underwent successful surgery for his abdominal wound and appears to have recovered fully. He returned to work on September 22, the same day that he and three other crew members received the Federal Aviation Administration's award for extraordinary service.

Another sequel is discovered in an Associated Press dispatch datelined Washington, June 8, 1970:

> The man who commandeered an airliner last Thursday in an unsuccessful bid for a $100-million dollar ransom matched perfectly the government's description of a potential hijacker, the Federal Aviation Administration said today. Had the new FAA weapons-detection system, of which the hijacker behavioral profile is a part, been in operation at the Phoenix, Arizona, airport gate involved, Arthur Barkley, the accused hijacker, almost certainly would have been apprehended before boarding the Trans World Airlines 727, an FAA psychiatrist said. . . . There has been no hijacking by an individual evading detection where the screening was in effect.

That Arthur Barkley was, at the time of his hijacking spree, the personification of the closely guarded behavioral profile has since been confirmed by FAA psychologist John Dailey.

So *that* is what a hijacker is like.

To us, this man is the extremist of the loser type.

There will be more sequels to the Barkley story, and perhaps one of them will explain the meaning of this oddity: Eight days after the hijacking, it was revealed that the $471.78 tax bill owed by Barkley had been paid by an anonymous benefactor. Arthur Barkley, Jr., said that he did not know who had paid the bill, and the IRS said they weren't going to tell.

Thirteen-year-old Eileen Story (hand to head) walks into Miami Airport terminal with other passengers of hijacked Pan Am jet released after being detained nearly four days in Havana. Eileen was threatened by knife-wielding hijacker when he commandeered the 707 airliner on May 29, 1971.—Pan Am Photo.

Captain John Priddy (center) and crew of Pan Am 747 destroyed by terrorists in Cairo on September 7, 1970, holding news conference in New York.—Paul Friend Photo.

Hijacked Olympic Airways 727 stands in remote corner of Athens Airport on July 22, 1970, with band of Arab guerrillas aboard while negotiations are conducted for release of passengers and crew in exchange for imprisoned Arab commandos.—UPI

Leon Beardon (center) and son Cody charged with hijacking Continental Airlines 707 on August 3, 1961, escorted to their arraignment in El Paso, Texas, by a U.S. marshal.—UPI

Leila Khaled—UPI

Raffaele Minichiello, hijacker of TWA jet on October 31, 1969, arrives at police headquarters in Rome following his capture at a country church called the Santuary of Divine Love.—UPI

The six who came back:

Raymond L. Anthony—UPI

Ronald T. Bohle—UPI

Robert L. Sandlin—UPI

Thomas J. Boynton—UPI

Joseph C. Crawford—UPI

Thomas G. Washington—UPI

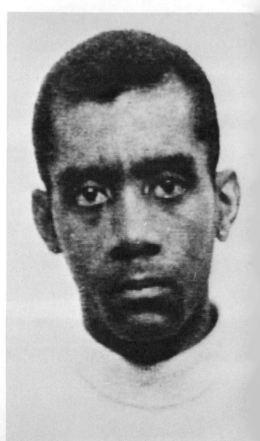

Eastern Air Lines stewardesses Arlene Albino, Christine Peterson, and Sandy Saltzer (top) tell newsmen how John J. DiVivo attempted to seize Boston-bound shuttle flight on March 17, 1970. Captain Robert M. Wilbur Jr. (below), seriously wounded in the attempt, is presented with Federal Aviation Administration award for heroism. His wife rewards her husband with a kiss while Transportation Secretary John A. Volpe (left), FAA Administrator John H Shaffer, and Wilbur's mother look on.—UPI

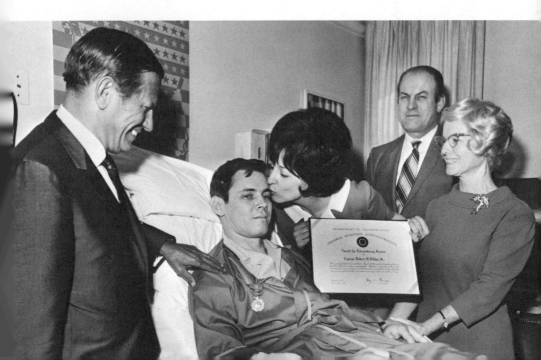

Sword-brandishing student hijacker urges passengers to hurry from Japan Air Lines 727 during refueling stop at Fukuoka, Japan, on March 31, 1970. Hijackers permitted 23 women and children to deplane before forcing the jet to North Korea.—UPI

JAL Captain Shinji Ishida meets with newsmen at Tokyo International Airport after bringing 727 back from North Korea.—UPI

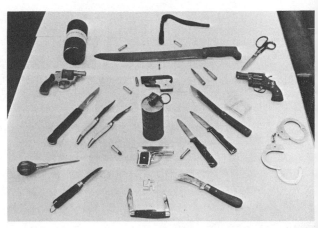

Sampling of paraphernalia collected by U.S. Customs agents during routine preboarding search of airline passengers.—Pan Am Photo.

G. Barkley (right) at cockpit door of
et he hijacked June 4, 1970. Photo was
y passenger.—UPI

Clipper 93 at Beirut Airport enroute to its destruction in Cairo.—UPI

Charred remains of Clipper 93 the morning after it was dynamited at Cairo Airport.—Pan Am Photo. PFLP guerrillas (below, left to right) "Diop," "Gueye," and demolition expert who hijacked the $24-million jet await interrogation in airport security office.—UPI

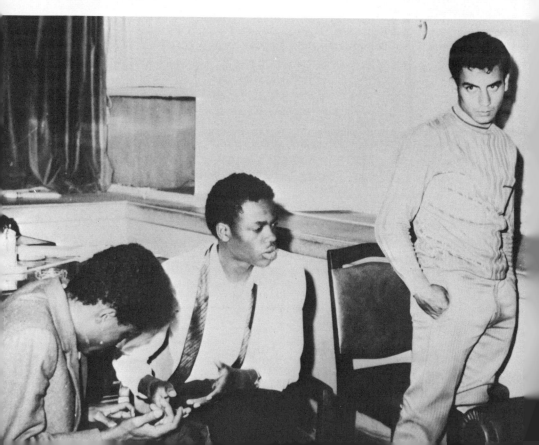

Debris flies through the air as the PFLP systematically destroys hijacked jets on desert airstrip at Amman, Jordan, on September 12, 1970. First to go is BOAC VC-10 . . . then TWA 707 . . . then Swissair DC-8. When the smoke clears there is nothing left but twisted metal and fire-gutted jet engines.—UPI

5/EMOTIONAL DISASTER CASES: THE SICK AT HEART AND SUICIDAL

The man who seems to have no haven or objective other than death itself has a far greater problem than joblessness, a domestic or a drinking problem, or a consuming grudge. There are such men among hijackers. (All hijackers flirt, consciously or unconsciously, with the idea of death, but most would infinitely prefer to live and keep on flirting or simply settle down after the first flirtation.) We venture to describe the tormented death-seekers as psychotic, or as emotional disaster cases.

The man who deliberately goes nowhere is a man under enormous stress, a man completely at odds with himself. He is not trying to settle his problems but put an end to them . . . and even this he cannot do by himself. Much as we condemn his act and much though we may fear him in the air, we pity him.

The Gunman Who Gave Up

The saga of Oran Daniel Richards unfolded during the relatively early days of the hijacking epidemic of 1968-69. Few American planes had yet been hit after the long, consoling lull of the years before, and Delta Air Lines had had only one previous experience. But those who were watching the evolving pattern could observe that the incidents were beginning to crowd upon one another's heels. On the morning that Oran Richards made his bid for nothingness, a private plane had already been diverted to Cuba. This was scarcely enough to inspire Richards, but something certainly did.

The second occurrence of that day—July 12, 1968—involved a Delta Convair 880, Flight 977 en route from Baltimore to Houston. Richards was one of forty-eight passengers aboard. Senator James O. Eastland (D.-Miss.) was another.

It was early evening and the stewardesses were clearing away the dinner trays. Flight 977, under the command of Captain Forrest Dines, was skimming across the sky over southwestern

Tennessee. Senator Eastland was on his way to the washroom after finishing his meal when he heard a man's voice: "Get back or I'll kill you. I'm a sick man." Eastman stared at the lanky six-footer with close-cropped hair and receding hairline, at the eyes behind glasses with clear-rimmed frames. Then he saw the pistol pointed at his own midsection. It was either a nickel- or a silver-plated gun, he observed, and it looked deadly. Without argument, and wisely, he returned to his seat. It seemed to him that there had been nothing personal in the man's threat, that the man had aimed the gun at him merely because "he wanted to get to the cockpit and I just happened to be in the way."

The pistol was a silver-plated automatic, and it was no toy. Stewardess Elaine Hawes didn't like the looks of it either. When Richards leveled it at her and demanded entrance to the cockpit, there was nothing she could do but let him in. He shoved her in ahead of him, gun at her back, then pointed the weapon at Dines.

"I'm a sick man," he said again. "I've got to get to Cuba. I'm dying of cancer." Dines saw a youngish man with a dark blue suit, blue-and-black striped tie, plastic-framed glasses, receding crewcut, pistol waving in his hand . . . and a troubled, almost tearful expression.

So it was to be Cuba again. Captain Dines eyed the gun. It looked big enough to crawl into. He changed course. But he also exchanged glances with his flight engineer, Glenn Smith. This fellow was no Cuban. Why should he want to go to Cuba? And wasn't there something irresolute about his manner? Maybe— just maybe. . . .

Glenn Smith was thinking of the same "maybe." He started talking softly. The pistol stayed trained at Dines's head, but the eyes behind it shifted slightly as the hijacker listened. Smith gently questioned him. What was his name? Where was he from? Did his family live in Cuba? What was his trouble?

Richards trembled, and his face worked spasmodically.

A number of people had seen the hijacker enter the cockpit and had noticed the change of course. Most of them assumed that they were going to Havana from the way the plane was turning and the position of the sun. Several American planes had already made unscheduled stops in Cuba since the beginning of the year. The trip was not yet a run-of-the-mill experience, but neither was it altogether novel. A sort of resignation set in, and there was no panic in the cabin.

Nor in the cockpit, though Richards himself was jittery and uncertain. But he was answering Smith's questions; he was listening to the friendly voice and replying readily. His name was Oran Daniel Richards and he was thirty-three years old. No, he wasn't Cuban and he wasn't a refugee. But he was a sick man, dying of cancer, and he had to get to Cuba. No, his family didn't live in Cuba either. They lived in Springfield, Ohio. So did he. Yes, he had a job. He was a forklift operator.

Smith suggested that perhaps he might be making a mistake. He could see that Richards had his troubles, but this was surely not the way out of them. And what about all the people on the plane who didn't want to go to Cuba, who might actually be afraid? Did Richards really think he was right in doing this?

Oh. Well . . . he certainly hoped he wasn't inconveniencing the passengers or frightening the children. He wouldn't want to do that, because that would be a sin. All he wanted was go to Cuba, and what could be wrong with that?

"Wrong . . ." He stumbled over that word, and then repeated it.

At times he was completely rational, and at times very irrational. It was hard to know just how to talk to him, but Smith kept trying and Dines kept flying, the pistol still at his head. At no time did the pilot attempt to reach around and grab the gun—a virtually impossible maneuver in the cramped space of the cockpit, even if he had thought it wise—and at no time did Smith try to jump him, although sometimes the pistol wavered and the man appeared indecisive and confused. Nevertheless Smith and Dines were taking action, cautious action: they were listening and talking. They felt that Richards knew that he was "sinning," and that he was not completely committed to going through with it. Smith concentrated on trying to convince him that his act was legally and morally wrong. After all, think of all the people involved. Think of how it would hurt his family. Think of how he would feel *himself* if something bad happened. . . .

About ten minutes after bursting into the cockpit, Richards

suddenly broke into tears and dropped into a crouch on the floor. Sobbing uncontrollably, he asked for his mother. He babbled wildly; he was completely incoherent. The two other men in the cockpit stiffened. The pistol was still pointing at Dines's back and now the man was raving through his tears. God alone knew what he was going to do next. To Dines, the situation was becoming untenable. It was very touchy. For moments, he feared for his life.

But Smith was still talking to Richards. Somehow he managed to re-establish some kind of rapport with the man. Richards gradually controlled his tears and his tongue, and listened again. Smith was tactful and quietly persuasive. It was obvious to him, he said, that Richards really wanted to do the right thing. Perhaps this wasn't it—neither for himself nor for all the other people involved. Of course he had no intention of jeopardizing the lives of others, but he might be doing just that. The fact was, the plane had been fueled to fly to Houston and might not be able to make it safely to Havana.

"I'm sick," mumbled Richards. "I'm a dying man . . . don't want to hurt anybody." But he still held the gun on the captain. It was now about fifty minutes since he had started holding Dines at gunpoint and, crouched on the floor though he was, he did not seem about to give up.

Again, the soft insistent flow of words: Clearly Richards was basically a good man who wouldn't deliberately harm anyone. But he *was* endangering lives, or would be if he went through with his plans. Fuel was low already. Wouldn't it be better just to put the gun on the floor and forget this Cuba business? Anyone could make a mistake. There was no reason why he shouldn't change his mind once he saw that he was going wrong. And he could see that Richards knew he was making a mistake. Besides, air piracy was a serious crime, a federal offense, for which the penalty was heavy. No reason why a good man should get into that kind of trouble. And hadn't Richards himself said something about a "sin"?

"Sin . . ." mumbled Richards. " 'S'crime. I'm doing wrong. Know I'm doing wrong."

Florida lay below; Cuba lay ahead, uncomfortably close and yet uncomfortably far away. Fuel *was* getting low.

And Richards dropped the pistol on the floor.

It was still cocked, and it lay there untouched while all breathing seemed to stop.

Richards spoke first. "You can land anywhere you think you should," he said to Dines.

Dines started breathing again. If it wasn't to be Houston at least it could be Miami, not Havana. For a few moments Smith let the gun lie on the floor. One rash movement now, and he could still blow the whole thing. He looked at Richards, and he waited.

Richards didn't move. He just crouched there, his face distorted and pale; tearful, but apparently in control of himself. Smith picked up the gun and handed it to the captain.

The aircraft started its almost imperceptible descent, and back in the cabin the passengers heard the pilot's voice over the intercom: "We are in a very ticklish situation, but it is under control."

Flight 977, which had been scheduled to arrive at Houston at 8:04 P.M., made an emergency landing at Miami International Airport at 9:44 P.M. with its passenger list intact and its crew unhurt. FBI agents handcuffed Richards, now expressionless and calm, and led him away.

Thus ended one of the few cases on record in which a hijacking attempt had been foiled in the air. But though the action was over, the story wasn't quite finished. Senator Eastland was photographed at Miami Airport after the ordeal and made several comments to the press. An Associated Press dispatch of July 13, 1968, notes: "Sen. Eastland said he blamed the Supreme Court's liberal decisions for letting 'criminals run wild,' and said no new laws are needed to curb plane hijackings.

" 'It's all the Supreme Court's affair—they make it possible for criminals to run wild,' Eastland said. Eastland said he saw no need for new laws against hijacking airliners.

" 'I don't think any new laws Congress might pass would have anything to do with it,' Eastland said. 'That's like these gun laws. We've got all the laws that we need. We just need courts to enforce the laws we've got.' "

The day after the attempted hijacking, Oran Richards was charged with air piracy. He was nervous and had little to say, though he did tell United States Commissioner Edward P. Swan that he had a $145-a-week job. "But I've probably been fired by now," he said.

Inquiries in his home town of Springfield turned up the information that Richards was a conscientious and religious young man. He had once gone voluntarily to the police and confessed that he felt a frightening compulsion to shoot somebody. As a result he was committed to the Columbus State Mental Hospital. On August 31, 1959, he was discharged after a series of psychiatric sessions, and was described at the time as "improved." He had never, so far as is known, actually attempted to shoot anyone.

Richards is once again a patient in a mental hospital. His physical health, his "cancer," is not his problem. But whatever the nature of his illness or obsession, he is not the classic example of a criminal running wild, nor is he a jobless misfit or a man with a consuming grudge. He is suffering from some kind of emotional disturbance of long standing.

The case of Oran Richards is interesting from a couple of other angles. Perhaps the most thought-provoking point is the way he was handled in the cockpit. It has frequently been suggested that the general airline policy of crew inaction, of passive nonresistance to any airborne hijacking attempt, has not only permitted but positively encouraged further such attempts. This question has been beaten almost to death, but one that is closely allied to it has scarcely been touched. That is the question of the pilot as a man, a compassionate and reasoning man, and of his crew as compassionate and reasoning people. There is obviously good reason for a general policy of restraint and caution by the crew. But the captain of an airliner *is* the master of his ship, as pilots frequently point out, and as such is the man responsible for assessing the hijack situation as it develops in the air. Is it necessary or advisable for him to do *absolutely nothing?* Pilots discuss this among themselves, and the weight of their opinion appears to be a resounding Yes. Their job is to bring the plane and passengers down safely—wherever they have to land—and that is *all* it is. Soft talk to hijackers is no part of their business.

But the critics among them, and elsewhere in the industry,

feel that pilots have been passive beyond the line of duty. They think it is not unreasonable to expect the men in the cockpit to make some effort to size up the hijacker and try to foil a hijacking attempt when an opportunity presents itself. Apparently Captain Dines agrees, or did at the time. He was not himself the one to apply persuasive pressure on Richards, but as the man in charge he permitted and encouraged Smith to try to reason with the hijacker, to talk to him as one man to another. And it worked.

It is quite widely felt that a number of other hijackings (especially those in which no weapon was in evidence) could have been averted if the men on the flight deck had similarly used a modicum of initiative and tact.

Another interesting point about the Richards case is the comment it made on the "good riddance" flights proposed to Castro by the U.S. State Department only the day before. The proposition was that planes going empty to Cuba on Freedom Airlift flights be used to return homesick Cubans so that they wouldn't have to hijack planes to get back. It was a reasonable offer, though it was not accepted, but the fact is that there were and are several legal ways for Cubans to get back home. Yet the Cuban hijackings continue. An easy ride home might cut down on the number of hijackings committed by Cubans, but it would be completely irrelevant in the case of a man like Oran Richards.

Richards wasn't going anywhere at all and he had nothing to take with him but his fears.

In this he was much like John Di Vivo.

The Shooting on the Boston Shuttle

John Di Vivo did not want to go to Cuba and did not ask to go there. He just wanted to *go*. . . .

He chose to shuttle into nowhere.

On the day after the happening on the Eastern Air Lines shuttle flight from Newark to Boston, the flight Di Vivo took, the United Press International carried a story which said, in part, that "Officials stressed it did not appear to be a hijack attempt, but Di Vivo reportedly told (Captain) Wilbur to 'fly east. I don't have any place to go. Just fly east until the plane runs out of gas.' "

The fact that the plane was already practically over Boston meant that there was nothing to the east but an awful lot of water. If it were to fly east it would be in desperately bad trouble very soon, because it was carrying only the normal amount of fuel required for the short shuttle flight. This was a hijacking, all right—forceful, violent, wrongful, and tragic. However anyone else cares to define it, this was hijacking enough— and more than enough—for captain and copilot.

It was Tuesday, March 17, 1970. The 7:30 P.M. shuttle, Number 1340, was carrying sixty-eight passengers and a crew of five—seventy-three persons who, for several crucial minutes, were in grave danger of being robbed of their lives. The action took place when the DC-9 was over Franklin, Massachusetts, about five minutes out of Boston, and the craft was actually beginning its final approach to the airport. Senior stewardess Christine Peterson and stewardess Sandra Saltzer were collecting the last of the fares. By now they had reached the next to the last row. There was a young man in sunglasses sitting by himself in that row with a little black bag at his feet. When Miss Peterson asked him for the fare, the man, later identified as John J. Di Vivo, muttered something that she could not quite hear. She thought, though, that he was saying he did not have enough money, and it seemed that she was right when he handed Sandy Saltzer less than the required fare. "I'm sorry, sir, but that's not enough," Miss Saltzer said, and told him the exact fare.

The passenger reached into the small black case on the floor. The stewardesses assumed that he was reaching for more money. Instead, he pulled out a gun. "Now, don't get excited," he said. "Don't be frightened."

They didn't get excited but they were nervous. For a few moments he did nothing but just sit there with the gun. They waited for him to make a move. He fidgeted slightly, but that was all. The two girls didn't know too much about guns, but they would not have been reassured to know that he held a stolen .38-caliber revolver—loaded.

Finally, he muttered something only half audible about wanting to see the captain. They could not quite hear what he said, though they more or less got the idea, and they didn't know whether he wanted to go to the cockpit or have the captain come out and see him. Neither prospect appealed to them. So they muttered something back, and went on waiting. Then Di Vivo repeated his statement, this time more audibly. He wanted to go to the cockpit and see the captain there. He rose, gun in hand, and looked expectantly at Miss Saltzer.

Miss Saltzer had a flashing prevision of a trip down the aisle with the gun in full view, passengers staring aghast. Very sensibly she asked Di Vivo to conceal the weapon so that he would not alarm the other people. Obediently, he put it inside his shirt and followed her down the length of the cabin to the cockpit door. There, she paused, telling him that the door was locked and that she would first have to talk to the captain on the intercom. Di Vivo nodded.

She got on the telephone and quietly told the captain that there was a passenger with a gun who wanted to see him. Captain Robert M. Wilbur, Jr., occupied with the final approach, did not absorb the message. All he gathered was that a passenger wanted to see him, and he knew this was no time for a visit. "I'm too busy," he said. Sandy tried again. Repeating her message, she made sure to emphasize that the passenger had a gun.

Perhaps it was the crackling of the intercom, or perhaps it was Miss Saltzer's attempt to speak quietly so as not to let anyone else hear, but Captain Wilbur still did not understand. The men inside the cockpit simply could not figure out what her problem was. So the first officer opened the door and looked out. "What's the trouble?" said copilot James E. Hartley . . . and the gun swung toward him. Di Vivo walked straight into the cockpit and growled something incomprehensible. Wilbur glanced around. Immediately it was only too clear what the trouble was.

He gave one order, the only one he had a chance to give. Miss Saltzer left the cockpit and closed the door behind her. It wasn't easy to pretend that nothing was wrong, but she did her best. She and the other two stewardesses—Christine Peterson and Arlene Albino—walked through the plane talking casually, even jokingly, trying to seem as normal as possible in accordance with the captain's wishes that no one be alarmed. Panic among passengers carries almost as much danger as a gunman in the cockpit.

Captain Wilbur, at gunpoint, was being ordered to turn the aircraft east. East? He must have wondered what Di Vivo thought he was going to find in that enormous stretch of ocean. Whatever he thought, Captain Wilbur turned east, after scrupulously asking the Logan Airport tower in Boston for permission to leave his approach pattern.

What happened next is somewhat hazy. Di Vivo seemed to be talking to the pilots quite rationally. True, he is reported to have said at one point that he had no particular destination in mind. "Just fly east. I don't really have any place to go. Just fly till the plane runs out of gas." That, however, was not characteristic of his behavior for the next few moments. For the most part he was making a sort of sense. His voice was low but clear, he was not apparently under the influence of drugs or any intoxicant, and he seemed to be listening to Captain Wilbur. The captain had made the turn to appease him, and with that one crisis point out of the way he felt he could at least talk to the hijacker. He explained that he had certain responsibilities, that to continue east would get seventy-three people absolutely nowhere, and that they would have to stop at Boston for fuel if they were to fly anywhere at all. Di Vivo appeared to understand that there was indeed very little fuel left and accept the need to do something about it. Definitely, he gave the impression of realizing that they would have to return to Logan.

Wilbur and Hartley really thought they had managed to convince him.

Yet when Wilbur banked the aircraft for the turn, Di Vivo seemed first surprised and then violently angry. His gun hand tightened and jerked. Some passengers heard "a couple of shots." Some heard "three or four." It was probably even more than three or four.

Captain Wilbur could not remember afterward—or perhaps he did not even know at the time—whether it was he or First Officer Hartley who had been shot first. But he did see blood on Hartley only seconds after feeling the searing jolt of his own pain. Wounded in both arms and the chest, he turned to see Hartley grabbing at a bloody circle in his own chest—and then lunging at the hijacker. In his agony, Hartley grappled with Di Vivo for the gun; and as Wilbur twisted from his seat he saw his copilot wrench the gun away from Di Vivo and shoot the hijacker twice. Then Hartley, now spilling his own blood and drenched in it, slumped into unconsciousness. Di Vivo writhed in pain on the cockpit floor between the two pilots' seats, but still he had the desperate strength to try to reach up and claw for his weapon, to flail his arms at Wilbur. Wilbur met him halfway. He took the gun from Hartley's limp fingers and slammed it down against Di Vivo. Di Vivo went down hard, badly dazed but not out cold.

At about this time the cockpit door flew open seemingly of its own accord. At least one of the passengers sitting up front saw a pair of legs, blood-splattered, stretched out on the floor, actually extending through the cockpit door; the copilot slumped in his own seat, sagging like a rag doll; the pilot upright with blood on his back and sleeves.

Sandy Saltzer went quickly forward when she saw the door swing open. A few people half-rose behind her and craned their necks. One or two started asked each other, "My God, is anyone flying the plane?"

A young man seated near the cockpit stood up in the aisle and said: "Sit down. Everybody sit down. Cool it. Don't say anything. Just let's everybody keep quiet."

"Yeah, but *is* anyone flying this plane?"

"Yes, there is. No need to get excited. It'll be okay."

Miss Saltzer was still standing at the cockpit door, wondering what was best to do—wondering whatever in the world it was possible to do.

The man on the floor moved under the jump seat, and it startled her. She backed away slightly, watching the man struggling up from the floor and hearing his groans; and the captain turned around and hit the man over the head.

The nose of the plane dipped briefly (though passengers said afterward that they had felt nothing). Within seconds, Wilbur regained control. He was in terrible pain but he was flying.

"Are you all right?" Miss Saltzer asked him fearfully.

"Yes," said Wilbur. The blood was spreading down his arm now, and his first officer was slumping lower and lower in his seat.

She asked if she could do anything. "No," her captain answered. "I'm trying to get the plane down."

Somebody—it is not clear whether it was a stewardess or a passenger . . . perhaps it was both—went down the aisle asking for a doctor. Nobody answered the call.

Even then, passengers in the main section had scarcely a glimmering of what was going on up front. Obviously they were not alarmed by the calm request for a doctor. Certainly they did not suspect what some of the others were witnessing. But a little curiosity stirred. Some of those in the rear of the plane started to leave their seats and move forward to find out what was happening; but stewardess Arlene Albino firmly ordered them back to their seats. She did not want them to be targets in case the action spread. For all she knew, the hijacker might even now be reviving. If he did, he might start shooting into the cabin. She made them fasten their seatbelts. Reluctantly they obeyed, particularly when they saw that the No Smoking sign had lighted up.

The No Smoking sign! Incredible. A pilot who can handle so small a detail in the midst of such stress is a pilot indeed. And the stress at that moment was more than anyone, including the stewardesses, could imagine. The pilot was very badly hurt, and he had no one to help him.

There was still some fight left in Di Vivo. Every once in a while he tried to struggle to his feet and Captain Wilbur had to reach over and whack him back down. And yet, bleeding profusely though he was, his hands full and his eyes beginning to cloud over, the captain continued his approach to Logan in a manner that was so normal, so usual, that the mind can hardly grasp how he could possibly do it. Calmly, the lives of seventy people in his agonized hands, dying himself for all he knew, he performed in the best tradition of airline captains—he kept his head, followed the book, flew the plane, said only what he had to, and concentrated on getting his plane down in one piece.

He requested emergency clearance from the tower, advising them that his copilot was wounded but making no mention of his own wounds. "My copilot's been shot," he said succinctly. "Where the heck do you want me to park this thing?" He requested an ambulance, a doctor, and the police; and when he had taken care of those important details he turned on the No Smoking sign because it was part of the routine and because it would reassure the alert ones back in the cabin that everything was under control. It was the stewardesses who really got the message, and though they had been extremely cool throughout they were more relieved than anyone. Only they knew the terrible danger that had passed . . . and perhaps was still not over. They hadn't landed yet. Among the passengers, no one had been much upset. A typical reaction was that of two ladies who finally became aware of some stirring in the atmosphere and mildly asked, as the plane was coming in for a landing, what was going on. Nothing was going on, because it was over.

The plane banked a little more steeply than usual and came in rather fast but so smoothly that the nonprofessionals aboard thought the landing was perfect. And it was; absolutely perfect in that it had been achieved at all, and safely.

Wilbur taxied the aircraft to Gate 12 at the Eastern terminal. Even before it stopped, one of the stewardesses opened the door to the cockpit and found the copilot still slumped and by now motionless in his seat, the hijacker subdued on the floor but moving and moaning, and Captain Wilbur pale with pain and bleeding but still managing to cling to consciousness. Christine Peterson opened the passenger door as soon as the craft stopped and let down the airstairs. State police and airline personnel were on board within seconds.

Stretchers and handcuffs came aboard with them. First Officer Hartley was placed on a stretcher but Captain Wilbur managed, with some assistance, to get down the stairs on his own two feet. Di Vivo, still resisting, was subdued and dragged away by state police. According to one passenger (former Air Force pilot Herbert F. Garland), he put up a fierce struggle in spite of his wounds. "It took at least six state policemen to get him under control. He was bloody. In fact, the whole cockpit was bloody."

It was only then that a stewardess told the passengers what had happened; and now, at last, she cried.

Now, it is said, some of the passengers shouted, "Kill him; kill him!" What they saw as he was being led away was "a rough-looking fellow" with moderately long hair, dark glasses and a fringed suede jacket; and they objected to the hair. "He's got long hair," they observed knowingly. "That's typical."

In fact, it was not typical at all. As Dr. Dailey of the FAA has observed, the typical hijacker does not have long hair. Di Vivo was not "one of those hippies or yippies or radical college kids." He was, simply, a rather strange young man known in his own neighborhood as "the Professor" because of his eyeglasses and longish hair.

This, of course, was not discovered until a little while later when the police started asking questions.

At the airport, before the questions began, a state trooper was trying to revive James Hartley by mouth-to-mouth resuscitation. But James Hartley was pronounced dead on arrival at the Massachusetts General Hospital. Captain Wilbur and John Di Vivo, both severely wounded and on the danger list, underwent surgery and were afterward pronounced in "satisfactory" condition.

Why did Di Vivo do it?

He had been employed as a short-order cook at Palisades Amusement Park in New Jersey. On the day of the attempted hijacking and the murder of James Hartley, he had spoken at the park to a friend known as Chic and told him, "I'm going to get into big trouble today." At another time during the day he told his mother that he was going to Boston, but did not say why. When he left the house his brother Frank got the idea that he was going to a party.

Di Vivo was a ninth-grade dropout, described as a "lone-wolf type" by the few people who knew him. He lived in West New York, New Jersey, with his widowed mother, two brothers and a sister, in a five-story brick apartment building that is well known to the local police. "House of horrors," they call it unofficially. Since 1967 the building has been the scene of two suicides, a murder, and a double murder and suicide. The latter and most recent incident involved a tenant who shot and killed his wife and two-year-old daughter and then jumped to his death. When police were making inquiries and conducting a weapons search in the Di Vivo apartment, an anonymous call was received at Police Headquarters saying that a bomb had been placed in the apartment house. The search spread through the building, but no bomb was found. Ordinarily a bomb warning results in a certain nervousness and the rapid evacuation of the building, but in this case the tenants took it as a commonplace occurrence. To them, it was just another incident in a series of macabre happenings that had already caused them to nickname their building "Rosemary's Baby."

These surroundings could scarcely have had a beneficial effect upon a young man who had for years shown signs of mental disturbance. One significant episode in his past casts some light on his later behavior. It would cast even more light if we knew exactly what happened and why; but all we really know is that Di Vivo wound up with a bullet in his head. Di Vivo's family is reported as explaining that he was shot in the head by holdup men several years ago during an abortive robbery attempt at Palisades Amusement Park where he was working at the time. But a West New York police detective says that when John Di Vivo was sixteen years old he tried to kill himself with a .22-caliber revolver. Whatever the cause of the gunshot, the bullet lodged in his head and was never removed. Di Vivo, once fun-loving and gregarious, became increasingly reticent and more and more of a loner.

A special report in *The New York Times* of March 18, 1970, bylined by Alfred E. Clark, gives this follow-up comment to the shooting event:

"As a result he was partly paralyzed and had to walk using a cane, his left leg dragging. He used a silver-topped black cane, and he frequently wore a top hat and a sweeping black cape." The story goes on to quote the owner of a delicatessen at which Di Vivo was a regular customer: " 'He would come in quite often with his cape and top hat and usually would have some books and magazines about astrology or magic. . . . Sometimes he would get off on the stars and the moon and talk a lot about how the moon and the tide affect human beings. He came in early last night but wasn't wearing the hat or cape. He just said to me, "I'm going to Boston." Then turned around and walked out. Boy, I was surprised when I saw it on television.' "

An immediate result of the Di Vivo skyjacking was a new nationwide call, spearheaded by the Air Line Pilots Association, for strong anti-hijacking measures. A pilots' strike was a distinct possibility. Robert H. Tully, first vice-president of ALPA, put it this way: "The patience of the pilots is fast diminishing. We've watched this fiasco progress into tragedy. We predicted it some time ago. The tragedy in Boston was small compared to what it could have been." He indicated that, unless some concrete action were swiftly taken by the Federal Aviation Administration to protect the lives of airline pilots, there would be a "complete shutdown of the air carrier system."

In a hastily called Washington conference with Transportation Secretary John A. Volpe, FAA Administrator John H. Shafer, and representatives of the airline companies, the pilots laid it on the line: Action *now*! They made their point. Volpe declared that "all possible measures will be taken to prevent hijacking and violence in the sky." A number of suggestions and decisions were made. Suggestions: Inspect all carry-on luggage or prohibit it entirely. Authorize the airline captain to make airborne arrests of suspected hijackers. Install onboard armed security guards. Permit pilots to carry firearms. Decisions: Step up preboarding detection system. Order bulletproof doors for airplane cockpits. Request Attorney General John Mitchell to speed up the prosecution of those already awaiting trial for aircraft hijacking as a deterrent to others with incipient hijacking tendencies. (At that time, twenty-one persons were awaiting trial on hijacking charges.) As a result of the conference a possible pilots' strike was averted and a fresh look taken at existing anti-hijacking procedures. What was generally considered most likely to succeed out of all the proposals made, and what Secretary Volpe declared to be the best protective measure, was the preboarding system designed to pre-select passengers likely to commit violence in the air. The "get them on the ground" theme was beginning to swell into a chorus. Eastern, TWA, and Pan American were already using the detection system, and three other airline companies had begun to discuss its use with the FAA. Volpe and others were seriously considering the possibility of making the system mandatory for all. This, however, would raise many problems in terms of cost, extent of coverage, training of personnel, delayed takeoffs, and inconveniencing of passengers; and it would impose a heavy burden on the smaller companies and the carriers flying low-risk routes. Still, the "mandatory" idea remained a serious consideration.

To be thoroughly effective the preflight detection system would require the screening of every single passenger for every flight at every ticket office and every boarding gate of every airline and every airport in the country—*and* airports outside the country. Unthinkable!

The question of how widespread the system should be, mandatory or otherwise, was pointed up very sharply by the Newark-Boston episode itself. Eastern, as the main victim of the shuttle-to-Cuba hijackings of previous years, was using the detection system as religiously as any line. But the system had *not* been available at the particular gate position from which the Boston shuttle had left Newark Airport. Already looking in the eye a problem now brought home to all airlines, Eastern had been undone by the impossibility of blanketing every facility— every gate and airport touched at by its vast fleet of planes— with magnetometers and personnel trained in the interpretation of the behavioral profile. If the law of probability was any guide, a shuttle plane on a mundane commuter trip from one East Coast city to another was among the least likely of all targets for a hijacker.

Well, it wasn't.

Eastern Air Lines, under the direction of its extremely able Chief Security Officer Michael J. Fenello, gave its security program a shot in the arm. Its system of electronic pre-inspection of passengers and carry-on bags was expanded at the Boston, New York and New Jersey airports to include air shuttle flights and presumably forestall any more Di Vivo episodes.

Next time a Di Vivo won't strike at Newark.

There are 524 other airports in the United States, counting only those served by commercial aviation. Total airports on record with the FAA number 10,847.

How many other Di Vivos are there? Guess.

Where do they live? Guess.

What airport and what airline are they likely to head for? Guess!

At that conference on March 19, 1970, the pilots considered

the possibility of carrying firearms themselves and came up with mixed reactions. Traditionally, they have always been against it, but now many of them did begin to entertain the idea seriously. The reaction of the FAA's John Shaffer was not mixed at all. He expressed strong disapproval for the idea of armed pilots or guards aboard passenger-carrying aircraft, saying, "The last thing we need on planes is more firearms." He would prefer, he said, someone trained in karate to handle situations of potential violence. Yes, this could include stewardesses. However, he did not press this as a directive or even a suggestion; it was merely a thought.

In Washington, the Air Line Pilots asked the Justice Department, and federal judges in general, to give priority to trials of accused hijackers.

In New York, the United Nations announced that the International Civil Aviation Organization (ICAO) would take up the question of attacks aboard civilian planes and other acts of air piracy at an Extraordinary meeting in Montreal in June.

Later in 1970:
ALPA's highest honor, its rarely given Gold Medal Award for Heroism, was bestowed upon two of its members.

"Whereas, although mortally wounded, First Officer J. E. Hartley disarmed and disabled the assailant and Captain R. M. Wilbur successfully kept him subdued and landed the aircraft, saving the passengers, crew and aircraft, and

"Whereas the EAL MEC has recommended that the Gold Medal Award for Heroism be awarded in recognition of these heroic acts,

"Therefore be it resolved that the Association's Gold Medal Award for Heroism be awarded posthumously to First Officer J. E. Hartley and a presentation made of such award to Captain R. M. Wilbur by the President of the Association."

Captain Wilbur made an excellent recovery and is back in the air.

Mrs. Hartley has her husband's medal.

John J. Di Vivo was released from a Boston hospital, arraigned on murder charges in Suffolk Superior Court, and ordered committed to Bridgewater State Mental Hospital for observation. He faded out of the news.

A United Press International report of October 31, 1970, reads as follows:

Boston—A man charged in the murder of an Eastern Airlines copilot and wounding of a pilot during an attempted hijacking was found dead today in his cell at the Suffolk County jail.

A spokesman for the sheriff's office said John J. Di Vivo, 27, of West New York, N.J., committed suicide by hanging.

Di Vivo was being held in the jail on charges stemming from the fatal shooting of First Officer James E. Hartley and the wounding of Capt. Robert Wilbur, Eastern Airlines employees. Di Vivo also was wounded.

The shooting took place on March 17 in the cockpit of a Newark-to-Boston shuttle plane as it neared Boston with 68 passengers aboard.

Di Vivo's body was found at 3:20 A.M. suspended by a neckerchief tied to the bars of his cell.

6/CRIMINALS:
FUGITIVES FROM THE LAW

All hijackers are criminals by definition—by moral definition, if not by the laws of every country. Whatever their motives, they are committing a crime when they commit the act of air piracy. But many a sky pirate or would-be pirate is a man who was already a criminal when he hitched his ride in the sky.

Skyjackers of this breed usually hijack because they want to escape in the old-fashioned, nonpsychological sense of the word. They are, in a sense, transportation thieves; they use the plane much as if it were a stolen getaway car. Often the takeover is the work of an individual runaway; sometimes it is attempted by two or more people acting together. How many of the successful hijackings listed as having been committed by unreturned "fugitives"—and there are over forty on record— were actually performed by escaping criminals is known only to the FBI, but a spot check of the data on hand turns up some interestingly diverse cases.

The first successful "criminal" hijacking on our master list was not really a hijacking at all. It was an act committed by a thief, and what he stole was the Beech T-34 Mentor which he himself flew to Cuba, from whence he has not returned. The man was a Cuban-born naturalized U.S. citizen, Airman First Class Robert A. Ramos Michelena, and he pulled his aircraft getaway theft on July 8, 1963. He may have been a homesick Cuban, but he really shouldn't have stolen the plane.

On February 18, 1964, two Cuban exiles, Enrique Castillo Hernandez and Reinaldo Juan Lopez Rodriguez (alias Reinaldo Lopez Lima), hijacked a small chartered plane from Miami to Cuba. They, too, may have been homesick, but they had a more urgent reason than homesickness to depart from the United States. Plane and pilot were permitted to return to the United States but Hernandez and Rodriguez remain in Cuba, where they are presumably safe from the charges leveled against them in this country for embezzlement and passing bad checks.

Charles Laverne Beasley is another occupant of the criminal category. On September 11, 1968, he hijacked a Canadian

146

Viscount at gunpoint and demanded to be taken to Cuba. This was the first hijacking attempt in the history of Air Canada and it naturally came as something of a surprise to our northern neighbors, particularly since their national airline does not have and never has had a service to Cuba. The plane landed for refueling at Montreal, where Beasley was talked out of his attempt by a Royal Canadian Mounted Police officer. Beasley told the officer that he belonged to a Black Power group and that he was fleeing from the United States Central Intelligence Agency. This was a dramatic story, but it was soon contradicted by a report from the United States that he was wanted in his home town of Dallas, Texas, on a bank-robbery charge. Nevertheless, Canada gave him a sort of asylum: Beasley is spending six years in a Canadian jail.

On January 28, 1969, two well-dressed young men armed with guns and dynamite commandeered a Miami-bound National Airlines DC-8 over the Gulf of Mexico and forced it to land in Cuba. This was by no means unusual for the times, but what made it a little out of the ordinary was the calm, professional manner in which the hijackers took over and the fact that they announced themselves as fugitives from a California prison. One of them thrust a .38-caliber revolver against the back of the chief stewardess and said that magic word, "Havana," and then they both walked into the cockpit after her. While one man held a gun on the pilot the other threatened to light a match to four sticks of dynamite which he said were concealed in the cigarette carton he was holding so carefully. The plane arrived in Havana, and left without the hijackers.

A dozen or more human-interest stories spring from every hijacking, but this one had an odd sidelight for one man and his family. Luis Sierra Valdes had planned to arrive in Miami in time to meet his parents, two of his brothers, and his brothers' wives and seven children, all of whom had been permitted to leave Cuba as refugees and were expecting to be met by Luis on January 28. Luis couldn't make it, however; he was on his way to Cuba aboard the hijacked plane, having cold chills about the sort of welcome he might get. Still, all was well that ended well. In Cuba he pretended that he was a Peruvian, and they believed him. He returned to Miami with the rest of the passengers about eight hours after his family had arrived.

Then there was the one about the self-styled Black Nationalist Freedom Fighter who, if he really had a cause other than himself, was no credit to it. Raymond Johnson did not have a record, nor was he wanted on any charges, when he hijacked a National Airlines 727 jet flying from Houston to Miami on November 4, 1968 (the twelfth hijacking of an American plane that year), and persuaded its crew to take him to Cuba; but he does seem to have had a streak of larceny that was appreciated neither by his fellow passengers nor by his Cuban hosts. Armed with a .38-caliber revolver, already practically standard equipment for the well-prepared sky pirate, he not only took sixty-five people out of their way but attempted to steal cash from fifty-seven of them. Johnson did not attempt to rob the crew, but under his gun stewardess Sandra O'Brien was forced to collect money from the passengers. The passengers did not have a great deal of cash in their pockets. By the time the plane landed, Miss O'Brien had collected $405, which Johnson took off the plane with him in Havana.

Cuban officials did not approve of his looting. They returned the money as soon as they heard of the robbery, thus stripping of his spoils America's first known skywayman.

Perhaps it is not fair to suggest that Ray Johnson had no true cause other than himself. During the flight he announced that he was naming the plane "Republic of New Africa." Later, in Havana, he identified himself as a Black Panther and became part of the black revolutionary community in exile. But he is not—unless he has changed considerably—the sort of man who might be expected to dedicate himself to any movement. Though he spouted leftist jargon he acted like a petty thief and part-time sadist. The FBI regards him as one of the more vicious skyjackers on record. He spent some of his air time reviling the passengers and calling them "economic devils" while waiting for the stewardess to take up the collection for him, and some of it in the cockpit standing over the pilot periodically tapping him on the head—quite roughly—with the .38. He also found it amusing to knock off the copilot's glasses and grind them underfoot.

But as a thief, Johnson had nothing on the "grubby-looking character" (thus described by an unadmiring passenger) who made his bid for fortune, fame, and freedom four months later.

The Flight of Fu Manchu

On March 5, 1969, a man who first identified himself as Tony Bryant and then as Jimmy Carver boarded a National Airlines 727 in New York to become one of its nineteen passengers. Of them all, he was the only one who did not plan on going to Miami. Anthony Garnet Bryant, as he turned out to be, was sporting a Fu Manchu mustache and beard, long hair, a dirty shirt, and the standard .38 weapon. It seems that he harbored some sort of notion about being a black Robin Hood, because what he did on the plane was steal from the rich and give to the poor—in the person of himself. But before collecting his grub-stake he made his destination known to the captain of the craft. "I would rather be a prisoner in Cuba than here," he said, waving his .38 around the cockpit but apparently referring to the United States, and Captain Ed Buchser quickly got the point. "He said he wanted to go to Havana, and I said, 'Fine.' "

But the captain, a man of experience with handguns, noticed that Bryant was not handling the weapon particularly well. For a while Buchser toyed with the idea of trying to jump him, and at one point he almost did. But eventually he decided not to; he was afraid Bryant might "get one of the girls."

Whether he could handle the gun or not, the skyjacker did seem to be in control of his emotions and nerves. Captain Buchser found him quite reasonable when told that there was more to changing their flight plan to Cuba than simply pointing the plane in a new direction. "He was very nice about it," Buchser comments. "He allowed me to use the radio freely and to figure out our fuel loads and navigational problems."

With these matters suitably settled, the sky pirate abandoned the cockpit for the cabin. Gesturing carelessly with the .38, he strolled down the aisle chatting with the passengers. He was from San Bernardino, California, he said, and he had been released from prison about three months earlier after serving eight years for selling narcotics. To both crew and passengers he announced that the reason he had sold narcotics was to support his wife and family. Now, it seemed, he required other means of support . . . for himself.

Going from one passenger to another, he put a gun to each one's head and asked, "Are you a rich man or a poor man?" A black soldier on leave from Fort Dix, New Jersey, Specialist 4 James Tucker, promptly replied: "Poor man!" and Bryant left him alone. One of the stewardesses, taking a look at the gun, offered him her wallet but he graciously refused it. Black passengers, a black stewardess, and anyone else Bryant thought looked "nice" were also exempt from his demands. But the rest were unlucky; they looked too white, or too unfriendly, or too affluent, or were simply too slow in claiming poverty. Bryant's pockets were filling up very nicely with valuables and money: $20 here, $30 there, and some interesting packages from a pair of mailbags which he also ransacked.

Then he hit the jackpot. "I thought it was a joke," said passenger Paul Rawman when he had recovered from it. He could not really have thought it very funny, because as a Cuban exile who was contented with his comfortable living as a salesman in Miami Beach, he had no wish to return to Cuba *or* be robbed. Yet for the moment he did not take it seriously; he didn't realize what was going on. "I was asleep. He put a gun at my head and so I gave him the money."

Seventeen hundred dollars! Some joke.

Bryant was delighted with his haul, so delighted that he returned smaller sums to two other passengers he had robbed earlier. "I've got plenty now," he cheerfully explained.

When the Boeing 727 landed in Havana, Bryant left behind him the packages he had filched from the mailbags but took along the $1,700, some smaller change, and a tasteful selection of valuables. He marched happily off the plane and into the arms of his new Cuban friends.

But this was the real joke. They didn't want to be friends.

They relieved him of his loot and returned the money and valuables to their rightful owners, expressing regret and sympathy over the shoddy little episode. Plane, passengers, and crew were promptly released, the once-customary side trip to Varadero by now being a thing of the past, and all but Bryant returned safely to Miami.

What happened next was a new twist in the Cuban hijack story and something of a breakthrough. On the day after the hijacking, the Communist party newspaper *Granma* announced the arrest of Anthony Garnet Bryant, age thirty, U.S. citizen and bandit. It was the first time that the Cuban government had ever publicly announced the arrest of a sky pirate, or had so much as disclosed any part of the fate of a hijacker who had come to roost on Cuban soil. It had become known through various indirect channels that some hijackers had been held for interrogation for many weeks and even months, but we had no certain knowledge of what Castro was doing with them. Thus the arrest and public announcement came as a surprise, and was regarded in some quarters as a hopeful sign.

It is possible that Castro had suddenly had his fill of hijackings and had decided overnight that this was the last straw, that now was the time to take action against this influx of dissatisfied Americans and other hijackers, particularly cheap crooks. Why should Cuba become the haven for every penny-ante pilferer, narcotics peddler, plane robber, or convict on the run? No doubt Castro *was* fed up with it. But his was no overnight conversion. He had already given some indication through diplomatic channels that he was giving thought to taking some action that would curb the hijacking habit, and we did have some idea that he was not rewarding hijackers with plush suites in the Habana Libre. What seems most likely is that Knut Hammarskjöld's visit of several weeks before was paying off again. Word of Bryant's background had reached Castro from the United States, through one channel or another, and he knew very well what kind of sky pirate he was welcoming to his shores.

The Cuban announcement, carried both on radio and in the press, made much of Bryant's criminal record. It said that he had been convicted twice in the United States, once for robbery and once for trafficking in drugs. It further noted, with transparent disapproval, that he had robbed a passenger of $1,700. (Which had naturally been returned by Cuban officials.) "The author of these acts," said *Granma* severely, "has been put under arrest in our country, at the disposition of competent authorities."

Neither newspaper story nor radio report gave any indication that Bryant might be sent back to face prosecution in the

United States. He has not, in fact, come back; but so far as is known he has not sent any wish-you-were-here cards to the United States and we suspect that he might be in prison. The Cuban account of Bryant's criminal history was altogether accurate. There are police records in San Francisco to show that an Anthony Garnet Bryant, born in San Bernardino, California, was convicted there in 1961 for first-degree robbery and in 1964 for possession and sale of marijuana. For both offenses he was sentenced to San Quentin, where he served eight years.

For the box-score buffs there was another point of interest in the skyjacking by the man with the Fu Manchu mustache. It was the forty-ninth hijacking of an airplane to Cuba since 1961, all but three of which had taken place within nineteen months. United States officials were not pleased with the box score but were gratified by the Cuban action, calling the sky pirate's arrest "a good step that should help deter hijackers." (Did it help? Worldwide, there were sixty-eight more skyjacking attempts during the rest of 1969, fifty-three of them successful. Of the latter, forty-one concluded in Cuba.)

The Case of the Red-Faced Guards

A little later in the year there was another criminal attempt. This time, nothing but a tiny piece of stainless steel was stolen aboard the plane, and since that had already been discarded by its owner its appropriation could scarcely be called a crime. But it was lifted by an accused criminal for a criminal purpose.

This time the seizure happened to Trans World Airlines, and in spite of the fact that they had inadvertently provided the weapon it was not their fault at all. They were not aware that the passenger listed as L. Perry was a prisoner under guard—not until he left the Boeing 727 at Havana's José Martí Airport.

On July 31, 1969, TWA's Flight 79 was proceeding routinely from Philadelphia to Los Angeles while Lester Perry was proceeding less routinely on another plane from Scranton to Pittsburgh. The TWA made a scheduled stop in Pittsburgh, and so did Perry. There, with the two federal officers who were escorting him to a California prison, he boarded Flight 79.

He is believed to have been charged with bank robbery.

The plane made stops at Indianapolis and St. Louis, after which it was scheduled but not destined to fly nonstop to Los Angeles International Airport. After the takeoff from St. Louis Perry asked permission to go to the washroom.

Perry was allowed to enter the lavatory alone. In his moment of privacy he found a used razor blade in the receptacle provided for that purpose. He emerged from the washroom, grabbed the nearest stewardess, and held the blade at her throat.

Radio message to ground control from Captain J. L. Wilmot: "There's a man in the cockpit who wants to go to Havana."

So Lester Perry went to Cuba and stayed there.

The plane returned home with the rest of its passengers, including a U.S. marshal and a prison guard who did not make themselves available for comment.

Shootout at El Paso

A case of an entirely different sort, although also within the criminal category, occurred during the first early-warning wave of American hijackings. Though almost buried by time, the avalanche of subsequent hijackings and the more recent cases of infinitely greater international significance, it is a classic of its kind.

It happened on August 3, 1961, when we in the United States were still licking our wounded egos over the two U.S. aircraft that had been diverted to Cuba earlier in the year. The Electra parked in Havana on July 24 had not yet been released; the Cuban mouse was twisting the U.S. lion's tail and there seemed to be nothing we could do about it. The situation was frustrating, and it was ominous. What had happened in the case of the Electra could happen again—but it had better not. There was a national outcry of bewilderment and rage not only over the seizure itself but the fact that one of our expensive planes was in Castro's hands while our own hands appeared to be tied. Federal authorities were grimly determined that there would be no more such seizures.

Leon Bearden, however, had no sympathy for federal authorities. He was, at the time, a thirty-eight-year-old ex-convict who had first seen the inside of a jail in 1941 after having been sentenced for grand larceny in Graham County, Arizona. In 1942 he drew three to five years for forgery in Maricopa County, Arizona, after which he rested for some time from his illegal labors and dabbled as a roofing worker and sometime car salesman. In 1957 he was back inside, this time on a sentence of five years to life for armed robbery in Los Angeles County, California.

He served less than three years before being paroled from Folsom Penitentiary. While still inside he had announced that he was sick of the United States, and had actually renounced his citizenship. He wanted, he said, to live abroad.

For a year or so after leaving Folsom he lay low and mulled over his plans for the future. Very early on the morning of August 3, 1961, he put them into action. With his sixteen-year-old son Cody, a ninth-grade dropout, he boarded a Continental Air Lines Boeing 707 on its stop at Phoenix en route from Los Angeles to Houston.

They sat in the coach section, Leon Bearden with his .38 and young Cody with his .45 casually concealed.

Minutes before their scheduled stop at El Paso they rose from their seats. Stewardess Lois Carnagey heard a low whisper, then felt something jab into her ribs. It was Leon Bearden's .38.

The march to the cockpit began.

Destination, Cuba.

Veteran Captain Byron D. Richards took a long, cool look at the two guns trained upon him and his flight crew, and then glanced at the fuel gauge. They didn't have enough fuel to get to Cuba, he told Bearden; they would have to land at El Paso.

Bearden thought it over. "Okay," he agreed. "Land and get gas. But use your head when we land." And, meaningfully, he leveled the .38 at the pilot's head.

They would use their heads, all right, First Officer Ralph Wagner fervently agreed, but Bearden must understand that El Paso was calling for acknowledgment of clearance and that the tower must be informed of what was going on so that the refueling could take place swiftly and without a whole lot of policemen swarming around. There was a deliberate flaw in his logic here, and he hoped Bearden wouldn't notice it. He didn't. It sounded like a good idea to him.

Down in El Paso, now only moments away, the tower operator received the message and relayed it immediately to a Continental official who called the FBI.

Some of the passengers had seen the forced march to the cockpit and had begun to murmur among themselves. By the time the big jet landed the murmurs had spread and, from some seats, the tones of near-hysteria were making themselves heard. No panic yet, but rising fear. People were not yet conditioned to the coffee, tea, or rum excursions that were later to become a sour sort of joke, nor had their senses been deadened by laconic newspaper accounts of gunmen demanding passage to Cuba and uneventfully getting there. They didn't even know the right sort of wisecracks to make; they were unashamedly afraid. Stewardess Antoinette Besset was doing her best with them, but she scarcely knew what to say. She, too, was new to the hijacking experience.

In the cockpit, the flight crew was trying to stall. They had never flown to Cuba, they told Bearden. They didn't know how far it was or how much fuel would be needed or how long refueling would take.

"Okay, so find out," Bearden said, "—and get on with it."

"How about my passengers?" said Stewardess Lois Carnagey. "They'll have to be told what's going on. Especially now that we've landed, they'll be worrying—"

"Okay, so go and tell them. And keep them quiet."

She went out and walked slowly down the aisle. There was still no panic, she was glad to see, but there was one pregnant woman who was sobbing uncontrollably and seemed ready to collapse.

She went quickly back into the cockpit and reported to the captain. The woman, she thought, should be permitted to leave the plane.

Richards agreed. Her husband should go with her. In fact, he told Bearden, he thought it would be best if all the passengers were permitted to get off. The crew would remain, but the passengers should be allowed to leave.

"Okay," said Bearden. "Let them get off. But not all of them. I want, say, four of them to stay. As hostages. Get volunteers."

There was an unbelieving silence when the call for volunteers came over the P.A. system; and then it seemed that something like half of the seventy-odd passengers were offering themselves as hostages because suddenly the aisle was full of people wanting to be stand-ins for others.

Four were chosen and the rest filed gratefully out of the main door and down into the cool darkness of the Texas pre-dawn—gratefully, because though many would have gladly stayed, they were just as glad to be free. Behind them the door thudded shut, sealing in the crew, the Beardens, and the chosen four.

As soon as the passengers were clear of the plane and safely in the main terminal area, the FBI moved in and surrounded the 707. With them near the plane, and deployed in various strategic places, were Secret Service agents, El Paso police officers, U.S. Border Patrolmen, deputies from the county sheriff's office, and agents from the U.S. Immigration and Naturalization Service. They had had their instructions from J. Edgar Hoover, who had been in contact with President Kennedy, and they were going to make sure that the plane would not leave the ground so long as the Beardens were aboard. No one knew, as yet, what the Beardens had in mind other than going to Cuba, but the one thing they did know was that the big jet was not going to be permitted to join the Electra still languishing on a Cuban airstrip.

So far they had no idea how to stop it, particularly with hostages aboard, but they were slowly formulating plans. It was up to the FBI men on the spot to decide what action to take and when. The President had made that known to them, and they were doing the best they could with their hastily recruited army and their vague idea of what manner of men the Beardens were.

They had to find out more about the Beardens; more about their background, their interest in Cuba, what they could be expected to do. They tried to go on stalling while they were finding out. The fuel trucks were near at hand but were not permitted to approach. Taking to loudspeakers and radio, FBI agents informed Bearden that the plane was too big to land in Cuba; that if he insisted on going, would he kindly go in a smaller plane?—they would gladly make one available to him.

Bearden wouldn't bite. He would go to Cuba aboard the very plane he had commandeered, and that was that.

The FBI tried reason, gentle persuasion, tough argument. Bearden stood his guns. Nothing doing. And why wasn't the plane being refueled?

Because it wasn't going anywhere.

Stalemate.

The day dawned. Being sealed up in an earthbound airplane in El Paso in August is not the most comfortable of conditions. Clammy already from suspense and strain, the people inside began to sweat from the heat and the growing strain. The air became stale. Bearden's face was getting uglier. Young Cody did very little talking, but his grip on the .45 was firm and his every move was dictated by word or glance from the older man. Cody wasn't going to be swayed.

By now the FBI had found out something about Bearden: thief, forger, armed robber, now with a group of hostages and a $5 million airplane at his mercy. And there was another sinister note: Bearden had recently visited the Cuban embassy in Mexico City. That suggested a number of possibilities, among them that this hijacking was part of a Cuban conspiracy against the United States. Maybe Bearden was in the pay of the Cubans, or possibly even the Russians; maybe he was stealing the 707 jet for them.

It got later. And hotter. Bearden got edgier. His patience ran out.

"Quit all this stalling! Let's get going—let's get the fuel in. Get a move on."

The FBI had run out of conversational ploys. Bearden was obviously very restive, and there seemed no alternative to refueling the plane. And so the job of refueling got under way, rather slowly, which gave the FBI another hour. And then . . .?

This plane was *not* going to leave the ground.

Near the runway several sharpshooters positioned themselves behind a building. FBI agents and other personnel climbed into cars and sat waiting.

Operations got the message from the first officer: "We're going to have to take off or somebody's going to get hurt!"

Operations gave a reluctant go-ahead.

Slowly, the engines started. Slowly the plane rolled down the taxiway away from the terminal building. Slowly it lumbered onto the runway . . . with the FBI cars creeping silently behind it and the sharpshooters following with the sights of their rifles.

When the Boeing was a little more than a hundred yards down the runway the agents fired. It was a staggering chance to take. Two armed men—Cody was young but even bigger than his father and totally under his control—in a plane with five crew members and four passengers helplessly at hostage to them! What the Beardens might do under fire was beyond imagination.

Bullets seared into the enormous tires and almost simultaneously all ten tires blew out. The plane lurched, and came to a floundering halt.

A lot of breath was being held around the terminal. Nobody outside the plane knew that Leon Bearden, white with rage, had rammed a gun against Lois Carnagey's head and was holding it there with his finger at the trigger, but they did know that if anything was going to happen to the hostages it was going to happen within the next few moments.

It was hotter than ever, both outside and in the plane. The sun at 10 A.M. might as well have been the high-noon sun of a western movie. It was as hot and still as noon, and it blazed down on a scene far more deadly than a gun duel. Leon and Cody Bearden between them could mow down the lot out of frustrated rage.

But if they did, then what? What could they do with themselves?

The minutes ticked by. Six of them. For six minutes, Bearden held the gun against the girl's head. Then he took it away.

He didn't know what else to do.

For about another hour absolutely nothing happened. An FBI man using the ground communication system identified himself and tried to get Bearden to talk. Bearden wouldn't.

He didn't know what to say.

The FBI men waited it out until it seemed pointless to wait any longer. The agent in charge firmly requested permission to board the plane and discuss the matter further. "Okay," said Bearden. "You come on in. Just you."

The agent went aboard. There was nothing for Bearden to do, said the agent, but surrender. There was no place for him to go. The show was over.

Bearden was not ready to give up, nor did he have the faintest idea what to do next. He talked. He wanted to go to Cuba, he insisted, and take his boy with him. He did not like the U.S. government or the type of life in the United States. Cuba appealed to him, and that was where he wanted to go.

"Then why," asked the agent, keeping Bearden talking, "didn't you take a commercial plane? You could have gone through Mexico."

"I couldn't," said Bearden. "I haven't any money. All I have is $25."

All he really had was a few minutes' talking time, and then his trip was over. While Bearden was talking to the agent, under the impression that he was negotiating, two more men climbed quietly aboard the plane, and the hostages—passengers and cabin crew—began just as quietly to leave. One hostage, a U.S. Immigration official, stayed behind with the cockpit crew to enjoy the final scene.

There was a knocking sound from somewhere in or immediately outside the plane, like someone knocking at a door. Bearden turned his head as if to locate the sound—and one single, solid punch slammed through the air and landed against the side of his jaw just below the ear, and Bearden dropped as if pole-axed. For a split second young Cody just looked on, open-mouthed; and then, before he could move, a pair of arms snaked toward him, grabbed him, and disarmed him.

The 707 did not go to Cuba.

Leon Bearden was eventually tried, convicted, and sentenced to twenty years imprisonment. Cody Bearden was sent to reform school.

During the interrogation of the Beardens it was discovered that Bearden had no interest in communism of either the Cuban or Russian variety. He was not defecting. He was unhappy with his life in the United States but not from a political standpoint. Nor was he anybody's agent. At no time had he considered stealing the plane for the benefit of any other country. No, he had tried to steal it for his own benefit, with a view to selling $5 million worth of plane to Castro and spending the rest of his life in luxurious retirement.

The Thieves Who Went to Baghdad

It need not be thought that all criminal hijackers are Americans.

On November 9, 1970, an Australian pilot named Sidney Strody Jordan was flying a twin-engine DC-3, owned by the Air Taxi Company of Iran and chartered to Iran Airways, when he encountered a group of criminals.

The reports of this incident are contradictory and confusing. What is definite is that Jordan was piloting the DC-3 from the sheikhdom of Dubai on the Persian Gulf coast of the Arabian peninsula to the port of Bandar Abbas in southern Iran, that he was forced by a group of men to divert the plane from its course, and that at least some of the men were later identified as criminals.

There were twenty-two persons aboard the plane on its 100-mile hop across the Gulf. Three of them were crew members. Of the nineteen passengers, only ten were ordinary, everyday travelers quietly trying to mind their own business. Of the other nine, it was first said that they were all criminals, then that six of them were criminals with three accomplices aboard, then that all nine were criminals who were being accompanied by two armed policemen from Dubai, then that six of them were "Iranian petty criminals, extradited from Dubai for trial" and that the other three were guards. It may be worth noting here that this conflict is not due to distortion or careless inaccuracy by the press. Rather, it is due to the inaccurate observations and faulty memories of the witnesses, who naturally were not expecting a crime to occur and probably would not have been more observant even if they had expected it, and to the different viewpoints of the various people involved. Pilot, copilot, innocent passengers, and the inevitable government spokesman all saw things through different eyes and reported what they thought had really happened.

What did happen was probably something like this: Six men, wanted in Iran for a variety of crimes, had some years previously fled Iran without passports or exit permits and settled in

Dubai where they managed to exist without the required work permits. Eventually they were discovered and expelled from Dubai under the escort of two or three armed guards whose assignment was to turn them over to Iranian authorities to stand trial for such crimes as smuggling and petty larceny. With or without the help of accomplices, they overpowered their guards, rushed the cockpit, and ordered the pilots to "fly to Baghdad or Basra."

Even if the weather had not been unpleasantly stormy, which it was, pilot Jordan would not have been happy about making the detour to Iraq. To turn a short commuter hop into a long flight over the Gulf was not the easiest thing in the world to do. Jordan didn't like the idea, the legitimate passengers weren't going to like it, and in all likelihood the Iraqi government wasn't going to like it either, particularly because of their strained relations with Iran. But Jordan had a pistol rammed against his head, and there were at least five other men who were brandishing knives and guns, so Jordan had no choice. Not even between Baghdad and Basra, because his next command was to get to Baghdad or else. As he said in his radio message to Teheran, "I have no choice but to use Baghdad International Airport and follow instructions."

Still, according to his copilot, he did try one maneuver. Changing course as subtly as he possibly could, he attempted to make for Bandar Abbas after all. But the hijackers quickly discovered his ploy and threatened to destroy the plane by pouring gasoline over the seats and setting fire to it unless Jordan straightened up and flew right. Jordan straightened up; surrounded by threatening criminals, he thought it best to turn immediately toward Iraq.

From Dubai to Baghdad is a much greater distance than from Dubai to Bandar Abbas. Jordan was going to be very pinched for fuel. Early reports on the hijacking indicated that Jordan was permitted to make a refueling stop, but these reports were erroneous. Jordan did not have the opportunity to refuel, and the flight to Baghdad was a race between him and the fuel tank. And as if things were not sticky enough already, he had to encounter two potentially disastrous delays. One occurred over Kuwait.

The hijackers had, by now, disconnected the aircraft's transmitter to prevent Jordan from exchanging possibly coded messages with any ground officials that might somehow lead to the foiling of the hijack attempt. Somehow the Kuwaitis got the idea that the DC-3 was going to attempt an unlawful landing in Kuwait, and when Jordan failed to explain the situation over the deactivated transmitter they reacted by sending up a delegation in the shape of Kuwaiti military aircraft, one of which became dangerously menacing. The hijackers themselves got alarmed by this and permitted the pilot to hook up the transmitter and contact the threatening planes. When the Kuwaitis understood that Jordan had no intention of trying to land in Kuwait they withdrew and permitted the Iranian plane to proceed.

Jordan neared Baghdad with a fuel tank that was scarcely more than damp. Here another hitch occurred, although there was no time for hitches. Iraqi officials refused him permission to land. He circled the city, pleading with them, explaining that he really would much rather go to Iran but had been forced into heading for Baghdad by a band of hijackers. The Iraqis were unsympathetic. They had already hosted two hijacked Iranian planes during the previous few months and they wanted no part of any more. On both occasions they had returned planes, passengers, and crews to Iran, in spite of their differences with that country, but enough was enough. Jordan could go somewhere else.

There has been a suggestion that Jordan's name caused some misunderstanding. Perhaps it is an apocryphal story, but rumor persists that the Iraqis' refusal to let Jordan land was due in part to a communications gap—the gap between the air and the ground, the gap between one language and another. He told them his name several times in the course of their questioning and his pleading. Did they think he was *from* Jordan? We don't know. But we have been told that that was one of the problems.

Whatever the real reason, the Iraqis did not want Jordan to land.

Jordan circled.

And, finally, had to report to the airport tower that he did not have enough fuel for one more circuit—that there was "not a single drop" of fuel left and that he would have to make an emergency landing.

They relented.

Emergency landing procedures were immediately ordered.

Jordan landed. He may actually have had a drop of fuel left, but only that; he was well into his last gallon when the plane rolled to a stop to be ringed by troops of the Iraqi militia. The hijackers and their guards were promptly removed from the plane by Iraqi officials. Crew members and the rest of the passengers were questioned over a period of about four hours and then released with the plane; hijackers and guards were detained. The hijackers asked for political asylum.

Relations between Iraq and Iran had been tense since January of that year, when Iraq accused Iran of attempting to foment a coup d'état. The first two Iran-to-Iraq hijackings that followed were political in nature, and there was reason to consider requests for asylum. But by no stretch of the imagination could the six criminals who arrived on that nonscheduled flight to Baghdad on November 9 be considered candidates for sanctuary on a political basis. Iranian government officials stated very firmly, with support from Dubai, that the hijackers were small-time criminals, smugglers, and petty larcenists who definitely were not political criminals. They added that some of the men had been accused of forging passports and customs documents in Dubai and had been living and working in that country on the strength of false papers, and thus were criminals twice over. Therefore the Iranian government wanted them returned.

The disposition of this case is not yet known. But if the hijackers are still in Iraq, they are almost certainly in jail.

Most of the hijackers featured in the above cases are petty little criminals, penny-ante people. Most of the above cases are petty little cases. But there are a lot of them, and that is why they are significant. Let us all look at this common type of hijacker again: He is forger, burglar, robber, pickpocket, two-bit smuggler, narcotics peddler, embezzler, check-kiter, chiseler, and punk.

Lest we forget our list of crooks, our little petty thieves, in the midst of the more internationally significant and exciting sky adventures of today, let us examine two more cases of criminals attempting to escape. And let us quickly relate the more recent one first, because it is so typical of the criminal category and because it was such an ignominious flop that we cannot help being cheered by it—even though it took eighty police cars, a forty-five-mile chase, and three helicopters to foil it.

Early on the morning of the day before Christmas, 1970, three bandits entered a bank in Locust Valley (Nassau County, New York), and swiftly bound and gagged three male employees after having persuaded one of them to open the vault. Shortly afterward, three female bank employees arrived and were also bound and gagged. The robbers stuffed a duffel bag and a small canvas sack full of money and headed for the door.

But the employee who had been forced to open the vault had somehow managed to set off a silent alarm at the same time. Police converged on the bank just as the robbers were leaving. Cops and robbers exchanged shots. The shooting stopped when the bandits grabbed the three women and headed for a waiting getaway car.

But the getaway car wasn't waiting. Apparently the fourth man panicked when he saw the police and made a getaway by himself. Quandary! What to do? Easy. Use the women as shields, and grab a car belonging to one of them. So three bandits and three hostages piled into the young woman's handily parked car.

Then the chase began. It led along a turnpike, and in and out of side streets, and toward Kennedy International Airport. Unmarked Nassau County and New York City police cars tore along after the fleeing car, and some lay in wait at intersections trying to head it off. Soon the three helicopters joined the chase. They hovered delicately within call but out of the immediate vicinity so that they would not be too obvious.

As the stolen getaway car zoomed down the pike and zigzagged through the side streets the robbers discussed their plans: they would hold their hostages until they reached the airport, where they would hijack a plane. They entered the airport and headed for a terminal building.

But then the three helicopters made their presence known. The bandits suddenly became aware of them chopping menacingly overhead and decided that their hijack plans would have to be changed. Tires screeching, they took the nearest exit and headed for Brooklyn.

They should have known better. It's easy to get lost in Brooklyn at the best of times. And it's only natural to get upset when the police are after you.

About forty police cars surrounded the getaway car on a Brooklyn street. The young lady who owned the car was roughly pushed out, perhaps as some sort of offering to the gods, but this maneuver availed the bandits nothing. The police closed in with revolvers, shotguns, and machine guns, and dragged the suspects out. One of them banged his head while scrambling from the car. He was the only one injured during the whole affair.

Later, their $19,200 heist went back where it belonged, and the suspects were booked in Mineola, New York, on charges of armed robbery, kidnapping, and assault.

With a little more luck and better planning they might have been charged with air piracy too.

"Hey, Paisan, Why Are You Arresting Me?"

Raffaele Minichiello thought he had been wronged. Perhaps he had been. Back in his birthplace, the little town of Melito Irpino, near Naples, people had for generations taken matters into their own hands when they felt injustice had been done. Perhaps Raffaele was still Italian enough to follow that tradition and genuinely feel that he himself was doing nothing wrong. Yet surely his reaction was extreme.

Because of a $200 misunderstanding he committed the dangerous act of transatlantic air piracy on a nontransatlantic craft, heavily armed and ready for a shoot-out with either FBI agents or Italian police or both; because of a grudge against the U.S. Marines he hijacked an airplane from San Francisco to Rome by way of Denver, New York, Bangor, and Shannon—a 6,900-mile flight lasting seventeen grueling hours—and played games with the lives of its kidnapped crew.

November 1, 1969, was Raffaele Minichiello's twentieth birthday. He had been due to appear the day before at a special court-martial at Camp Pendleton, California, the Marine base at which he was stationed, but instead he had gone AWOL and boarded TWA Flight 85 at Los Angeles. Now, on this Saturday that was his birthday, he was celebrating aboard the hijacked craft by repeatedly taking apart his rifle, cleaning it, and putting it back together again. His growing resentment over his treatment by the Marines had become too big for him to handle.

He had enlisted in the Marine Corps and served honorably in Vietnam, taking part in twenty-eight combat missions, being decorated with the Vietnamese Cross of Gallantry and promoted to lance corporal. On being shipped back to the United States he signed up for another Vietnam tour, not because he had any burning desire to return to Vietnam but because it was a way to reduce his enlistment term.

It was in January of 1969 that Minichiello was first provoked into bewildered anger. During his year in Vietnam he had saved some money. Now, back in the States between tours, he wanted it. So he asked the paymaster for the $800 he had saved, and the paymaster told him that he had saved no more than $600. Minichiello objected; that was wrong. It was supposed to be $800, and $800 he was going to get. But you do not win arguments with Marine Corps paymasters. Minichiello took the $600 and went away furious, sure that he had been cheated.

Weeks, even months, went by. The wrong rankled within him; his bitterness and anger grew. The Marines owed him $200 and, by God, he was going to get it.

One night in May, he tried. It was a night when he was drinking a little too much beer while waiting for a buddy who never showed up. After the first few beers he began brooding over the injustice done to him. In the course of seven or eight beers, he achieved a state of righteous anger and a mood for action.

Reeling slightly, he broke into the Camp Pendleton PX (according to pre-court-martial records) and helped himself to some watches and radios. Beer-befuddled but still thinking in terms of what was only right and fair, he took what he judged to be just about $200 worth of goods and propelled himself unsteadily into a recreation hall. There he passed out. The MPs who aroused him found the goods on his person.

In August he was told that he would be court-martialed on a charge of theft of government property. The date of the trial was set for October 31. His lawyer advised him that a not-guilty plea would likely result in a six-month sentence followed by a bad conduct discharge and that he would therefore do better to plead guilty and settle for thirty days. Minichiello could not accept this. He felt he was not guilty and that he did not deserve a bad conduct discharge after serving honorably in the Corps.

He waited it out until the day before the scheduled court-martial. Then, on Thursday, October 30, he drew out all the money he had (about $460), did some shopping, and took a bus to Los Angeles. At L.A. International Airport he bought a ticket to San Francisco, where TWA's Flight 85 was supposed to terminate, and stepped aboard the plane. It was now late at night.

The plane was an early model of the Boeing 707. Its navigation equipment and other instrumentation did not qualify it—at least in TWA's view—to fly internationally, nor was its captain qualified for international flights.

No matter. Minichiello had wanted some form of transportation, and this was to be it.

Most of the passengers were asleep inside the darkened plane at about 2:25 (Pacific Standard Time) in the morning of October 31. Captain Donald Cook was at the controls. James Findlay, a TWA pilot deadheading back home after a vacation in Honolulu, was on his way out of the cockpit after a talk with his friend Don Cook, whom he had not seen in some time.

One of the stewardesses had just stopped to talk to a young man seated in the rear of the plane. In the dimness she could see him working with something, or reaching for something down under the seat. She asked him if he needed any help. "No, thank you," he said politely. "I'm just putting together a fishing rod." And she saw the long, rodlike shape.

The stewardess, Charlene Delmonico, proceeded to the galley. The young man followed her a moment later. She half-turned, saw what he was pointing at her, and gasped, "You're not supposed to have that!"

It was about twenty minutes before ETA at San Francisco that Findlay, now walking through the coach section, saw against the light of the galley the silhouette of a man holding a rodlike shape against the back of the stewardess. It was not a fishing rod. It was an M-1 carbine.

Findlay noted rather absently that it was some kind of short-barreled rifle. His first thought was that the man must be showing her the rifle. His next thought must have been: "In the *back?*"

"I mean business," Minichiello was saying with quiet ferocity. He looked as though he did. Also, although they did not know this, he was very proficient with the M-1, having had much practice in the Marines.

The stewardess turned carefully toward Findlay. "Sir," she advised, "you had better go sit down."

Minichiello briefly swung the gun away from her and pointed it at Findlay. "You *better* go sit down," he said emphatically.

Findlay sat down. And watched.

All his customary politeness briefly stripped away, Minichiello thrust the gun at the stewardess's back and gruffly demanded to see the captain. They marched briskly up the aisle, stewardess with gun at her back and Minichiello pushing from behind. There was a brief pause while the stewardess whispered into the intercom, and then Captain Donald Cook opened the cockpit door to let them in.

Minichiello's tension was almost tangible. He was like a loaded gun himself: deadly dangerous and ready to explode, a trembling trigger-pressure away from letting himself go. Captain Cook managed to appear unmoved and yet amenable. A madman, he thought; and turned without argument and headed east. Sure, they would go to New York, he said, but they would have to stop for fuel somewhere along the way. . . . In the face of Cook's unruffled serenity, Minichiello himself calmed down. His manners came back, and he apologized to Miss Delmonico for frightening her.

A few minutes later he politely requested the girl to go back to the coach section and pick up his gear. She went back and told Findlay, "He wants all his things up in the cockpit."

Findlay looked at Minichiello's gear. He saw a vinyl suitcase, a military duffel bag, and a leather case containing a pair of high-powered binoculars. "Let me take a quick look through these things first," he said to the stewardess, and while she waited nervously with one eye on the cockpit door and the other on Minichiello's gear, Findlay tried to look into the suitcase. His idea was that he might find another gun, not necessarily for his own use but something to be kept away from Minichiello. One catch was undone but the other was locked, so he could not open it all the way. But he did see some camouflage-type military clothing and some canned food.

The stewardess was getting restive at the delay, so Findlay said: "Take these—the suitcase and binoculars—on up to him, and tell him there was too much for you to carry." The duffel bag was heavy, so this should seem reasonable to Minichiello.

She went up front and Findlay looked rapidly through the duffel bag. It was jammed full of canned goods (including soup, goose liver, anchovies, and cocktail sausages), civilian clothing, cigarettes, and ammunition, the latter including a magazine or clip for the rifle. There was also a military field manual on how to use the rifle. The contents indicated that Minichiello had carefully planned on some sort of lengthy siege, or for holing up somewhere when he got to his destination. But there was no other weapon in the bag; Minichiello must have all his weapons on him.

By this time most of the thirty-nine passengers knew that something extremely irregular was going on, and those who had an idea what it might be began to spread the word. Along with the word grew spreading concern.

Cook, with perfect timing, came on the intercom. The hijacker seemed to have settled down. It was safe, now, to communicate with the passengers without sparking off some kind of outburst.

"There's a man here who wants to go some place," he said drily, "and he's just chartered himself a plane. To New York." This kind of unofficial chartering, he added lightly, might very well be due to the high cost of travel. He would announce the estimated arrival time in New York as soon as he had worked it out, and in the meantime booze was on the house.

There was a slight relaxation of tension among the passengers. Cook was good, very good; smooth, reassuring, totally in control of his own emotions and reactions.

A few people made use of the availability of free liquor, though none to excess. The stewardesses circulated quietly, offering free drinks, food, blankets, and playing cards to any takers. Four men in the first class compartment began an intense card game.

Cook came out once to check on his charges and chat with them. Satisfied that there was no hysteria and that everybody was being looked after, he went back to the cockpit for another chat with Minichiello. They could stop at Las Vegas, Salt Lake City, or Denver. Denver was the farthest east that the plane could go on its remaining fuel. Minichiello preferred to go as far east as possible before stopping, and elected Denver. Cook radioed ahead, then talked again, persuasively, to Minichiello.

A few minutes later he went back on the intercom. He had made a deal with the hijacker, he said, to stop in Denver for fuel, and to let all the passengers off the plane when they got there. "I wish I could go with you," he remarked, "but unfortunately I can't."

Denver got ready to receive the hijacked plane. No plans were made to seize the hijacker there, but the word was passed to the FBI and other agencies in New York that they could expect uninvited guests at JFK Airport some time late in the New York morning.

Top FBI agents in New York got busy.

Cook kept in touch with his passengers over the intercom. At one point he told them that the group in the cockpit was busy playing bridge and that "he's offered us chewing gum and we're all having a smoke." At another he came on and announced, "Well, this is old blabbermouth again. . . . It's twenty-eight degrees in Denver and for those of you who thought you were going to land in California where it's warmer, just take a blanket when you leave the plane and if anybody stops you, you just tell them that they are compliments of TWA."

The captain's amiable chitchat was not merely for the purpose of maintaining calm in the cabin. He had discovered that his studied casualness was having a soothing effect on the young gunman. A kind of rapport was beginning to develop between them, a desirable circumstance in view of the fact that Minichiello was not only armed with the loaded rifle but had a pistol and a knife stuck into his military cartridge belt.

The plane landed in Denver shortly before 5:30 A.M. Mountain Standard Time. There was a brief rise in tension while those aboard the plane and on the ground wondered whether the hijacker would go through with his promise to let the passengers debark. Cook again eased the situation: "The hostesses won't help you with your wraps. Everyone get his own and please make as little noise as possible leaving the plane. Please have as little confusion as possible. We have enjoyed having you on TWA today and we hope to see you again."

The passengers quietly left the plane without a menacing move from Minichiello. Findlay got off with them, as did three of the stewardesses. The fourth stayed behind at Cook's soft-pedaled request. None of them had to stay, he had told them after calling them all into the cockpit, but he would certainly like it if one of them would. Just to serve them coffee. It was going to be a long trip and they were going to need a lot of coffee.

They were going to need a lot more than he knew.

Minichiello eyed the stewardesses and opted for Carlene Delmonico. Perhaps he felt he knew her better than the others. But Cook suggested that it might be fairer to ask first for volunteers, and Minichiello agreed. Stewardess Tracy Coleman said she would like to stay aboard because she wanted to go to New York anyway, and again Minichiello agreed. By this time his manner was generally agreeable.

With the passengers out of the way and the refueling completed without incident, the plane took off about an hour after landing and headed for New York.

There, elaborate plans were being made by the FBI. Sharpshooters were to be hidden in the weeds at JFK. Other agents were to be disguised as truck drivers and mechanics. The top New York agent himself was to don a bulletproof vest and lead the charge. Forwood C. Wiser, president of Trans World Airlines, urgently requested that a shoot-out be avoided. The FBI said "Uh-huh," and went on with their preparations to ambush the plane. Wiser expressly instructed Cook, via radio, to "play it cool and not do anything heroic."

Cook played it cool. He had several hours in which to get to know the young hijacker, and he used them as well as he could. To try to disarm the boy was out of the question. All he could do was talk to him and listen, and he realized that Minichiello was not going to be talked out of his attempt. But where did he really want to go? Surely not New York. There wasn't much sense in an American hijacking a plane from one American city to another, least of all someone who seemed to be equipped for a hunting trip. . . .

Minichiello told him then that he wanted to go to Cairo.

Cook reported this news. It meant a long transoceanic flight and he would have to pick up a pair of internationally qualified pilots. The plane, though not properly equipped, could probably make it; some modifications had been made on the ten-year-old craft, and the load was light now that the passengers and their baggage had been discharged. He would be able to take on plenty of fuel and, if lucky enough to get tailwinds, should be able to manage the trip in a series of hops.

TWA officials sent out a quick call for volunteer pilots. It was answered by Captain Billy Williams, manager of the line's international pilots, and Captain R. H. Hastings, an international supervisory captain.

In the meanwhile, a relationship of trust and confidence was developing between hijacker and crew on that strange flight to New York. They drank coffee together; they told each other things about themselves; they reached the familiarity of using first names. They found they liked each other.

"We sat with that boy for six hours," Cook said afterward, "and had seen him go from practically a raving maniac to a fairly complacent and intelligent young man with a sense of humor. And then . . ."

And then they landed in New York to be met by the FBI. Many hours later, when the hijacking was over and Cook was tired and jangled, he made some irate comments about the FBI and used some ill-chosen words which he later regretted. But he felt when he made his remarks that the FBI had "irresponsibly made up their own minds about how to handle this boy on the basis of no information, and the good faith we had built up for almost six hours was completely destroyed."

Whoever was right and whoever was wrong, the fact is that the FBI did manage to antagonize and unnerve Minichiello. They were out in force, with coveralls and crowbars, riding around in trucks and lurking in the tall weeds, moving in on the plane in such force that it was obvious to crew and hijacker that they were considerably more than the "minimum ground crew" requested. Some were carrying weapons openly and wearing military-type flak jackets. It is not surprising that Minichiello started to panic. "Get those people away from the airplane!" he screamed. "Get them away!"

Cook stuck his head out of the cockpit window and did some yelling of his own. "We want everyone away from this plane! This boy is going to shoot us."

But the agents ignored him and continued to move in.

Minichiello watched them, his jaw tight and his eyes blazing. Cook watched them too. There was a man in a TWA maintenance outfit moving in under the wing. Cook was sure he was no maintenance man. He was even more sure when the man just stood there looking up, not trying to maintain anything but a purposeful look. Still, maybe he was worth talking to. Time was ticking by, and Raffaele was getting increasingly touchy. Something was delaying the fuel truck.

Cook yelled down at the man: "We've got to get out of here! Get us moving!"

The man in the maintenance outfit looked up at him.

Cook is probably still furious over this incident. "And this clown—I wish I could get my hands on him—shouted back, 'We'll get you moving when we're ready to.' "

And he meant it. *They* had decided what *they* were going to do.

But so had Minichiello. He had decided that he was leaving the country, and he wanted to be on his way. Time dragged by and nothing happened except for a great deal of unproductive milling around outside the plane. When he realized that the refueling of the plane had not yet even begun, he lost his manners for the second time, along with much of his control.

He erupted violently. "I'm going to kill you!" he screamed. "Get me out of here!"

Cook would have been glad to move at once, but they did need the fuel and they did need the two pilots.

Frustrated almost beyond reason, Minichiello fired a shot up into the ceiling of the cockpit. Such a shot could have seriously damaged the aircraft, but either by good luck or good aim the bullet bounced harmlessly off an oxygen bottle. The shot, Cook was sure, was not for the crew's benefit. The crew already knew Minichiello meant business. Rather, it was a warning to the agents encircling the plane.

Minichiello was crouching behind the galley door, only the muzzle of his carbine visible, ready to fire again. But his warning shot seemed to take effect. The agents withdrew, speeded on their way by shouts from Cook.

By now the marine had had enough of JFK Airport. He wanted to leave immediately. Never mind the refueling. Get those pilots on the plane—and *pilots* is what they'd better be.

He was suspicious when Williams and Hastings approached. First, he ordered them to remove their coats and hats before boarding; then he searched them expertly after they had boarded; and finally he ordered them to take over the controls and start the engines. If they had been FBI men and unable to start the engines, that would almost certainly have been the end of them. Luckily for everyone, they were real.

Watchers saw the plane start suddenly down the runway. Quickly, it was airborne, heading northeast for some as yet unspecified stopping place. Stop they would have to, because now, more than ever, they needed fuel.

It was now about ten minutes after noon, New York time. There was scarcely a soul in New York who had not heard the news of the hijacking through radio reports—nor in California, nor points between. The hijacker was rumored to be an AWOL marine, young, good-looking, likable but unpredictable. No one knew where he was going. It was all rather exciting.

And getting more exciting all the time. They had missed him in New York! The plane hadn't even been refueled! The hijacker was shooting mad! What was going to happen next?

Next, the plane was refueled at Bangor, Maine, about an hour after leaving Kennedy. Now where? A stop in London? "I doubt if it could make London," said a TWA vice-president. "After it leaves Bangor, it might stop at Iceland, or a number of other places."

Three questions were being asked: What was the ultimate destination to be? Was there any way to halt this runaway flight without endangering the lives of the crew? How long was the hijacker going to be able to stay awake and alert?

The hijacker was taking No-Doz tablets. While the world waited for news, Raffaele chatted and played cards with the crew, loaded and unloaded his carbine, took the gun apart to clean it, walked away from his seat in the cabin leaving the gun behind him, and even closed his eyes and dozed in spite of the No-Doz. Williams was flying the plane and Cook was watching Minichiello. At times it seemed that that Minichiello was daring Cook, who was closest to him, to make a grab for him or the carbine. He even asked Cook, after giving him several such opportunities, why he had not done so.

Cook was in no mood for dares. He was very conscious of the knife and pistol stock sticking out of the cartridge belt, and he could only guess what kind of combat training Raffaele had gone through in the Marines. He could also only guess at the boy's emotional state. Minichiello's behavior seemed very erratic to him. At times the boy seemed coolly rational and he showed good planning ability; and then again he would seem to be extremely disturbed, and obsessed with death. Cook told him that he had not gone for the weapon because he and his crew, like Minichiello, had fought in wars and had no more desire to fight or kill. "I wouldn't consider it unless it was a mandatory thing. Besides, we've gotten to like you and we really think we can bring this to a conclusion without our being killed and without your being killed."

Minichiello told him, then, that he would have killed himself if he had had to struggle with the crew. Graphically, he showed Cook how: he jammed the rifle barrel under his chin and squeezed his trigger finger.

He also told Cook that he did not want to go to Cairo at all. That had simply been a verbal decoy. He wanted to go to Rome.

His mood swinging from one extreme to the other, he talked about how he was going to get away, about the gun battle he would probably have with the police upon landing in Rome, about having only one or two days to live no matter what happened. He worried about the crew. He thought he might need hostages when he got to Rome and brooded over which members of the crew to select. They would have to be single people, he insisted. Cook, a bachelor, told him that all the crew members were married. (Of the four original crew members, three were single.) Then he worried about what might happen to the crew if he took a policeman as hostage upon landing—whether they would be treated well and be comfortable, and if he could afford to give them money to stay at "the best hotel." And what would the FBI say if they found out that the crew had not attempted to take the gun away from him? Cook reassured him on that score. "Don't worry about that. It's my duty to look after the safety of the crew and the plane." Well, he hoped it would be all right. But: "I've given you guys an awful lot of trouble."

They were not taking it personally. But ground officials and the public of two continents were completely in the dark as to Minichiello's attitude and ultimate intentions.

The aircraft reached the skies over Rome. Minichiello, by radio, ordered an unarmed police official to be waiting for him with a car when the plane landed.

The news crackled electrically around the world—and continued crackling after the plane touched down and the main door opened. Police official Pietro Guli, who was the deputy commander of customs police at Rome Airport, waited for him in a car. Minichiello got into the car, brandishing pistol and carbine, and ordered the policeman to drive him south toward Naples.

Next news: Four police cars are following Guli and Minichiello. Minichiello flares nervously, orders his hostage out of the car, drives on, abandons the vehicle, runs into the hilly Italian countryside.

Hundreds of Italian policemen, using helicopters and police dogs, spread out over the Appian hills and fields . . . and cannot find him. For five hours, they search. They know he cannot be far away.

In the United States, charges are placed and extradition steps are already being considered. The existing extradition treaty between the United States and Italy does not specifically cover the return of air pirates, but does cover kidnapping and armed robbery. The warrant against him in the United States charges him with air piracy, kidnapping, and interference in the operations of a commercial airliner. Conviction for air piracy carries a mandatory minimum of twenty years in prison and the possibility of a life sentence. Further, the jury may recommend death.

The Italian police have caught an innocent quail hunter. They let him go. They are ready to abandon the search.

Minichiello has been found! It is All Saints Day, and mass is being celebrated at a country church called the Sanctuary of Divine Love. Minichiello is seen wandering about the church, aimless and weary, seeking refuge perhaps but making himself conspicuous by his "suspicious" behavior and his attire. He is wearing either undershorts or Bermuda shorts topped off with a white shirt.

He resists briefly and without enthusiasm. He is very tired and has come to the end of the road. The policeman slaps a pair of handcuffs on him, and Raffaele—genuinely puzzled? surprised? mentally wandering? too tired to care?—says plaintively, "Hey, paisan, why are you arresting me?"

He has come home.

His countryman did not immediately detail the charges, but it was the end of the odyssey for Minichiello. Shortly after his arrest, Italian police found some of his gear stashed away on a nearby farm. It consisted of Minichiello's carbine and pistol, and a knapsack containing food, cigarettes, a hunting knife, ten dynamite caps and 250 rounds of ammunition. Later in the day the chief of Rome police announced that the "suspect" would be held for trial by Italian authorities on charges of hijacking, kidnapping, armed threats and illegal possession of arms. (The maximum penalty might be twenty to thirty years; there was no possibility of a death sentence.)

Extensive questioning by police and a few queries by reporters elicited blurred replies. Minichiello was rambling and vague. Either he had temporarily slipped off the tightrope of mental control or he was being deliberately evasive and trying to give the impression of mental disturbance. He would, or could, give no reason for wanting to come to Italy, even though his aged father (separated by many years and many miles from Raffaele's mother and sister, who lived in Seattle) was living near Naples at the time. Interviewers thought he had an ambiguous attitude toward his family, and were struck by his attempts to shut out all memory of the hijacking.

"The boy should be helped," said Captain Billy Williams. "I

don't think he was totally rational." To Cook, he was a boy who had gone to Vietnam at the age of seventeen and a half and had had, too young, about all that he could take. "He just blew his top."

Raffaele's stateside friends said much the same thing. They told of his shyness as a youth, of the way he had been taunted by his classmates for his Italian accent, the way he worked to improve his English, his love for flying, and his return from Vietnam.

Paul Carosino, a year his senior, had befriended Raffaele on his arrival with his family in Seattle from Italy in 1963. His English, then, had been almost nonexistent, and for some time the two friends communicated in sign language. When they were old enough, and speaking English freely to each other, they went flying together a few times in a small plane—Raffaele, Paul, and the pilot. Raffaele wanted to be a pilot himself, but he couldn't make it. He was having a hard time in high school. He didn't like it, wasn't good at his school work, and dropped out in the third year. Instead of becoming a commercial pilot he joined the Marines and went to Vietnam.

"He is a person that when he became nervous at times—like anyone else—he got panicked and riled up." This is how Paul Carosino describes him. "After he came back from the Vietnam war, last January, he was worse. He was a kid when he went in and when he came back he was a grownup man. But the war made him real kind of jumpy and not himself . . . I think the war affected him in many ways."

Italians, too, sympathized with the young vet. An Italian Citizens Committee, spearheaded by Italian novelist and journalist Carlotta Mandel, rallied to Minichiello's defense, determined to do all in its power to prevent his return to the United States for trial and a possible death sentence. In their view, he was a victim of the war in Vietnam and a refugee from the American system, a tormented young man seeking salvation in the land of his birth.

In his birthplace, Melito Irpino, Minichiello was acclaimed as a hero. Young girls offered to marry him if that would be of any help to his cause, or even if it wouldn't. They found him both fascinating and handsome. His flight, to them, represented a protest against a cruel and unjust war—though at no time did Minichiello make this claim for himself—and, as such, was not only justified but truly magnificent. "And he didn't kill anybody," the girls said gratefully, as if that made everything all right. "I admire him," they said. "I would do anything for him and above all I would love to marry him."

Olimpia Barrello, the seventy-four-year-old midwife who had helped bring Raffaele into the world, said: "I know him well. He comes from an honest family and was always a good boy. He should be set free. He is a hero. Who else could do what he did?"

What was it again that he did? Save a life, commit an unselfish act, prevent an aerial disaster, make his family proud and happy, give $200 to the poor, take a step toward ending the war? No, he did not. He got high on beer, broke into the PX and stole what he thought was coming to him, threatened compassionate people, committed the longest and most hair-raising hijacking in history, abducted a police chief, and then, when found, said innocently, "Hey, paisan, why are you arresting me?"

Minichiello was not extradited to face the death penalty in the United States. Nor was he found insane. In November of 1970 he was tried in Rome on an eight-count charge: two counts of kidnapping the crew of the airplane and an Italian policeman; two counts of using coercion, by threatening armed violence against the crew and the policeman; one count of using violence against a public official; and three counts involving the illegal importation of a military weapon, its possession, and carrying it without a license. The maximum penalty, if he were to be convicted on all counts, would be thirty years in prison.

He did not get the maximum penalty, but the sentence he drew must, at the time, have seemed a very heavy one to a young man who has not even yet accepted the fact that he had done anything "so serious." On November 11, 1970—a few days more than a year after his reckless escapade—Minichiello was sentenced to seven and a half years in prison and a fine of $580. He would have to serve only four and a half years, because a general amnesty proclaimed several months earlier had automatically reduced by two years the sentences for nearly all crimes committed prior to it and because he had already been in custody for a year by the time he was tried. In late April, 1971, an appeals court cut his original sentence to a three-and-a-half-year stretch. Thus, the amnesty having already knocked off two years, he was left with a total term of eighteen months. And by that time he had served his eighteen months almost to the day. On May 1, 1971, he walked out of Rome's Queen of Heaven prison a free man—still wanted in the United States for air piracy, but cheerful, unrepentant, and with no intention of returning to face charges.

Minichiello had spent $15.50 for his air ticket from Los Angeles to San Francisco. An economy class ticket for a Los Angeles-to-Rome flight would have cost him $435.60, including tax. He could have paid for it. If he had stayed in the United States to face his court-martial for burglary, his sentence would have been about thirty days to six months, depending on his plea. In the end he paid only a slightly higher price for his fare to Rome—but his junket cost TWA more than $50,000.

It is a pity that Minichiello is so young, so attractive, so appealing. While the more responsible of the American editorialists were crying out, "Skyjackers are not heroes!" the Italian prosecutor—repeat, prosecutor—was describing Minichiello as "a good boy, a timid boy," who had only wanted to return to his native land to see his father and find peace. And that was nothing to the perorations of the defense. Here was a "rustic and uneducated Don Quixote, without Sancho Panza and without Dulcinea, who instead of his horse Rosinante, flew through the skies of the world following his dream and his goal." What stirring stuff this is! How can we fail to be moved, especially when we are further told that Minichiello is a pathetic and romantic being, a young man who desired merely to "flee the injustices of the great America." Guiseppe Sotgiu, for the defense, was clearly in fine form. "He is a romantic figure, for pining and yearning with nostalgia drove him to this improbable adventure, like an ancient crusade."

Well. Maybe. Or perhaps breaking into the PX had something to do with it.

See Minichiello: A real devil-may-care of the sky, cleaning and recleaning his rifle while the aging 707 flew high over the sea with its cargo of kindly hostages . . . who, time and time again, were very close to death at the hands of a likable thief.

Postscript: On November 10, 1969, fourteen-year-old David L. Booth threatened a young woman hostage with a butcher knife in an attempt to hijack a Delta DC-9 from Cincinnati to Sweden or wherever else he could get it to go. David was persuaded to give up his attempt and was taken into custody before the plane left the ground. There may be no tie-in with the dazzling Minichiello exploit, but the boy's mother, Mrs. Anne Booth, did suggest that her son might have been influenced by the young marine's spectacular flight to Rome the week before. "He had been reading and watching televison about the hijacking with interest all last week," said Mrs. Booth.

We have seen this happen more than once; we have seen it since the Minichiello case: A young man with whom kids can identify attempts to hijack a plane, and a few days later an adolescent tries to emulate him.

In this, the hijacker-idol commits yet another crime.

7/POLITICS IN THE SKY

Hijackings with a political motive fall into two categories: those that are committed for personal reasons by individuals who are alienated from the mother country, or need to make a desperate break for freedom, or wish to offer a gesture of defiance toward a disliked establishment; and those that are committed by groups or members of groups for a larger political purpose, such as the propagandization of a cause or the furtherance of a guerrilla war.

POLITICAL RUNAWAYS: PERSONAL SEARCH FOR ASYLUM

It is not easy to select pure examples of individuals who hijack for personal political reasons. Not every man who runs down the aisle of a U.S. airliner yelling—"Black power! Havana! Black power!"—and claiming to be on his way to join fellow Black Panthers in Cuba is an honest-to-goodness Panther seeking asylum with his brothers. Nor does every escapee from an iron curtain country turn out to be the victim of political persecution. Escaping criminals, and misfits too, often claim to be seeking political asylum when in reality they are dodging the police or running from themselves or crying out for attention. Similarly, the motivation of the returning Cuban exile is not essentially political. He returns because he has made a mistake. The United States is not the paradise he dreamed of. He simply does not like it here and his longing is for home.

The great majority of skyjacked flights originating in the United States have been basically apolitical. For most people there are several ways to leave this country other than via hijacked plane; and it is still possible to get into Cuba, visa or no visa, without resorting to air piracy. Thus many cries of "Black power!" are open to skepticism. Eldridge Cleaver did not find it necessary to skyjack.

Yet in 1968 and 1969 a number of Black Panthers did make their way to Cuba on the skyjack route. Perhaps for them it was the only practical way. It is conceivable that the motive of the runaway Panthers was group political action of some sort, but all available evidence suggests that in each case the actions of the individuals were their own idea. They were disaffected with the United States for personal sociopolitical reasons. As individual Panthers, they had usually tangled with the police in so-called shoot-outs or other confrontations, they wanted to go elsewhere, and if they met their friends at the other end of the line, so much the better.

Black Panthers on the Run

Tyrone Ellington Austin is a disappointing example for those who look for their heroes in the ranks of people claiming to be Black Panthers. Very few other instances come to mind in which a skyjacker has snatched a child for use as a combination shield and hostage.

Tyrone Austin and his wife, Lynda, twenty years old and nineteen, respectively, boarded the Eastern Air Lines New York-to-Miami flight on the evening of January 2, 1969. Mr. Austin wore an Afro-style hairdo and a conservative business suit. Mrs. Austin carried her baby strapped to her back in a manner described by observers as papoose-style. Actually, Indian women do not carry their babies thus; but African women do.

Somewhere along the way Mr. Austin went into the washroom and changed from his conservative suit into an outfit that featured a Nehru shirt, heavy boots, and a white, beanie-type cap. The flight was almost on its last leg when Mrs. Austin leaped up from her seat in the rear of the plane, where she and her husband had settled themselves, and ran screaming up the aisle with her baby on her back. This was quite attention-getting, and no one immediately noticed her husband jumping up from *his* seat and waving an automatic pistol. They did take note when he started yelling, "Havana Black power, Havana! Black power, Havana!" and were thunderstruck to see him grab two-year-old Alan Levy from his mother's lap, jam the gun against the child's head, and threaten to kill him—*if*. Then he followed his wife toward the cockpit, flaunting the automatic. Mrs. Levy, in her turn, bounded up from her seat in pursuit of little Alan. Austin turned on her, pointed the gun into her face, and sternly said, "Havana!"

Mrs. Levy froze.

The Austins continued up the aisle. Husband, wife, baby, and captive child were all yelling by this time. A stewardess standing in the aisle of the first class cabin saw them coming and could scarcely believe her eyes. "The hijacker's wife ran by screaming and he was right behind her. I half-turned around, and he grabbed me by the neck. I'm afraid I panicked a little and tried to get away, but I couldn't." A passenger describes her action much more charitably, if not with total clarity. "This lovely little stewardess went up to him to try and get the child, and he started choking her with the pistol around her neck."

He then released the stewardess and barged into the cockpit with his wife and the stolen child.

Moments later, Captain Dennis Vanhuss radioed Jacksonville and said: "I am going to Havana." Then, according to passengers' reports, he got onto the intercom. "This is the pilot speaking. I'll do the best I can. All I'm on this wire to say is—to the mother—that her son is sitting on the lap of the engineer, that he has calmed down, is fine, and actually enjoying it."

The little boy was released when the plane landed at José Martí Airport. The hijacker and his small family were apparently well received by the usual Cuban welcoming committee with perhaps a little more enthusiasm than was customary. One of the passengers, socialite Christina Paolozzi Bellin, described the arrival scene thus:

"When we landed in Havana the hijacker was treated like a hero." (Perhaps she looked upon the scene with jaundiced eye, but this is the way it looked to her.) "He paraded up and down, strutting, with a sort of honor guard of Cuban militia of about thirty. He marched so much he even bumped into them. I didn't see anybody leading him away, either."

Maybe they had mistaken him for someone else. Maybe they thought he was one of the leaders of the new American Revolution. But to the FBI he is a Black Panther gunman and air pirate, and to New York City police he is a man who allegedly shot and wounded a cop and then jumped bail. To the people aboard Eastern's Flight 401 to Miami, he is the man who snatched a baby boy as hostage.

Is political asylum without punishment a just reward for this man? It is doubtful that Fidel Castro would think so.

But whatever Castro thinks or might have thought, Austin was apparently not comfortable in Cuba. Somehow, some time ago, he made his way back to the United States. On April 21, 1971, Tyrone Ellington Austin was shot to death by a New York City patrolman shortly after holding up a Manhattan branch of the Manufacturers Hanover Trust Company and making off with $6,000. Clearly, the man was a criminal—but still a criminal of political stamp.

A slightly different breed of cat was Willie Lee Brent. Even he has the taint of criminality about him, not only as a hijacker but as a man already looked upon with disfavor by the law. But, in a society that tends to regard all Black Panthers as criminals by definition, it is hardly to be wondered at that he is more often described as a criminal than as a political defector.

On June 17, 1969, William Brent hijacked an Oakland-to-New York TWA 707 and forced it to fly to Cuba, thereby achieving the longest United States hijacking to that date. Those who saw him in the cabin described him as tall, dapper, bespectacled and nervous. He took charge of the plane somewhere over Nevada (over Wilson Creek, to be precise) and made his requirements known to the pilot, who then invited him to remain in the cockpit "for safety's sake." The suitcase that he kept with him at all times contained black clothing and a copy of *Black Panther*, by fugitive Eldridge Cleaver, who was still reportedly in Cuba at that time. Possession of such a book is scarcely evidence of a man's political beliefs, but those who saw it found it suggestive under the circumstances.

The skyjacker was taken into custody by Cuban authorities who described him only as a tall Negro wearing a dark suit and a dark felt hat. By the time his arrival was announced without enthusiasm by Havana radio he had been whisked away. A few days later the FBI identified him as Willie Lee Brent, a Black Panther captain accused of taking part in a shoot-out with San Francisco police in November of the year before.

Brent vanished into the Cuban silence and may still be in Cuba. But it was not long after his arrival that rumors of Panther discontentment with conditions under Castro began to filter back to the United States. Probably Brent, among others, soon decided that if there was a Panther haven anywhere in the world it was not to be found in Cuba. The land of promise, it was beginning to seem, held no promise for the Panther skyjacker.

Exit from East Germany

Skyjacking episodes were becoming so widespread by the fall of 1969 that it was hardly a surprise when two young East Germans were reported to have gone over the Berlin wall by air. Iron curtain escapes were on the verge of becoming almost as common as unauthorized expeditions to Cuba. But this was a first: no East German had ever before succeeded in fleeing aboard a commercial airliner.

The two young men had made their way quite legitimately to Warsaw. There, on October 19, 1969, they took a chance and boarded a Polish Lot Ilyushin 18 bound for Brussels via East Berlin. Some time after takeoff they forced their way to the cockpit, brandishing pistols, and told the pilot to take the plane to West Berlin instead of East Berlin because they wanted to seek asylum in the West.

When the crew refused to cooperate, the young skyjackers struck both the pilot and the copilot over the head with the guns. Thus injured, the pilots did what they were told and took the plane in to a landing at Tegel Airport in the French sector of West Berlin. French police and soldiers sealed off the area as soon as the plane touched down. No civilians were permitted in the immediate vicinity. It was a bright, sunny day when the skyjackers stepped cheerfully to freedom on Western soil and announced to French authorities that they were defecting. Among the passengers watching them debark were at least twenty other East Germans, none of whom attempted to follow the example of the two young men and seek asylum in the West. After a three-hour stopover, the slightly injured pilot and copilot recovered sufficiently to take off again and complete the journey as far as East Berlin. And the two air pirates left behind in the French sector received the asylum they had asked for.

But there was a sequel: A month later they were tried by a French military court for "endangering air safety and having hindered air traffic." Each received sentences of two years imprisonment. The French prosecutor had demanded a minimum of three years for each. There was a need, he said, for "exemplary punishment," and he called on the court to consider the growing incidence of the severe crime of air piracy and the dangers involved in it for so many otherwise uninvolved people. The court was lenient, but at least sentence had been passed. At last there was some Western recognition of the fact that a hijacking for purposes of political asylum, with us as well as with them, is nonetheless a criminal act.

The Plot that Failed

The newspaper *Leningradskaya Pravda* reported the alleged plot in two sentences: "On June 15 [1970], in Smolny Airport, a group of criminals trying to seize a scheduled airplane, was detained. An investigation is being carried out."

It was difficult for outsiders to piece the story together because official sources were playing it very close to the chest, but dissident informants filled in some of the details.

At about 8:30 in the morning of Monday, June 15, 1970, eleven men and a woman were arrested at the Leningrad airport while walking from the terminal to the small (twelve-seater) commercial Aeroflot AN-2 craft that was bound for Soviet Karelia near the Finnish border. The group was allegedly intending to divert the craft across the border to Finland and thence to Sweden, from which country they would subsequently make their way to Israel. This, under Soviet law, was treason—not the intended hijacking, but the attempt to flee the country.

Let it be noted that they did not so much as board the plane.

Yet some of the group were said to have tried, unsuccessfully, to escape, and authorities apparently found several knives and two pistols among them. Later, when Tass eventually got around to describing a hijack plot surely far more lurid than the would-be skyjackers had ever dreamed of, the armory swelled into a fearsome collection of revolvers, ammunition, knives, axes, rubber truncheons, clotheslines shaped into nooses, gags, and even knuckle dusters. Who were to be the victims of all these devilish devices? Tass didn't say. Nevertheless, some of the accused were armed, and some did try to run.

Not all of the twelve were immediately identified, but it was disclosed that several had served time together in labor camps for "anti-Soviet propaganda" in the 1960s, that several among them had made repeated attempts to obtain exit visas to Israel and had been turned down, that six were among the signers of a letter to United Nations Secretary-General U Thant appealing for his assistance in getting Soviet authorities to permit them to go to Israel, and one was very active in her home town of Riga in her efforts to win permission for Jews to emigrate to Israel.

Immediately after the arrests at the airport, eight Jewish residents of Leningrad were reportedly seized at their homes, at their places of employment, and even in one case at a vacation spot. These people were all known to have been active in protesting the limitations set by the Soviet Union on the ability of Jews to leave the country and go to Israel . . . or anywhere else, for that matter. Security agents searched another fifty Jewish homes within the next few hours. The apparent purpose was to round up the friends and acquaintances of the alleged plotters. Scores of Jews were detained for interrogation in Leningrad, Riga, Moscow, and Kharkov, after which they were released. Toward the end of the month, twenty-six more Jews were arrested in Riga, Kishinev, and Tiflis for alleged political crimes. And still there were no reports of these events in the Soviet press; all the news came from the so-called dissident sources. The Russian public knew nothing of the events, not until the first of the trials.

That trial opened in Leningrad on December 15. There were eleven defendants, nine of whom were Jews: Eduard Kuznetsov; his wife, Silva, of Riga, who had been so untiring in her efforts on behalf of Russian Jews: Silva's brother Izrael Zalmanson; Mark Dymshits, a former air force pilot; Alexei Murzhenko; Arye Khnokh; Anatoli Altman; Boris Penson; Iosif Mendelevich; Mendel Bodnya; and Yuri Fyodorov. Apart from those immediately involved in the proceedings, the trial was attended only by close relatives of the defendants and a select group of spectators supposedly representative of the "Leningrad public." The spectators were openly unsympathetic, even downright hostile. At the close of one day's proceedings, shortly before the end of the trial, a woman spectator berated the weeping wife of one of the defendants. "Are you sick?" she asked. "If you are not sick, you should not be crying."

The stiff sentences asked, the mass interrogations and arrests that had been made after the supposed hijack attempt, and the reports that leaked out about the unpleasant atmosphere of the trial led people outside the Soviet bloc to strongly suspect that this was no hijacking trial but an anti-Semitic or anti-Zionist persecution campaign. In some quarters the case was said to be a deliberate frame-up; or if not a frame-up, then a vicious anti-Semitic reaction to a desperate gamble attempted by a group of Jews who wanted only to be free to leave a land in which they had little freedom. It was said in these quarters that the Kremlin intended to make scapegoats of the defendants and use their purported crime as justification for a determined drive against all dissenters, particularly freedom-seeking Jews, in the Soviet Union. "Not so!" raged Tass. "Zionist circles abroad are whipping up anti-Soviet propaganda!"

However it was being whipped up, anti-Soviet feeling ran even higher when the sentences were passed by the three-judge court on the day before Christmas 1970. Mark Dymshits and Eduard Kuznetsov, said to be the ringleaders of the plot, were sentenced to death before a military firing squad. For the others, sentences ranged from four to fifteen years—most of them closer to fifteen than four.

While defense lawyers appealed for lighter sentences, an outcry went around the world. The Pope announced that he would do all he could to obtain clemency for the two men sentenced to death. Mass protest rallies were held in the United States and Israel. American rabbis said: "The gross inhumanity of the death sentences . . . must cause decent men to recoil in horror and outrage," and, "We call on all men everywhere to raise their voices in protest against this barbarism the Soviet Union calls justice." In Jerusalem, thousands of angry, grim-faced people flocked to the Wailing Wall early on Christmas morning to stage a spontaneous demonstration against the severity of the sentences. Israel, of all nations, holds no brief for hijackers, but in this case the punishment was monstrous. The defendants had tried repeatedly to leave the country legally but all requests had been denied. They were virtually (so thought Israelis and non-Israeli Jews) trying to break out of prison. And they had not even boarded the plane!

Israeli Premier Golda Meir, her voice charged with emotion,

said in a radio broadcast that Israel would not rest until the right of every Jew wishing to immigrate to Israel was recognized.

Tass roared back angrily. The sentences were *not* unjust. Soviet justice was not only fair but merciful. Why, several persons involved in the plot had not even been prosecuted! (In fact, they had not even been to the airport.) For instance, the wife and daughter of Dymshits had been totally spared because it was recognized that they had been under Dymshits's influence. Further, kindness itself had been shown to Mary Mendelevitch, who was pregnant and whose husband had been sentenced to fifteen years. As for the fact that the hijackers had been apprehended before boarding the plane:

"If they were not able to carry through the plot, if the plane never left the ground and the members of the crew were not attacked, it was not at all because the criminals had given up. It was because of circumstances beyond their volition that kept the criminals from acting.

"Can one consider a bandit or murderer caught one minute before dealing a blow to his victim an innocent man only because he did not have time to deal the blow? The very question sounds strange, and contradicts the very foundation of law, logic and common sense. But that is the posture taken by Zionist propaganda, which is trying to use the so-called Leningrad case to fan anti-Soviet hysteria." Furthermore, said Tass, the severe sentences were in the spirit of an anti-hijacking resolution endorsed a short time before by ICAO.

Be that as it may, the defense appeal was handled with unprecedented dispatch. On December 31 the two death sentences were commuted to fifteen years in labor camp, and the terms of three other defendants were reduced.

The trials were not yet over. On January 7 a Leningrad military court sentenced Lieutenant Vulf Zalmanson, brother of Silva and Izrael, to ten years in prison on charges of participating in the planned hijacking. One of the twelve originally arrested at Smolny Airport, he was tried separately in the military court because he was a member of the armed forces. Other trials were in the offing for a score or so of other Jewish "troublemakers." By the time they were ended, thirty-four "plotters"—all but two of them Jews—had been tried and sentenced in the wake of the alleged plot.

Left over were two questions: Is there ever a legitimate excuse for hijacking or attempting to hijack a plane? Was the Soviet Union attempting to use this episode to justify and expand its alleged anti-Semitic policies? Only one thing was clear: The Soviet Union had contributed absolutely nothing to the solution of the hijacking problem and had in fact unwittingly reminded the world that the crime of hijacking may be the desperate man's only way of reacting to even greater crimes.

In March 1971 an underground account of the first trial was received and published by the Washington *Post*. It reported that the main accusation against the Leningrad eleven was not attempted hijacking but attempting to go to Israel without permission. So much for the Soviet crackdown on hijacking. Also in March of 1971, the Western world received reports from "reliable Soviet sources" that Soviet Jews were suddenly "being allowed to go to Israel in a wave of emigration unprecedented in the fifty-three-year history of the Soviet Union."

The Family Skyjack: Soviet Style

For the most part, Soviet hijackings are given minimal publicity. If the trial of the Russian Jews made news around the world it was for one of three reasons: Dissident sources were determined to be heard; the Russians had deliberately decided upon a "show trial" to prove that they meant business against all dissidents; Soviet authorities had genuinely become perturbed by two successful Soviet hijackings that had occurred between the Lengingrad attempt and the trial, and were using the trial in part to show all future would-be hijackers that they would be severely punished.

This exception aside, hijackings or attempted hijackings of Soviet airliners are usually played down for one reason or another. The most acceptable reason to foreign observers, even though they might not agree with it, is that splashing such events on newspaper front pages might inspire further attempts. It has long been government policy in the USSR to give brief, contemptuous, back-page treatment to all acts of violence with possibly political overtones so as not to put ideas into the heads of politically disenchanted or unstable individuals who might be stimulated by the efforts of others to duplicate such acts as hijacking planes or taking potshots at public figures. Even foreign hijackings receive very little coverage in the Soviet press.

Therefore, the event of October 15, 1970, was given only four short paragraphs on the back page of *Pravda*. Though by no means a major international incident, it was important as the first known successful hijacking of a Russian plane. Also, it was the kind of skyjacking that made skyjack watchers ponder once again over some of the deeds that are done in the name of political asylum.

The abbreviated accounts of hijackings that had filtered down to the Soviet public suggested that no one but a fool would attempt the seizure of a Soviet craft. There were military guards at Russian airfields, Soviet flight crews were inclined to take violent countermeasures against hijackers, and any hijack attempt would be followed inexorably by retribution at its most severe.

None of these factors discouraged Pranas Brazinskas-Korejevo and his teen-age son Algedras from boarding a Soviet Aeroflot turboprop plane with intent to divert it. The plane was on a domestic run between the two Black Sea ports of Batumi and Sukhumi with fifty-one persons aboard when father and son broke into the cockpit and thrust a note at the pilot demanding to be taken to Turkey. They were carrying an arsenal of shotguns, pistols, and grenades, enough to deter the most stouthearted of pilots, but still Captain Valery Adeyev immediately took evasive action.

He started with a sudden, steep banking turn that should have taken the hijackers completely by surprise. But, as his copilot afterward explained, "although he did air acrobatics with dives and flips, the air pirates did not lose their balance but started shooting instead." One shot slammed into the pilot, who was still flying aerobatics, and seriously wounded him. Stewardess Nadezhda Kurchenko fell dead just outside the cockpit door, a bullet through her heart. Another crew member and a passenger were wounded. The agonized captain wrestled with the controls, but by now the plane was doing its own wild acrobatic spins in the sky. It was enough, and more than enough, for copilot Surikov. He grabbed the controls and "did what the pirates told me."

They told him to land in Trabzon, a Turkish Black Sea port a hundred miles from Soviet territory. The plane made a normal landing but was immediately surrounded by police. The hijackers walked off first, looking very happy in spite of having committed murder, and meekly surrendered their weapons and ammunition. Then they asked for political asylum in Turkey.

What followed were all kinds of rumors and a series of sharp exchanges between Russia and Turkey. The rumors said that father and son were Jews escaping from the Soviet Union; fact said that they were Lithuanians who had been living in Uzbekistan. Another rumor then said that as Lithuanians they had objected to the Soviet absorption of their country and the restrictive conditions under which they were obliged to live; the counter-story claimed that the father was a fleeing criminal who had "corrupted his son, armed him with a sawed-off shotgun and drawn him into crime and murder."

They were indeed not Jews but discontented Lithuanians, although the cause of their discontent will probably never be completely clear.

Russia demanded the extradition of the pair. Turkey thought it over for some time and then refused. But, Russia objected, these were criminal murderers! Beside the point, said a Turkish court; Turkey has no criminal extradition agreement with the Soviet Union, and in any event these men had committed a political crime for which they could not be extradited. Humanitarian considerations were involved; the principle of political asylum must be observed. But, Russia insisted, not only had they committed treason by hijacking their way out of Russia but had actually committed crimes in the Soviet Union before their departure. We will look into that and reconsider, Turkey replied; and then ruled that the crimes known to them had been committed in an effort to obtain political asylum. "The murder of an air hostess and the injury of two pilots were committed while the father and son were trying to reach a free country," said the Trabzon court; and that, for the time being, was it so far as extradition was concerned.

Again there were questions and dissatisfactions left hanging in the air. *Pravda* described Brazinskas-Korejevo as a thief and embezzler, and said that he had not only been dismissed from several jobs for these activities but had actually served five years for theft and other "economic crimes." Another report on the man said that he had been convicted of abuse of state funds and black marketing, and had never been involved in political activities. It was therefore impossible, according to the Soviets, to consider the man a political offender. He had, they said, amassed $6,500 through his illegal activities, and had decided to flee Russia with his spoils and his corrupted son.

By the time the Russians made their accusations the Trabzon gendarmes who had met the plane had already described what the hijackers had had in their possession: shotguns, pistols, cartridges, explosives, and $6,300 in cash. Had they stolen that money or had they earned it? Had the Russians found out for themselves about the missing monies, or did they seize upon the Turkish report of finding $6,300 to bolster their claim that the defector was a thief? Was he really a criminal, or did Russian authorities invent a sordid past for him as part of a campaign to prove that no one who is fool enough to attempt to flee Russia can possibly be a genuine seeker of political asylum? Had he in fact been a political activist for some time, and victim of a number of previous frame-ups that had branded him as thief, embezzler, and black marketeer? We do not know, and probably never will.

What we do know and cannot condone is the murder of the stewardess and the violence done to others on the plane. By extension, we cannot condone the hijacking itself, for every hijacking carries with it the threat and risk of danger or death for persons other than the hijacker. It is not as if a pilot or a stewardess or a passenger were in any way like a brutal guard at a concentration camp. Those who go over the wall for their own private political or other reasons would do well to consider whom they knock down on the way.

Whose life and freedom is worth more—the hijacker's, or his victims? To each his own, of course.

Shortly after this episode, it was announced that two thousand armed guards were to fly on Soviet planes traveling near

Soviet borders or from airports from which a plane might conceivably be hijacked abroad. Another five hundred specially trained detectives were to be posted at airports to check passengers and luggage.

Russia had joined the club.

The question of asylum is a knotty one. If a man escapes from one country for reasons of political persecution and throws himself upon the mercy of another, it is hard for the sanctuary country to turn him down and toss him back to the wolves from which he claims to have escaped. National pride and pity inevitably enter the picture. In the opinion of Dr. John T. Dailey of the FAA, "Nobody is going to return all hijackers. There will always be cases where the hijackers will be thought of as legitimate political refugees." Referring to the Brazinskas-Korejevo case, he says: "If they had gotten out without killing somebody, I think they might have been regarded as heroes and worthy people who were escaping from tyranny. I think even as it is the Turks are not going to send them back to Russia. They may try them for murder or something or they may just slap their wrists." (Or, according to recent news reports, they may decide to extradite them after all.)

"Any conceivable agreement that nations will really sign must have an escape clause, that if they think he's really a political refugee they'll give him political asylum then try him and punish him for whatever he has done—for the hijacking, the shooting, the murder, the kidnapping, or whatever it is. But in some cases they might give him a very light slap on the wrist, such as if it were an uncomplicated hijacking to Cuba and they figured the guy was a political refugee. Then they might give him token punishment and political asylum. However, it's very unlikely that very many American hijackers would be deserving of political asylum. Cuba has actually said that. On the other hand, almost any hijackers *from* Cuba—and this would have to include hijackers of boats—would be legitimate political refugees in the sense that it is illegal to leave Cuba freely. So they leave any way they can, and they leave under threat of severe punishment if caught."

So long as there are countries from which it is illegal to depart freely, we will be obliged to consider the legitimacy of a search for sanctuary elsewhere. But we will not be obliged to condone armed threat, murder, or any other form of violence.

ORGANIZED POLITICAL ACTIONS

Although several hijackings of a personal-political nature have been committed by groups, they differ from the true group-political hijackings such as those committed by the PFLP in that the individuals involved are acting for individual if similar reasons whereas the organized political group performs *as a group* for purposes of political demonstration or to commit acts intended to further a revolutionary or extremist movement.

The first such act to capture worldwide attention was the hijacking of the Tel Aviv-bound El Al 707 on July 23, 1968, by three Arab guerrillas, one of whom is said to have assisted in landing the plane after the pilot was hit on the head with a gun butt. Not long after the plane set down in Algiers the world was informed by the Popular Front for the Liberation of Palestine that one of its units was responsible for the hijacking. Algeria, which considered itself at war with Israel at the time, held the plane as well as twelve Israeli passengers and the crew until September 1, 1968. Although the Algerian government had had no advance knowledge of the hijacking, they cooperated whole-heartedly with the guerrillas after the fact. The PFLP wanted the Israeli passengers held as hostages to be exchanged for "our fighting brothers inside the prisons of the enemy" and the Algerians obligingly did the holding.

While Israel waited for her citizens to be released, an Israeli newspaper editorial commented that, "With every hour ticking by without the release of the passengers, the crew and the plane, the Government of Algeria is becoming more and more of a partner to this act of piracy."

It was an outrageous situation, and it could have set an alarming precedent. Here for the first time we saw a government enthusiastically collaborating with sky pirates from another land. This is Barbary Coast piracy in modern dress.

Israeli outrage turned rapidly to thoughts of retaliation. The morning *Davar* said ominously: "What happened to the El Al plane yesterday can happen to any plane tomorrow—in the passenger planes of the Arab countries."

When Israel did eventually retaliate it was after a great deal of further provocation, and retaliation did not take the form of hijacking but of the wholesale destruction of parked Arab planes. The action was ugly and had a strongly negative effect on world opinion. And it only brought more terror in return. Nevertheless a truth remained: What had happened to the El Al plane that day could happen to any plane in the days and months and years to come—any plane in any country of the world. It has happened many times since then. The most spectacular of such organized political acts were the PFLP seizures of September, 1970; but the most bizarre was the one that brought Japan into the widening hijack arena.

The Affair of the Samurai Swords

This one started happening on March 31, 1970. It was only about 7:30 A.M., still a sleepy hour, and the Japan Airlines 727 was making its way from Tokyo to Fukuoka on what is ordinarily only a forty-five-minute flight. For the first few minutes it was one of those routine trips (coffee, tea, or sake?), and those who had not already done the flight so often that they no longer bothered to look out a window were peering down to admire the majestic beauty of Mount Fuji before settling back to drowse or enjoy the gracious charm of a Japanese flight. There were over a hundred passengers aboard; mostly Japanese, a few Americans, a smattering of tourists, a number of businessmen, quite a few women and children, some students, a group of Japanese doctors on their way to a three-day medical conference in Fukuoka, a minor official or two, and a Maryknoll priest—a standard complement for a short domestic flight.

The seat-belt sign had just been turned off and the four stewardesses were distributing the customary hot towels to the passengers when one of the neatly dressed young students stood up and shouted, "We are the Red Army!" And he waved a glittering samurai sword. Suddenly the aisle was full of students, or seemed to be. There were nine of them, ranging in age from sixteen to twenty-seven, all conservatively dressed in coats and ties and looking for all the world like young office workers. But instead of briefcases they carried swords and pistols and home-made bombs.

They came down the aisle in a rush, wielding their samurai swords like warriors of old and pointing their pistols at the passengers like sky pirates of today. "Hold up your hands!" they shouted as they ran and took up their various positions. Some of them burst into the cockpit. One pointed a gun at the pilot, another stood guard and another tied up the copilot. Then, waving their swords threateningly and announcing again that they were members of the Red Army, they demanded to be flown to North Korea.

The Red Army is the most extreme of Japan's many radical student organizations. It is dedicated to the violent overthrow of established order. Captain Ishida, the pilot, did not try to argue with them but pointed out reasonably that the short-hop plane could not reach Pyongyang, which was their desired destination, without stopping at Fukuoka to refuel. This much reason they could see, but they were not about to take any chances. While the pilots sat there with swords over their heads and pistols at their necks, some of the young men busied themselves in the cabin by tying up the male passengers and warning the women not to try to leave their seats. A few of them gave candy to the children.

Ishida continued toward Fukuoka with the guns and swords and threats hanging over his head. Two escort planes joined him in the sky to keep the jet under surveillance. That was all they could do. Any attempt to force the airliner down would multiply the danger to the passengers and crew. As it was, the presence of the escorts was an additional strain on the pilot.

He radioed Fukuoka a few minutes before landing: "The hijackers threaten to blow up the aircraft with bombs in case the hijacking fails. Please do not bring people near the aircraft."

The plane landed at Fukuoka and stayed on the airfield for five hours while pilot and airport authorities pleaded with the hijackers to free the passengers, and police mulled over plan after plan to keep the plane on the ground. How about disconnecting the electric system? Disabling the fueling system? Pumping tear gas into the ventilating system? But most of the proposed plans could not even be attempted. Those that were tried, failed.

Expert riot police-squad marksmen stationed themselves behind airport buildings. They took great care not to be seen, but they themselves could see passengers peering anxiously from the windows with looming shadows behind them. Eventually they decided that gunfire could only worsen the situation. Newsmen and police officers using binoculars could see right into the cockpit. What they saw was a student hijacker, and perhaps the shape of another, standing behind the pilot and copilot with upraised samurai sword. Definitely, no gunfire.

The passenger cabin was getting unbearably hot as the spring sun shone down upon the craft. The men, tied to their seats, were becoming extemely warm and uncomfortable, and the women tried to help them by mopping their brows. Men who did not have wives or other women seated next to them were out of luck and had to sweat unmopped. Very little movement was being permitted. Passengers who needed to go to the restrooms were allowed to do so, but only one at a time and under nervous, watchful eyes.

Time dragged on and the war of nerves continued. On the one hand airport officials were begging: "Please do not harm the passengers or crewmen. Let the passengers go." On the other the hijackers were threatening: "Let this plane leave here or we will explode a bomb."

The hijackers were getting tense and restless. Their manner toward the passengers was still fairly cordial, but their politeness was beginning to slip a little. The swords were being waved about a bit too freely and were looking bigger and deadlier all the time. The impasse had to be broken somehow. It was, and the hijackers won most of the chips. The police finally gave up trying to keep the plane grounded and the young Reds permitted twenty-three of the passengers to get off the plane: twelve children, ten women, and one ailing elderly man. One of the hijackers stood on top of the boarding stairs, samurai sword raised high and flashing in the sun, to see them safely off. Husbands, fathers, doctors, businessmen, tourists, minor officials, Maryknoll priest, crew, and Red students stayed aboard.

The plane, refueled, took off for Korea. For a while it was

tracked by two Japanese Self-Defense Force jets, but these turned back when they reached Korean airspace and the 727 flew on alone. There was still no panic aboard. "The young men kept repeating that as soon as we got to North Korea we would be allowed to go home unarmed, and somehow we believed them."

It is a short flight from Fukuoka to the North Korean coast at the 38th Parallel, and all indications were that the plane would soon be landing. There was no reason to suspect that the North Koreans would harm anyone aboard. Therefore it came as something of a surprise when Communist shore guns met the Japanese 727 with bursts of anti-aircraft fire. Apparently the North Koreans were not about to welcome the plane to their territory. It looked as though it would be much too dangerous to try to fly on to Pyongyang.

The jetliner banked away and slid swiftly out of North Korean airspace.

Fighter planes soared into the sky. They looked as though they might be North Korean planes, and perhaps that is what all or most of the passengers thought they were.

The planes closed in on the airliner in the first move of an elaborate ruse and escorted it in the direction of an airport which identified itself from the control tower as Pyongyang. It was actually Kimpo Airport at Seoul.

South Korean skies look no different from those of North Korea. Nobody on board asked any questions.

Below and to the south there was much activity at the airport.

All Western flags were removed; all identifying names and English-language signs were covered up. Quickly, placards were produced proclaiming welcome to North Korea's Pyongyang Airport. Thirty South Korean paratroopers disguised themselves as customs officials and prepared to board the aircraft when it landed. Other South Korean soldiers and policemen quickly changed into North Korean uniforms and stationed themselves strategically about the airport.

Floodlights were blazing as the plane approached. It was not yet dark but soon it would be, and perhaps the blaze of light would help to fool the eye and blot out the view beyond the airfield. The voice from the control tower to the aircraft went on talking in its usual cool, laconic way, "Pyongyang tower calling Japanese aircraft, Pyongyang tower calling Japanese aircraft . . ." and filling the captain in on such necessary details as wind velocity, runway length and elevation and the like. Thus did the "Pyongyang" tower talk the plane down to Seoul.

Captain Ishida brought the plane in to a smooth landing and a gentle stop. (He really thought, he said, that he was landing in Pyongyang. His copilot had been told by an unidentified radio station that the Pyongyang airport's frequency was 131.4 megacycles. He tuned into this frequency and was guided down to—what do you know!—Kimpo.)

In front of the plane official greeters waved the Welcome-to-Pyongyang placards. Loudspeakers blared a similar message: "This is Pyongyang, and we welcome you!" Soldiers with smiling faces and Communist insignia appeared on the tarmac and took up positions alongside the plane as if in formation of an honor guard. Girls carrying bouquets of flowers scampered gaily along the runway with glad cries of "Welcome to Pyongyang!"

The hijackers peered suspiciously out the windows. Was there something perhaps a little overdone about this enthusiastic welcome? The doors of the airplane remained closed. An official approached with a megaphone. "This is Pyongyang and we welcome you," he called out engagingly. "Come down!"

Well, perhaps it really was Pyongyang after all. One of the hijackers went to the main entrance door and was about to open it when another yelled at him to stop. Wait—something was wrong! He had seen a car of American make parked near the terminal building. And just then another hijacker turned on his transister radio and heard English voices and jazz music.

"This is Pyongyang!" the official on the ground shouted insistently through his megaphone. "The landing ladder is ready. Come down!"

"This is not Pyongyang," one hijacker shouted back through a cockpit window. "This is Seoul. If this is Pyongyang, show us proof!"

For proof, they wanted photographs of Pyongyang to compare with what they were seeing at Kimpo. South Korean officials replied that they were not running a photographic bureau. The airport was a military base and photographs were not available.

Something must be available, the hijackers insisted, and demanded instead to be shown a portrait of North Korean Premier Kim Il Sung.

In South Korea there are not many portraits of the North Korean Premier. Certainly there was not one to be found at Kimpo Airport or anywhere near it. For five hours the South Koreans kept on trying to provide some sort of proof. None was to be found. The flowers wilted and the girls trooped off disconsolately. The welcoming placards were removed. The plane doors remained closed. Finally, South Korean officials gave up.

A note was passed through the cockpit window from outside explaining to the hijackers (in case they harbored any resentment against the captain) that the pilot really had thought he was landing in Pyongyang, and that the hijackers would be allowed to leave for the North after the passengers had been freed.

But this was not what they wanted. They wanted hostages. Furthermore, they wanted to take off for Pyongyang without another moment's delay. The soldiers, who had long since lost their smiles, drew closer to the aircraft. Others joined them, until about two hundred South Korean troops were surrounding the plane.

The pilot urgently radioed the control tower: "Please do not bring people near the aircraft. The hijackers are prepared to blow up the aircraft with bombs if there is any obstruction to takeoff."

But in the meantime the pilot himself was still trying to stall. He told the student hijackers that it would be difficult to take off from Kimpo at night and suggested that any decision should be postponed until morning. For some reason, the hijackers agreed, and the plane was permitted to move to a quiet corner of the airport so that normal traffic might resume. A tape-recorded message from the tower repeated a warning to the hijackers that they would be held there and the plane would stay on the ground so long as the passengers remained aboard. The hijackers countered with a message of their own. They would be willing to wait three or four days if necessary . . . and then they would blow up the plane.

During the night the young Reds flicked the passenger cabin

lights on and off, on and off, a childish but nerve-racking tactic that was apparently designed to demoralize the occupants. And still they waved their swords about. Attempts were made to send food aboard, but even this effort was turned down and only a few sandwiches were accepted. There was not much in the galley for those who were beginning to feel empty; the plane had left Tokyo with only light snacks for the short trip to Fukuoka.

Morning came, and, with it, growing unease and sharpening pangs of hunger. Still the swords and pistols were being brandished, and still the passengers were confined to their seats. Two of the student hijackers were standing in the cockpit with pipe bombs in their hands. Outside, South Korean troops maintained their vigil, though there was really nothing they could do but keep the curious sightseers away. For a while the plane was kept supplied with electricity to keep the air conditioning going, so that even if food was scarce and the cabin was beginning to get rumpled and uncomfortable at least the air was fresh and cool.

At one point mechanics wheeled a battery cart toward the plane to recharge its batteries. Watchers from afar thought that they were trying to remove an engine, and apparently the Red students got the same impression because they screamed at the mechanics to stay away and moved in threateningly upon the captain. No attempt was actually made to remove an engine, though South Korean officials were seriously considering the possibility of cutting a hole in the belly of the jet and flooding the cabin with tear gas. But this proposition did not get beyond the discussion stage. Nor did any others that involved possible danger to the passengers . . . and it seemed that all conceivable solutions held that danger. South Korean officials were determined to take a hard line with the hijackers and were strongly tempted to prevent the departure of the plane by virtually any means. But humanitarian considerations and the Japanese ambassador prevailed. Japanese Ambassador Masahide Kanayama, who was stationed in Seoul, urged the greatest caution and said that the plane must be allowed to leave with its present load if it became obvious that this would be the only way to avoid loss of life or injury to anyone aboard.

Thus it was a waiting game, and for a while it was not too bad for those aboard except for a natural tension. Then the electricity cut out. The air conditioning went with it.

The day passed, then a hot and stuffy night. The toilets began to overflow. Stubble appeared on men's faces, and shadows beneath the eyes of all. Food and supplies were down to near-starvation rations. People dozed uncomfortably when they could, but it was impossible to get any restful sleep. Dawn again . . . and the heat of another day. At one stage the cabin temperature rose to 107 degrees. The doors remained closed.

"It was just like in hell." This from stewardess Junko Kubota. "The hijackers kept swinging their samurai swords around. We were haunted by hunger and terror. We were in constant tension because we could not even move or stand up. They would shout out right away when we made the slightest move."

The tape-recorded message from the tower kept reminding the Red students that they could leave as soon as the passengers were released, but that mechanics must then be permitted to approach the plane because the engines would have to be ignited from outside. The skyjackers ignored the message.

It was a vicious impasse. Both South Korean and Japanese authorities were fully aware of the nature of the Red Army and its policy of violence. They could not predict what the young Reds might do to plane and passengers in a final spectacular gesture upon landing at the place of their choice—and neither could they guess what sort of reception might be given the passengers in Communist North Korea. But the plane couldn't just sit there at Kimpo forever. Something was going to have to give, and very soon.

Worst of all was the discomfort and the hunger. Even the students were feeling the pinch. Tired and hungry themselves, they drafted a message asking for food, water, cigarettes and blankets for all. Captain Ishida passed their message on by radiotelephone. Sushi, sandwiches, and other supplies were promptly sent aboard by airport personnel.

All kinds of discussions were going on in Tokyo and Seoul. As a result of the Tokyo discussions, Japanese vice-transportation minister Shinjiro Yamamura flew to Seoul and spent hours negotiating with the pirates. His offer was this: If the hijackers would let the passengers go, Yamamura would stand in as a substitute hostage and the hijackers would be permitted to fly to Pyongyang in the stolen plane. Also, it should be understood by the hijackers that Captain Ishida and his flight crew were by now too exhausted from lack of sufficient rest and food to risk the flight into Communist territory, and that therefore it would be advisable to permit a relief crew to take their place.

These suggestions were received with limited enthusiasm. Japanese Ambassador Kanayama and Minister Yamamura, in radio contact with the hijackers and occasionally with the captain and one or two of the passengers, found the hijackers to be "in a very excitable condition" and that they could be expected to do just about anything at any moment. Since they were reported to be armed with pistols, swords, daggers, pipe bomb and other explosives, they obviously held a very strong bargaining position.

By no means would they accept a relief crew. They wanted the crew that was already aboard, no matter how stale and tired that crew might be. And they would not exchange their passenger hostages for Yamamura. How could they know that the man who was bargaining with them really was Yamamura, and that Yamamura was actually the vice-minister for transportation? He had better prove it. And the only proof they would accept was in-person verification of the man's identity by Sukeya Abe, a Socialist member of the Japanese parliament. If Abe would vouch for Yamamura, then perhaps some sort of agreement might be reached. *Perhaps*.

Abe was flown from Tokyo to Seoul to make the identification.

The hijackers recognized him, accepted his credentials, and decided to settle for Yamamura. Agreement was reached on three points: The aircraft was to be promptly moved to takeoff position for North Korea, with departure to take place on the following day. Passenger baggage was to be removed from the cargo holds to await the owners of the bags at the terminal building. Fifty of the passengers were to leave the plane at one time, at which time Mr. Yamamura was to board; then the other fifty would be freed, after which the aircraft would depart for Pyongyang.

This agreement was made late on the Thursday afternoon of April 2. The hijacking had begun early on Tuesday morning.

That evening there was an almost festive atmosphere in the cabin. Japanese politeness reasserted itself and the young sky-jackers decided that, since their companions were to leave them on the morrow, it was now time to introduce themselves and offer entertainment. Tamiya, the twenty-seven-year-old leader of the boyish band, performed the introductions, starting with himself as the oldest and ending with "Boya," who at sixteen was a sort of terrorists' apprentice. "Boya," or Little Fellow, had played hooky from Kobe High School to participate in the junket. All the boys acknowledged introduction graciously and made long speeches to their captive audience, many of whom were still tied to their seats. Tamiya recited a long Chinese poem in the high-pitched, lugubrious chant customarily employed by declaimers of Oriental classics, and a good time was had by all.

The exchange of hostages took place without a hitch on Friday morning. Passengers and the four stewardesses got off, and Mr. Yamamura got on; flight deck crew and nine commandos made preparations to depart. North Korea was ready to receive the Japanese aircraft. Just what they were ready to do was an open question. Japanese negotiations with the North Koreans through the Red Cross had elicited a guarantee of the prompt return of the passengers and plane. But as the plane took off from Seoul with a weary captain in command, the North Koreans started singing a different and somewhat hysterical tune to the effect that the Japanese authorities were seeking to "lay on our shoulders what they should have done, and arrest the so-called criminals with our help." According to them, "the situation has changed." Neither Japanese nor South Korean authorities could understand how or why it had changed, unless it had something to do with the release of the passengers. But they got very worried indeed. Implicit in the fiery comment from Pyongyang was the threat of possible torture and imprisonment for the three crewmen and Yamamura. Returnees from a plane previously pirated to North Korea had reported having been beaten and tortured; and the Pueblo and a south Korean airliner were apparently in permanent Communist custody.

Thus the so-called change of situation hung like yet another sword over the hostages' heads

The flight to Pyongyang was a strange one. Yamamura, the main hostage, found the hijackers quite cordial as soon as they were sure the plane was on its way to North Korea and as long as he was careful about what he said. "As individuals they were very pleasant and polite companions—but once you rubbed them the wrong way you couldn't be sure what they would do. They were like madmen."

Captain Ishida, who should have been almost dropping from exhaustion, was too busy to make conversation with his captors and too angry to be tired. "Inside, I was boiling. As the saying goes, don't give swords to madmen! If I could, I would like to have killed them."

But the madmen already had the swords, and fortunately did not use them to kill.

The unpredictable North Koreans received the aircraft courteously. They were quite friendly to the hijackers but by no means unfriendly to their four hostages.

At the airport to observe the arrival of the plane was the Pyongyang correspondent of the Japanese Communist party's official newspaper. He described the youths as in high spirits when they landed, but—"utterly arrogant! swinging their arms and kicking the air in karate fashion, striking karate poses, and behaving like heroes." Perhaps the correspondent was just being sour because he was over thirty, or because the Red Army group favors revolutionary violence and has accused the Japanese Communist party of revisionism, but anyway he was not impressed by the hijackers. He was more impressed with the pilot. "Captain Ishida," he reported, "seemed in unbelievably good health and spirits as he descended from the ramp, almost as if he had never been cooped up in the narrow cockpit for over eighty hours, nor exposed to the danger of being killed."

Japanese and South Korean fears about the fate of the plane and the hostages soon proved to have been groundless. Hijackers and hostages alike were politely interrogated and then taken to a Pyongyang hotel. There they were hosted at dinner by an official of the Security Ministry, after which Mr. Yamamura and the crewmen were separated from the hijackers. The hostages did not see the hijackers again throughout their short stay in North Korea, which was perfectly all right with the crewmen and Mr. Yamamura, and were advised that they would be permitted to leave with a minimum of delay.

On Saturday, April 4, two announcements were made. One came from a Red Army leader speaking from his Tokyo hideout, and he said: "I think we succeeded. Our objective was to reach North Korea. We had no advance contacts with the North Koreans, yet now it is clear they are going to let our people stay there. World revolution is our ultimate goal, while our immediate objective is to set up revolutionary bases overseas. . . . We are no longer just a student organization, but a revolutionary organization in the real sense. We have to show that violent revolution is not only possible but necessary in an advanced industrialized country like Japan."

The other announcement, an official statement by North Korean authorities, was broadcast over Pyongyang radio. It declared that the young Reds had said that they never wanted to return to Japan, and that they would be kept in North Korea and investigated. "Investigated" was a rather weasel word, in light of the rest of the statement and the ambiguous attitude of the North Korean authorities toward uninvited guests. What North Korea was going to do with the young men, the statement concluded, "is our own business and is not a question to be interfered in by the Japanese authorities."

Captain Ishida, his two fellow crew members, and Mr. Yamamura arrived safely at Tokyo's Haneda Airport in the hijacked plane on Sunday morning, April 5. No one had been held or tortured; the plane had not been impounded. But something had been achieved. The Japanese Red Army had made personal contact with the North Koreans with whom they felt an ideological bond as fellow revolutionaries. Two of the tentacles of a worldwide movement had met and touched. That the North Koreans had described the nine young Japanese students as "strangers who came uninvited" and said that "our officials concerned will take appropriate steps after necessary investigation" did not unduly concern the Red Army members who had encouraged the hijacking from Tokyo. So far as they were concerned, everything had worked out very nicely.

Official Japan was also—officially—pleased. Japan thanked the North Koreans for returning the plane, the crewmen, and Mr. Yamamura, and acted forthwith as though the incident was closed.

Which, apparently, it was. The objective had been reached, and that was that. Tentacles do have a way of reaching out and meeting.

The Latin American Movement

There was an aborted hijacking on July 1, 1970, which, though far from being the most thrilling of aircraft seizures, was interesting to skyjack buffs and people who like to put together political jigsaw puzzles and come up with sinister patterns.

A Brazilian jet airliner, a Cruzeiro Do Sul Caravelle, took off from Rio's Galeão Airport at nine o'clock in the morning bound for São Paulo and Buenos Aires. Brazil had already suffered eight commercial aircraft hijackings since the previous October and had put into effect a number of security measures that were not, apparently, entirely successful. The thirty-four passengers who boarded the plane in Rio managed to pass through the police search of clothing and hand baggage that customarily preceded every Brazilian flight as a precaution against hijacking, but somehow or other three men and a woman managed to get aboard with a machine gun which they used to commandeer the plane.

The details of this affair are sketchy, but it is the punchline of the story that is significant. Though the hijackers were almost certainly bound for Havana, the seizure of the plane and passengers was more important than the destination. All the hijackers needed was some friendly and hospitable country, *any* one, to give them shelter while they used the captured passengers for barter. There is nothing on the record about how the pirates stormed the cockpit, or whatever it is that they did (Russia is not the only country that does not tell us everything); the only thing that is known for certain is that they commandeered the plane before it reached São Paulo and for some reason or other did not realize that the pilot was turning back to Rio. When the plane landed and they saw that they were right back where they'd started from they were naturally outraged, and demanded furiously that the plane take off again at once.

Brazil had had enough hijackings and related acts of terrorism. Furthermore, the Brazilian government does not and did not tend to handle crisis situations with kid gloves. The President himself gave orders that the plane was not to be permitted to leave the ground. Federal police and members of the Brazilian Air Force swiftly appeared on the scene and demanded that the sky pirates give themselves up. The sky pirates in their turn threatened to kill the passengers one by one unless the plane was allowed to take off. This cut no ice with Brazilian authorities. Probably they reasoned that the danger to the passengers at this stage was no greater than it would be if the aircraft did depart under criminal control. Air Force policemen, creeping quietly through the underbrush near the taxiway, froze into position and took aim. Ten minutes after the plane had landed, they shot out two of the four tires under the right wing.

Inside, nobody moved. Not even the machine gun wavered.

Three hours passed. Then, finally, the action began. Vehicles and loading ramps were driven into the vicinity of the aircraft and parked there—not too many of them, and not too close together; just enough, strategically placed. Men in coveralls began creeping up from behind the plane to disappear under the fuselage. Airport fire engines suddenly sped past the grounded plane to spew out billows of fire-fighting foam, and military policemen pumped out clouds of dense white smoke. More than thirty officers, armed with machine guns and other weapons, darted out from the cover of the parked vehicles and filtered through the heavy smoke screen. In the carefully created confusion, four of the coveralled men managed to get on top of the fuselage and then down along a wing to launch an assault on the front cabin door. But they could not get it open.

For those within the cabin, it was the moment of truth. As soon as the attack started the hijackers had threatened again to kill the passengers unless all action stopped immediately. Now there were bursts of gunfire from outside and a heavy hammering at the main door. The hijackers hesitated just a few seconds too long, and their victims took matters into their own hands. Someone opened the main door from within and someone else opened an emergency exit. Passengers burst out of the aircraft from one side and military police burst in from the other.

The hijackers were all about twenty years old, defiant, earnest, unafraid. With some pride, they identified themselves as members of the so-called National Liberation Action which had previously claimed credit for kidnapping U.S. Ambassador C. Burke Elbrick and West German Ambassador Ehrenfried von Holleben, whose lives had been put on the line in exchange for fifty-five political prisoners. This time the plan had been to skyjack the plane out of Brazil and exchange the passengers for other prisoners described as "terrorists" by Brazilian authorities.

This case would undoubtedly have made very much bigger news if the skyjack attempt had not been aborted. Yet the lack of headline value does not disguise its significance: the kidnapping of diplomats or other handy victims for purposes of political blackmail, and the hijacking of airplanes in order to use both planes and passengers as pawns in a war game, are part of the same revolutionary package.

A failure here or there does nothing to permanently dampen the spirit of rebellious violence in those who feel they have a vital cause. Wherever they are in the world, they keep on trying. Success is also a spur. No doubt the PFLP seizures of 1970, though embarrassingly overdone and not applauded by underground fighters of every stripe, were an inspiration to many revolutionary groups. (The Iran-to-Iraq hijacking of October 10, 1970, in which three hijackers threatened to blow up the plane with all passengers and crew aboard unless Iran released twenty-one political prisoners, was almost certainly inspired by the PFLP performance of the month before.)

Whatever the source of their inspiration, five men and two women successfully commandeered a Costa Rican LACSA turboprop on October 21, 1970. The plane was seized at gunpoint during a domestic flight that had originated in San José, the Costa Rican capital. Destination: Cuba. The change in the flight plan was only the first and least of their demands, as the pilot and the Costa Rican government discovered later.

Because there was not enough fuel to get to Cuba the pilot flew to the Colombian island of San Andrés to refuel. In the course of the flight the hijackers learned that four United States citizens were aboard. This gave them a new idea, or a fresh twist on a plan they had already been nursing. When the plane landed they passed a note out to airport officials who promptly turned it over to Colombian authorities. Diplomatic wheels began to turn. Colombia referred the problem to Costa Rica, and Costa Rica began urgent talks with Mexico.

In the hijackers' note was a demand for the release of four Nicaraguan guerrillas who were being held in a Costa Rican jail. The plane and its hijackers were to continue to Cuba regardless of what happened, but if the imprisoned guerrillas were not released the four American passengers would be killed and the plane blown up after landing in Cuba.

The negotiations took time. Mexico entered the picture when the Costa Rican government started making arrangements for releasing the prisoners. It was not intended for them to join the LACSA craft grounded in San Andrés; rather, they were to be released to Mexico as political exiles on their way to Cuba.

Hours dragged by, as hours do when ransom arrangements are under way. Thirty-two people were permitted to disembark from the plane, but the four American hostages, the crew, and the hijackers remained aboard.

The four jailed guerrillas who were being sprung were leading members of the Sandinista Front of Nicaragua. The Sandinistas take their name from César Augusto Sandino, a Nicaraguan guerrilla hero of the thirties who successfully eluded U.S. Marines who sought to hunt him down only to be shot to death in ambush by his enemy Somoza after the departure of the Marines. Ordinarily the Sandinistas operate in Nicaragua, where they devote their efforts to warring with President Anastasio Somoza (son of the original), but occasionally they slip into Costs Rica. One of them, Carlos Fonseca Amador, fled into Costa Rica in 1969 to dodge pursuing Nicaraguan National Guardsmen and had the ill luck to be picked up for unlawful possession of a firearm. For this he was jailed. Shortly afterward a group of fellow Sandinistas launched an attack on the prison in an attempt to free him. Two guards were killed but the rescue attempt failed and several of the would-be rescuers were captured.

Now Carlos Fonseca Amador and three of his comrades were to be released together. The note had meant business; the only way to prevent the murder of the four United States citizens was to release the four guerrillas.

The story wound down to an unspectacular and fortunately bloodless ending. The hostages were released after Fonseca and his fellow guerrillas left their Costa Rican prison. The seven hijackers were taken care of, one way or another, in Havana. The four guerrillas arrived in Mexico on the first lap of their journey. One said: "We want to get to Cuba as soon as possible so we may continue the fight against the government of General Anastasio Somoza."

Thus ended another guerrilla extortion plot.

These, then, are the five faces of the skyjacker. He may have more, for all we know; or perhaps one or two of the faces are less distinct from the others than we have suggested. Maybe our dividing lines between categories need relocating. Nevertheless the skyjacker type is not that of one man but many types of men.

None of them are normal.

We look closely into the five-faced picture and we try to merge the faces into one; and there is a point at which all five images do blur into one another. What we see then is a desperate and unhappy man.

We cannot get away from this. But we also cannot get away from the fact that there are many different kinds and degrees of desperation and many different causes. We do not find it easy to slot the political activist into the "psychotic" column or brush him aside as just another misfit whose mind is slightly out of kilter.

The man who hijacks to get out of what, to him, is political prison is of course a misfit. He doesn't fit into that prison. The guerrilla who hijacks as an act of war is also a misfit. He and his fellow fighters are misfits in a society that has not provided for them—not provided the basic needs of life for all instead of just for some, not provided a government of and for and by the people; not, in some cases, provided a homeland at all. These are the really dangerous misfits.

For all that we would like to think that our five-faced creature is a fumbling, pitiful amateur, we must see him in part as a deadly, dedicated professional. Picking up all the nuts and bolts we can get our hands on will not wipe out this type of skyjacker or solve this phase of skyjacking.

8/THE WORLD FIGHTS BACK

The stirrings of anxiety and counteraction that followed the American skyjackings of 1961 did not have a lasting effect. Government agencies trying to attack the hijack problem found the public and the airlines rapidly losing interest during the long hijacking lull. Even when the lull was over, the Federal Aviation Administration found it extremely difficult to drum up national enthusiasm for an anti-skyjack program. One of the stumbling blocks was that somebody had to pay for it, and nobody was too eager to do that. Another was that any drive to educate the would-be skyjacker into realizing that skyjacking is a risky business might carry with it a backlash effect and persuade passengers that flying was too risky. It was a fine line to tread, and so it was trod with very careful steps.

"We started out," Dr. Dailey says, "with a tremendous amount of public apathy. And we had to operate within the restraints of doing something that, among other things, wouldn't slow down the loading of aircraft, would not be very expensive in terms of total effort and would have minimum impact on the attitude of the public. Starting out under these constraints, what we did first was a very basic study of the characteristics of hijackers. Then we developed and tested our passenger screening system for a long period until we were sure we had developed the right thing."

But something else was happening while the FAA was quietly developing and testing its anti-hijack program: the public was beginning to lose its apathy. Toward the end of 1968 the FAA and the airlines began to receive a flood of letters offering hijack-prevention suggestions. The flow of ideas has not stopped yet and show no signs of letting up.

The Helpful Public

One proposal that popped up repeatedly during the take-me-to-Havana days was to build a fake Havana airport in Florida and then have the pilot land there under the pretense of humoring the hijacker. This suggestion has lost some of its steam of late. Another inspiration, received with equal lack of enthusiasm by the FAA, was to have the pilot depressurize the hijacked plane so that all passengers including the hijacker would be rendered unconscious by anoxia (and get the bends too, presumably). If this were to be done the pilot would have to be pretty quick about putting on his own oxygen mask before being confronted by the hijacker, who might wonder why he was doing it.

Very popular was the idea of flooding the cabin with some sort of gas that would immobilize everyone outside the cockpit. This one presupposed that the pilot would receive a few seconds advance warning from a stewardess, by some as yet undevised signal, that a hijacking was in progress. He would then instantly seal off the cockpit, cut off communications from the cabin to the cockpit, and throw a switch to pour gas into the cabin. The flight deck crew could then put on their gas masks and one of them could go into the cabin and take care of the hijacker.

There are many variations on the gas and depressurizing themes. Some of them are very imaginative indeed and all are, in the end, impractical.

Again and again the suggestion is made that, if the cabin crew cannot communicate with the pilots, the hijacker would have no way of getting his wishes across to the people who fly the plane. Thus the communication system would be one-way. The pilot would be able to make announcements to the passengers but he would receive no messages from the cabin. The only possible exception might be a signal light that the purser or stewardess could flash in case of an emergency such as a serious illness aboard the plane, which would alert the pilot to land at the nearest airport. But what, one wonders, would the hijacker be doing in the meantime? He might, with his .38, be picking off crew and passengers one after the other. For this reason, locked and bulletproofed cockpit doors are not the answer either, although they are in use. Sooner or later the determined hijacker is going to get in one way or another.

Even more popular has been the idea of equipping the crew with mace chemical spray or tranquilizer dart guns of the type used to subdue wild animals to tag them or capture them for zoos. The crew member most strategically positioned would then trigger the little dart and watch the would-be hijacker slump helplessly to the floor. One James Bonded letter writer recently suggested that a marshal impersonating a passenger carry the dart cunningly concealed in a cigarette. Then, when a hijacking attempt got underway, the marshal would pretend to light up his ever-handy weed and neatly blow the dart at the hijacker. *Zap!* Down goes the skyjacker. The trouble with the dartgun idea is that the paralyzing action is far from instantaneous. First there is the "ouch!" reaction, then the angry staring around to see who did it, then the slow spreading of the tranquilizer through the blood stream. The delay gives the hijacker plenty of opportunity to stagger around and grab stewardesses and fire shots.

Dropping sleeping pills or a Mickey Finn into whatever the hijacker might be persuaded to drink holds similar drawbacks. It works too slowly, if it works at all. One man's mickey might be another man's benny. Furthermore, few hijackers drink on the job, so even the most effective knockout drop would be unlikely to get past the lips. A related suggestion is to ply the hijacker with deadly poison in his coffee or jab him with an instant-death dart. Apart from the difficulty of administering such poisons—which, as all mystery and thriller fans know, really do exist—there is the serious drawback of overkill. We do not necessarily want to kill hijackers. We simply want to stop them. More particularly, we do not want to kill the vacillating hijacker who might instead be dissuaded from his attempt, or the man who is merely trying to make a stupid joke. (Incredibly, some passengers, especially those who have had too much to drink, still persist in making silly remarks and half-threatening gestures that can easily be taken seriously.)

The trapdoor idea, too, has been frequently advocated. Its supporters suggest installing a hidden trap either immediately outside the cockpit door or right behind the pilot's seat, so that he can swiftly push a button and dump the hijacker neatly into a bombproof compartment below. (Too bad if he were, mistakenly, to dump a stewardess that way.)

A super-refinement on this plan engages the use of a metal plate on the cabin floor in front of each passenger's seat. The plates would be so devised as to look both decorative and practical, as if to protect against carpet wear and tear, but they would be electrically wired. Each plate would be cued in with a switch on a concealed board accessible to the cabin crew. Then, if a passenger in any particular seat were to rise up and utter a hijack threat, some member of the crew could quickly throw a switch electrifying the plate under that seat and shock the hijacker into submission.

A number of bright minds have come up with the idea of having all passengers strip before they board and checking in all clothes, stockings, wigs, kerchiefs, purses, hand luggage and other possessions in exchange for pajamas, smocks or kimonos. On reaching their destinations they would change in the arrival terminal and have their possessions returned to them. The smock idea has a little twist of its own: No need to undress the passengers but simply zip them into smocks over their clothes. Only the stewardess would be able to unzip them, and passengers would not be able to reach into sinister pockets underneath the smocks. (Nor would they be able to get to the rest room by themselves.)

Tying all passengers down has been another frequent suggestion. Security guards would guide the passengers aboard and lock them to their seats by the legs so that they cannot walk around. Anyone requiring to leave his seat during the flight would be accompanied by a security guard. The pilots would be the last to board and the first to get off, so that no hijack-minded passenger could possibly get at them.

As skyjacking got more sophisticated, so did some of the anti-skyjacking suggestions. One lively thinker suggested blacking out all of the windows of all airplanes. Then, in the event of a skyjacking attempt, security men could switch off all the regular lights and turn on the special infrared lighting system. Nobody would be able to see anybody—except the security men, who would quickly put on their infrared goggles and subdue the night-blind hijackers.

Then there was the interesting idea proposed by the man who loved computers. He suggested programming the flight plan in an onboard computer that would control the airplane and that could not be reprogrammed in flight. Thus nobody on board, pilots included, would be able to divert the flight from its programmed flight corridor no matter what happened in cabin, cockpit, or at the destination airport. So the plane flies through an electrical storm and lands in the midst of an earthquake; so be it. It beats hijacking.

A more primitive solution-seeker suggested that the airlines arm all passengers with guns as they board the plane. Any hijacker attempting to commandeer the craft could then be shot by the quickest passenger on the draw. Maybe, at first, a few bystanders might be shot and a couple of airplanes might even be lost, but sooner or later the hijackers would get the message that hijacking is not so easy after all. Also, a lot of people might give up flying altogether.

Yet another suggestion involved more stringent preflight checking procedures. All travelers should carry fingerprinted cards to serve as identification at the check-in counters. Before each flight, all freight, baggage, carry-on luggage, passengers, and the aircraft itself should be subjected to a thorough search. After the search, all passengers should be kept in a quarantined area to prevent any contact with other people until takeoff time. No uncleared passenger should be permitted to join a cleared flight by connection from any other flight or any other airline.

And still the suggestions come in. Crews should be trained in karate. Rewards should be posted for the apprehension of air pirates, dead or alive. Stewardesses should be provided with gunbelts and hunting knives. Trained dogs should be used to sniff out explosives. Electronic detection devices should be employed at boarding gates. Armed sky guards should be placed on air carriers. But wait! We have some of those now, don't we?

Sometimes the public comes up with ideas that are not bad at all.

This is not to say that public inspiration or pressure is responsible for the anti-hijack measures now in use. It is only to say that individual citizens and the various agencies concerned with aircraft security have been and still are thinking—with some crackpot exceptions—along very similar lines. There may even come a day when Pan American, for example, will be warned by El Al, for example, against ticketing certain passengers regarded as possible security risks.

The Passenger as Pest

Once in a while a passenger will get a little obstreperous or silly. But considering the number and types of people who fly, the proportion of nuisance passengers is very small. We are talking, now, in the context of a skyjack situation, in which passengers other than the skyjacker himself may feel the urge to contribute. On an extremely rare occasion, a passenger may turn out to be an FBI man or a Brink's guard, and can do a professional job of subduing the skyjacker when the moment is ripe—usually after the plane had landed for refueling. The passenger with a gun against his ribs or head does not go in for heroics. Not a single one has yet. Once in a great while one or more passengers may help to subdue a hijacker after the gun has been turned away from the head or after the gun has been emptied into the floor, but this sort of thing happens so seldom that it doesn't even put a dent into the records. Again, the occasional male passenger has to be talked to very sternly to be persuaded not to launch a physical attack upon the skyjacker or forcibly rescue the beautiful stewardess from his clutches . . . but only the very occasional one. The overwhelming number of passengers recognize that the sky is an alien milieu to them and that action is not their forte, and have the sense to quietly mind their own business.

The passenger most likely to be a pest is the company employee. Not a deadheading crew member (who knows the score too well to get underfoot), but a passenger agent, a vice-president in charge of something or other, or an airline marketing or public relations man. Some of these people are so anxious for the paying customers to have a good flight that in a crisis situation they outdo themselves to be helpful. Perhaps they also like to feel important. What they often succeed in doing is getting in the way.

Patricia Redner has for more than seven years been a stewardess with one of our major domestic airlines. We stress her length of service because we feel it useful to point out that she knows her job and her company obviously knows she knows it.

On June 25, 1969, the flight she was working was diverted from its Los Angeles-to-New York path and forced to go to Cuba. It was not the world's most spectacular skyjacking, although it probably sounds less exciting than it actually was because of the matter-of-fact manner in which Pat tells the story:

"It started almost as soon as we got in the air, say a minute or two after the seat belt sign had gone off, and we were still climbing. I was the B stewardess in the first class cabin, so I was sitting by the jump seat that was adjacent to the main cabin door, also adjacent to the cockpit. And as I looked down the cabin—because I was facing aft—I saw two men coming up the aisle. The one in the front, who was a passenger I'd seen before, was very pale and ashen. My first thought was, He's ill, and the man behind him's helping him to the bathroom. But they bypassed the bathroom—this was on a DC-8—and came up to me. Our lounge, by the way, was filled; in the first class cabin every seat was taken. And the hijacker said, 'I'll give you three seconds to open the cockpit door.' I didn't believe him; it didn't occur to me at the time that this was a hijacking attempt. The passenger said something like, 'Please do it—he's got a gun.' And I still really thought it was just two passengers hamming around. So I unfastened my seat belt, got up from my jump seat, and he *did* have a gun against the passenger's neck.

"So—all airlines say, do what the hijacker wants. So I knocked on the cockpit door, and he pushed myself and the passenger into the cockpit. As soon as we got into the cockpit he transferred the gun from the passenger's neck to the captain's neck and then held it against the captain's neck for the first, say, two and a half hours of the flight. But as soon as he had the gun on the captain's neck he shoved the passenger and myself back into the cabin. Since it was so soon after takeoff, the pilots were still doing their visual check out the window; they didn't even turn around when I knocked on the door. It was totally unexpected for them!"

The flight lasted over six hours. Most of the conversation that went on in the cockpit was a secret to Mrs. Redner until the flight was over. The hijacker did not seem unbalanced, and after the first couple of hours he relaxed enough to move his gun slightly away from the captain's neck and just loosely point it at him. There was no opportunity to change the hijacker's mind about diverting the plane.

What else happens when a hijacker is in the cockpit—specifically, this hijacker?

"He didn't do anything but sit in the seat behind the captain, holding the gun. Once or twice he'd open the door for us when we went in with food. The hijacker himself had nothing to eat or drink. The captain and the copilot were hungry, so he let them eat. But we had to remove the knives and forks. They could only eat with spoons and have cold water to drink. I guess the idea was that he didn't want to be attacked with anything sharp and he didn't want any hot liquids thrown into his face. We'd just knock on the door and the hijacker would open it a crack and we'd put the meal tray in and close the door.

"As for the cabins, we tried to keep everything as normal as possible. One thing we did—the stewardesses, that is—was to move the people sitting in the lounge area back into the coach cabin. We thought it best for them to be back away from the cockpit. But we ourselves didn't make any announcement to the people—just quietly asked them to move, and they did. We assumed we were going to Cuba, but we didn't *know.* The people who had been in the lounge area, and most of the people in the first class cabin, had seen an unauthorized person— someone not in uniform—go into the cockpit. And most people, if they travel at all, realize that's unusual. But the whole thing affected the passengers very, very little. Nobody was distraught; there were no fainting spells or anything like that. After a while the pilot did make an announcement on the public address system, and he said, 'We have a slight diversion . . . we'll be landing in Cuba.'

"Still nobody got upset. The only thing was, we had several businessmen who were concerned because they had important business meetings in New York the next morning that they were going to miss. But nobody was afraid for their lives. I didn't feel fear; none of the girls felt fear. It took him only a few seconds to bundle me into the cockpit. There wasn't time to feel fear then, or later. This particular hijacker stayed in the cockpit all the time. We had absolutely no association with him. He didn't interfere with us at all, didn't give us any trouble.

"We kept normal flight service going on. I stressed this, because I didn't exactly know how soon we'd be leaving Havana once we got there, and I certainly know we weren't equipped to reservice the plane when we landed. So I told the passengers if they felt at all like eating, it would be a good idea to eat now because I didn't know when they'd be able to eat again."

A practical girl, this Patricia. She knew what she was doing. In fact, there was considerable delay in Havana, and some of the passengers were very glad that they had listened to her.

Things on the whole were going quite well. But there happened to be three fairly high-echelon airline employees on the flight for public relations reasons. Briefly, it was their function to ride the flights to see how a certain new service was going over with the passengers.

"Stewardesses, as you know, are the bottom rung of the ladder," Pat says wryly, "so that when a P.R. man tells you that Mr. Soandso is aboard, he is one of our vice-presidents, you better treat him like a god, you do. You're very nice to him, you do everything in your power not to offend him even if he gets difficult. Now there was one man in particular on this trip—a marketing representative—who did get rather difficult. Not unpleasant, but. . . . And of course he meant well. After we were hijacked he was going out of his way to make the passengers feel comfortable and for them not to be concerned."

As a result of Mr. Soandso's efforts, Pat, when she got home, prepared a little list of her own. Much of it applies just as well to regular passengers as to the Mr. Soandsos. We quote her document verbatim because we think it is the only one of its kind and it may be helpful to passengers of all varieties as well as to the crews of hijacked planes:

Because I was a stewardess on (a) hijacked flight to Cuba I have compiled a list of definite DO NOTS for any company employees who may be involved in a future hijacking.

DO NOT "assist" crew members unless you have been asked to assist.

DO NOT "blame" stewardesses for admitting hijacker to cockpit. An inconvenient diversion is more desirable than injury or death to passenger or crew members.

DO NOT suggest drugging the hijacker. The drugged food or drink may be fed to one of the pilots.

DO NOT ask for cockpit key. This key is only for crew use.

DO NOT unnecessarily alarm passengers. They are already aware that the hijacker may be mentally unbalanced.

DO NOT suggest unlimited liquor. An intoxicated passenger is not always a happy one—certainly not an alert or dependable one.

DO NOT interfere with stews or passengers during the meal service. It may be a long time before passengers or crew members have the opportunity to eat again.

DO NOT try to be a hero and physically overpower hijacker. In this case the customer is right!

DO NOT suggest stews remain out of cockpit area on landing (on grounds that the hijacker may come out shooting). Stews *must* sit at assigned emergency exits.

DO NOT concern pilots with questions as to what happens when plane lands. The pilots have other things to think about.

—PLEASE—

DO assist when asked by crew. In many instances employee cooperation may be invaluable in emergency situations.

(signed) *P. A. Redner*

"It's only a list of things I don't think you should do if you're a company employee," Pat says mildly. "Employees should definitely identify themselves and volunteer their assistance, but not initiate any action or interfere with what we are trying to do. Give us credit for knowing what we are doing, along with the pilots, because we are trained to do what we are doing and we really know what should be done. Sometimes helpful people can get to be a hindrance. The list looks corny, but everything here I've said not to do, this man did. And everything we tried to do, he would. . . . Well, let me give you an example.

"As soon as he saw me let the man into the cockpit and come out again, he called me over and said: 'Pat, how come you opened the cockpit door?' And I said, 'Well, because he had a gun against Mr. X's neck.' And he said: 'Are you sure it was a real gun?' I said, 'No, I didn't ask to examine it.' He said: 'Well, what kind of a gun was it?' I said, 'I don't really know.' He said: 'Do you think the gun was loaded?' And I said, 'I had to assume it was!'

"When that was over, he kept trying to assure the people that everything was all right. This was fine, but there is such a thing as overdoing it. Too much reassurance isn't always very reassuring."

Pat very tactfully avoids the comment that he was also helping to clutter up the aisles and getting in the way of the meal service that the stewardesses were trying so hard to maintain on a normal basis.

He went his rounds for a while, and then:

"Several minutes later he asked: 'Do you girls have a cockpit key?' I said, 'Yes, we do, but it's only for crew use.' He said, 'Well, I want it.' "

This put her in a quandary. He was, after all, a company official.

"So I went up to my flying partner, who was the senior stewardess, and I said, 'Beth, what do you think?' Now he'd given us a lot of aggravation—plus we'd had this same man on the trip going from New York to Los Angeles the day before, during which he was full of ideas and suggestions, too. We decided that perhaps this man was the sort that, if you gave him a toy or whatever, he would sit down and that would satisfy him. But it didn't. As soon as he got the key he went up and down the cabin, both first class and coach, saying: 'People, please don't be alarmed if you hear shots or screams from the cockpit. You don't have to worry about a thing, because I've got the cockpit key right here in my pocket.' Which didn't assure the people, I don't think, at all. And it was possible that the hijacker had an assistant or someone else in one of the cabins. That wasn't the case, but it could have been; it was possible."

Pat Redner, more than her VIP passengers, knows the score. Stews do. She is quick to admit that non-VIPs can be a problem, too, but seldom because they try to interfere with the hijacker. "A drunken passenger can be a danger, or someone who's high on drugs and doesn't know what he's doing. We've had quite a bit of that lately—we've had a lot of young kids with marijuana. But the only other case of interference I personally know of, though it wasn't my flight, involved another company employee. This one was a passenger agent. He was really big on the drug thing. He kept saying, 'Let's drug the hijacker! Let's take him unawares!' And that is definitely not the answer; that is dangerous. Anyway, the only drug we had on the plane at the time was Dramamine, and we don't even have that any more."

So much for the drug scene.

Pat's closing advice to passengers: "Don't do anything to the skyjacker. Just stay in your seat and keep calm."

Once in a great while we run across an exception to this very practical rule. On second thought, the unique case we have in mind was not really an exception, because the passenger did stay in her seat and did keep calm . . . but she also acted. And "acted" is the operative word.

On August 19, 1970, Sachio Inagaki hijacked a Japanese jetliner and ordered it to land at a Japanese Air Force base where he demanded a rifle, ammunition, and two drums of gasoline in exchange for the seventy-four passengers aboard the plane. Reports have it that he was planning an elaborate suicide scene because of his despair and frustration over a girl who no longer wished to share her life with him.

The captive airliner remained on the military runway surrounded by baffled soldiers for two hours after the hijacking. Those were two long hours, and as the third hour approached one woman passenger decided that she had had enough. Calmly sitting there in her seat, thinking things over but paying no attention to the hijacker, she suddenly achieved an advanced state of pregnancy. Her muted cries and little moans of agony brought a swift response from the crew. What was her problem, what could they do for her? Alas! she was so sorry, but the labor pains were becoming too much to bear. Could she possibly be taken off the plane? And quickly, too?

The pilot went into a rapid huddle with the hijacker. Something must be done—the moans were rising into screams—the woman must be removed from the plane at once before—as man to man, please! The hijacker agreed.

When the ambulance arrived just moments later, a plainclothes officer arrived with it and hastened up the rear ramp of the aircraft. Rushing past the moaning woman, he pounced upon the hijacker, clapped cuffs upon his wrists and hustled him away.

And the lady just as promptly recovered from her instant pregnancy.

The View from the Pilot's Seat

The pilot rarely receives this kind of cooperation, nor expects it. He would frankly prefer not to need it, or any other kind of emergency help, although he does appreciate intelligent assistance when he gets it. The pilot as an individual is a cool-headed businesslike man who wants to get on with the business of flying and not have to be concerned with such extracurricular problems as tackling skyjackers or participating in airborne gun battles. Traditionally, he has always been opposed to having armed guards aboard or carrying a gun himself. But gradually, his position has been changing. The current stand of the Air Line Pilots Association is that pilots who wish to carry guns should be free to do so. Such episodes as the one-sided shoot-out on the Boston shuttle and the ransom attempt culminating in bloodshed at Dulles Airport made a lot of pilots stop and think about a problem that they had never before been forced to deal with. The long-run implications of the Middle Eastern hijackings gave further pause for thought; and at the end of the pause the concensus of the pilots was that, sky marshals or no sky marshals, those pilots who were qualified to use firearms and wanted to carry them should equip themselves accordingly.

When they made their decision they were fully aware of the dangers that might be involved. They had been aware of these dangers for years. But how much more dangerous can it be to be armed rather than unarmed when threatened by the gun-crazed, suicidal skyjacker? Captain Charles H. Ruby, until recently the long-term president of the Air Line Pilots Association, puts it this way: "When you are exposed to people of this character, you've got to make a choice between total destruction *for sure*, and maybe part or total destruction in an attempt to *prevent* the deliberate, total destruction of an airplane."

The public has become accustomed to thinking of pilots as efficient, well-built, neatly uniformed, highly skilled men with pleasant intercom voices; men who are near-machines on the job and probably daredevils with the stewardesses on the side. (That most pilots not only have a wide range of nonflying interests but are also among the most conservatively domesticated of men is beside the point.) It is only recently that news-conscious people, and passengers of skyjacked planes, have realized that the pilot even up there in the cockpit is a living, breathing, sometimes fearing and sometimes bleeding man who occupies a hot seat. He, personally, is in great danger in the event of a skyjacking. But there is one danger to some pilots that we have given little thought to, and that is the danger of being skyjacked into the hands of his own enemies. This is not something that happens often, but we can foresee it happening more frequently as more and more skyjacker-havens (or hoped-for havens) open up around the world, and more and more terrorists seize planes wherever they may be from and wherever they happen to be and force them down into territories inimical to the legitimate occupants of the plane. We have seen this happen time and time again to passengers, but it happens to pilots too.

A classic case is that of George Prellezo.

On June 30, 1968, Captain George Prellezo wound up in a Cuban jail.

He had left Miami on the day before as the pilot of a Southeast Airlines DC-3 twin-engine plane bound for Key West. He had intended to take the day off to celebrate the eighth anniversary of his defection from Cuba, but when one of his co-workers reported sick he agreed to fill in for him and take the plane on its routine Miami-to-Key West flight. There were fifteen passengers aboard when it took off from an intermediate stop at Marathon in the Florida Keys, and one of them was a man with a gun who entered the cockpit and ordered Prellezo to fly to Havana.

We can only begin to imagine how Prellezo's heart must have flip-flopped. He had defected to the United States while he was a pilot for the Cuban airline Aeropostal. His last flight from Cuba in 1960 had also been a routine run, because at that time Havana-to-Miami flights were still under way, but when he arrived he got off and stayed. He told immigration officials that he was fearful of arrest in Cuba, and asked for political asylum. The plane was flown back to Havana the next day by another

Cuban crew, and in the course of time George Prellezo became an American citizen, married a Puerto Rican girl, and started building a family. So far as the Castro government was concerned, Prellezo was still a Cuban—an enemy of the state and a deserter.

The passengers were returned the day after the Southeast Airlines hijacking and the plane followed the day after that. But Prellezo remained in Cuba under arrest. Havana radio announced that he was to be tried for desertion.

It was a dismal situation for Prellezo in the Cuban jail and for his family waiting, terrified for him, at home. It was also a knotty problem for the United States. Could the U.S. government protect a naturalized citizen against trial and incarceration by a government that the United States did not recognize and which, in its turn, might not recognize the validity of Prellezo's American citizenship?

Mrs. Prellezo begged the State Department to let her go to Cuba to be with her husband, "to plead for him, to do any necessary thing to get him back," and finally, on July 12, they permitted her to go and Castro let her enter. The hassle continued. The Swiss Embassy in Havana was doing its best, on behalf of the United States and George Prellezo, to work out a release with the Cuban Government. Prellezo himself was not hopeful. Friends of his in Key West remembered that he had often wondered aloud what might happen to him if a hijack situation were to land him in Cuba. The Pueblo case was heavy on his mind, for the United States had still been unable to secure the release of the captured crew. "I'm just one, and they are eighty-three . . ." Would the United States be able to rescue him if he were captured?

Now all his fears had come home to roost.

But George Prellezo was freed from his Cuban jail on July 22 and was flown to Mexico City with his wife, Olga, on his way back to the United States. It was an extremely unpleasant experience for him, but nevertheless he was lucky.

As the incidence of hijacking took an upturn the airlines started working overtime to provide their crews, and particularly their captains, with updated information and instructions in regard to such matters as the permissibility of weapons

aboard aircraft, what to do when ordered to an unfamiliar airport, and how to get along with the hijacker. We offer in example a couple of pages from a route manual carried by Pan American pilots. The section is dated June 19, 1970, and the runninghead is "Flight Information: Emergency."
Beneath that, read:

HIJACKING

Until some long term solution is found to the problem of hijacking, Pan American aircraft, particularly those operating into the Caribbean area, are subject to this act of piracy. This section provides information and guidance to aircrews on this subject.

I. *Pan American Policy on Hijacking*

In the event a flight is subjected to an act of piracy, the safety of the passengers and crew are the most important considerations. Any other factor is of secondary importance. Neither the crew nor the passengers should initiate actions which would in any way jeopardize the safety of flight. Therefore, if subjected to an act of piracy, the continuation of flight should be conducted in accordance with the foregoing principles.

II. *Air Traffic Control*

FAA has concluded that a hijacked aircraft is in an emergency situation and entitled to the full cooperation of the ATC facilities. In order to facilitate identification, routing and handling of hijacked aircraft by the FAA ATC facilities, Captains of hijacked aircraft are directed to *switch to Transponder Code 3100*. ATC facilities receiving this hijack code will not question the pilot but be immediately responsive to his requests. Additionally, they will take action to notify all appropriate agencies concerned, including the owner/operator of the aircraft being hijacked. Canadian Department of Transport authorities have agreed to their ATC facilities employing the same procedures as described above.

III. *Communication With Hijacker*

In the event the hijacker does not speak or understand

English, the following typical phrases are translated into Spanish and French: [We offer, here, only the English phrases.]

English

1. We do not have enough fuel to get to _____.

2. The airport is not large enough at _____ for this airplane.

3. The airplane has a mechanical problem and we cannot proceed to _____.

4. The weather is not good enough for a safe landing.

5. What you are requesting is not possible—we must land first.

6. We do not have required information for that airport necessary to conclude a safe operation.

IV. *Terminal Information*
Approach plates to José Martí Airport, Havana and other Cuban airports are contained in the Emergency Airport Section of this Manual.

V. *Release of Hijacked Aircraft*
The U.S. Government has made informal arrangements through intermediary Governments for the release, by the Cuban Government, of aircraft hijacked to Cuba for departure from the José Martí Airport. The captain of a recently hijacked airliner was requested to complete a "Declaration" reciting the airline's assumption of responsibility for the flight and committing the pilot to proceed to the stated destination in the U.S. Any Pan American captain of a hijacked airplane may be asked to and if necessary, should sign a similar declaration . . . [Here follows a sample format, which we will omit.]

VI. *Recommended Procedures for U.S. Air Carrier and Commercial Pilots Flying Aircraft Hijacked to Mainland China*
If it is possible to do so without jeopardizing the safety of the flight, the pilot of a hijacked American aircraft after departing from the cleared routing over which the aircraft

was operating will attempt to do one or more of the following things, in so far as circumstances may permit:

a. Maintain a true air speed of no more than 400 knots, and preferably an altitude of between 10,000 and 25,000 feet.

b. Fly a course toward the destination which the hijacker has announced.

c. At appropriate intervals fly the international pattern for lost communication—left-hand triangles—and transmit the international distress signal, may day, on any of the international distress frequencies available to him. . . .

We will leave the document at this stage, something the pilot cannot do. The volume of emergency information grows larger every day. No longer can the man at the controls simply carry route information for his destination; he has to carry maps and approach plates to places 'way outside his normal flight plan. But no pilot carries a complete route manual to cover all possible contingencies and all points on the map. There are master copies of such things, but to issue them to all pilots of all planes everywhere would be impractical and extremely expensive. The information issued to each pilot depends on the type and range of the craft, and its scheduled destinations—with reasonable alternatives. Once a pilot is in the air and heading for some place he had not intended to go and for which he does not have detailed approach information, he must fill in the gaps in his knowledge via operations advice from the control towers below. Thus Captain John Priddy, in his 747 that was not by any stretch of the normal imagination supposed to go within hundreds of miles of Beirut or Cairo, had to get the details of latitude, longitude, airport elevation, runway length and direction, wind velocity, and so on by radio from ground control.

The language of even the short-form route manual contains its mysteries for the layman, which is of no importance to the public unless the content happens to be particularly interesting. Take, for example, the reference to "Transponder Code 3100" in the paragraph headed "Air Traffic Control." This does not leap immediately to the eye as something of absorbing interest, yet it is a nugget of a story in itself.

Airplanes are equipped with a number of devices to assist ground-control stations in keeping track of them. One such device is the transponder. The transponder emits radio signals on various frequencies. Clearly, all aircraft cannot be sending transponder signals on the same frequency at the same time, therefore an air traffic control center will instruct the pilot to, for instance, "squawk ident on 1900." The receiving pilot, in his turn, tunes his transmitter to the 1900 frequency and pushes a button which sends the signal to the ground station. The signal flares on the ground controller's radar screen, and the controller is thus able to identify the aircraft.

A special transponder code of 3100 has been established by the airlines to let ground control stations know that an aircraft is under hijack. Instead of waiting for any requests from below to go to such-and-such a frequency, the pilot immediately hits 3100 and keeps sending out the code signal for as long as he feels it advisable. Ground control, in the meantime, does nothing but keep track of the distress signal. This is one of the particulars of the 3100 code: radio silence between ground and aircraft. Ground control is supposed to keep its nose out of things and wait for further word from the pilot, or a request for route information, before attempting to make contact with the plane. Ordinarily there is an almost constant gabble of radio sound from ground to air, but not when the pilot goes to 3100. It could be too distracting for a man already under extreme stress.

Thus, not so long ago, when a Pan Am pilot sent out the 3100 signal, it was picked up several hundred miles out of Shannon and relayed to every air traffic control center in Europe. The advisory read, in part, that Pan Am Clipper 114 was sending a 3100 transponder signal and apparently was being hijacked.

Everybody, quiet!

Everybody was quiet.

Minutes ticked by—five . . . ten . . . fifteen . . . twenty . . . twenty-five. . . .

The captain of Clipper 114 became restive. Why wasn't he hearing anything from the ground? There was maybe something wrong with his radio? Had the world ended out there?

Nothing of the sort. Little did he realize that, in demonstrating the use of the 3100 code to his copilot in a sort of dry run, he had inadvertently sent out the 3100 signal and there wasn't a ground station in the area that was about to bug him.

After half an hour of not hearing from the ground he had had enough. The silence from below was eerie. He got on the radio and said querulously: "This is Clipper 114—is anybody there?"

Instantly, at least three ground control stations came on the air to find out why he was sending out on 3100.

In the meantime, concerted high-level efforts were being made to combat the hijack menace.

The Passenger Screening System

In February, 1969, the Federal Aviation Administration established a Task Force on Deterrents of Air Piracy. Under the chairmanship of Dr. H. L. Reighard, that Task Force developed the two-phased anti-hijacking system which is still the main thrust of the American battle against the skyjacker. Sky marshals came later. That the use of sky. marshals was not seriously considered for another eighteen months was due not only to the expenses and possible dangers involved in their use but also to the strong feeling of government agencies, airline security officers and pilots' associations that the best thing to do with hijackers is to *get them on the ground.* Nobody has changed his mind about that. Our main objective, still, is to get that hijacker *before* he boards the plane.

When the FAA rolled up its sleeves and really got to work in 1969 we already had an epidemic going full blast. Nobody had been able to come up with any effective plan. Almost everyone involved with the problem had given up on it. All sorts of ideas were still being bounced back and forth but no one had been able to suggest a practical program of action. The only practical proposal to come out of a series of Congressional hearings on the subject was that of the FAA. That proposal was to try a psychological approach. What eventually emerged was the behavioral profile and the weapons-screening system.

Hijacking, at that time, was regarded primarily as a United States problem, since most hijackings were originating in the United States and terminating in Cuba. Therefore what the FAA and its team of experts started out to do was to minimize the hijackings of aircraft to Cuba. Note the word "minimize." Throughout the airline industry there seems to be absolute agreement that we cannot totally eradicate the skyjack bug. To quote the FAA's Dr. John T. Dailey:

"I think it is a mistake to believe you can 'stop' hijacking. Just as with efforts to control other crimes, perhaps the most we can hope for is to reduce the number of events. There are too many people who have motivations for violence. We cannot really hope to eliminate this disease entirely—at least for the time being. A more practical goal would seem to be to develop a number of techniques through which we might reduce this very serious problem with which we are faced. If we were to place our reliance on developing a single 'solution' we would be doomed to failure. . . . What you need to do is think of this as a total problem, a people problem as well as a technique problem, and approach it from that point of view."

Which is precisely what Dr. Dailey and his associates did.

They started by making studies of the kinds of people who were committing the skyjackings, and were able to conclude quite early in the game that most of the culprits to that date were amateurs, not very resourceful ones and in many cases not even particularly determined. There was little evidence of organized conspiracy or conspiratorial activity. Political tie-in was at a minimum; and the planning of the hijackings was on the whole haphazard and inept. The skyjackers themselves appeared to be generally incompetent, insecure, and frightened people. This assessment led to the hope that the greater the number of difficulties placed in the path of the potential skyjacker, the greater the likelihood that he would be deterred from making his attempt. This was more than a hope. It was an assumption, and a reasonable one. A further and equally reasonable assumption was that the more that was publicly known about these difficulties, the more likely it was that the would-be hijacker would be dissuaded.

The business of dissuading the U.S.-to-Cuba skyjacker became a question of undercutting the hijacker's motivation, placing plenty of obstacles in his path, and giving maximum publicity to all the difficulties, horrors, and hazards that lie in wait for skyjackers.

If the hijacker was motivated by a desire to find sanctuary, then it must be made clear that there was no sanctuary to be found. One very important part of the program was to make every effort to find out what was happening to hijackers when they got to Cuba. In the beginning no one knew, because Castro wasn't sending us reports, but eventually some of the hijackers came back with some very sour comments about their treatment there. What they told us has been repeatedly confirmed through indirect channels by others who elected to go on to Europe or Africa rather than come back to the United States, and by lines of intelligence that have since been established. We started getting some very interesting hard information as to the fate of the runaways, and it didn't sound good. Jail, hard labor, cane-cutting, isolation—that, for the most part, was Cuba for the hijacker. The FAA made every effort to disseminate this information as widely as possible.

Having learned that hijackers were not being treated well, the FAA decided to capitalize on their knowledge in yet another way. Says Dr. Dailey: "We thought it might be possible to accelerate that process, by preparing and sending to the Government of Cuba, through diplomatic channels, a concise statement of the facts about many of the hijackers, namely, that one had held up a liquor store here and was a fugitive from justice, that another had been dishonorably discharged from the Navy, and so on." (Or had "robbed the Bank of Texas," as Mr. Hammarskjöld would say.) "There have been indications that information of this type has had a very important impact on the Cuban government, which does not like to receive hijackers who are criminals."

A number of agencies cooperated in this area of the FAA's project. The FBI has been particularly effective in identifying the fugitives, no matter what false identities they assume, and providing background information from date of birth to criminal record. All this is grist for the FAA, *and* for Fidel Castro, and for the traveling public. The potential hijacker's motivation cannot help being undercut if he realizes how he is likely to be rewarded.

The obstacles placed in the path of the would-be hijacker consisted of certain pre-boarding procedures and various kinds of hardware. Procedures and hardware together made up the detection-deterrent system devised by the FAA and its consultants. The first step of the system called for the identification of suspects, or "selectees," by their behavioral characteristics, and the second called for the screening of the selectees with a detection device. It was found that the great majority of people would be cleared by the first step, and most of the rest by the second. The very few individuals who remained uncleared after this process were interviewed by airline officials who would inspect credentials and ask a few polite questions. Any selectees who still looked suspicious after such an interview would then be searched by authorized agents. Arrest could be the result.

Full descriptions of these procedures, excepting only the details of the behavioral profile, have been and still are being given as much publicity as the media will take. The hijacker, no matter how feeble, used to know that hijacking was easy; now he was being told that he would have to run an unnerving gauntlet to get aboard the plane and that, even if he succeeded in his hijacking attempt, he wasn't going to like the way he would be treated at the other end of the line.

The FAA team was flying by the seat of its pants in coming up with this approach. They could not be certain of success, not by any means, but they felt, in Dr. Dailey's words, that they were dealing with "a free-running epidemic, completely out of control, and that almost anything positive we tried would have some effect."

As the phenomenon spread in new directions, became more complex and attended by an increasing degree of professionalism on the part of some hijackers, so did the program enlarge and change. It is still being modified as hijacking characteristics change. The goals for the passenger-screening system, however, remain the same. These goals are spelled out in the FAA handbook entitled *U.S. Efforts to Deter Hijackings*, which originated as a verbal presentation to foreign countries and airlines in explanation of what this country is doing to deter hijacking of U.S. aircraft.

To quote:

GOALS FOR PASSENGER SCREENING SYSTEM
ENSURE SAFETY
  —Identify passenger carrying weapon
      Apply behavioral characteristics
      Screen with detection equipment
      Interrogate suspects
  —Deny passage
APPREHEND POTENTIAL HIJACKER
  —Search of suspect
  —Take violator into custody
PREVENTION OF HIJACKING ATTEMPTS
  —Publicize results of detection efforts
  —Improve detection system.

One thing that was done very early in the game was to post signs at airports so that no traveler might be in any doubt as to his right to take aboard his .38 or wander into the cockpit. For those readers who haven't done much air travel of late, this is what the sign says:

IT IS A FEDERAL CRIME TO:
—Carry Concealed Weapons Aboard Aircraft
—Interfere with Flight Crews

PASSENGERS AND BAGGAGE SUBJECT TO SEARCH UNDER:
—Federal Laws
—FAA Safety Regulations
                    Federal Aviation Administration
                    U.S. Department of Transportation

Dr. Dailey expands on this in the FAA handbook:

". . . We post(ed) signs stating that hijacking is a serious crime, subject to severe penalties; that carrying concealed weapons on an airplane is a serious crime; and that search and inspection of passengers would be done under some circumstances. There was some controversy about this at the beginning. Some people thought that signs might stimulate people to hijack, through the power of suggestion. We felt that this would not happen and that the signs would be a positive factor. Also, we had the feeling, based on some research we had done, that passengers would react favorably to this. So we had signs designed to carry this message. . . .

"On the passenger search proposal, this is the first time that anybody had said publicly that passengers might be searched. Actually, however, the airlines have the right to do this, under the conditions of the tariff. When people contract for transportation with an air carrier, they agree voluntarily to submit to search or inspection, if necessary. If they then choose to withdraw from this agreement, the contract is void, and the airline is under no obligation to carry them as passengers."

The searches, incidentally, are not conducted by airline personnel but by U.S. marshals. With extremely rare exceptions, people with nothing to hide do not object to being searched. Only the occasional DPL or VIP raises a bit of a fuss. Undeniably, such search *is* an invasion of privacy, but the overwhelming majority of passengers are heartily in favor of search when it seems necessary and magnetometer screening wherever it is in use. It gives them a sense of security. Some say that the program should have been instituted long ago.

Dr. Dailey also explains the clearing system as a whole in more detail:

"Here in detail is how our system works. The signs are posted. This is essential, as there must be substantial warning to a person, if there is going to be surveillance. This is an important legal requirement. We also have a law enforcement officer either standing at the exact gate or very close by, to be quickly available if needed.

"We screen the passengers for selectees, as we call them—not suspects. These are the people who are left after you have cleared as many people as you can from the information [behavioral profile] you have on them. The magnetometer itself clears some people. You then interview the people failing the magnetometer test. Most selectees, when informed about their high magnetic reading, will show the interviewer the item which caused the reading and they can then be cleared to board. This is an interview which results in a voluntary search. An uncooperative selectee would have to be forcibly searched."

Forcible searches have been very rare. When they do occur, they usually turn up firearms or narcotics. But most people with a plane to catch and something to hide prefer to change their plans rather than go through the search. Either they quietly ditch their weapons under the potted palms at the airport, or they fold their tents altogether and just as quietly steal away. An amazing number of odd objects have been found in hastily sought-out hiding places near the boarding gates: knives, pistols, pieces of lead pipe, filthy pictures, glassine envelopes, packages of pot, and so on. One man who was actually searched had an arsenal of guns strapped around his belly; another had a knife hidden up his pants leg; another had diamonds sewn inside his coat; another had a case bulging with banknotes; and yet another carried a fortune in heroin. At one overseas boarding gate of a American airline company a woman was discovered with an assortment of firearms concealed beneath her clothes. It turned out that she had no intention of doing any such thing as hijacking an aircraft. All she had wanted to do was have something to sell, and thus live off, when she got to her destination. Another individual at a boarding gate in another land was found to be carrying a lifetime supply of salami, apparently under the impression that you can't get good salami in the United States.

As for the legendary behavioral profile, it does not so much pinpoint suspects—rather, selectees—as identify and eliminate people who are "low risks." Those who are eliminated go ahead and board; those who are not are given a closer look. It's as simple as that—even simpler.

Dr. Dailey: "The way we have it set up now, it [the behavioral pattern] is highly simplified. We have a small number of criteria and the way it works now he must meet every one of them." (That is, any individual who is to qualify as a selectee must fit into every one of the points in the pattern.) "If we were to find it necessary to put in additional criteria, to emphasize the difference between hijackers and other passengers, we might then require the passenger to meet some but not all of the criteria. With the smaller number we now use, the passenger must meet them all to be cleared."

The effectiveness of that part of the system employing the

profile as a screening device is dependent on the fact that the general public is unaware of the nature of the behavioral characteristics. If the characteristics, simple as they are, were to be disclosed, the system would be compromised. Any hijacker with sense would be able to use the knowledge to his own advantage. Thus it would be a serious mistake for any scoop-hunter to spell out the profile. It can be said, though, that the basis of the system has nothing to do with ethnic considerations or physical appearance.

Dr. Dailey: "There isn't any common denominator except in their behavior. Some will be tall, some short, some will have long hair, some not, some a long nose, et cetera, et cetera. There is no way to tell a hijacker by looking at him. But there are ways to differentiate between the behavior of a potential hijacker and that of the usual air traveler. This is what we depend on: this is what we call our profile of the behavioral characteristics of a hijacker. We stress it is behavior—things they do or don't do, or their style of doing it or not doing it."

Frank Cardman, director of security for Pan American World Airways, has something to add to this: "The profile is not a psychological measurement. It simply qualifies the person by age and characteristics of ticket purchase—not as somebody who is a potential hijacker, but as somebody who should be looked at further. This is what it does. Then, as you move into other sensitive areas, such as the Middle East, we start looking for other characteristics. Primarily, we look a little harder at the origin of the passport and the veracity of the passport in relation to the person. It best singles out a person as being someone you look at yet once more before letting him aboard the aircraft."

But who measures the passengers against the profile? There cannot be a trained psychologist at every ticket counter or boarding gate. Airline people, and not necessarily senior personnel, are saddled with this job. But are they qualified? Here we enter a controversial area. Perhaps they are not as fully qualified as one would like them to be. But they are briefed and trained by those who *are* qualified, and furthermore they have experience with the traveling public—or, if they are new employees, they are getting it on the job. People who meet people may or may not be the luckiest people in the world, but they do get to know people. Customs, for example, has run itself almost entirely for many years according to a sort of behavioral profile check, an unofficial one that is based on sixth sense based in its turn on experience. And, though customs officers sometimes miss they more often hit. This sixth sense born of experience is not confined to customs men. Police officers, FBI agents, department store detectives, industrial security officers—all have it. So do airlines personnel. The longer they stay on the job, the more of it they have.

Cardman: "For twenty-five, thirty-five years, passenger agents or flight service supervisors have gone to a captain and said, 'I don't like the look of this guy,' and he's been taken off the plane. They haven't been especially trained for this. It's just been done by experience. We've shaken down people—just by virtue of experience, say sky marshal or customs experience— we've shaken down any number of people that we've found thoroughly undesirable to have aboard an airplane, but are not basically hijackers. Narcotics!—we're knocking off people day after day carrying the hard stuff. The general public thinks of the behavioral profile as a slick device of behavioral measurement, much more in the area of cosmetics and psychological behavior and that type of thing. It's anything *but* . . . yet as long as they think that, well and good. The mere fact that the public knows you're operating a behavioral profile and magnetometer provides a psychological deterrent. There is no question about it—operative or inoperative, it has been a deterrent."

Something certainly has been. Though we still have far too many hijackings, the U.S. rate has slowed down quite considerably while the foreign incidences have been accelerating.

Of course, to be really useful, the profile must be sensitive to current problems in our own country and to happenings in other regions. In its most simple form it cannot take in the professional hijackers who now—in their impact on the public if not in numbers—seem to be dominating the scene. But, as Dr. Dailey says, "We have a large number of characteristics in reserve to crank in whenever we need to." The profile, like hijacking, can expand.

Before the magnetometers were put into operation a great deal of exploratory work was done by the FAA and other agencies, some of them private companies, in connection with weapons detection. At least ten basic approaches were actively investigated.

Back to Dr. Dailey and the FAA handbook: "Nonlinear scattering is one of these approaches, but its precise nature is classified. Another is short-pulse X-ray. Here a very short low-energy burst of X-ray is used, supplemented by an image intensifier to build up the image. The minute amount of X-ray that is used is no more than the radiation you get by being around a brick building. When magnified by the image intensifier, it will show clearly the profile of a weapon inside a suitcase or on a person, if we wanted to use it. This technique is not advanced to the extensive trial stage yet, but it has shown a great deal of promise.

"Other possible screening devices include polarization imaging radars, ultrasonic imaging, chemical detectors, infrared, visual optics, ultraviolet, physiological measures, and even animals. On the possible use of animals, some of our information looks fairly discouraging. The British, however, think they may have some use for them, based on the animal's keen sense of smell. . . .

"Magnetic devices are the ones we are using. We chose these because they were sufficiently developed so that it appeared that they might be suitable for use. People said . . . that magnetic devices were worthless for stopping the hijacking problem. Used by themselves, this would appear to be true.

"However, we found that by combining the magnetometer with several other things we had a system that would be useful for passenger screening."

The metal detection device currently in use is the magnetic gate. There are several different models. One looks like a doorway, one is more of an archway, another consists of a pair of pillars, and yet another looks like a couple of upright poles. The last-named is the one thus far in most common use in the United States. The ticketed passenger walks between the poles on his way from the departure lounge to the aircraft. If he has on his person a particular amount of ferrous metal that is above the established threshold, the detection device activates a buzzer or a flashing light. Little things like pens, keys, and the like are below the threshold and do not affect the magnetometer. Other equally innocent things sometimes do, such as heavy cigarette lighters or the metal supports some women use in undergarments. Well, nothing in this world is perfect, and the magnetometer sometimes embarrasses perfectly innocent people. When this happens, a discreet interview serves to straighten matters out.

Also in occasional use is a nightstick type of magnetometer, a little hand-held device that is used much like a divining rod. The inspector holds it within a few inches of the person being searched and traces a pattern (invisible, of course) over the surface of the body to seek out lurking metal objects. A needle on the dial of this gadget jumps nervously when the stick comes within half an inch of the location of any magnetic material. The passenger is then given the opportunity to explain what the object might be: metal brace, cigarette case, pocket flashlight, stainless steel teeth (yes, there was such an incident), steel arch supports, or postoperative skull plate. The advantage of this system is that the stick is highly directional, which the poles are not; the disadvantage is that it is slow and must have the cooperation of the passenger. The disadvantage of both types of magnetometer is that they cannot distinguish between a weapon and any other object of equivalent magnetic properties. So long as we are using these devices, passengers are simply going to have to leave their ferrous metal home.

There are, of course, such things as non-magnetic metals and nonmetallic weapons. Is there any way that these can be detected? Yes, there is. There is already a Finnish metal detector that can spot all metal objects whether magnetic or nonmagnetic; and a number of devices currently undergoing final tests are proving very useful as detectors of nonmetallic weapons. In the middle of 1970 Dr. Dailey announced that such things were under development. "The short-pulse X-ray would show up a plastic dagger, or a nonferrous weapon, and there are other things under consideration. I would say that within a reasonable period of time we will have additional hardware that would help in that type of detection."

Unfortunately, it is costly.

Obviously, the system in use today is not foolproof. It is still possible to smuggle lethal weapons aboard, including explosives, and people do. Knowing this, as she cannot help it, the hostess in the sky is not prepared to assume that the bottle of colored water being waved in front of her face cannot possibly be nitro or some sort of disfiguring acid, or that the stick-shaped objects wrapped in paper are not sticks of dynamite. More often than not, these objects turn out to be phony, but sometimes they are the real, the deadly thing. How can she possibly know the difference? Her doubts are due partly to the fact that no weapons-detection system yet devised can spot all the murderous weapons known to man, and partly to the fact that not all airport boarding gates are covered by the screening system. She *knows* that it is possible under some circumstances to get aboard with real nitro, real dynamite, or a real .38. Now, the determined hijacker need only scout ahead for an unguarded boarding gate, buy a round-trip ticket, dress and act like a businessman on a routine business trip, and take one or two simple precautions (including a type of weapon) that we do not choose to describe. If he really wants to do the thing in a professional manner he will do a little studying beforehand and familiarize himself with the general structure and operations of an aircraft, but in truth all he really needs to know about any plane is that the cockpit is up front and the stewardess is the smiling girl in the shapely uniform—the girl with the perfumed neck.

Sounds too easy, doesn't it? Well, it is. In spite of everything that has been done, it is still too easy for a person of moderate intelligence to hijack a plane.

And yet the screening system has been effective. During a typical sixteen-month period ending mid-February, 1971, U.S. marshals tipped off by airport detection devices arrested 273 undesirables, confiscated sixty-seven guns, one grenade, two rifles, and $1,500,000 worth of narcotics. The magnetic gates, when used, have proved to be so effective that a woman who tried to sneak aboard a plane with a puppy zipped up inside her tote bag was stopped cold in her attempt when her dog's collar triggered off the metal detector.

In very few of the recent American hijackings were the airport gates guarded by the behavioral profile plus weapons-detection system. The airlines concede that there are many gaps to be filled, but claim that they are moving as quickly as possible to plug those gaps. The magnetometer gates run close to $1,000 apiece, the slow-moving nightstick costs about $100, and the more sophisticated pieces of equipment now under test may cost a few thousand dollars each. And somebody has to pay: the airlines, the airport authorities, to some extent the federal government—and probably, eventually, the public. Thus far the airlines have been bearing as much of the brunt as they feel they can stand. Airline business did not flourish in 1969, 1970, and 1971, for reasons completely unrelated to skyjacking, and the prospect of paying out more money when less was coming in did not and still does not fill the airline with elation. Yet, as we say, somebody is going to have to pay; and somebody is also going to pay in some way if money is not spent.

Enter the President of the United States

The shock wave generated by the PFLP skyjackings of September, 1970, went around the world and struck deep into the heart of Washington. On September 11 of that year President Richard M. Nixon issued a strong statement announcing the United States position in regard to "international blackmail" and outlining a specific course of action to meet "the menace of air piracy—immediately and effectively." Specially trained armed guards would be placed aboard U.S. commercial airliners. Efforts to develop new security techniques and equipment were to be accelerated, and the use of electronic surveillance systems was to be extended to all "gateway" and key airports in the United States and—wherever possible—in other countries. Appropriate U.S. agencies would go into immediate consultation with their foreign counterparts to share anti-hijacking techniques, and the United States government would urgently press for international acceptance of multilateral conventions and agreements providing for the swift extradition or punishment of hijackers.

In all, President Nixon announced seven major steps, which

summed up and emphasized his determination to implement all possible security measures with the least possible delay and his conviction that the international community must take united action to combat "this international menace."

"These are not the only steps we will take," the President said. "But they do provide a decisive program for the immediate future. . . . Piracy is not a new challenge for the community of nations. Most countries, including the United States, found effective means of dealing with piracy on the high seas a century and a half ago. We can—and we will—deal effectively with piracy in the skies today."

The world still waits for the "community of nations" to come together in multilateral agreements regarding the prompt extradition of all hijackers. It still waits, even, for bilateral agreements between such countries as Cuba and the United States, India and Pakistan. These pairs of countries, at loggerheads for many years, can do much to spearhead one-to-one agreements until such time—millennium!—as the world community can get together to tackle this crime against all people.

But at least, with President Nixon's statement, we had declared all-out war against the skyjacker.

9/NO HAVEN ANYWHERE

Item: An airline ticket agent thrusts his hand into a flight bag during a preboarding check and grasps a bare double-edged razor blade. It slashes his thumb severely. Later, bandaged, he goes back on the job. It is the second such occurrence of the day at that terminal. Preflight inspection procedures are under way—but they have their hazards.

Item: On November 14, 1970, Russia, after years of dilly-dallying, joins the International Civil Aviation Organization.

Item: Passengers checking their luggage with certain airlines note a new procedure. The agent is writing the passenger's name on each luggage destination-claim tag. He is doing this because of what the airlines call "gate no-shows." These are passengers who check in their luggage and then for some reason do not show up at the gate to board the plane. Through cross-checking of the airline's computer passenger list, and the hand-tally by agents at the boarding gate, a "gate no-show" can be pinpointed within minutes and the passenger's luggage can be off-loaded rapidly. Why? Because a passenger who does not care to travel on the same plane with his luggage may have something in that luggage which should not be up in the air at all.

Item: An airline agent finds lettuce leaves in the purse of a young girl. He does not regard this as particularly sinister, for as a hijacking tool lettuce has never yet been used; nevertheless he is curious about it. What can be the purpose of this lettuce? The answer lies, crouched, in a cardboard box clutched under the young lady's arm. It is a pet guinea pig. Reluctantly, the girl turns over both the guinea pig and lettuce to a relative and boards alone. Strange things are beginning to turn up in passenger baggage.

Item: The question of in-flight security comes under increasingly close scrutiny. All agencies, airlines and aviation organizations agree that the prime objective of any anti-hijack system is to *get them on the ground*, but at the same time there is a growing feeling that an effective onboard system or combination of systems must be devised. Armed guards are only part of the answer. Teams of specialists redouble their efforts to probe into the onboard problem and come up with the optimum procedure for apprehending skyjackers who do succeed in getting off the ground. The requirements are stringent: No hazard to passengers or crew; minimum danger of any damage to aircraft; under the direct or indirect control of the crew; usable in a reasonable number of cases; fast and effective when used; and capable of being kept secret.

Item: Fort Dix, New Jersey, October 7, 1970—A five-day crash program to train 880 military men to serve as armed sky marshals on an interim basis began here today in a stepped-up attempt to foil would-be hijackers. Lt. Gen. Benjamin O. Davis, Jr., now retired, is director of the training program started by the U.S. Department of Transportation. Davis, who heads the program as the department's new civil aviation security director, said the trainees were mostly enlisted personnel with law enforcement or military police backgrounds who volunteered for the program.

The battle had been joined in earnest.

Ghost Riders in the Sky

Some two hundred civilian government guards had been rushed immediately and somewhat unceremoniously into sky duty immediately after the Arab skyjackings. These were men whose background in security work qualified them to step aboard and get to work at once with little more than a briefing. There is a slight element of mystery here, or perhaps merely confusion, about the exact number of those deployed and where they had been found. It seems that we began with two hundred men, federal agents drawn from such sectors as the Federal Bureau of Investigation and the Treasury Department, but that another one or two or three hundred were added as swiftly as they became available. The suggestion of hush-hush surrounding these apparent additions may be due to honestly conflicting reports or may have something to do with the nature of some of the agencies from which they were recruited: The FAA (not notoriously close-mouthed, although it does have its own intelligence system); customs; the FBI; the Treasury Department's Secret Service, and the Central Intelligence Agency.

Whatever their exact number and wherever they were drawn from, the first emergency contingent of shotgun riders was a drop in the bucket. To spread them over our domestic and overseas flights was to spread them very thin. Thus the crash program at Fort Dix. But the crash program in itself was a stopgap measure designed to fill in some of the holes until all interim marshals—federal agents and special military deputies—could be replaced by a permanent force of between 2,100 and 2,500 freshly trained federal air security specialists. And these specialists had still to be recruited, screened and instructed.

The crash program swiftly went into high gear. Before the end of October, well over two hundred military deputies were riding shotgun aboard commercial airliners, and every five days a new batch went into the air. General Davis noted that these men had passed an exacting screening process indicating that they were capable of exercising careful judgment under stress. He told his trainees and reminded his graduates: "Although you will be armed, the use of guns should be only as a last resort. And even though you will be using special ammunition designed for minimum harm to persons, you must always remember that the safety of passengers and crew is paramount."

They left sky marshal school after an intensive course of instruction in the psychological approach to skyjackers, the innards of an aircraft cabin, the basics of the aircraft's most vulnerable parts, the rudiments of judo and other forms of hand-to-hand combat, and the workings of a .38-caliber revolver with special reference to total accuracy of aim. They grew their hair a little longer because, though hijackers rarely have long hair, only the military these days sport completely clean-shaven faces and crewcuts. Their sideburns began to sprout a little. They hung up their uniforms, put nondescript looks upon their faces, loaded up their snub-nosed .38-caliber detective specials with dum-dum bullets, and merged quietly in with the rest of the passengers. Only to the crews of their assigned flights were they to be identified as special riders.

They went aboard knowing that they were to lose their identity until called upon to act, knowing that they were considered a last resort, knowing that theirs alone was the responsibility to shoot to kill if necessary. Over and over again it was drummed into their heads that the primary battle against hijacking would still be fought on the ground. Down there, behavorial scrutiny of every passenger, newly developed weapons and explosives detection devices, and selective searches would be the first and main line of defense against the madmen of the sky. Great stress was placed upon their responsibility while operating aboard the aircraft. They would be expected to try all alternative means of subduing the hijacker, such as reason or judo, before resorting to weapons; they would be expected to use their heads and remember at all times that they were working within the confines of an expensive, vulnerable airplane and with many lives at stake. Their weapons would be loaded with special low-velocity bullets that would not penetrate deeply and would thus minimize potential injury to innocent persons or damage to an aircraft.

Though the concept of sky marshals was accepted because we felt that something must be done and because our President had said that this was one of the things we must do, it did not receive wholehearted support. Traditional opposition was still strong. The reasons: impracticality and danger. The cost of putting armed sky marshals aboard all air carriers would be astronomical. "Take Florida alone," suggested those who were cool on marshals. "There are fifty-seven cities in the United States with direct, nonstop air service to Miami. Now, Miami International Airport has approximately 1,200 landings and takeoffs a day. Even if the armed guards were used selectively they would probably have to cover five hundred flights a day. And these guys would have to be paid, plus they are going to be running up additional expenses. What will the tab be—$5 million a year? That's Florida flights alone, don't forget. Now we've got other flights and other cities to consider, some of them not even in the United States. Some of these are just as vulnerable as any domestic flight. Look what's already happened to TWA and Pan American. Add sky marshals to their flights, and I ask you, who is going to pay these people?"

Never mind; that's been taken care of. Our sky marshals, by now well over two thousand of them, *are* being paid . . . by the public, through an airfare tax. They are not getting any huge sum of money but the fringe benefits are most attractive and their training qualifies them for a nice future in customs or some related career. (And the tab, incidentally, runs to about $51 million a year.)

Something that has always been considered much more of a drawback than the financial factor is the possibility of setting the scene for a wild gun battle several miles up in the sky—as, for instance, in a 747 loaded with 362 passengers. The big fear has been that a bullet or two, penetrating the cabin structure, would lead to what aviation experts call "explosive decompression" . . . and rip the plane apart in midair. This is a bit of a misconception. The design and structure of today's airplanes are such that the fuselage skin will not rip or tear over a wide area even if penetrated by several bullets. A plane flying at current maximum commercial altitudes (30,000 to 42,000 feet) will not lose its total pressurization if its skin is penetrated by a spray of bullets or even if a window is blown out. When young Thomas Robinson fired nine shots into the skin of a pressurized cabin, all he did was scare a lot of people; he did not harm the plane. If an entire passenger cabin window is blown out there may be some minor, temporary passenger discomfort until the pilot makes a descent to a more comfortable level, but again there is more discomfort than danger. Explosive decompression will not occur under these conditions. Small-arms fire makes practically no difference as far as pressurization is concerned. Again, if one or more windows are blown out and the pilot for some reason does not respond by descending to around 10,000 feet, oxygen masks drop automatically when cabin altitude dips to 10,000 feet. And if they don't automatically drop, they can be made to drop via electrical command from the flight deck. But the big point here is that *the plane does not decompress and explode.* The sound of a bullet puncture or a window blowing out might be deafening and would make many a heart seek refuge in the stomach, but it would not be the signal of an explosive decompression.

The only time a small-arms bullet could cause serious trouble to the aircraft itself would be if it struck a vital aircraft component such as fuel, hydraulic, oxygen, or electrical lines or other critical equipment.

But the greatest danger of a shoot-out on an aircraft is what it might do to an innocent passenger or two or three ... or to a pilot desperately concentrating on a final landing approach to a busy metropolitan airport.

Therefore, the sky marshal is taught to shoot only when he has to. He is taught to know and recognize the vulnerable areas of the plane and avoid shooting anywhere near them—and that includes the flight deck. He is taught to draw the hijacker's fire away from those areas and away from passengers if shooting does begin. He is taught to be adept in his use of the special .38 with its low-velocity hollow-pointed bullets that can effectively halt a man in his tracks but have little power to penetrate. He is taught to aim right down the middle with 100 percent accuracy; and, if he cannot achieve that kind of accuracy, he flunks the course.

Today's sky marshals are the new crop of professionals. The temporaries, already trained to some degree before they offered their services, received only the five-day course of special instruction at Fort Dix, New Jersey, before taking to the air and trying to forget that they were primarily military men or special agents. The present semi-civilian corps has undergone a far more prolonged and rigorous training course, some of them in Washington, D.C., and others—the more recent graduates—at Fort Belvoir, Virginia. In background and style they are not unlike their predecessors, although many of them are younger. Still, the age ranges from the early twenties to the late fifties. Some can pass as college students and some as middle-aged businessmen. Among them are former customs inspectors, former pilots out of their regular jobs because of airline cutbacks, onetime policemen, detectives and security officers, and an assortment of people with little or no experience in law enforcement or aviation but with the necessary qualifications of marksmanship, toughness, and stability. Any candidate who upon application shows any sign of wishing to be in the game for the glory of it is promptly scratched. Any candidate who, in training, cannot quickly achieve the desired standard of marksmanship or shows himself to be inept in a cabin situation is washed out.

It is impossible, and always will be impossible, for sky marshals to man all the daily flights of all U.S. passenger airlines. Perhaps one out of four flights will eventually be covered. Top priority is given and will continue to be given to those flights regarded as "high risk" trips. Heaviest protection is given to flights to Florida and Europe. At least two marshals, and more often three, are assigned to each flight that is chosen for protection. When the risk is considered especially high and the plane is of the jumbo type, one or more additional marshals may be assigned to work the aircraft.

The would-be hijacker may find some comfort in the fact that not all flights are protected by armed guards. But, like the stewardess who cannot afford to assume that the sinister-looking bottle in the hand of the aerial holdup man does not contain nitro, nor can the skyjacker assume that the plane he has boarded does not carry a sky marshal. Thus while it is still technically—or perhaps we should say theoretically—easy to hijack, there is a big new "maybe" up there in the sky for the man who is tempted to try. What if it does come to a confrontation? Today's sky marshals are infinitely more intelligent, cool-headed, and well-balanced individuals than most of today's skyjackers. They also know a great deal more about airplanes, firearms, hand-to-hand combat, and ways of overpowering and disarming sky pirates than the sky pirates themselves will ever know—except perhaps those sky pirates who have been especially trained in guerrilla camps and airplane mockups of their own.

Meet three fairly typical sky marshals who recently flew a fairly typical protected flight. (No single sky marshal is truly "typical," and this particular flight was aboard a 747 which still is novel and impressive enough to most people that it cannot really be described as typical. But soon it will be.)

First let it be said that we are not meeting these three men aboard the plane. They do not talk to each other while flying, they most certainly do not confide in passengers at any stage, and they make every effort to avoid being seen together under any circumstances other than the preflight briefing.

With that understood, we introduce ourselves to Goldberg, Larsen, and O'Shea, none of whom will recognize themselves under these names.

Goldberg is twenty-seven years old. He is, by trade, an aircraft mechanic with four years experience at JFK. He is about five foot ten, broad-shouldered, slightly shaggy-haired. He is single but engaged and lives in New York. His hobbies are gymnastics, skeet-shooting, and flying light planes.

Larsen, at forty-five, is the eldest of the three. He is a former Treasury man who spent twenty-five years as a Treasury enforcement officer. His home base is Baltimore, where he lives between assignments with his wife and two of their three children. In looks he is so ordinary as to be almost invisible, but if we observe closely we will realize that he is taller than he seems at first, is in extremely fine physical trim, and sometimes lets that gimlet-eyed T-man look flicker briefly over his face.

O'Shea is thirty-one, a college-educated former G.I. who put in his time with the Military Police. He is a chunky-looking man with gingery hair and an exuberant mustache. Like Larsen, he lives in the Baltimore area and is a family man.

"We've all had many previous flights," says Larsen. "Not many on 747s, but enough so we know our way around pretty well. We've all had extensive training on 707s and we've made numerous flights on those. Of course we always travel incognito, and we have to have convincing cover stories in case we get some chatty seatmate. This happens every once in a while. Your story's got to be good—people are still trying to play the game of 'spot the sky marshal.' In a way it's a drawback that a couple of us can't sit together and talk like businessmen traveling together so as to discourage anyone else from chiming in, but of course we can't do that. We've got to be in different parts of the plane. We could use more personnel. Maybe when the lady sky marshals come in we'll be able to double up once in a while. As it is, the number of sky marshals are spread too thin over the number of flights we have to cover. When the load is light, that's okay . . . but on a fully loaded 747, for example, three guys have got a lot to handle."

"On light flights we actually travel alone," Goldberg says. "It makes me feel kind of conspicuous, traveling alone. If there were any deadheading crew members on a flight—you know, our airline personnel—it would be good if they could ride with us, sit with us, to pose as a wife or at least a traveling companion to make our setup look more natural."

All agree to this, with some reservations. Maybe a passenger would recognize a "wife" as a stewardess from another flight. Still, they all like the idea in principle.

One wonders how, if they are to maintain anonymity at all times, they are able to make themselves known to the crew.

"We're briefed beforehand," Larsen explains. "We know in advance which flight we're supposed to take. We go to the service control unit for a briefing by the duty controller. He gives us the passenger load and the cargo load and the names of all the crewmen. Of course we don't write them down or anything like that. But we do know who the essential personnel are going to be. Then we ourselves are properly identified before the flight at a crew briefing. At the briefing the in-flight service director makes us known to all of the flight service crew. Our part of the briefing deals with setting up signals between ourselves and the crew so that we'll be able to communicate unobtrusively when any one of us becomes aware of any impending hijack attempt."

And what happens if someone does become aware of such a threat?

There is a pause. The three men look inscrutable.

"This is classified information," O'Shea says finally. "All we can say is that we have certain game plans worked out for various contingencies. We use hand signals for communication when necessary and we do have coded word clusters worked out for exchanging information. What do I mean by 'game plans'? Well, maybe there'll be some sort of prearranged action for the pilot to go into sharp turns and dives to throw the hijacker off-balance—*if* that sort of action seems practical under the circumstances. And other things . . . but I can't tell you any more than that."

"And that's plenty." Larsen looks slightly disapproving. "We can't give away our method of operations any more than we can give away our identity."

But how does a pilot or stewardess alert a security marshal of trouble?

"That's classified, too. But some of the more obvious signals might be to bring the marshal a drink he didn't order; give him a magazine he didn't want; pass a few magazines out to the passengers, and give the marshal his magazine upside down or with a napkin tucked inside, or a timetable, or a note. Or make a public announcement—say, a routine position report, and have a coded word to tip off the sky marshal, like, "Ladies and gentlemen, we are now passing over *Gunsmoke*, Wyoming. . ."

Can they tell us anything about their physical setup on the plane, such as where they sit and how much they can move around?

"I can tell you about the flight we just got off," says O'Shea. "But don't get the idea that we do exactly the same thing every time. On this flight, one of us sat toward the extreme rear of the airplane—I won't even tell you the row number—and another sat in the first class section near the stairs leading to the upper deck. The other one sat in the upstairs lounge and stayed there throughout the entire flight—lucky devil."

"Not so lucky," Goldberg disagreed. "It may be a cushy spot, but it's boring all the same. Especially on these long flights. That's about the toughest thing about these trips—the boredom. Obviously you can't get too engrossed in what you're reading, or anything like that, or talking to some chick, or you're simply not going to be alert. No matter where you sit, you've got this problem. You've heard about these guys complaining they've seen the same old movie a dozen times? I've never watched a movie. Pretended to, sure, but that's not what I'm paid to do. We've got to be on the ball."

"Right. It can get tough. We're not permitted to sleep at all, obviously. We've got to be awake throughout the flight. That trip we just got off of—we were on it for the round trip and we had a weather delay of over five hours, during which time we still had to be awake and alert. So we've actually been without sleep for about twenty-four hours."

"We don't get to move around much, either—any of us, not just the guy in the lounge. We have to be where the crew expects us to be. On the whole, the thing isn't very entertaining. I'll tell you—we're not supposed to have anything alcoholic on the flight, but we do take a drink once in a while. It doesn't look natural for a grown man to fly six or seven hours and drink nothing but coffee or Coke."

Can they tell us anything about what they're supposed to do if a hijacker does make a move?

"Not in detail. But, first off, not all of us would jump up and go into action if we see something start. Whoever is closest to the situation or spots it first acts alone, and the other two stay put just as if they were passengers. The reason for this is that if one hijacker makes a move, there may be one or more others elsewhere on the plane who are staying put and won't do a thing until they are ready to act. And when they're ready, we've got to be ready, too."

"Another thing—only if we have a really good opportunity, a perfect opportunity, to take the man off-guard when he first starts his action, do we make any kind of move at all. Then it's got to be something quick, like a karate chop or grabbing him from behind or tripping him up. In fact, that's always preferable action to gunfire. But ordinarily we would have to look very, very, very carefully, and wait and watch so that the time and the place would be right for us to try to subdue the hijacker. This could be one, two, three, four or more hours after the hijacker takes over the airplane."

"Right. As a matter of fact, on short flights of, say, half an hour, we wouldn't attempt to overpower the guy where there was any chance of endangering a life—except maybe his. But on a longer flight we would have a better chance. After a while when the hijacker sees that everything is going smoothly for him he tends to relax his vigilance. It may be a considerable length of time before any of us would act. But a long flight increases our chances of getting him with his guard down. Even then, of course, we've got to be extremely careful. There are ways we can get the guy, which we can't go into, but I'll say that if it looks like we cannot take a safe action, it's better to go where the man says than to endanger the passengers or the crew or the aircraft."

But you fellows are armed, are you not?

"Sure. We'll shoot if necessary, like when a situation gets so critical that that's about all you can do. Especially if we can get a clear shot right down the middle, as is sometimes possible."

You shoot to kill?

"We shoot to kill. But, you've got to understand, only as a last resort. This whole sky marshal program can be defeated if some young, insufficiently experienced, trigger-happy marshal would start some kind of unnecessary shoot-out in the air. If people get hurt, we'll undermine everything we're trying to do."

Each man states without prompting that the best deterrent to hijacking is to catch the potential hijacker on the ground. But they also agree that it would be reasonably easy for anybody to hijack an airplane provided he had made a study of it, knew what he was doing, and had a good plan of operation. The sky marshals think of themselves as the final filter in our anti-hijacking system. They do feel that they are necessary, and that there should be many more of them. They know that some day they will be phased out, and they hope that in the meantime they will have become unnecessary, but until such time as better solutions are found they hope to stay on the job.

To a man, they insist that appropriate background experience, a cool head, thorough training, and a willingness to keep on learning must be the profile of the sky marshal. These men have been given extensive training on the airplanes which they ride, and yet they continue to talk from time to time with the pilots to learn as much more as possible about the working parts of the airplane. They are primarily concerned about people, but they are also concerned about the plane, and one senses in them a willingness to sacrifice themselves when it comes to the crunch. They are always concerned with the possibility that a pistol or hand grenade or some other form of explosive will go off in the wrong part of the plane and interfere with the workings of the craft. This cannot be allowed to happen. They will do their best to see that it will not.

One thing we would like to see, as long as we are going to have a sky marshal force, is a little more care in the deploying of it. Sure, oversights and errors are bound to creep into the best of programs, but we really cannot afford to have many of them in the air. Take, for example, an incident in Teheran, Iran, back in December, 1970. There had been plenty of skyjackings in the previous weeks, and the world was rife with rumors and warnings that skyjackers might be planning to board here, there, or anywhere. So, at the Teheran Mehrabad Airport that day, the stewardess was very glad when the pair of sky marshals she'd met at the pre-flight briefing boarded the 707 jetliner. It made her feel secure. She was less pleased when a couple of suspicious-looking characters came aboard. Somehow she got the feeling that they were armed. So, quietly, she made her suspicions known to the sky marshals. Since the plane was still at the boarding ramp they could afford to act immediately. Just a little discreet inquiry first, and then, lower the boom. . . . But—the men who had seemed to be acting suspiciously were sky marshals too! Through a scheduling mixup. . . . Well, no need to go on. One set got off the jet, and that is the end of the story. But it does suggest a little oversight somewhere.

Whatever the flaws in the current onboard anti-hijacking system and whatever the alleged faults of some of the sky marshals, doubtless the sky itself is much less of a haven for the skyjacker than it used to be. The man who passes the ground barriers and pulls a gun on a crew member is no longer sure, no matter how determined he may be, that he has found safe passage.

Nor is he sure of a haven when the trip is over. He started finding this out long before there was serious international discussion about extradition or point-of-landing punishment for the successful hijacker.

The Six Who Came Back . . . and Other Stories

It seems that life in the Cuban cane fields is not so sweet after all.

Neither is life in a Cuban jail. Nor is job-hunting in a Cuban city.

On November 1, 1969, six Americans wanted for separate airplane hijackings sailed into Montreal on the Cuban freighter *Luis Arces Bergnes*. One of the men brought with him a little girl, his daughter Jennifer. All had apparently left Cuba on their own volition, and all were apparently fully aware that the charges of air piracy and kidnapping carry heavy sentences.

At Montreal they asked Canadian authorities to escort them to the international border at Champlain. On the following day they were rearraigned at Plattsburgh, New York, turned over to United States marshals, and jailed in lieu of bail.

They were "fed up" with Cuba and wanted to return despite the consequences. Each had fled the United States for a different reason: job problems, marital difficulties, emotional instability, disenchantment with life in the United States; and each came back for the same reason: disenchantment with Cuba.

We have met a couple of these men before. Now let us meet them all.

Thomas J. Boynton of Kalamazoo, Michigan, lost his job as a researcher at the Fort Custer Job Corps Center in January, 1968. A month before that, his wife had filed for divorce. On February 17, he hired a small charter plane in Marathon in the Florida Keys and hijacked it, at gunpoint, to Havana.

Thomas George Washington, an unemployed Philadelphia chemist, took his daughter for a walk on December 19, 1968, and boarded an Eastern Air Lines Philadelphia-to-Miami flight which he diverted to Cuba.

Ronald T. Bohle of Michigan City, Indiana, a promising young student, used a knife to divert an Eastern Air Lines craft from its Miami-to-Nassau flight plan and forced it down in Cuba. It landed there on January 9, 1969.

Robert L. Sandlin of Vernon, Texas, not yet twenty at the time of his departure, skyjacked a Delta Air Lines plane scheduled from Dallas to Charleston, South Carolina, on March 17, 1969. The plane touched down at José Martí Airport almost simultaneously with one that had been hijacked from Peru. Young Sandlin and the Peruvian hijackers promptly got together at the airport restaurant and compared notes.

Raymond L. Anthony, unsuccessful and reportedly heavy-drinking car salesman of Baltimore, used a pocket knife to force an Eastern Air Lines Baltimore-to-Miami flight to take him to Havana on June 28, 1969.

Joseph C. Crawford of St. Simons Island, Georgia, boarded a Continental Air Lines flight at El Paso, Texas, on July 26, 1969. The aircraft was scheduled to fly from Los Angeles to Lubbock, Texas, but Crawford wanted to go to Cuba.

Boynton had gone with high hopes of finding a new life and a way of putting his talents to work. Instead, he was used as a common laborer. He did not like the climate, he did not like the food, he could not stand the work for which he was heavily overqualified as a sociologist, and he felt virtually imprisoned. Indeed, he *was* imprisoned from time to time. The Cuban authorities did not altogether trust him, and suspected that he might be CIA agent or something of the sort. Thomas Washington, in his turn, managed to get himself a fairly satisfactory job for a while at least, but decided that Cuba was no place to bring up a child. Between the lines of the little he said upon his return was the suggestion that Cuba is no less racist than the United States.

Ronald Bohle had wanted to move to another society where he could start afresh. He was well received in Cuba at first but was later held in a political prison for several months. Robert Lee Sandlin spent his first six months in Cuba in a jail, confined to a cell block with a number of other Americans. Raymond Anthony reported on his return that Cuba is a "terrible and horrible place," from which he was only too happy to return. His daughter described him as a sick man, emotionally and physically, who sorely needed help. We know nothing of Joseph Crawford's reasons for hijacking or returning; but return he did.

These are not the only hijackers who have returned. How they managed to get out of Cuba is not precisely known. The United States had no direct role in their release. It is probable, though, that "general diplomatic efforts" undertaken through the Swiss have somewhat eased the path of some hijackers wishing to return; they have come back through Canada, Algeria, Spain, Berlin, through many a point in Africa, Europe, or the Americas that they have reached in the course of their wanderings away from Cuba. Alben Barkley Truitt came back. So did Willis Jessie. Also James Oeth and Charles Healy, Leonard Bendicks, Lorenzo C. Ervin, Lawrence Rhodes, and former Green Beret Robert McRae Helmey. And others, still being counted.

It was once thought the United States would be helpless against our particular breed of hijackers unless Castro were to send some of them back in disgrace. In 1969, we discovered that his diplomatic cooperation was not absolutely necessary. It seems that the Cuban experience—for hijackers—is its own worst advertisement.

Alben Truitt, who hijacked a small chartered craft from Florida to Cuba in October, 1968, was among the first to suggest that the Cuban hijack haven was no bed of roses. He was under arrest in Cuba until January, 1969, when he was put aboard a ship bound for France. He left the ship at St. John, New Brunswick, and was arrested at the border at Champlain. According to him, Cuba treats hijackers as undesirables rather than as heroes. Perhaps there are exceptions. But, as he said: "Some, I was told by people of the Department of State Security, were imprisoned immediately. Others, I was told, were sent to work camps."

This turned out to be a typical observation. As Dr. Dailey of the FAA puts it, "When some of the hijackers started coming back, many of them said things that indicated that going to Cuba was a very poor way of trying to solve their personal problems. They also revealed that hijackers, when they got to Cuba, were often jailed. They ended up doing very hard manual, physical labor, like cane-cutting."

Swiss diplomat Alfred Fischle, who served as ambassador to Cuba for four years, added his own brief comment when he arrived in Mexico City on a new assignment at the end of January, 1971. He stated that plane hijackers are not well received in Cuba. "They are sent to prison or to mental hospitals." (Which usually happens to them in the United States. We just don't go in so much for cutting cane . . . and working on the chain gang is no longer the fashion.)

A bilateral agreement between the United States and Cuba would seem to be a very useful measure. At its simplest, we could agree to do a trade-off of some hijackers and guarantee to prosecute the others. In regard to a future, better understanding with the Castro government, Dr. Dailey has this to say: "I am hopeful that Castro is fed up with hijackers. There are conversations about a possible bilateral agreement under the terms of the Cuban anti-hijack law. About a year ago [as of October, 1970] they passed a law making hijacking a crime against Cuban law. This decree called for negotiating bilateral agreements with other countries for the return or punishing of hijackers. We made a very thorough study of the terms of that decree, and it is our judgment that it is pretty favorable to us—in that, if we have an agreement, we would have to return very few Cuban hijackers and they would have to return almost all of the U.S. hijackers to us. We don't feel under any circumstances that they would send back a Cuban citizen, but that under the agreement they would have to punish them if they didn't send them back. And we do know that even without the agreement they are punishing Cubans who go back—they are prosecuting them."

In fact, without the agreement, they have already sent us back, *through direct channels*, one American hijacker whom they did not want. They found him extremely undesirable, and told us so; we found him mentally incompetent. Robert Labadie is in a mental institution.

There are other suggestions that Cuba is no haven for those who are disaffected with the United States, even when they hijack for "personal-political" reasons. It may be presumed that Castro would enjoy receiving people who are self-proclaimed enemies of the United States, and perhaps in the beginning he did relish the opportunity to poke a finger in Uncle Sam's eye. He may, even yet, encourage or condone Latin American guerrilla activity, including hijacking, that helps to cement relations between the various Latin American guerrilla groups and eats into the hearts of "oppressive" reigning governments or "unjust orders." But we cannot be sure even of this: many signs indicate that Castro has no wish to protect any kind of hijacker.

His disposition toward Black Panthers and other black militants is not particularly friendly. During 1969, when there must have been quite a little colony of American blacks in Cuba, reports kept leaking out that the quality of brotherhood in Castro's country was distinctly strained. Blacks, including Cleaver himself, seemed to be bitterly disappointed. One who made his position very clear was Raymond Johnson.

Remember Raymond Johnson? He was the somewhat unsavory, self-styled Black Nationalist freedom fighter who hijacked the National Airlines flight on November 4, 1968, and whiled away his time directing the stewardess to collect cash from the passengers.

By June 25, 1969, he had apparently become just as disenchanted with Cuba as he had earlier been with the United States. In an interview to reporters in Havana, he complained that American black militants had not been treated as the revolutionaries they felt themselves to be—that Castro did not appreciate their revolutionary spirit. Worse: The blacks were literally isolated and imprisoned in Cuba. They had no freedom of movement, and though they sought to settle down and work as part of Cuban society and the Cuban system of socialism, they were not permitted to use their talents and rise to positions of importance. They were even subjected to arrest if they dared to offer criticisms of life in the Cuban paradise.

Worse yet: Castro was mistreating blacks *as blacks*. The Castro regime was racist. Blacks were being made to feel like slaves.

Possibly Johnson was only expressing his personal dissatisfaction. Maybe Cuban officials remembered him as a petty skywayman. Yet it is unlikely that he would have been permitted by his fellow Panthers, and least of all leader Eldridge Cleaver, to air his complaints unless they reflected general feeling among Panthers about life in Cuba for black militants. It is also unlikely that he would have asked, as he did, that Panthers in the United States should stage protests at the Cuban Mission to the United Nations on behalf of Panthers in Cuba, unless he had been given the go-ahead by Cleaver.

We have never suggested that there has been anything conspiratorial about Panther hijackings to Cuba. They have been, we feel sure, individual efforts. Yet it is a fact that since Cleaver publicly changed his mind about Cuba and traveled on to seek a better atmosphere in Algeria, there has been very little black militant hijacking to Cuba. It cannot be stated flatly that there is a real relationship, but some sort of relationship seems to be there. Word gets around. Castro is not soft on Panthers.

This in itself is a deterrent to some hijackings. There is another: the prospect of the law getting its firm hands on the hijacker who gets caught or otherwise reaches the end of his rope.

The Greatest Deterrent of All?

Severe punishment may not be the answer. Nevertheless would-be hijackers would do well to remind themselves that their eventual haven is very likely to be prison.

The "six who came back" were sentenced as follows:

Thomas J. Boynton—twenty years.

Thomas G. Washington—two years; other charges still pending in Philadelphia.

Ronald T. Bohle—twenty-five years.

Joseph C. Crawford—fifty years. At the time of his conviction on September 14, 1970, this was the stiffest sentence meted out.

Raymond L. Anthony—fifteen years.

Robert L. Sandlin—committed to a mental institution.

It is not an inspiring future for the skyjacker, nor for the individual who is thinking of planning a skyjacking caper.

Sentences have also been passed in other lands. These have ranged from small fines to fifteen years in labor camp to twenty-five years imprisonment to summary execution. We will comment no more on them. It is enough to cite a few other typical examples from the American list of convictions for U.S. piracy. If these fail to make a point, no more detailed list will succeed.*

Bruce Britt—twenty years.

Leon Bearden—twenty years.

Cody Bearden—correctional school.

David Healy—twenty years.

Leonard Oeth—twenty years.

Thomas Robinson—correctional school.

Willis Jessie—ten years.

Alben Truitt—twenty years.

Oran Richards—committed to a mental institution.

Lorenzo Ervin—life imprisonment.

Anton Funjek—twenty-five years.

John J. Di Vivo—committed suicide in jail.

Many other sentences have been passed; many are pending; many mental examinations are still being held. Once in a great while the sentence is light, and once in an even greater while, the defendant is acquitted or prosecution is declined.

But the trend today is toward increasingly stiff sentences, and it is very seldom that the skyjacker finds a haven in an American court, any more than he finds one in Cuba.

No haven anywhere . . . ? It is a comforting thought for the hijack-weary public, so far as it goes. Fortunately for us, most of the world's hijackers are amateurs who hijack for purely

* The crimes of these individuals are listed in the Chronology, Appendix A.

personal reasons and generally lack both planning ability and skill with weapons. These people usually are looking for a haven in the commonly accepted sense of the word. They hardly ever find it, either because it never existed for them or because we have learned how to snatch it out of their grasp.

But for other people there is another type of haven, one that cannot be defined as a place so much as an ideal or the fulfillment of a cause. Their haven is the realization of a dream or one small fragment of a dream. How can we extradite a guerrilla-hijacker from his dream-haven on a desert landing strip 1,000 miles from nowhere? What country is responsible for the man or woman without a country? What fanatic will be deterred by the threat that he has no place to go?

We have a fairly strong anti-hijack program now, as do some other countries, and the present dip in the hijacking graph indicates that it is effective . . . when all systems are operative. We realize that the old-time hijackings are on their way out, and will probably fade out almost altogether unless we get smug and careless. But there are still loopholes in our system, and in a way even larger loopholes than before because *American* hijackings have become inextricably tied in with *international* hijackings. Our aircraft may be targets wherever they fly; and our citizens are vulnerable whether they fly on American planes or on flag carriers representing virtually every other country in the world.

There is still opportunity for the demented, suicidal human being to take to the sky with gun or plastic bomb in hand. There are still people who feel imprisoned and enslaved in their own land, and who know no other way of getting out than commandeering a plane. There is still scope, and plenty of it, for guerrilla or other activist groups to extend their battle plans into new air space and down onto new soil. The professionals and their apprentices have not yet given up.

How much opportunity do these people have? Maybe the experts can answer that. Now is the time, while we have some breathing space between hijacking streaks, to assess our present anti-hijack program in terms of what it has accomplished so far and what it may have to cope with in the future.

10 / WE'VE COME A LONG WAY, BUT ...

Let us postulate a round-table discussion among several people who have probably never participated in such a discussion, though some have met each other, but would surely make a good conversational team. (Some will talk more than others, as is usually the way.) The participants are Dr. John T. Dailey of the Federal Aviation Administration; Frank Cardman, director of security, Pan American World Airways; Captain Charles H. Ruby, past president of the Air Line Pilots Association; Knut Hammarskjöld, director general of the International Air Transport Association; General Benjamin O. Davis Jr., director of Civil Aviation Security for the Department of Transportation; an airline publicity officer who prefers not to be named and to whom we shall refer as the "P.O."; and a high-echelon official of a federal investigative agency who similarly prefers anonymity and whom we shall call the FIA man. Their comments have been garnered from personal interviews and telephone conversations with the author and from public statements and official documents. The subject of the discussion is the effectiveness of our current security posture in the light of today's events, and what we can expect to see in the hijacking picture of tomorrow.

The P.O., something of a cynic although he is an industry man to the core, is the one with the most questions and the fewest answers. It is he who starts the conversational ball rolling.

The P.O.: "Do you gentlemen really think our anti-hijacking system is effective? That it's good enough?

Cardman: ". . . Let me put it this way. What we've got now is a fairly good posture. Dealing with hijackers and sabotage is a question of keeping the wrong things and the wrong people off airplanes. And in keeping the wrong people off airplanes, you've got to realize the problems are inherent and stem from the fact that, in the first instance, a passenger with a properly purchased and validated ticket has a right to board an airplane. You go from there to the question of qualifying that man as a potential threat, or not qualifying him. Now, the FAA's screening program, largely headed up by Dr. Reighard and Dr. Dailey, has tremendously reduced the number of hijackings out of this country, primarily to Cuba. Evidence of this lies not only in the leveling-off rate, but is to be found in such simple things as the experience of airlines in which a whole host of devices—knives, guns, and so on—have been found after having been thrown or stashed away before passengers board aircraft.

"The program has been a good one and I think it should continue. As far as magnetometers are concerned, the technique is improving constantly, and the behavorial profile program is constantly under review. It's being updated as rapidly as possible, and it's being extended to take care of individual characteristics by study in foreign areas where characteristics are different—this, of course, in the light of various types of threats, such as the Middle East threat, which to some degree is different from our own.

"In consequence of the September 6, 1970, hijackings, a whole new dimension was put on the problem. We had witness to the first taking of hostages for severe and serious political purposes. As a result, two things happened: In the United States, we had the instant mounting of the U.S. air guard program where flying marshals are aboard aircraft—on certain international aircraft and in certain segments of domestic operations. Then, customs came in to help with the searching of in-cabin baggage carried by passengers. This, combined with the behavioral profile program and the magnetometers, substantially lowered the threat of in-aircraft hijackings—in not letting the wrong people get aboard the craft."

Dr. Dailey: "We do think that approach has been effective; the level of hijacking has been reduced. But in the evolution of hijacking, the thing is evolving in all directions and we don't know what the future is going to hold. But it is quite probable that it won't be at all what we had in the past, where it was a stream of planes going to Cuba. I'm quite hopeful that the Cuban thing now may really settle down, on several grounds . . . one, our own anti-hijack system, two, they're finding a lot of other places to go, and three, Cuba doesn't seem to want them and actually sent one hijacker back under circumstances that would seem to me to be very deterrent. . . . Of course, while the United States rate slowed down, the foreign incidence began to accelerate at a pretty fast rate—largely people looking for asylum. I would think that an agreement about the return and/or punishment of hijackers would be a strong additional deterrent."

The P.O.: "My understanding of our present anti-hijack posture is that it is largely psychological—from signs at the airport to magnetometers to the behavioral profile and even to the sky marshals. Is more publicity the answer—or less? And what is your view of the value of sky marshals?"

Dr. Dailey: "We *have* taken a psychological approach, and obviously the media have to play a very important part. There must be a right way of publicizing the profile, the sky marshals and the other measures to the right people—the people who might be contemplating a hijacking—so that it gives them the image that they might fail in their attempt, that they might be caught if they try. Our thought here is that if we are really successful in this we will never catch anybody, because they'll be afraid to try and therefore won't try; but that if they do try, to make every effort to catch as many as possible . . . knowing that we can't catch all of them. Some are bound to slip through the screen. No matter what, even if your policy were one hundred percent search, after a couple of weeks people would let down and be careless and there would still be some of them that would get through.

"This is like anti-submarine or anti-aircraft warfare. What you try to do is put as many obstacles as possible there to raise the risk of failure as high as you can. Then, in addition—and I want to stress this—through the use of public information to make this as vivid as possible to the right people so they would perceive these obstacles as maximally discouraging. The final thing is, if they get through the screen, to do something about it and try to terminate some of the hijackings in the air. This is what the air guards are for—the last line of defense."

General Davis: "I believe very strongly that what goes on in people's minds has an awful lot to do with what people do, and that there is a deterrent effect in our strong stand and in the press spreading the word about the fact that you have armed sky marshals aboard aircraft—that Cardman is taking very careful precautions there at JFK and Frankfurt and other places. I think that you get the impression from Dailey that certain types of hijackers are not very strong people. Those people are dissuaded. Of course, when you get down to the terrorists, they are strong people, and that is something else again. Still and all, if you didn't have any guards in banks you'd have a helluva lot more bank robberies than you have today, and that's what I mean—deterrent action."

The P.O.: "But isn't the sky marshal program risky? Couldn't it create a disaster in the air in the shape of a bloody gun battle? Or would you say that the disaster is already in the air once the skyjacker is up there?"

Davis: "There has always been the possibility of a gun battle when you have a hijacker standing in the cockpit with a gun at somebody's head. The sky marshal is a carefully selected, thoroughly trained, mature individual who is concerned primarily with the safety of the airplane and the passengers. He is not going to try to stop a hijacking by destroying the airplane or killing passengers."

Captain Ruby: "In my view, the sky marshal program is a very strong deterrent. I don't know of but one instance where a so-called sky marshal has been exposed to identification. So, really, they are not identifiable per se, they're just another passenger. And until we get the complete world set up with adequate screening equipment for pre-boarding, not only for passengers but also mail cargo and anything that is put aboard the airplane, it's our view that the sky marshal is the best interim solution to the problem. And when I speak of interim I mean just that—because you can put manpower aboard airplanes much faster than you can put sophisticated ground equipment in every place that it is needed and do an effective pre-boarding screening job. With our volume problem, this is about the only way it can be dealt with at this time. Our overall use of air transportation, inside the United States as well as international, is of such a total crush it just takes a long time to produce all the necessary equipment it takes to do the job. In the United States we've got about five hundred airports that have to be dealt with."

The P.O.: "Suppose we do eventually get all the equipment and personnel we need, having somehow found the money to set them into operation, it seems to me that we would still be vulnerable to the professional hijacker. I'm sure we're deterring a lot of amateurs right now—I know we are—but I'm not so sure that the system we have is going to be effective against professional teams, organized groups such as the PFLP."

Cardman: "You can't protect yourself one hundred percent, not against a quasi-military operation. That's not what we're trying to do. Oh, we're trying to do that, too, through the Middle East, and we've been thoroughly successful. You'd be amazed how many people we've kept off airplanes who *were* professionals, who were politically charged with taking an airplane away. There's a lot of that. We've turned back an awful lot of people who didn't want to confront the simple procedure of going through the screening system and boarding an airplane, knowing that they weren't equipped to handle it—although they were professionals. We've seen guys take off on us like ruptured ducks when they saw what they were going to have to get through in order to board our aircraft. But, short of a military operation, short of a total military posture on the part of an aircraft, its owners and its operators, you can't keep every hijacker in the world off an aircraft. Definitely not. You can reduce it to minimums, which minimums become acceptable.

"I would say that ninety per cent of the world's hijackers are nonprofessional in the sense that they do not have military backup or capability. These are people who can be sorted out to a reasonable degree with our present programming, and as technological development goes further down the road we'll be able to sort them out even more—I can assure you of that!"

The P.O.: "What do you mean by 'acceptable minimums'?"

Cardman: "If you get back to the early days of aviation, the thing that made international aviation possible was the four-engine airplane, because a four-engine airplane reduced the risk factor to acceptable minimums, in regard to passengers, operators, investors, and the general public. Now, that's not to say that you can't lose three or four engines. You can. But you reduce the entire proposal to acceptable minimal levels of risk in terms of business and pilots and what have you. Now, one of the problems of security is the constant endless conflict between being secure and facilitating the movement of passengers and goods, which is the single largest justification for air transport. I think what we're working toward is reducing the entire hazard to those minimal acceptable levels of risk.

"Now, we're willing to spend a great deal of money on security, no question about it. But there has to be a hard evaluation as to where and when your risks lie. The object of security is to meet the threat by a proper evaluation of where and when, never losing sight of the fact that you've got to move airplanes and people. Security must be flexible."

The P.O.: "But some airlines have been notoriously lax. What they've been doing, they've been weighing their financial self-interest against the likelihood of being hit by hijackings, and then deciding that they can more easily afford a few hijackings than pay to put the detection system into operation. Of course, it isn't wholly an airline problem. Government has to help. It seems to me that everybody's letting down a little bit lately—particularly those who never did anything in the first place, probably because we're going through some kind of lull. Does anyone think that this hijacking thing is going to peter out?"

The FIA man: "Oh, no. It won't peter out unless you people at the airlines get your hand into your pocket and start spending some money. You've been waiting for Uncle Sam to finance all these preventive measures and let somebody else . . . I saw something today that, of the major airlines, there's only one or two that have put screening things in their terminals. Most of them have got a few in some terminals, and six of the airlines don't have *any yet*. And they're waiting for someone to pay for them, I guess, and I don't see why Uncle Sam should do that."

The P.O.: "Well, it's kind of a hard line to draw, particularly with an international carrier. Of course, government agencies think that the airlines should pay for it and the airlines think that government should bear a good part of the burden. After all, the seizures of our aircraft are not attacks upon the airlines or their passengers, as such. Many of them are, directly and indirectly, attacks on government policies. I believe it is the position of the Air Transport Association, for example, that this whole thing has now become a government problem. The major thrust of the threat today is professional, it is political. It's international blackmail. So it's a problem for governments to solve. Certainly, a lot of airlines agree on this.

"On the other hand, you have someone like the managing director of Munich Airport accusing the airlines of the world of complacency and carelessness. He has been known to say that the airlines against which the attacks are directed should be the people most concerned about the introduction of security measures, but that they have taken hardly any action to protect their aircraft and their passengers. . ."

Hammarskjöld: "The airlines are actually the most vulnerable line of defense. Today, I think they are doing enough. The only way to stop hijacking is for all governments to extradite the hijackers to the country of the airline concerned or to punish them severely at the point of landing. The cause of continued hijackings is the failure of many governments to fulfill their responsibilities in this respect—including some governments who, although they have punished the hijackers, have awarded such light sentences that they have no deterrent effect. The individual states are, or should be, responsible for the safety and welfare of their inhabitants."

Ruby: "Personally, I'm highly critical of the courts for not always imposing anything from long prison terms to death penalties for persons who are caught and found guilty. I'm dead set against a police state, but maybe that's better than . . . ? It's my judgment that the governments of the world should bear down, and let people know they're not going to get away with it. As for extradition of hijackers, they should be returned to the country that is responsible for the operation of the aircraft. For example, suppose Pan Am leased an aircraft to the British. Then, the hijacker should be returned to the U.K. for trial. Or if it is a Pan Am plane operating, say, between Beirut and Bangkok, the hijacker ought to be returned to the United States for trial."

The P.O.: "I couldn't agree more, but that's government responsibility on an international level. For the moment, I am thinking more of costs and local responsibilities. We heard a while ago that only one or two of the major airlines are really doing anything at all to protect their customers. Now, I'm very much against any kind of foot-dragging, but I would like to point up two things: One, airline costs have been going up and up and up, and airline income has been going down—deep down into the red in many cases. Security equipment and procedures, boarding delays and so on, these cost money. The money just isn't all that readily available. Two, I wouldn't want to split hairs, but I would say that better than just one or two U.S. airline companies have put security systems and equipment into effect. There are twelve major U.S. carriers. Three of these—the biggest and the best, with the most to lose—have very fine security operations. Two others have a fairly good setup; they cover their high-risk areas pretty well. Another two are just fair, and about four or five of them, I would say, are definitely lax; they have done literally nothing. Without excusing them I would say that their hijack record has not been bad. They do not as a rule fly the high-risk routes. I would very definitely say that more security has *got* to come from somewhere—the airlines must be more vigilant, and the governments ought to do more to protect their citizens."

Cardman: "You have to break down security into those two broad categories: the obligation of government, obviously airport authorities, and the obligation of the industry itself for air carrier security. I think prior to the time when we lost the Swissair aircraft and the Austrian aircraft it was generally felt that the responsibility was almost exclusively that of the operators. Governments were considerably less involved, particularly the airport authorities. They have, now, become more involved, though not to the degree that I think they should. I'm not satisfied that governments are doing all they can at the airport level.

"For example, protection for aircraft parked in government areas—that is, in a terminal complex—and ramp-site protection in terms of patrol and strike force capability in order to make certain that those in and around aircraft, or servicing aircraft, are qualified to be there.

"These are two of the areas. Perimeter control around airports in the general broad context of security is something they haven't done much about. And one of the most important things that governments haven't approached really adequately is the question of identification systems. They are doing more than they were, but still not as much as they should. . . . One of the key things in getting a permanently increased security posture is to understand that it is going to cost money. And in the ultimate, the airlines will have to pay for it, I suppose. But, while the airlines are prepared to pay their proper part of the user charges, landing fees, et cetera, I think security is in many respects a pure government obligation. They should assume a greater responsibility—including costs."

The P.O.: "*And* legislation? For example, what about countries that simply do not have laws to deal with hijacking, or air piracy? They have to try skyjackers for kidnapping, illegal possession of weapons, 'deprivation of liberty' of the passengers, coercion of the pilot, illegal entry into the country, and so on. These, except for kidnapping, are lesser crimes and they often draw only token punishment in certain countries. Governments could and should do much more in this area."

Hammarskjöld: "Here you get to the very core of the problem, and this is where, since 1968, we [IATA] have been trying to push and concentrate our efforts. This whole activity—hijacking—has been made possible because of the absence of legislation. When aviation started to develop after the war, everything was covered by law—the technical aspects, the commercial aspects—but they completely forgot the criminal side of it. This is not only international, but also national. In many countries, when the hijacking problem gets to them, the court has no law for it.

"Some time ago you had a case of an Algerian aircraft going to Yugoslavia. The Yugoslavs were very firm, but they had no law to apply. But I think they finally extradited the hijackers in such a way that they got into the hands of the Algerians again, and now they are in custody. The Turks discovered that *they* had no law when they got a case. Now there *is* a law in Yugoslavia; there is a law in Turkey; and the Japanese, after the Korean case, immediately made a law. So this is now coming, not fast enough in my mind, but it is coming. From this point of view, the spread of hijacking has been very good. More and more governments are getting enlightened. They admit that 'this can happen to us.' Some rather civilized countries just closed their eyes to it until they got very close to the matter. They just said, 'This is political business.' But there are now countries which have declared by national law that any hijacking, whatever the reason for it, is a crime of nonpolitical nature. I read again yesterday of a country having adopted this as their national decision, and this, I think, is right."

Ruby: "Yes, an act against an aircraft is a crime. It is not a political act. Fortunately, the Russians and the United States agreed on that at the ICAO meeting in the Hague not long after Russia joined ICAO—that such acts be classified as criminal offenses, as common crimes, and not related to requests for political asylum. This is the first step that I've seen from the two biggest powers that makes sense on how to deal with hijackers.

"The existence of complete international agreement for extradition and severe penalty for those who are caught and found guilty would be a tremendous deterrent—because if anyone has the idea that they can divert an aircraft to some so-called safe haven, naturally, they're going to do it. So the world community is going to have to take cognizance of this fact and deal with it accordingly, and by this I mean all countries of the world, not just some of them."

The P.O.: "Something that we are going to have to live with for a while is the question of whether or not it is ever legitimate to skyjack a plane, as for example when that is the only way to escape injustice and repression in the home country. In all humanity, we must give some thought to motivation. The difficulty of course is that, though motivations differ and we feel more sympathy for some hijackers than we do for other hijackers, methods differ very little. Every hijacking, no matter why it is committed, is a crime against passengers, crew, and airline company. Are we going to set a double standard and say that some hijackings are not as bad as others? I don't see how we can. And yet the idea of political asylum is practically sacred. It is going to be difficult to reconcile these two opposing viewpoints: sanctuary for those in need; no asylum for the skyjacker."

Hammarskjöld: "My philosophy is that there *is* the element of political asylum which is so holy in certain countries that you cannot touch it, because if you try, this wrecks your whole effort. So my philosophy is that either people have to be extradited or they have to be punished. If the government takes upon itself the responsibility of not extraditing them, then it must take the responsibility for punishment. And I think this is now being accepted. Only the Egyptians, the same as some other Arabs ... they are only to a limited extent masters in their own house, the Egyptians perhaps more so than the Jordanians. And there are certain things they can do and others that they don't dare."

The P.O.: "Yes, they are in a peculiarly difficult position. But as to the general picture of hijacking and other threats against civil aviation—has the overall pattern changed? What is our main concern for the 1970s?"

Cardman: "I think we will have the hijacking threat pretty well solved in the very near future. When I say 'solved,' I mean reduced to absolute minimums to the point where we can operate with comfort. Sabotage is with us for another three or four years—maybe five. Security will turn more and more toward antisabotage."

Davis: "Both hijacking *and* sabotage are part of the world pattern of violence and transgressions against the law that, in the main, are exemplified by the kidnapping actions in Uruguay and the FLPQ in Quebec. I personally feel that we require in this country—and in all countries—a very strong wall of defense that takes into consideration the threat of sabotage, of political terrorism that would seek on the part of interested people to bring world attention to a particular cause. To put it briefly, though there have been fewer hijackings lately, I still don't think it's under control. I wish it were. I wish I had the confidence that some people do have in the recent statistics. I believe very strongly that President Nixon took a firm stand last September [1970], which is responsible for the decrease in the incidents of hijackings. Unless the pressure is kept on, as Secretary Volpe has pointed out, that vigilance really is going to be the only thing that is going to keep us out of trouble in the future. I just can't believe that if you open a door wide, that somebody isn't going to walk in.

"In the case of two or three airlines, they are probably very, very effective in watching over their property and being very careful in their security operations, and doing the things that their management should do to protect themselves. But this is not the case throughout the industry. And it is this type of opportunity for hijackers that I am worried about.

"If you look at world events, you will find that things like hijackings, like assaults against constitutional authority, and the very strong increase in violence in itself, come right along together. Hijacking is part of the pattern. . . . Until everybody gets to understanding that mass violence, or violence against large numbers of people and valuable property, is not going to be acceptable, we stand in danger."

The P.O.: "If I may bring up the question of costs again—we are locked into a darn tight economic situation. The airlines have been losing money; the traffic forecasts haven't been up. How does this play a part?"

Davis: "It plays a big part without any question whatsoever. However, I myself divide the subject into more than one big part. Passenger screening of the type the FAA has strongly endorsed, and that we recommend very, very highly to all of the airlines, costs very little. It's really very slight in cost. Now when you get into building fences, developing segregated areas, restricting the movement of employees at an airport and all those other things that represent a higher plane of security, then you are running into the face of economics. I myself think that a tremendous lot can be done without economics really being involved that isn't done in a lot of places—but I do recognize that some of the things that we'd like to see done will take several years. All that I'd urge, frankly, is that we get on with it at least from the standpoint of planning and programming. . . .

"Everybody is trying to uncover promising technological leads. We ought to do that without any question. But for today and tomorrow we have a magnetometer that is within price range that can be bought. When you run into some of the more exotic and expensive appliances, it ought to take a long time before you decide what you are going to buy and what you are going to recommend to the airlines. What we need today is an *attitude of awareness* that we have a continuing problem."

The P.O.: "I think we have that attitude of awareness on the part of Cardman, and Fenello of Eastern. If we had a Cardman or Fenello in each airline, with the confidence of airline management, we'd be a long way ahead of where we are now.

But I think that that attitude of awareness is contagious—as contagious as hijacking seems to be. We were a bit slow getting started, but I am encouraged by the fact that the industry has established a network of intelligence on the subject of hijacking. The network includes double agents, pilots who have been exiled, prisoners in federal prisons, and a whole string of law enforcement and investigative agencies."

The FIA man: "We are a part of that. We do have informants in a lot of so-called subversive-type groups. It's not for the sole purpose of thwarting hijackings, of course—it's just a usual part of our intelligence coverage of these groups."

"The P.O.: "But useful to the airlines nevertheless. It helps us keep abreast of the changing scene. We can't just sit around and wait for things to happen. We have to be watching trends and trying to predict what may happen in the future. I know that Dr. Dailey considers that an important part of the FAA program is information acquisition and analysis. We have to know not only what the threat is but what it is *likely* to be."

Dr. Dailey: "We know that the past isn't necessarily going to repeat itself. We base our estimates on what the threat is and where it is likely to come from partly on past statistical studies but primarily on the up-to-date intelligence information we get. We realize that our system has to be changed as appropriate, as the nature of the phenomenon changes, and intelligence—that is, information acquisition and analysis—is a very important part of that. And we have seen a very great alteration in the pattern of events since we started."

The P.O.: "What about IATA? Does it have its own intelligence system or security force?"

Hammarskjöld: "Yes and no. We have a security office which is dealing with defense against aggression, defense against property loss, and what we call fraud prevention. This office has spent almost all its time on hijacking problems. We have a worldwide network of communications and information. We work through our members, our IATA members, through the chief security officers of strategically placed airlines. They are in constant touch with us on our behalf, and we coordinate. They, in turn, are of course in contact with the police and different forces in their areas. And also we work very closely with Interpol."

The P.O.: "Does anyone here have any particular fears or predictions for the future? I myself live in dread of the day when one of the jumbo jets, or perhaps even an SST, gets blown out of the sky with hundreds of people aboard. It could be the result of some maniacal act—either deliberate, or a terrible accident. Or it could be the result of an airborne takeover. For example, say a PFLP group in a pursuit plane tries to force a commercial airliner to the ground under threat of blowing it out of the sky. The airliner could crash as a result of the pursuit, or it could even get shot down. Or suppose that the bombs and grenades carried aboard by hijackers to intimidate the crew were to go off prematurely. There are any number of things that might cause a terrible catastrophe. I'm surprised that it hasn't happened already. I think it is inevitable."

Hammarskjöld: "Yes, we are deeply concerned about that probability of disaster. We at IATA are saying that with every new hijacking incident, the statistical risk increases. We have seen some incidents already that have been bad. The big disaster is, in a way, overdue."

Cardman: "One of my greatest fears today is not only for that disaster, and not only for the Middle East, but for the Indo-china area—the fear that, some day, somebody is going to take a 747 and make another Pueblo incident out of it . . . take it behind the bamboo curtain. Also, we are concerned that sabotage is going to be the next thing. There are so many ways of getting the wrong things aboard aircraft. We are, in this country, concerned about the Weatherman, and groups like that. I'm already looking down the road toward sabotage attempts by urban guerrillas and other forces.

"Now, in the Middle East, and in through those areas, the fear is that sabotage attempts might destroy the whole bloody airplane even if you take it down—you know, with passengers aboard. The urban guerrilla threat here is quite something else again. It's not a threat against people—it's a threat against things. We expect harassment by anti-war groups, such as over-loading reservations, preaching at people not to fly, tying up airport traffic in some way, perhaps through sabotage. Then the bomb threats and the hijacking threats coming over the tele-phone—that's something that constantly keeps you keyed up, that's one of the most hellish things you can imagine for an airline to worry about and to evaluate. Then we believe they may occasionally show up with a little incendiary device here and there—nothing big, nothing huge, but just enough to use as a threat. . ."

The P.O.: "Is there a possibility that the type of action pulled off by the Palestinian Arab group could take similar form in the United States? There were press reports and rumors when Angela Davis was taken into custody that an extremist group might hijack an aircraft and hold the passengers hostage until such time as she might be freed."

Davis: "There is—that *is* the political activist threat. That is exactly what is going on down in Uruguay, Brazil, Spain, Quebec, and other places, and that's what can be made to happen here by any group of extremists that considers itself so strongly dedicated to a cause that they think it requires an attention-getting act or a resort to blackmail. With extremist groups of any kind, we have to be concerned about their actions. An extremist is an extremist. It doesn't make any difference if he is a Weatherman or a member of the KKK or a Minuteman or what he is, he is an extremist, and extremists are likely to be misguided. And when you get a misguided person, heaven knows what he may do."

Listening to the experts, we realize that though we have come a long way, we still have a long way to go. The echoes of what they have to tell us are not altogether reassuring. . .

"When you get down to the terrorists, that is something else again. . ."

"We are concerned that sabotage is going to be the next thing. . ."

"Hijacking and sabotage are part of the world pattern of violence that is exemplified by the kidnapping actions in Uruguay and Quebec. . ."

"Say a PFLP group in a pursuit plane tries to force a commercial airliner to the ground under threat of blowing it out of the sky. . ."

"The big disaster is, in a way, overdue. . ."

"Some day, somebody is going to take a 747 and make another Pueblo incident out of it. . ."

"We are concerned about the Weatherman, and groups like that. . ."

"In the Middle East, the fear is that sabotage attempts might destroy the whole bloody airplane—with passengers aboard. . ."

"Extremist groups? That *is* the political activist threat. That is exactly what is going on . . . that's what can be made to happen here. . ."

We've come a long way, *but. . . .*

11/TOMORROW THE WORLD?

In the spring of 1970, which seems a long time ago because of the catastrophic events that have crowded upon us since then, it was still possible for us to smile wryly at the antics of the occasional hijacker. It was almost funny when a would-be skyjacker hijacked a bus to the airport at Petosky, Michigan, and then tried to skyjack a DC-9. His attempt failed.

For sheer one-upmanship it is hard to beat an event that occurred elsewhere on the same day. Not content with public transportation, Ira and Dianne Meeks hijacked a taxi to take them to the Gastonia Airport in South Carolina. There they hired a private Cessna and successfully skyjacked it to Cuba. This one produced definite snickers. There was something about the absolute gall of it that made people shake their heads ruefully and laugh at the same time.

We have had very little to laugh about since then.

Although we have witnessed a decline in the incidence of hijackings, we have seen a mushrooming of guerrilla and other revolutionary-type activities involving aircraft. The skyjack war encroached upon new territory on January 30, 1971.

On that day, two young members of the Kashmiri Liberation Front hijacked an Indian Airlines F-27 with thirty-two persons aboard and diverted it from its normal flight plan to Lahore, Pakistan.

The two Kashmiri skyjackers, though armed with pistols and hand grenades, made no attempt to intimidate the passengers or hold them hostage when the plane landed at Lahore. Instead, they promptly released all passengers and crew members—and stayed on the plane themselves. They would remain aboard, they said, until the Indian government released thirty-six imprisoned Kashmiri "freedom fighters," and until they themselves were guaranteed freedom from prosecution by the Pakistanis. Furthermore, they said, they would blow up the plane if the Indian government did not meet with their demands.

People rushed to the airport to catch a glimpse of the hijackers. Police reinforcements rushed after them. The crowd at the airport was very excited. This ought to show India a thing

284

or two! And the citizens demanded that Pakistani authorities keep the Indian passengers "as hostages for Moslems kept in Indian jails."

It was a very sticky situation. Behind the skyjacking lay the Kashmir issue, an issue that has long festered between India and Pakistan and over which those two countries have fought two bitter wars. For Indians, Pakistanis, and Kashmiris the dispute over Kashmir is one that carries with it all the fierce emotionalism and desperate bitterness characteristic of the Palestinian guerrilla cause.

The Indian government ignored the skyjackers' demands and hotly accused the Pakistanis of stalling the return of the plane and being lax in their efforts to persuade the skyjackers to leave it. They were also angered by the Pakistani refusal to permit a relief plane to go to Lahore to pick up the passengers. Pakistani authorities, in their turn, said that they were doing their best to get the skyjackers off the plane and that, when they succeeded, the aircraft and passengers would be free to leave Lahore. However, they added, they could not allow an Indian relief plane to fly in to pick up the stranded passengers. "Crowds at the airport are hostile," they said, "and it might jeopardize the safety of Indian pilots."

The crowds were undoubtedly hostile to India but they managed to keep their animosity within bounds. Although they had voiced the suggestion that the passengers be kept as Pakistani hostages, they were intrigued by the very sight of an Indian plane on their soil and were curious enough to see real live Indian passengers and crewman to be almost friendly. As for the hijackers, the Pakistanis thought they were marvelous and tried to drape garlands around their necks.

But the hijackers weren't sticking their necks out. They kept inside the plane and waited for action.

Two days later the passengers and crew were returned to India. They went back by road.

In New Delhi, hundreds of Indians demonstrated in front of the Pakistan High Commission to demand the return of the hijackers and protest the fact that Pakistan had not released the plane.

In Lahore, the hijackers were still aboard with their pistols and their explosives. The Pakistani government had already granted them political asylum, but that was not enough; they said that their main demand was the "release of all political prisoners rotting in Indian jails for refusing to succumb to India's repression to accept its sovereignty over Kashmir."

Once the passengers were safely home, India flatly refused the hijackers' demands. The Pakistanis permitted the two young men on the plane to have a quick conference with a Liberation Front leader who joined them at the airport. The visitor left, and the skyjackers blew up the plane.

So far as is known, they had nothing more destructive than hand grenades at their disposal, and since these do not provide the devasting detonation power of carefully wired loads of dynamite they had decided to remain aboard until they were quite certain that the plane would be effectively destroyed. They did so, keeping Pakistani fire engines at bay until the plane was burning fiercely, after which they jumped to safety. Both were placed under guard in a military hospital. One was seriously injured; the other suffered minor wounds.

The Pakistani Foreign Office deplored the firing of the plane.

India was outraged, claiming that Pakistan's military government could have prevented the destruction of the plane. The government of Mrs. Indira Gandhi immediately and belatedly raised an outcry against sky piracy and condemned it as a "crime against all civilized people." Also, it promptly canceled the right of Pakistani planes to fly over Indian territory—military planes for starters, and then commercial craft—in retaliation for the loss of the Indian plane.

With this, another new element was added to the skyjacking picture: a specific hijacking had directly contributed to the disruption of air traffic over a specific area for an indefinite length of time. For Pakistan, it meant that the two parts of Pakistan—East and West—were even more isolated from each other than before (though the civil strife that later occurred did much more to increase the estrangement). For the air traveler and the aviation community in general, it means that a sky-jacking has already interfered with the routine interchange of air traffic between countries and the routine overflying of planes from one place to another. It is a very small indication, but a very pointed one nevertheless, of what might happen in the future if countries that are already at loggerheads become further inflamed by a hijacking: no more overflights, no more service between the two countries, no more stopovers in either or both of the countries by airlines of other countries serving either of them.

It could turn into an extremely awkward and complex situation. Let us hope that we will have some workable bilateral agreements going for us before something like the India versus Pakistan episode occurs again—perhaps next time on a very much larger scale.

In a way, this incident has its positive side. It made Mrs. Gandhi protest to Pakistan for giving the two hijackers political asylum instead of treating them as "common criminals"; it made Mrs. Gandhi come right out and condemn, at long last, the practice of air piracy. She might have done so earlier, when the Palestinian guerrillas hijacked and blew up four planes, but she overlooked that opportunity. It has long been India's policy to support the Arabs in the Middle East, including Arabs belonging to such guerrilla organizations as Al Fatah; thus India, without openly supporting the actions of the PFLP, did not find it necessary or convenient to denounce the Palestinian skyjack-ransom monstrosities.

But when skyjacking came to India, it suddenly became a "crime against all civilized people"!

It is only when it happens to *us* that we realize how much it can hurt.

What is significant about the India-to-Pakistan skyjacking, aside from the dual reaction of the Indian government, is that it was committed by yet another "national liberation front."

And there were still new fields to conquer. On March 30, 1971, news reports came out of Hong Kong and Red China the likes of which we had never heard before, although we did hear echoes in them of the skyjack flight by the nine Japanese Red Army students who had wanted to make contact with their fellow ideologists in North Korea.

This time the skyjackers were "six long-haired Filipino youths" who described themselves as Maoists and said they were taking over the plane for "ideological reasons." The craft was a Philippine Air Lines twin-jet BAC-111 on a domestic flight between Manila and Davao with forty-four passengers aboard and a crew of five. Armed with pistols, a carbine, and scissors, the youths seized the jetliner and took it to Hong Kong for refueling. According to initial reports, they belonged to "some young radical group, some rebel group" in the Philippines. During the refueling stop they released twenty passengers and an infant not included on the passenger list. The crew and the rest of the passengers, including four Americans, remained aboard as hostages.

The hijackers were hoping to fly on to Peking, but no charts were available for a Peking flight and they were obliged to settle for Canton. The plane took off for Canton without awaiting clearance from Communist Chinese authorities.

Passengers, crew and hijackers were courteously received at Canton's White Cloud Airport. Chinese officials appeared to be surprised by the visit, and not at all in favor of the seizure. The legitimate occupants of the plane spent the night in one of the dormitories of a compound at the airport, and during their twenty-four-hour stay in Communist China they were given regular meals and reading matter consisting of Communist publications in a variety of languages. Their hosts were at all times extremely courteous.

Peking radio, in referring to the incident, charged that the plane had "illegally violated Chinese air space" and did not mention that it had been hijacked. But the broadcast did say that the government had decided to deal "leniently" with the matter and let the plane go.

The next day, they did. But before doing so they gathered the passengers together with the hijackers, made the hijackers apologize to their victims, and firmly announced that they themselves did not approve of the hijacking. Then the plane and its passengers returned to Hong Kong without the six young hijackers.

"I couldn't see that the hijackers got any different treatment from us while we were in Canton," said one of the passengers. "They were made to apologize, but they didn't seem to be in any trouble."

Yet the Chinese had made it clear that they wanted no more pirated planes coming to China. According to Captain Antonio

Misa, "They themselves impressed it on us that they don't approve of air piracy, and that they don't want this kind of incident of going to China on a hijacked aircraft."

After the hijackers made their apology they wished the passengers good luck. Maybe the passengers should have wished *them* good luck. Yet, according to one of the passengers, the spokesman for the hijackers told them that this was not going to be the last hijacking. Russell Ebersole, an American missionary, quoted the young man as saying that the group had gone to China for "training" and would later return to the Philippines.

Whether or not they get their "training" remains to be seen. Perhaps they will be severely punished. Or perhaps, in spite of official Chinese disapproval, they succeeded in reaching out another tentacle. . . .

Although the actions of the PFLP and other revolutionary and radical groups have not been universally admired, they have had conspicuous effect. It should not be at all surprising if—or rather, *when*—other groups borrow the tactics of the PFLP, either emulating them right down the line or refining them to suit local circumstances and the needs of the moment. Kidnapping for ransom, the holding of hostages or the seizure of a piece of property, sabotage or other destructive attacks on buildings and airplanes, potshot sniper fire or deliberate assassination . . . all these are in the catalogue of the professional guerrilla or "freedom fighter" who treads the path of the PFLP.

The PFLP itself appears to be lying fairly low these days, both in regard to its hijacking activities and its public statements. We should not be encouraged by this. The Front has had its problems: disagreement within the ranks, changes of leadership, a degree of estrangement from some groups that enthusiastically supported them until they pulled their audacious political skyjack-blackmail act, and increased harassment and counteraction by establishment fighting forces. One result of their skyjackings was King Hussein's decision to crack down severely on commandos operating in and from Jordan. All this has put them somewhat on the defensive—which, according to all handbooks on guerrilla warfare, is not the proper posture for the well-organized guerrilla group. Yet none of this should serve to indicate that they will not repeat one or more of their vicious attacks involving aircraft and airlines: sabotage of airplanes, shoot-outs at airports, murderous raids on airline ticket offices, hijacking jetliners, kidnapping their occupants, and holding hostages for barter.

There is no evidence that the PFLP feels any regret for its September, 1970, spectacular. In the weeks following their achievement, its members repeatedly congratulated themselves, claiming that "the headlines have shown that our cause is now clearly publicized" and implying that this in itself was justification for what they had done. But they not only made news; they wheeled and dealed with human lives in a massive extortion plot, and in this, too, they largely succeeded. Why should they not cap success with success when the time is ripe? Early in February, 1971, a PFLP spokesman declared: "Hijacking is one of our weapons, and when the proper time and target turn up we will use it again."

Confirmation of sorts followed shortly afterward. Here is a United Press International dispatch dated Feburary 18, 1971:

Zurich—Swiss federal authorities have warned police and airline officials in Zurich, Bern, Basle and Geneva of increased danger of aircraft hijackings by Palestinian guerrillas.

The warning, based on information from the French embassy in Amman, said that the threat comes from the Popular Front for the Liberation of Palestine, which could try to restore its weakened ranks and influence by dramatic hijackings like those it carried out last September.

And another UPI dispatch, this one dated February 24, 1971:

London—International police warned airlines today that seven militant Palestinian guerrillas are known to have reached Europe where they are suspected of planning a new wave of aircraft hijacking attempts.

Officials at London airport said airlines tightened security checks on boarding passengers after receiving the hijack alert from the international police organization, Interpol.

This is not hard evidence of impending action. It is merely suggestive. Suggestive, too, are the increasing numbers of scares, rumors and dire warnings that have cropped up during the last few months. These, according to IATA's director general Knut Hammarskjöld, indicate that the PFLP is capitalizing on its own reputation. "The PFLP has a great psychological factor going for them—and this is the way they keep their flag up," Hammarskjöld told this writer.

On March 29, 1971, Leila Khaled gave a press conference in Kuwait. Her comments were briefly reported on the following day in Beirut, in the Lebanese-Arabic newspaper *Al Anwar*. Due to the continued and consistent support of Israel by the United States, she said, hijackings were planned in the near future for Geneva, Munich, Hamburg, London and Edinburgh. Truth, or scare warning?

The scare tactic is another integral part of guerrilla warfare. To what extent we can take these threats, whispers, and announcements at face value we do not know. But we had better be prepared: "When the proper time and target turn up, we will do it again."

There *is* evidence, according to Hammarskjöld, that some of the scares are more than threats and rumors deliberately spread by the PFLP. Some are based on solid fact and have been traced to the source with good results. As Hammarskjöld puts it: "There are certain ones we keep very close tabs on . . . but I can't elaborate further. We are constantly on alert, and the airlines have to have security organizations to deal with this. We have been able to follow developments very closely. Through very diligent surveillance of certain people, *potential hijackings have been stopped."*

We would like to think that, if some of the more basic demands of the Arab guerrillas were to be met, the threat of the PFLP would be defused. To this, Hammarskjöld comments: "I think there will always be fanatics, for one reason or another. Once they find out how easy it is to exploit this kind of activity—and how spectacular it is—anyone can hijack or terrorize an airplane."

What is true of the PFLP is equally true of other, similar groups. Even if established governments were to make honest, wholehearted efforts to meet the demands of one or another or all their dissenting groups, not all of those groups would be satisfied. Probably none of them would be. Surely, there will always be fanatics. But as of now, with scarcely any effort being made to accommodate or even listen to the demands of anti-establishment extremist groups, we have far more fanatics than we need.

The Body Snatchers

The Popular Front's action was so outrageous that it all but eclipsed—at least while the immediate shock lasted—the hijackings and hostage-takings that had preceded it. The *New York Times* of October 4, 1970, commented: "The Palestine guerrillas seem to have put together the techniques of the Latin American kidnappers and the Fidelista airplane hijackers." This was an interesting comment, followed by the observation that the practice of taking hostages, of human tribute, and of ransom is nothing new, that it goes all the way back to the time when "Athens had to offer its youths and maidens to the Minotaur in Crete until Theseus appeared."

But what seems to have been overlooked in the general excitement at the time was that a number of Latin American guerrilla groups had already *themselves* combined hijacking with the taking of hostages—an act that is otherwise known as kidnapping. That combination was not an innovation of the PFLP. In fact, one—fortunately unsuccessful—skyjack-ransom attempt was made by members of the same Brazilian terrorist group that had kidnapped two foreign ambassadors. (We should also not forget what happened to Moise Tshombe. It wasn't quite the same, but it was close.)

The implications here are very frightening. Political kidnapping has become one of the most widely practiced and effective terrorist weapons. We have seen it time and time again in Brazil, Uruguay, and Guatemala, carried out by groups whose ideologies and tactics are very similar to those of the PFLP. We have seen it, too, in Canada, and it is not beyond the realm of possibility that we may see it in the United States. Now that political kidnapping has taken to the air, we should be prepared for it to happen anywhere. There is a growing uneasiness in the United States that terrorists may some day seize a plane with an American official aboard and hold him to ransom until certain exorbitant demands are met. This could happen in the Middle East, or in Europe, or it could happen here.

This is not alarmism. If such a thing were to happen, it would only be part of a pattern that is gradually spreading across the face of the world.

If we cast our minds back over 1970 and the early months of 1971, we begin to recall some of the non-airborne kidnappings that occurred during that time:

Guatemala's foreign minister, Alberto Fuentes Mohr, is kidnapped and held for several days before being released in exchange for an imprisoned student-guerrilla leader.

Guatemalan guerrillas hold Sean M. Holly, U.S. diplomat, for some forty hours as hostage for jailed rebels.

Dominican guerrillas kidnap Lieutenant Colonel Donald J. Crowley, U.S. air attaché in Santo Domingo, and free him upon the release by the Dominican government of nineteen political prisoners.

Left-wing group in Argentina kidnaps Paraguayan diplomat but frees him without obtaining release of two political prisoners demanded in ransom.

Body of West Germany's ambassador to Guatemala found after Guatemalan government remains firm in its refusal to bow to ransom demands for $700,000 and the release of twenty-two political prisoners.

Former President Aramburu of Argentina disappears from his home, apparently kidnapped. His body is found several weeks later, buried in a farmhouse basement.

West German Ambassador von Holleben is kidnapped by Brazilian terrorists in Rio de Janeiro. Kidnappers demand that Brazilian authorities call a halt to the torture of political prisoners, and release some of them.

U.S. Ambassador to Brazil, C. Burke Elbrick, is kidnapped

by the same group responsible for the kidnapping of von Holleben. The two men are eventually exchanged for a total of fifty-five political prisoners.

The Tupamaros of Uruguay kidnap Aloysio Dias Gomide, a Brazilian consul, and demand a ransom of $1 million. Eventually they lower their demands to $250,000, and release him.

Daniel A. Mitrione, an American aid official, is kidnapped by the Uruguayan Tupamaro guerrillas and murdered by them several days later.

Claude L. Fly, a U.S. soils expert, is captured and held by the Tupamaros, who try to extort $1 million ransom money in exchange for him. After long captivity and a heart attack, he is released and left on the steps of a Montevideo hospital.

Quebec separatists kidnap Pierre Laporte, Quebec Minister of Labor and Immigration, and James Cross, British Trade Commissioner. Laporte is murdered. James Cross is eventually found alive.

The Tupamaros kidnap Geoffrey Jackson, British Ambassador to Uruguay. They also "execute" a Uruguayan policeman.

An American Air Force sergeant is kidnapped by leftists in Ankara, Turkey. Several days later, four more airmen are seized and threatened with "execution" if they are not bought back for $400,000. The plot fails.

Tupamaro guerrilla kidnappers snatch Uruguayan executive Ulysses Pereira Reverbel from a dentist's chair, saying, "We have come to take you to be judged by the people's court." This is the second time in three years that Pereira has been kidnapped by the Tupamaros.

Diplomats and other officials in various parts of the world are fully alive to the possibility that they might be kidnapped. The American ambassador to Jordan carries a .38-caliber Smith & Wesson, travels in an armored car accompanied by a bodyguard, and drives to and from his residence by different routes each morning and night. He is determined not to become a hostage of any of the guerrilla groups operating in Jordan. Some half-dozen American embassy aides have already been held by Palestinian guerrillas for various lengths of time, and one military attaché was murdered. The possibility of a kidnap attempt against the ambassador is very real.

Knut Hammarskjöld of IATA himself lives in fear of being kidnapped. He is calm about it, but he is fully aware of the possibility. As a man who is not only in the midst of the international aviation scene but also is acquainted with the members of at least one active guerrilla-hijacker group, he is an unenviable target. His position as head of the world aviation body demands that he travel a lot. His travel itineraries are known only to himself and one or two close aides . . . yet he could just as easily be kidnapped in the air as on the ground.

So could some very prominent international or American "pigs," as we are reminded by the Berkeley *Tribe* and other papers representative of the alternative press; they could just "be hijacked from the U.S. to parts unknown. By, say, freaks." Or by other revolutionaries, more fanatic than freaky.

In the past we were able to take some comfort in the supposition that the various little struggling separatist, guerrilla, or radical student groups operating here and there around the world were struggling alone. The NLF of Vietnam had nothing to do with the ELF of Eritrea; the FLQ of Canada had not so much as heard of the Tupamaros of Uruguay; the Black Panthers couldn't care less about the PFLP; New Left student groups in the United States didn't know the difference between China's Red Guard and Japan's Red Army; and none of these groups knew anything about Angola's Popular Liberation Army or the Kashmir Liberation Front or the radical Maoist students in the Philippines.

If that was ever true, which we doubt, it isn't any more. There are hands across the sea, and there are hands across the air, and they are joining. These groups talk to each other. They exchange letters and communiqués. They read each other's newspapers. They visit back and forth, within the limits of their mobility. They teach each other what they have learned through their own experience. The more organized and well-entrenched groups even offer courses at training camps to eager neophytes from other countries. Obviously these groups are not all from the same rubber stamp, and there are differences among them. Some are more Marxist than Maoist; others are more Maoist than Marxist. Some are ready for all-out guerrilla warfare; some kill their kidnap victims; some destroy planes; some have not yet passed the stage of trash-bombing. But there is an interrelationship between all these groups. From Canada to Algeria, from Brazil to Lebanon to Spain to Syria to Germany to Japan to Uruguay to the United States to various countries in Africa, they study the same basic material, share roughly the same purpose, and are beginning to look more and more alike in method.

We call again upon Dr. Dailey of the FAA:

"The Middle East hijackers have really made a study of their job. They are the professionals, just like the ones who took the Japanese airliner to Korea. These groups are all interrelated. The Red Army is of course the ultra-militant left fragment of the Communist party in Japan and is roughly equivalent to our Weatherman group here. They are all linked through contacts in Havana. The focus, at least symbolically, is all this business about groups going to Cuba to participate in the sugar harvest. These groups have included the ultra-militant groups from our country, this group in Japan, the ultra-militant Arab groups, and other groups from some South American and African countries. Roughly speaking, it's sort of a loose affiliation of all the ultra-militant Maoist-type groups in the world—including, probably, the Quebec Liberation Front—and in this country, it includes the Black Panthers, the Puerto Rican Liberation Front, the Weathermen, some of the wilder women's liberation groups, and the like.

"We know that these terrorist groups, worldwide, have certain doctrines and tactics in common. We have seen copies of procedural manuals that they study; they've been published in Havana. There is one here, called the *Mini-Manual for the Urban Guerrilla*, about sixty pages. In it they spell out their tactics in great detail. This does include hijacking; it includes kidnapping people to ransom your comrades out of jail; it includes bombings, and so on. . . . This particular manual was written by a fellow named Marighella, a Brazilian, specifically for Brazil, but it's been adapted by all these groups as their basic manual."

Life in These United States

To Dr. Dailey, Captain Ruby, General Davis, a high-ranking official of the FBI who does not wish to be directly quoted, and a number of deeply concerned aviation authorities interviewed by the author, there is a distinct possibility that a terrorist-type hijacking *may* take place in the United States. Obviously, no one can say, "Sure, it will happen—it's bound to." It is not bound to. But we have to look at the possibility in terms of the climate of violence in which we live, the anything-goes hatreds which spill over in the form of verbal virulence and terror bombings and vicious attacks against anything that represents authority. We do not like to admit that urban guerrilla warfare is already being waged in the United States. But it is. Thousands of incidents of guerrilla-type activity have occurred in the form of trashings, bombings, arson, and other acts of sabotage. Sniper attacks against police officers, vehicles, and stations are common. Almost every day we read about some terroristic act that can only be ascribed to a guerrilla group or individual. Guerrilla tactics used in other countries are undeniably being used here. Banks, homes, stores, business firms, colleges, schools, churches, state and local offices, federal buildings—all these have been bomb targets. The U.S. Capitol itself was torn by a bomb blast on March 1, 1971. In 1970 alone there were 1,096 bombings across the nation, 176 attempted bombings, and 592 bomb threats. Ninety-seven policemen were killed in criminal assaults. In January, 1971, seventy-nine bomb explosions were reported; in January and February together, twenty-three policemen were killed and 246 were wounded.

Civilian lives have not yet been seriously threatened, although there have been some "accidental" casualties. There will probably be other deaths and injuries, and they may not all be accidental. Violence breeds violence, and one form of violence leads to another.

Talking about guerrillas in general, Dr. Dailey comments:

"The interesting thing is that during the first phase of a terror campaign, their doctrine is not to kill anybody. They use small mini-bombs, or they use bombs that will go off when they know people *won't* be there. Or they will telephone and give warning so the people can get out."

"The first phase. . ."?

This is exactly what is happening here.

Does that mean that terrorists in this country may escalate their activities and perhaps resort to hijacking?

"We feel, yes, there is a real threat there. It's been demonstrated that hijacking can be a very effective terror weapon. We feel that, as part of terroristic campaigns in the future, they'll undoubtedly try it."

In November, 1970, the director of security for a United States airline company expressed this fear: "What would happen tomorrow if a couple of Weathermen or Panthers got hold of an airline and hijacked it to Cuba or some place else and said, 'We're holding all passengers as hostages until Angela Davis is released'? That, to me, is a bloody immediate worry, and I don't know what to do about it."

There is a sense of apprehension throughout the airline industry that the United States may suffer that kind of attack some day, and soon. We have had more than our share of hijackings, so the fear is not for the threat of hijacking per se. The fear is of deliberate terrorism in the air, carefully planned and executed by a group that might even now be taking lessons in the art of airborne kidnapping.

Scene: Minneapolis, Minnesota. Date: November 13, 1970. Police, acting on what they describe as "bits and pieces" of information, arrest Ronald Lindsey Reed, a twenty-year-old black man, on conspiracy charges for allegedly planning to kidnap the governor of Minnesota and hijack an airplane to force the release of black militant political prisoners such as Miss Angela Davis and Black Panther national chairman Bobby Seale.

Reed is arrested at his apartment on the basis of warrants sworn out in Omaha, Nebraska, charging him with attempted robbery and attempted murder. He surrenders without resistance. Notes are found in his pocket allegedly outlining the kidnap-hijack plans. He is then formally charged with conspiring to steal an airplane.

Police say that the plans include the possible kidnapping of Governor Harold Levander and St. Paul councilwoman Mrs. Rosalie Butler and the hijacking of an airplane out of the Minneapolis-St. Paul International Airport. News reports quote one note as reading: "Liberate prisoners, kidnap Governor, hijack." (Just a reminder, we suppose.) Another note is said to consist of an apparent itinerary which spells out plans to hijack the plane on November 13, the day of the arrest, and reads in part: "Message to control tower to be relayed to Governor Levander, Police, FBI or any agent of Government concern. We our [sic] revolutionaries. Take heed to our first and last warning. If there is any attempt to interfere or stop us, we will blow up this airplane and everybody on it." The note continues with a demand that the black leaders, the "political prisoners," be released from jail, that the government give the Black Panthers $50,000 "in gold," and that the party be given national television time to explain its position.

It seems that none of this comes as much of a surprise to the police. Apparently they were aware of the alleged plot even before finding the notes and have already put a close watch on the airport, on the governor's mansion, and the home of Mrs. Rosalie Butler.

How were the police tipped off? We do not know.

Is this a genuine kidnap-hijack plot? The FBI is disinclined to think so. But again, we do not know.

Since then there have been a number of purported plots and threats to "blow up" certain minor public figures, kidnap others, and hijack airplanes with a view to securing the release of one or more black militants, primarily, of course, Angela Davis. So far there has been no proof of any concerted move or conspiracy on the part of Black Panthers or Weathermen or any other U.S. extremist group to go in for hijacking as a matter of policy. In fact, the FBI tends to downgrade the possibility. But obviously, there is concern; there is alarm; there is "information" that it "may" happen. Whether the hijacking takes place as a result of group policy or individual extremist decision

makes very little difference; it does not take a large-scale conspiracy to create a large-scale airborne disaster.

Nor will we be particularly encouraged if we do not see
close-to-home political kidnapping or assassination or skyjacking in 1971. Violence engulfs us and will not vanish at the
turn of 1972, 1973, or 1974.

It is only now that we are finally waking up to the fact that
we *are* in the midst of violence—a type of violence that has little
in common with conventional crime.

Pictured below is a sample of the material contained in one of
the hundreds of guerrilla manuals freely available throughout
the United States. When we say freely, we don't mean that you
can pick one up at any friendly neighborhood paperback store.
You may have to check as many as three or four bookstores
before you find what you are looking for. If you want to do it
an easier way, you can pick up an occasional copy of an
underground or streetcorner newspaper, and sooner or later you
are bound to find out everything you always wanted to know
about subverting the establishment but were afraid to ask.
Actually you don't even need to be afraid to ask. Asking is the
easiest way, even easier than going to the nearest well-stocked
library. Someone always knows someone, and before you know
it you will have in your hands the blueprints for total guerrilla
warfare, or any particular guerrilla tactic you would like to try,
or any bomb you feel like making.

These things have been filtering through the States for years.
Of late they have virtually swamped the country. We have been
astonished by the multiplicity of publications available and the
detail of their instructions, complete with admonitions to be
very, very careful. These are all supposedly "underground"
materials. Lately we note that equally deadly material is being
released on the open market in expensive, aboveground
publications.

But we are more interested in publications that are not quite
so openly and commercially circulated and which are made
available to readers for 25 cents or for nothing. (If you sincerely
want to offer instruction to fledgling revolutionaries, you don't
try to make a profit out of them.) We have in our possession
hundreds of diagrams for making bombs and other weapons of a

very simple but very deadly type. They have to be simple; the ingredients must be inexpensive and non-extraordinary. Questions may be asked when would-be terrorists and saboteurs go around asking for sophisticated explosive or incendiary materials. You want to make a pipe bomb, fire bomb, pipe pistol or shotgun, hand grenade, auto bomb, delay timer, fuse igniter, or telephone booby trap in your spare time? Fine. Just follow the simple directions, and be careful.

We do not intend, however, to fill in the details of bomb construction for those whose targets are banks, campus buildings, government offices and so on. Our concern in these pages is for airplanes and their passengers.

The accompanying diagram shows only a switch—an altimeter switch to be employed with explosive material described on other pages of the guerrilla manual from which we borrowed it.

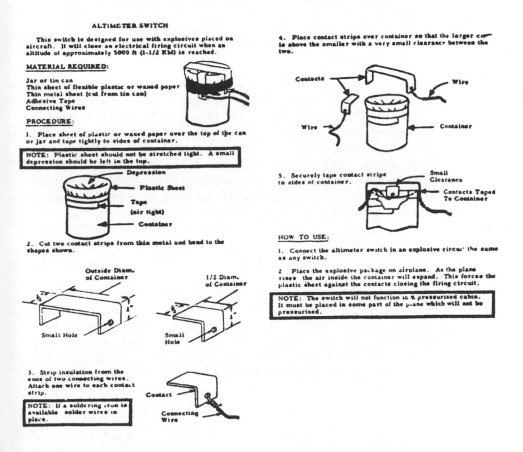

ALTIMETER SWITCH

This switch is designed for use with explosives placed on aircraft. It will close an electrical firing circuit when an altitude of approximately 5000 ft (1-1/2 KM) is reached.

MATERIAL REQUIRED:

Jar or tin can
Thin sheet of flexible plastic or waxed paper
Thin metal sheet (cut from tin can)
Adhesive Tape
Connecting Wires

PROCEDURE:

1. Place sheet of plastic or waxed paper over the top of the can or jar and tape tightly to sides of container.

NOTE: Plastic sheet should not be stretched tight. A small depression should be left in the top.

2. Cut two contact strips from thin metal and bend to the shapes shown.

Outside Diam. of Container

1/2 Diam. of Container

Small Hole

Small Hole

3. Strip insulation from the ends of two connecting wires. Attach one wire to each contact strip.

NOTE: If a soldering iron is available solder wires in place.

Contact

Connecting Wire

4. Place contact strips over container so that the larger is above the smaller with a very small clearance between the two.

Contacts

Wire

Wire

Container

5. Securely tape contact strips to sides of container.

Small Clearance

Contacts Taped To Container

HOW TO USE:

1. Connect the altimeter switch in an explosive circuit the same as any switch.

2. Place the explosive package on airplane. As the plane rises the air inside the container will expand. This forces the plastic sheet against the contacts closing the firing circuit.

NOTE: The switch will not function in a pressurized cabin. It must be placed in some part of the plane which will not be pressurized.

For those who cannot read the slightly blurred type, we will spell out the heading:

ALTIMETER SWITCH
This switch is designed for use with explosives placed on aircraft. It will close an electrical firing circuit when an altitude of approximately 5000 ft (1-1/2 KM) is reached.

The closing comments, too, are quite interesting and helpful. Thus:

How to Use:
1. Connect the altimeter switch in an explosive circuit the same as any switch.
2. Place the explosive package on airplane. As the plane rises the air inside the container will expand. This forces the plastic sheet against the contacts closing the firing circuit.
Note: The switch will not function in a pressurized cabin. It must be placed in some part of the plane which will not be pressurized.

We can't help thinking that there must be some sort of demand for such a design, or else it would not be in supply.

Even while peering into the future and seeing there the possibility of an American-based skyjack spectacular, complete with hostages and ransom demands, we cannot afford to overlook other contingencies. There are revolutionaries in this country, as there are in other countries, who have such a sense of powerlessness and desperation that they are willing to attack the System in any way that hurts it. Big Business has already been a target, particularly Big Business that lends itself directly or indirectly to the pursuance of the war in and around Vietnam or the support of anti-Arab groups. Airlines are Big Business.

There are many ways of harassing and hurting the airline industry. The most obvious is sabotage. Sabotage does not always require bombs. As General Davis remarks, "It is very glamorous and very flagrant of course—the violation in security is very flagrant—when somebody is able to put a bomb in the belly of an airplane. But there are other types of sabotage that can quite easily be done by people and which won't be detected except perhaps as material failure."

There is a hole, here, in our security system; a hole of which airline security directors are very much aware. There are fanatics among airline employees, too, and airline employees are in a highly strategic position to compromise the safety of an aircraft. This means that we still need a much better system for the screening of potential employees, and it also means that we need very much greater control of the movements of people throughout the air site in general and in the ramp and cargo areas in particular. All-over airport security still leaves much to be desired. People in uniform are able to operate very freely on an air site . . . and if they have not been properly screened or identified, they can do their own thing with comparative ease.

Outsiders can be equally dangerous, and perhaps even more so if they organize. We have seen what anti-noise and anti-pollution and other anti groups can do to paralyze business, construction, and the movement of traffic when they put their minds to it. What might be the result of a series of massive lie-downs on airport taxiways and runways? Can we envision a concerted attempt to block off roads leading to airports so that passengers cannot reach the terminals? How could airlines fight a bombardment of thousands upon thousands of telephone calls claiming that bombs have been placed on X number of planes or threatening a wave of skyjack attempts? What if the airlines were treated to a gigantic and prolonged Do Not Fly campaign by mobs of people stalking about with picket signs and yelling anti-airline slogans or, worse, screaming out dire warnings about what might happen to people who take to the sky? What would happen if groups of extremists converged on various airports throughout the United States, made their illegal way to loaded aircraft still at the boarding ramps, surrounded the planes, whipped out their weapons, and shouted out, "Meet our demands . . . or else!"

Not too long ago an airline security officer sat at his desk, puffed energetically on his cigar, and said to this author: "If the kids were to try to do to any American airline what they have done to Dow Chemical and even the ROTC—!" He didn't finish the sentence. He didn't have to.

But we are not concerned only about kids. Our revolutionaries are growing up and they do not seem to be settling down. It seems to us that they are more and more coming to believe, along with the PFLP, that revolution has no rules. And more and more *we* are coming to believe that revolutionary zealots, desperate to secure what they consider their own basic human rights, will not hesitate to sacrifice casual bystanders or people who just happen to be sitting on a plane.

We have to consider the economic implications of a well-organized attack against our national or international aviation system. It could be disastrous for our airlines and their employees; it could be disastrous for all businesses dependent in any way upon the use of airlines. In the ultimate, it could be disastrous for the international community. The mind cannot grasp what the world would be like without air service. To put it very mildly, the worldwide establishment would be in exactly the state of chaos and, we would suppose, disintegration that must be the guerrillas' dream.

Yet we cannot honestly envision that sort of disaster. We have enough safeguards so that worldwide paralysis of our airlines, and the economic catastrophe that would follow it, looms as a very dim and unlikely possibility.

A much more likely possibility is a dreadful catastrophe in the air. It is more than a possibility. It is a probability, perhaps an inevitability. Considering that more than 1,500 crew members and 15,000 passengers have been involved in aerial hijackings as of the end of March, 1971, it is astonishing that we have been as lucky as we have. Yet there have already been airborne catastrophes, some planned and some unplanned, some due to hijacking and some to sabotage. Perhaps there are some we do not even know about, just as there must be hijackings that have not made the record books. Most of those we do know about have not been of any great magnitude. This is no consolation; it simply adds to the suspense, and to the statistical probability of a major disaster.

There have been passengers injured in forced landings and sudden evacuations, as in the incidents at Cairo and Amman. Crew members have been wounded. Pilots, copilots, and a stewardess have died. Seventeen people were killed in the

Cubana crash of November, 1958. Nobody was killed in the airborne explosion of February, 1970, when a bomb ripped through the cargo compartment of an Austrian airliner, but the plane and its occupants came within a hairbreadth of disaster. That narrow margin of safety was tragically missing in the case of the Swissair craft that exploded in the air on the same day. All forty-seven persons aboard were torn to pieces. Nobody was killed on August 26, 1970, when a man with a bomb tried to hijack a Polish aircraft to Vienna, but eleven people including the hijacker were injured when the bomb exploded in the man's hands. The blast tore off the door to the flight deck, damaged electrical equipment, and set the plane on fire, but the pilot managed to bring the craft down safely.

An incident that occurred on January 23, 1971, holds some sort of lesson for us if we can only determine exactly what it is. It may be that too much interference is more dangerous than too little, which is exactly what the anti-armed-guard elements have been telling us and what the sky marshals themselves maintain. A young man hijacked a South Korean airliner and tried to divert it to North Korea. He was armed with four hand grenades and a razor-sharp kitchen knife. With the first of his grenades he blew open the cockpit door, after which he made his demands known to the pilot. The pilot sent out a radio message and proceeded to fly false patterns in an attempt to convince the skyjacker that he was flying as directed. South Korean fighter planes took to the air and tried to head off the airliner as it zigzagged closer and closer to the border, and ground positions fired warning shots. The pilot finally made a belly landing on a lonely beach moments before reaching the border, considerably shaking up the plane and its passengers. The plane's security agent then reportedly shot the hijacker twice with his pistol; and the hijacker dropped his remaining hand grenades. They all blew up, killing the hijacker and the copilot and injuring at least thirteen others, four of them seriously.

We also recall hand grenades that have fizzled because of faulty springs; shoot-outs in the air and on the ground that have been fatal for one or more members of the crew and nearly fatal for all aboard; and attacks on pilots that have caused planes to go momentarily out of control. Looking back over these things, we know we have been lucky, although there have been tragedies enough.

In dwelling upon the possibility of skyjack attempts and other revolutionary attacks against air service by our homegrown guerrillas, we cannot permit ourselves to be sidetracked from what is happening in other countries of the world or from the fact that deranged and other desperate individuals are still slipping through the screening process. We are sending jumbo planes into the air these days, and the catastrophe will be just as great if they are blown up or crashed down by a madman with a bomb or a guerrilla group with a cause; just as great whether it happens here, out over the open sea, in Africa, in Europe, in the Middle East, in Latin America, or anywhere. If, by some fortuitous circumstance, we do not see another skyjacking for three months, six months or a year, the next one could still mark a day of catastrophe. And it may not be the only one.

We have got to keep the war of the misfit and the madman, of the revolutionary and even the refugee, out of the civilian sky. There is war enough already. The lives of travelers and those who transport them should never have to be endangered by someone else's cause. It makes no difference what side you are on, or they are on, or we are on, or I am on. Skyjacking is a crime against humanity. There are other crimes against humanity, but it seems to us that at least this one crime can be tackled by the community of nations acting together.

EPILOGUE / AND THE WAR GOES ON

In endorsing the new anti-hijack treaty of the International Civil Aviation Organization, which formally recognizes hijacking as a crime, President Richard M. Nixon commented that the hijacking and destruction of four airplanes in the Middle East in 1970, the continued hijackings to Cuba and the hijacking of Soviet and Eastern European aircraft had "brought the world to an awareness of the fragility of the network of international air traffic."

He added: "But we think that additional action is necessary. It should include sabotage, and an international agreement to suspend air services to countries which refuse to cooperate in the release of hijacked aircraft and the punishment of hijackers. ... The world cannot permit the boon of air travel to become the tool of criminals."

What is the world to do about it? Opinions are virtually unanimous that there is no single solution. In bringing together a multiplicity of observations we find a general agreement in regard to a multi-level approach.

1. Every individual and group with any share in the world aviation community—the community engaged in civil air traffic—must push for ratification and signing of bilateral and multilateral agreements, international treaties and conventions, regarding the swift extradition or on-the-spot punishment of skyjackers. We in the United States and every country of the world should treat skyjacking as an international threat to air safety and an infringement on human rights, wherever and for whatever reason the skyjacking occurs. The act of skyjacking must be recognized as a crime by all aviation bodies and all governments; severe punishment should be swift and inevitable. Punishment should not include the death sentence, because that penalty is unlikely to have any effect on extremely unbalanced or other desperate individuals. It should consist of long incarceration in a prison or mental institution. Sentences should be made as uniform as possible throughout the world.

2. Though extradition to the point of origin is preferable in most cases, we cannot overlook the element of political asylum. Incorporated in any agreement must be an understanding and definition of "political asylum." We must acknowledge the legitimate aspirations of all people, their political beliefs, their need and right to make a bid for freedom. Though we would like to say that skyjacking is *the* unforgivable crime, on a par with kidnapping and murder, and that people who commit it must forfeit their right to asylum anywhere, we cannot be so harsh. We have to recognize that, in some cases, there probably is no other visible way out. Yet even political refugees should be tried and punished, in the country of asylum, for the crime or crimes they have committed—air piracy, kidnapping, interference with the operations of an aircraft, coercion, assault, murder—and punished accordingly in that country.

3. We would request the governments of the world, including our own government, to take heed of the aspirations of the people on their soil. Our young revolutionaries *are* frustrated to the point of desperation; the ELFS, the PFLP, the Tupamaros, and their counterparts in other countries of the world *do* have their legitimate grievances; individuals who are not granted exit permits to leave for another land *are* captives in the country that holds them back. It is time for us all to listen, and try to get down to the root cause of these problems. We would request an international body such as the United Nations to bestir itself and try to make it possible one way or another for "rebel" groups to present their case on a world platform before turning, as a last resort, to kidnapping, sabotage, and skyjacking.

4. We, the people of every country served by aviation, must urge our national governments to bear a much greater responsibility, in a financial as well as a supervisory sense, for aviation security. Skyjacking and other security problems have gone beyond the scope of airline management; they are international problems that cannot be solved by private or semiprivate industry. The airplane is a common carrier; the central government of every country has a considerable degree of regulatory control over its airlines in such matters as routes, safety standards, and fares. That control should be extended to protecting the services rendered by these carriers. The airlines cannot afford to

pay for the required protection, nor are they able in themselves to establish uniform security procedures. Security would be more uniform if governments were to pay for it and control it. At best, we might even see a greater *worldwide* consistency, and a more effective interchange of information between airline and airline, country and country.

5. All countries and airlines should agree to provide at least their high-risk terminals, gates, and routes with modern detection systems and equipment, and make their *air sites* as secure as possible so that cargo and maintenance areas are also under protection. Again, government should bear much of the responsibility, not only in terms of cost and control, but also by assisting company efforts to screen potential employees thoroughly and effectively. Air sites, security equipment, detection systems, and search procedures should be periodically inspected and spot-checked by representatives of an international body such as IFALPA, IATA, or ICAO.

6. All members of the international aviation community must, working together with the help of government, develop a fail-safe means of communication—an intelligence network—between all the airlines of the world. Thus, if one airline spots a security risk, that airline should warn other airlines of their suspicions, and as specifically as possible. There must be an international exchange of information about uncovered hijack plans, hijack attempts, individuals who have been refused passage for substantial reasons, acts of sabotage, and the like.

7. The use of sky marshals should be continued on a scheduled basis. Existing sky marshals should be phased out and replaced by *airline personnel* after comparable if not more extensive training than that received to date by recruits from outside the industry. These new sky marshals would have the advantage of thorough familiarity with the operations of airlines and aircraft, and would be well equipped to assess and handle airborne emergencies with all regard to the safety of passengers, crew, and craft.

8. Airline crews should be given the benefit of all available information in regard to hijackings and related events. As part of their training and continued briefings they must be psychologically prepared to assess hijack attempts and the

nature of the hijacker, and to take cautious action whenever there is room for such action. When airline management receives any relevant current information it should disseminate it to their crews through security personnel, and *immediately*. Any captain of any airliner that is about to take off, or any captain of any airliner that is already in the air, must be informed by top-priority advisory of any hijack attempt taking place in any part of the world and given full details.

9. Crew members should be forbidden to carry arms. So should all passengers, whether diplomats or generals or non-airline private security guards. The crew has its job to do and cannot take effective armed action against hijackers. Armed passengers, no matter what their rank or profession, can only add to the danger of an unnecessary shoot-out. If on a rare occasion an armed passenger (such as a private guard or law-enforcement officer) has been able to subdue a hijacker, his success has been a matter of luck; his action could have led to serious consequences. Only the duly designated air marshal, familiar with plane, crew, and coded signals, should be permitted to carry any weapon aboard. Passengers should never initiate action, but if they have any security training they should stand ready to assist when asked—and only then.

10. Neither pilots nor any other groups or individuals assigned to handle airplanes—such as mechanics, fuel handlers, commissary handlers, baggage handlers, dispatchers, and so on—should consider or attempt boycotts in relation to any hijack situation. Such boycotts are counterproductive. Pilots, particularly, must be urged not to take such action. The only result would be to aggravate the situation even more and complicate matters beyond unraveling. The boycotted country or countries would retaliate; and we would see the breakdown of bilateral agreements which are very difficult to obtain in the first place and almost impossible to re-establish. The web of negotiation is so delicate that we cannot afford to have it disturbed. The aviation community, in the process of negotiating, must take special care to avoid disruptive action.

11. The world aviation community should make a point of working with the press and all news media so that the public is

kept informed about the positive side of the security picture rather than only the spectacular aspects of the successful hijacking. Dull news is no news, but in fact the airline industry, with some help from government, has achieved a remarkable reduction in the incidence of hijackings. The press, in its turn, owes it to the world community to point out how rarely the skyjacker is other than a pitifully disturbed human being, how obstacle-strewn is the path of the would-be skyjacker, and how seldom a skyjacking accomplishes its aims. This is a two-way street: We expect our airlines and our government to give us full information; and we expect our press to exercise judgment in giving us not only the drama of the event but also the stupidity and the monstrosity of it.

"The world cannot permit the boon of air travel to become the tool of criminals."

ACKNOWLEDGMENTS

Since becoming associated with commercial aviation, first as a wire-service newsman and later as an airline employee, I've had great admiration and respect for the men and women who make up the group called Schedule Control (in some airlines called Operations Control). The Schedule Control Center is the heartbeat of every airline, and to see a controller at work is to see coordination in motion. Controllers must know *where* their company's aircraft are at any given moment ... they must know where they are going, how they are getting there, what to do with them when they get there, how to get them there on time, how to get them home, how to make the best of a weather diversion ... and a dozen other things to make the daily operation run smooth. In short, a schedule controller is a pilot on the ground.

To an airline like Pan Am, with a fleet of 172 aircraft circling the globe, or TWA, whose fleet numbers some 224, this can be quite a job.

The accuracy, detail and color in the first chapter of this book which described the waning hours of the Clipper *Fortune* were provided in large measure by Pan Am's Schedule Control at John F. Kennedy International Airport, New York. For the sake of writing for the laymen, some of this material may seem grossly oversimplified to professional schedule controllers ... but, under the circumstances, I'm sure they will understand.

The material in this book has been under research since 1961 and the list of people who made contributions would be far too long to note here. However, I must mention David H. Brown of the U.S. Department of Transportation who served as my statistician; Donald Pengelly of the International Air Transport Association; David T. Parsons of Pan Am in New York; and Robert E. Wick of Pan Am in Washington for their efforts in arranging critical interviews.

Also, special thanks to Donald Bain, who convinced me that this book had to be written and to Lilla Tognelli for long hours of manuscript typing and proofreading.

The words in this book make sense because of Valerie Moolman, whose truly professional literary skill and ability to

312

grasp the highly complex subject of aerial hijacking made it a sheer delight to work with her as my editorial consultant.

And finally, I would like to comment on a line written by my former UPI colleague, Robert J. Serling, who said in dedicating his last book to his wife: ". . . stewardesses make wonderful wives."

That goes double for my Elizabeth Ann.

James A. Arey
Scarsdale, New York

APPENDIX A

CHRONOLOGY

Aerial hijackings, successful and unsuccessful, from 1930 to mid-1971

KEY:

* Successful to Cuba
† Unsuccessful to Cuba
‡ Successful to countries other than Cuba
§ Unsuccessful to countries other than Cuba
(J) Juvenile
(S) Military personnel

This list is compiled from data furnished by the U.S. Department of Transportation, Federal Aviation Administration, American Air Transport Association, International Air Transport Association, International Civil Aviation Organization, thousands of press clippings, and the personal files of the author.

DATE	NAME	AIRLINE	TYPE OF AIRCRAFT	FLIGHT PLAN	COMMENTS
‡ 1930		Foreign	F-7	Peru/Local Flight	Peruvian revolution
‡ 7/25/47		Foreign (Private)		Rumania/Turkey	
‡ 4/8/48		Foreign		Czechoslovakia	Landed U.S. Zone, Germany
‡ 5/4/48		Foreign		Czechoslovakia	Landed U.S. Zone, Germany
‡ 6/4/48		Foreign		Yugoslavia/Italy	
‡ 6/17/48		Foreign		Rumania/Austria	

DATE	NAME	AIRLINE	TYPE OF AIRCRAFT	FLIGHT PLAN	COMMENTS
‡ 6/30/48	2 men	Foreign		Bulgaria/Turkey	Pilot, copilot wounded; landed Istanbul
§ 7/16/48		Foreign		Hong Kong	
‡ 9/12/48		Foreign		Greece/Yugoslavia	
‡ 4/29/49		Foreign		Rumania/Greece	
‡ 12/9/49		Foreign		Rumania/Yugoslavia	
‡ 12/16/49		Foreign		Poland/Denmark	
‡ 3/24/50		Foreign (Czech)		Brno/Prague	Landed U.S. Zone, Germany
‡ 3/24/50		Foreign (Czech)		Ostrava/Prague	Landed U.S. Zone, Germany
‡ 3/24/50		Foreign (Czech)		Bratislava/Prague	Landed U.S. Zone, Germany
§ 12/3/52		Foreign		Phillippines/Red China	
‡ 3/23/53		Foreign		Czechoslovakia/W.Germany	
‡ 2/16/58		Foreign		S.Korea/N.Korea	
§ 4/10/58		Foreign		S.Korea/N.Korea	
* 10/22/58		Foreign		Cuba—domestic	

DATE	NAME	AIRLINE	TYPE OF AIRCRAFT	FLIGHT PLAN	COMMENTS
† 11/1/58	5 men	Cubana	Viscount	Miami/Varadero	Plane crashed, 17 killed; 3 rescued
* 11/6/58		Foreign		Cuba—domestic	
‡ 4/16/59		Foreign		Cuba/USA	
* About 5/15/59		Foreign		Haiti/Cuba	
‡ 10/2/59		Foreign		Cuba/USA	
‡ 4/12/60	4 men	Foreign	Viscount	Cuba—domestic	Landed Miami
‡ 7/5/60	2 men	Cubana		Madrid/Havana	Landed Miami
‡ 7/18/60	1 man	Cubana	Viscount	Havana/Miami	Landed Jamaica
§ 7/19/60	1 man	Trans-Australia	Electra		
‡ 7/28/60	3 men	Cubana		Cuba—domestic	Landed Miami
§ 8/21/60		Foreign	USSR		
‡ 10/29/60	9 men	Cubana	DC-3	Havana/Isle of Pines	Landed Key West
§ 12/8/60	5 men	Cubana		Marathon/Key West	All executed
* 5/1/61	Antilio Ortiz	National	CV-440		Fugitive
‡ 7/3/61	14 men	Cubana	DC-3	Havana/Varadero	Landed Miami
* 7/24/61	Wilfredo Oquendo	Eastern	L-188	Miami/Tampa	Fugitive
† 7/31/61	Bruce Britt	Pacific Air	DC-3	Chicago/San Francisco	20 years prison

DATE	NAME	AIRLINE	TYPE OF AIRCRAFT	FLIGHT PLAN	COMMENTS
† 8/3/61	Leon Bearden, Cody Bearden(J)	Continental	B-707	Los Angeles/Houston	20 years prison, Reform school
* 8/9/61	Albert Cadon	Pan Am	DC-8	Mexico City/Guatemala	Mexican prison—8 years, 9 months
§ 8/9/61	Group of men	Cubana	DC-3	Havana/Isle of Pines	3 killed, 6 wounded
§ 9/10/61	3 men	Foreign (Private)	YAK-13	USSR/Armenia	1 killed, 1 injured in crash
‡ 11/10/61	6 men	Transportes Aeros (Portuguese)		Casablanca/Lisbon	Refueled Tangier, landed Brazil
‡ 11/27/61	5 men	AVENSA (Venezuelan)	DC-6B	Caracas/Maracaibo	Landed Curacao, hijackers extradited
§§ 3/17/62		Foreign		France	
* 4/13/62	David Healy, Leonard Oeth	Private	Cessna	Miami—local	20 years prison, 20 years prison
§ 4/16/62	1 man	KLM (Dutch)		Amsterdam/Lisbon	Landed Holland
† 8/5/63	Roy Siller	Private	Beech T-34	Miami—local	$150 fine
* 8/8/63	Robert A. Michelena	Private			
‡ 11/28/63	6 men	AVENSA (Venezuelan)	CV-440	Ciudad Bolivar/Caracas	Landed Trinidad, hijacker extradited
* 2/18/64	Enrique Hernandez, Reinaldo Rodriguez	Private	Piper PA-23	Miami—local	Fugitive, Fugitive

DATE	NAME	AIRLINE	TYPE OF AIRCRAFT	FLIGHT PLAN	COMMENTS
§ 10/19/64	2 men	Foreign	AN-2	USSR	Pilot wounded
§ Spring 1965	1 man, 1 woman	Foreign	AN-2	USSR	
‡ 8/31/65	Harry Fegerstrom (J)	Hawaiian	DC-3	Honolulu	Correctional School
§ 10/11/65	Lawrence Heisler (S) Richard Boyd (S)	ALOHA	F-27	Molokai/Honolulu	4 years hard labor, dishonorable discharge for both
† 10/26/65	Luis Perez	National	L-188	Miami/Key West	Acquitted
† 11/17/65	Thomas Robinson (J)	National	DC-8	New Orleans/Florida	Correctional School
§ 3/27/66	Angel Bentancourt Cueto	Cubana	IL-18	Santiago/Havana	2 killed after pilot used trick to land Cuba
§ Spring 1966		Foreign		USSR/Turkey	
‡ 7/7/66	9 men	Cubana	IL-18	Santiago/Havana	Landed Jamaica, co-pilot wounded
§ About 8/66		Foreign		USSR/Turkey	1 passenger wounded
‡ 9/28/66	Maria Varrier and 18 men	Foreign (Argentine)	DC-4	Buenos Aires/Rio Gallegos	Landed Falkland, all extradited and jailed
‡ 2/7/67	Riyad Hajjaj	Foreign (Egyptian)	AN-24	Egypt	Landed Jordan

DATE	NAME	AIR LINE	TYPE OF AIRCRAFT	FLIGHT PLAN	COMMENTS
‡ 4/24/67	5 men	Foreign (Nigerian)	F-27	Benin City/Lagos	Landed Nigeria
‡ 6/30/67	1 man	Foreign (Private) (UK)	HS-125	Spain/Majorca	Landed Algeria; Moise Tshombe passenger
* 8/6/67	5 men	Aerocondor (Colombian)	DC-4	Barranquilla/San Andres Island	
* 9/9/67	Ramiro Garcia Fernando Garcia Joaquin Garcia	AVIANCA (Colombian)	DC-3	Barranquilla/Magangue (Colombia)	
* 11/20/67	Gabor Gabler	Private	Piper PA-10	Hollywood, Fla./Bimini	Fugitive
§ 2/9/68	William Clark (S)(Marine)	Pan Am (Military charter)	DC-6B	Vietnam/Hong Kong	Hard labor, dishonorable discharge; conviction set aside on appeal 12/69
* 2/17/68	Thomas Boynton	Private	Piper PA-24	Marathon/Miami	20 years prison
* 2/21/68	Lawrence Rhodes, Jr.	Delta	DC-8	Tampa/W. Palm Beach	Pending—mental exam
* 3/5/68	Sani Analaye Jaico Acosta Aristides Villalobos	AVIANCA (Colombian)	DC-4	Rio Hacha/Barranquilla	

DATE	NAME	AIRLINE	TYPE OF AIRCRAFT	FLIGHT PLAN	COMMENTS
* 3/12/68	Jesus Armenteros / Gilberto Gonzales / Ramon Martin	National	DC-8	Tampa/Miami	Fugitive / Fugitive / Fugitive
* 3/16/68	1 man	Foreign (Private) (Mexican)		Marida/Cozumel	
* 3/22/68	3 men	AVENSA (Venezuelan)	CV-440	Caracas/Maracaibo	
* 6/19/68	Radhames Mendez Vargas	VIASA (Venezuelan)	DC-9	Dominican Republic/Curacao	20 years, Dominican court
* 6/29/68	E. H. Carter	Southeast	DC-3	Marathon/Key West	Fugitive
* 7/1/68	Mario Fonseca	Northwest	B-727	Chicago/Miami	
§ 7/4/68	John Morris	TWA	B-727	New York/California	5 years prison
* 7/12/68	Leonard Bendicks	Private	Cessna	Key West/Miami	Pending
† 7/12/68	Oran Richards	Delta	CV-880	Baltimore/Houston	Committed mental hospital
* 7/17/68	Rogelio Leyva	National	DC-8	Los Angeles/Miami	Fugitive
‡ 7/23/68	3 men	EL AL	B-707	Rome/Tel Aviv	Landed Algiers
* 8/4/68	Willis Jessie	Private	Cessna	Naples, Fla.—local	10 years prison
* 8/22/68	1 man	Private	Cessna	Nassau/Exuma (Bahamas)	

DATE	NAME	AIRLINE	TYPE OF AIRCRAFT	FLIGHT PLAN	COMMENTS
† 9/11/68	Charles Beasley	Air Canada	Viscount	St. John/Toronto	6 years Canadian prison
* 9/20/68	Jose Garcia	Eastern	B-720	San Juan/Miami	Fugitive
* 9/22/68	Ramon Garcia	AVIANCA (Colombian)	B-727	Barranquilla/Cartagena	
* 9/22/68	Carlos Londono	AVIANCA (Colombian)	DC-4	Barranquilla/Santa Maico	
* 10/6/68	Judy Vazquez	Aeromaya (Mexican)	HS-748	Cozumel/Merida	
* 10/23/68	Alben Truitt	Private	Cessna	Key West—local	20 years prison
§ 10/30/68	J.F. Garcia-Zurita	SEASA(Mexican)		Tampico/Brownsville	Landed Brownsville, Texas
† 11/2/68	Roger Pastorich (J)	National	DC-9	Mobile/Chicago	Probation
* 11/4/68	Raymond Johnson	National	B-727	New Orleans/Miami	Fugitive
‡ 11/6/68	M. Rabuya	Foreign (Philippines)		Philippines—local	Electrocuted
‡ 11/8/68	G. Umberto	Olympic (Greek)	DC-6B	Greece—local	8 months; Greek prison
* 11/18/68	Hugo Torres	CMA(Mexican)	DC-4	Merida/Mexico City	

DATE	NAME	AIRLINE	TYPE OF AIRCRAFT	FLIGHT PLAN	COMMENTS
* 11/23/68	Irardo Viera Teresa Demendoza Moises Rodriguez Aramis Garcia Miguel Valasquez Alberto Quintero	Eastern	B-727	Chicago/Miami	
* 11/24/68	Jose Cruz Luis Soltern Miguel Custro	Pan Am	B-707	New York/ San Juan	Fugitive Fugitive
* 11/30/68	Miguel Sanchez	Eastern	B-720	Miami/Dallas	Fugitive
* 12/3/68	Eddie Canteras	National	B-727	Tampa/Miami	Fugitive
* 12/11/68	James Patterson Gwendolyn Patterson	TWA	B-727	Nashville/Miami	Fugitive
* 12/19/68	Thomas Washington	Eastern	DC-8	Philadelphia/ Miami	2 years; additional charges pending in Philadelphia
* 1/2/69	Tyrone Austin Linda Austin	Eastern	DC-8	New York/Miami	Shot to death 4/21/71 in bank holdup attempt in New York; woman still at large.
‡ 1/2/69	G. Flamourides	Olympic (Greek)	DC-6B	Crete/Athens	22 months prison
* 1/7/69	1 man	AVIANCA (Colombian)	DC-4	Rio Hacha/ Maicao	Landed Santiago

DATE	NAME	AIRLINE	TYPE OF AIRCRAFT	FLIGHT PLAN	COMMENTS
* 1/9/69	Ronald Bohle	Eastern	B-727	Miami/Nassau	25 years prison
* 1/11/69	Robert Helmey	United	B-727	Jacksonville/Miami	Acquitted
* 1/11/69	Jesus Anala	ASPA(Peruvian)	CV-990	Panama City/Miami	
† 1/13/69	Kenneth McPeek	Delta	CV-880	Detroit/Miami	15 years prison
* 1/19/69	Aristo Payano	Eastern	DC-8	New York/Miami	
* 1/19/69	3 men	Ecuatoriana (Ecuadorian)	L-188	Quito/Miami	
* 1/24/69	Johnny Coulter (S)	National	B-727	Key West/New York	Fugitive
* 1/28/69	Byron Booth Clinton Smith	National	DC-8	New Orleans/Miami	Fugitive Fugitive
* 1/28/69	3 men	Eastern	DC-8	Atlanta/Miami	Fugitives
* 1/31/69	1 man	National	DC-8	San Francisco/Tampa	Fugitive
* 2/3/69	Wilfredo Garcia Joaquim Estrada	Eastern	B-727	Newark/Miami	
† 2/3/69	Michael Peparo (J) Tasmin Fitzgerald (J)	National	B-727	New York/Miami	Correctional school Correctional school
* 2/5/69	Leonardo Fuentes	SAM (Colombian)	DC-4	Barranquilla/Medellin	
† 2/8/69	Victor Romo	Foreign (Mexican)		Mexico City	

DATE	NAME	AIRLINE	TYPE OF AIRCRAFT	FLIGHT PLAN	COMMENTS
* 2/10/69	Pedro DeQuesada	Eastern	DC-8	San Juan/Miami	
* 2/11/69	3 men	Aeropostal (Venezuelan)	DC-9	Maracaibo/Caracas	
* 2/25/69	Lorenzo Ervin	Eastern	DC-8	Atlanta/Miami	Life in prison
* 3/5/69	Anthony Bryant	National	B-727	New York/Miami	Fugitive
† 3/11/69	Juan Caro Montoya	Sociedad (Colombian)	DC-4	Bogota	
* 3/15/69		Aerocondor (Colombian)	DC-6	Barranquilla/San Andres Island	
* 3/17/69		Faucett (Peruvian)	B-727	Lima/Ecuador	
* 3/17/69	Robert Sandlin	Delta	DC-9	Dallas/Charleston, S.C.	Pending; mental exam. Committed to fed. mental inst.
† 3/19/69	Douglas Dickey	Delta	CV-880	Dallas/New York	Pending; mental exam.
* 3/25/69	Luis Frese	Delta	DC-8	Dallas/San Diego	Fugitive
* 4/11/69	6 men	Foreign (Ecuadorian)	DC-6	Guyaquil/Quito	Fugitive
* 4/13/69	Hiram Sanchez Manuel Aguero Jose Claro Esmeraldo Castanedo	Pan Am	B-727	San Juan/Miami	Fugitive Fugitive Fugitive Fugitive

DATE	NAME	AIRLINE	TYPE OF AIRCRAFT	FLIGHT PLAN	COMMENTS
* 4/14/69	3 men	SAM(Colombian)	DC-4	Medellin/Barranquilla	
† 5/3/69	John Kivlen	National	DC-8	Los Angels/Miami	Prosecution declined
* 5/5/69	Jean Charette Allain Allard	National	B-727	New York/Miami	Fugitives
* 5/20/69	3 men	AVIANCA (Colombian)	B-737	Bogota/Pereira	
* 5/26/69	Crecencio Zamora Robert Garcia Marino Samon	Northeast	B-727	Miami/New York	Fugitive Fugitive Fugitive
† 5/30/69	Terrance Neimyer	Texas Intl.	CV-600	New Orleans/ Alexandria, La.	Pending; mental exam.
‡ 6/4/69	1 man	DIA(Portuguese)	DAKOTA	Angola/Cabinda	Landed Congo
* 6/17/69	William Brent	TWA	B-707	Oakland/New York	Fugitive
* 6/20/69	3 men	Urrago (Colombian)	DC-3	Colombia— local	
* 6/22/69	Medrand Esquivel sick wife & daughter	Eastern	DC-8	Newark/Miami	Fugitive
* 6/25/69	John Marques	United	DC-8	Los Angeles/ New York	Fugitive
* 6/28/69	Raymond Anthony	Eastern	B-727	Baltimore/Tampa	15 years prison
* 7/3/69	1 man	SAETA (Ecuadorian)	DC-3	Ecuador— local	

DATE	NAME	AIRLINE	TYPE OF AIRCRAFT	FLIGHT PLAN	COMMENTS
* 7/10/69		AVIANCA (Colombian)			
* 7/26/69	David Canbera	Mexicana (Mexican)	DC-6	Veracruz/Tabasco	
* 7/26/69	Joseph Crawford	Continental	DC-9	Los Angeles/Lubbock, Tex.	50 years prison
† 7/29/69		Foreign(Nicaraguan)			
* 7/31/69	Lester Perry	TWA	B-727	Philadelphia/Los Angeles	Fugitive
* 8/4/69	3 men	AVIANCA (Colombian)	DC-4	Santa Marta/Rio Hacha	
† 8/5/69	John McCreery	Eastern	DC-9	Syracuse/Tampa	Committed mental hospital
‡ 8/12/69	7 men	Ethiopian Air	DC-3	Bahr Dar/Addis Ababa	Landed Khartoum; 2 weeks jail for passport violation
‡ 8/14/69	Domingo Diaz Julio Perez	Northeast	B-727	Boston/Miami	Fugitive Fugitive
‡ 8/16/69	Dr. V. Tsironis	Olympic(Greek)	DC-3	Athens/Agrinion	Landed Albania
‡ 8/18/69	M.S. Al-Muniri	Misrair (Egyptian)	AN-24	Cairo/Luxor	Landed Egypt; sentenced to life
* 8/23/69	2 men	AVIANCA (Colombian)	AVRO-748	Burcarmanga/Bogota	
* 8/29/69	Jorge Delgado	National	B-727	Miami/Houston	Fugitive

DATE	NAME	AIRLINE	TYPE OF AIRCRAFT	FLIGHT PLAN	COMMENTS
‡ 8/29/69	Leila Khaled Salim Isawi	TWA	B-707	Los Angeles/Tel Aviv	Landed Damascus
* 9/6/69	6 men, 1 woman	Foreign (Ecuadorian)	C-47	Ecuador—local	
§ 9/6/69	6 men	Foreign (Ecuadorian)	C-47	Ecuador—local	Co-pilot killed when refueling in Tumaco; plane abandoned
* 9/7/69	1 man	Eastern	DC-8	New York/San Juan	
† 9/10/69	Jose Medina	Eastern	DC-8	New York/San Juan	Pending
§ 9/13/69	3 men	Ethiopian Air	DC-6	Addis Ababa/Djibouti	1 hijacker shot, other 2 arrested when plane landed Aden
‡ 9/13/69	Carlos Huete	SAHSA (Honduran)	DC-3	Honduras—local	Arrested after landing in El Salvador
‡ 9/16/69	Sadi Toker	Foreign (Turkish)	Viscount	Istanbul/Ankara	Land Sofia; committed mental institution
* 9/24/69	Alfred Hernandez (S)	National	B-727	Newark/Miami	Fugitive
* 10/8/69	1 man	Cruzeiro do Sul (Brazilian)	Caravelle	Belem/Manaus (Brazil)	
* 10/8/69	E. Ugartteche	Aerolinas (Argentine)	B-707	Buenos Aires/Miami	

DATE	NAME	AIRLINE	TYPE OF AIRCRAFT	FLIGHT PLAN	COMMENTS
* 10/9/69	Francisco Perry	National	DC-8	Los Angeles/Miami	Fugitive
‡ 10/19/69	P. Klemt H. V. VonHof	LOT(Polish)	IL-18	Warsaw/E. Berlin	Landed W. Berlin Each sentenced 2 years
* 10/21/69	Henry Shorr(J)	Pan Am	B-720	Mexico City/Miami	Committed suicide in Cuban hotel 9/28/70
* 10/28/69	2 men	Aerotaxi (Colombian)		Buenaventura/Bogota	
‡ 10/31/69	Rafael Minichiello(S)	TWA	B-707	Baltimore/San Francisco	Landed Rome; tried on non-hijacking counts; sentenced to 7½ years; released after 18 months
* 11/4/69	2 men	Lanica (Nicaraguan)	BAC-111	Miami/Mexico City	Stop in Grand Cayman where all but crew deplaned before going on
* 11/4/69	5 men, 1 woman	VARIG (Brazilian)	B-707	Buenos Aires/Santiago	
* 11/6/69		East-West Airlines			
† 11/8/69	Luis Melgarejo	Austral (Argentine)	BAC-111	Cordoba/Buenos Aires	Talked into surrendering at refueling stop in Montevideo; sentenced to 1-2 years

DATE	NAME	AIRLINE	TYPE OF AIRCRAFT	FLIGHT PLAN	COMMENTS
§ 11/10/69	David Booth(J)	Delta	DC-9	Lexington, Ky./ Chicago	Used girl as hostage in terminal; committed to mental hospital
† 11/12/69	2 men	LAM(Chilean)	Caravelle	Chile—local	Overpowered by crew
* 11/12/69	1 man	Cruzeiro do Sul (Brazilian)	YS-11	Brazil—local	
* 11/13/69	6 men	AVIANCA (Colombian)	DC-4	Colombia—local	
* 11/18/69		Foreign(Mexican)			
† 11/20/69	W. Szymankiewicz R. Zolotucho	LOT(Polish)	AN-24	Wroclaw/Warsaw	Landed Austria; Szymankiewicz 24-27 months hard labor; Zolotucho, 2 years; both expelled
* 11/30/69	1 man	Varig(Brazilian)	B-707	Lisbon/Rio de Janeiro	
* 12/2/69	Benny Hamilton	TWA	B-707	San Francisco Philadelphia	Fugitive
† 12/11/69	3 men	Foreign (S.Korean)	YS-11	Kangnung/Seoul	Landed N. Korea
§ 12/12/69	2 men	Ethiopian Air	B-707	Madrid/ Addis Ababa	Both hijackers slain by security guards; landed Athens

DATE	NAME	AIRLINE	TYPE OF AIRCRAFT	FLIGHT PLAN	COMMENTS
* 12/19/69	1 man	LAN(Chilean)	B-727		
§ 12/21/69		TWA	B-707		
* 12/23/69	1 man	LACSA (Costa Rican)	C-46	Puerto Limon/ San Jose	Released 30 passengers at San Andres Island
* 12/26/69	M. Martinez	United	B-727	New York/Chicago	Fugitive
* 1/1/70	4 men, 1 woman	Cruzeiro do Sul (Brazilian)	Caravelle	Montevideo/ Rio de Janeiro	Stopped in Peru, Panama
§ 1/6/70	Anton Funjek	Delta	DC-9	Orlando/Atlanta	Wanted to go to Switzerland; overpowered on ground, sentenced 25 years
§ 1/7/70	Mariano Rodriguez	Iberia (Spanish)	CV-880	Madrid/Zaragoza	Wanted to go to Albania; surrendered in Zaragoza, sentenced 6 years, 1 day
‡ 1/9/70	Christian Belon	TWA	B-707	New York/Rome	Took over after Paris; landed Beirut, fined $7; later re-arrested and sentenced to 3 years which was reduced to 9 months

DATE	NAME	AIRLINE	TYPE OF AIRCRAFT	FLIGHT PLAN	COMMENTS
† 1/9/70	Jorge Medrano	RAPSA (Panamanian)	C-47	David City/ Bocas del Toro	Slain by militia when return David City to refuel
* 1/23/70	2 men, 2 women	ALM (Netherlands Antilles Airlines)	F-27	Santo Domingo/ Curacao	
† 2/6/70	Pedro Bravo Oscar Vasquez	LAN (Chilean)	Caravelle	Puerto Montt/ Santiago	1 hijacker slain, 1 wounded; stewardess wounded by detectives disguised as crew
§ 2/10/70	3 men	EL AL (Israeli)	B-707	Tel Aviv/ London	Grenades hurled at passengers while plane parked at Munich; 1 passenger killed and 11 wounded
* 2/16/70	Daniel Abad	Eastern	B-727	Newark/Miami	Armed with gun and homemade bomb; could not speak English; fugitive
§ 3/10/70	1 man, wife	Interflug (E. German)	AN-24	E. Berlin/ Leipzig	Couple reportedly committed suicide when attempt failed
* 3/11/70	Clemente Stubbs	United	B-727	Cleveland/ W. Palm Beach	Refueled Atlanta; fugitive

DATE	NAME	AIRLINE	TYPE OF AIRCRAFT	FLIGHT PLAN	COMMENTS
* 3/11/70	4 men	AVIANCA (Colombian)	B-727	Bogota/Barranquilla	
* 3/12/70	1 man	Varig (Brazilian)	B-707	Santiago/London	Similar flight hijacked 11/4/69
§ 3/17/70	John DiVivo	Eastern	DC-9	Newark/Boston (Shuttle)	Wanted to go "east"; copilot killed, pilot wounded but landed safely Boston; held for murder, committed suicide 10/31/70
* 3/24/70		Aerolinas Argentinas (Argentine)	Comet IV	Cordoba/Tucuman (domestic)	9-hour repair stop in Lima, Peru; landed Cuba next day
* 3/25/70	1 man, 1 woman	Foreign (Private)	Cessna	British Honduras	Refueled in Mexico
‡ 3/30/70	9 students	Japan Air Lines	B-727	Tokyo/Fukuoka	Wanted to go to N. Korea; armed with swords; land S. Korea by trick; after 4½ days, passengers exchanged for hostage; land N. Korea 4/3/70; crew and hostage return 4/4/70

DATE	NAME	AIRLINE	TYPE OF AIRCRAFT	FLIGHT PLAN	COMMENTS
† 4/6/70	Lynn L. Little	TWA	B-707	San Francisco/ Pittsburgh	Surrendered to crew
§ 4/16/70	Group young men	Foreign(Czech)		Prague/Karlovy	Overpowered by crew
† 4/18/70	Marvin Right Lindon and brother	Foreign(CRNA)	C-46	Puerto Limon/ San Jose	Surrendered to police
§ 4/22/70	Joseph Wagstaff	North Central	DC-9	Detroit/Sault Ste. Marie	Hijacked bus to Petosky, Mich., Airport; boarded plane but was subdued after threatening crew; pending mental exam
* 4/22/70	Ira Meeks Dianne Meeks	Private	Cessna	Gastonia, S.C.—local	Hijacked taxi to airport; then hired plane; refuel Rock Hill, S.C., Jacksonville, Fla., and Fort Lauderdale, Fla., both fugitives
* 4/25/70	1 man	Viacao Aerea de Sao Paulo (Brazilian)	B-737	Domestic	Refueled Guyana where 36 passengers deplane; 1 "hippie" asked to remain in Cuba
* 5/1/70	2 men	Foreign (British West Indian)	B-727	Jamaica/Senegal	Wanted Algeria at first

DATE	NAME	AIRLINE	TYPE OF AIRCRAFT	FLIGHT PLAN	COMMENTS
‡ 5/5/70	Pavel Verner	Foreign(Private) executive plane (Czech)		Domestic	Junior executive for Czech uranium plant knocked out boss and stabbed pilot; wanted W. Germany to look for a job but diverted to Linz, Austria; sentenced to 1 year
* 5/12/70	8 men	ALM(Netherlands Antilles Airlines)	F-27	Santo Domingo/	Dutch revolutionaries
§ 5/14/70	T.N. Perrotis	Ansett Airlines (Australian)	DC-9	Brisbane	While hijacker allegedly threatened pilot with what proved to be toy gun, girl, 6, accidentally opened exit door while plane on ground at Sydney Airport, allowing police to board; 5 years prison
* 5/14/70	1 man	Viacao Aera de Sao Paulo (Brazilian)	B-737	Brazilia/Manaus	Refuel Guyana, Curacao; hijacker armed with gun and explosives

DATE	NAME	AIRLINE	TYPE OF AIRCRAFT	FLIGHT PLAN	COMMENTS
* 5/21/70	4 men	AVIANCA (Colombian)	DC-3	Yopal/Sogamozo (Domestic)	Stopped unexpectedly in Barrancabermeja and later refueled in Barranquilla
* 5/24/70	3 men, 1 woman	Mexicana de Aviacion (Mexican)	B-727	Cozumel/Merida (Domestic)	
* 5/25/70	Graciella Quesada	Delta	CV-880	Chicago/Miami	Armed with .38 revolver; took over after Atlanta; fugitive
* 5/25/70	Nelson Molina	American	B-727	Chicago/New York	Refueled New York where passengers deplaned; fugitive
§ 5/30/70	15 members Sinn Fein group	BEA	Trident	On ground at Shannon	Occupied aircraft; evacuated by police
‡ 5/30/70	Gianlocca Stellipi	Alitalia (Italian)	DC-9	Genoa/Rome	Toy pistol; landed Cairo
* 5/31/70	2 men	AVIANCA (Colombian)	Avro-748	Bogota/Bucaramaga	Refueled Barranca-bermeja
§ 6/4/70	Arthur Barkley	TWA	B-727	Phoenix/Washington, D.C.	Landed Dulles where hijacker sought $100 million ransom; $100,000 was paid; departed for up-state New York but

DATE	NAME	AIRLINE	TYPE OF AIRCRAFT	FLIGHT PLAN	COMMENTS
					returned for more ransom, tires shot out when aircraft landed again at Dulles, FBI board; armed with gun, knife, can of fluid; pilot, hijacker wounded; pending mental exam
§ 6/5/70	Z. Iwanicki	LOT(Polish)	AN-24	Szczecin/Dganst (Domestic)	Armed with 2 grenades; landed Copenhagen; 6 years sentence, later reduced to 3 years
‡ 6/8/70	4 men, 4 women	CSA(Czech)	IL-14	Karlsbad/Prague (Domestic)	Landed Nuremberg, ask asylum but sentenced to terms ranging from 8 months to 2½ years
§ 6/9/70	A. Rybak R. Jasinski	LOT(Polish)	AN-24	Katowice/Warsaw (Domestic)	Foiled by crew
§ 6/15/70	12 persons	Aeroflot (Soviet)	AN-2		Tried by Soviet court; given sentences ranging from 3 yrs/life;
§ 6/21/70	2 men, 1 youth	Iran National	B-727	Iran/Iraq	Landed Baghdad

DATE	NAME	AIRLINE	TYPE OF AIRCRAFT	FLIGHT PLAN	COMMENTS
‡ 6/22/70	Hexhi Xyaferi	Pan Am	B-707	Beirut/New York	Landed Cairo
* 6/26/70		AVIANCA (Colombian)	B-727	Cucuta/Bogota	Refueled Barranquilla
* 7/1/70	Bob Serra	National	DC-8	San Francisco/ Miami	Taken over after stop in New Orleans; 4 servicemen passengers roughed up at Jose Marti Airport; hijacker apparently boarded at Las Vegas; fugitive
† 7/1/70	3 men, 1 women	Cruzeiro do Sul(Brazilian)	Caravelle	Rio de Janeiro/ Buenos Aires	Had hoped to ex- change hijacked passengers for jailed terrorists
* 7/4/70	2 men	Cruzeiro do Sul(Brazilian)	YS-11		Refueled French Guiana where 37 passengers left
‡ 7/11/70	1 man	Foreign (Arabian)	B-707	Saudi Arabia/ Syria	
§ 7/22/70	George Hardin (S)	Air Vietnam	DC-4	Pleiku/Saigon	Held pilot at knifepoint for 2 hours before sur- rendering at Ton San Nhut Airport;

DATE	NAME	AIRLINE	TYPE OF AIRCRAFT	FLIGHT PLAN	COMMENTS
					air had been let out of tires; escaped from military custody 8/10/70, tried to hijack C-141 from Bienhoa Air Base, recaptured
‡ 7/22/70	5 men, 1 woman	Olympic (Greek)	B-727	Beirut	Arab commandos released passengers after Greek government promised to release 7 Arab terrorists from jail; landed Cairo
* 7/25/70	4 men	Aeronaves de Mexico(Mexican)	DC-9	Acapulco/Mexico City	30-minute refueling stop Mexico City
† 7/28/70	Germin Albornoz	Aerolinas Argentinas (Argentine)	B-737	Salta/Buenos Aires	Armed with 2 guns; refuel Cordoba where 23 passengers left and at Mendoza; Andes snowstorm forced plane back to Cordoba where hijacker surrendered
* 8/2/70	Rudolpho Rios	Pan Am	B-747	New York/San Juan	Displayed "gun" and bottle of fluid;

DATE	NAME	AIRLINE	TYPE OF AIRCRAFT	FLIGHT PLAN	COMMENTS
					he and stewardess hostage stayed outside cockpit door; fugitive
§ 8/3/70	Johann Huber	Pan Am	B-727	Munich/W. Berlin	Wanted Budapest but was talked out of it by crew who said plane did not have sufficient fuel
§ 8/7/70	Waldemar Frey	LOT(Polish)	AN-24	Szczegin/Katowice (Domestic)	Armed with grenade but denied entry into cockpit; landed E. Berlin but wanted Hamburg; 13 years prison.
‡ 8/8/70	Vladimir Rehak and sons, Vladimir, Jr., and Jaromir	Foreign(Czech)	IL-14	Domestic	Landed Vienna
* 8/19/70	Jose Arrue	Trans Carib	DC-8	Newark/San Juan	
‡ 8/19/70	Sachio Inagaki	All Nippon (Japanese)	B-727	Nagoya/Sapporo (Domestic)	Ordered plane land at Hamamatsu Air Defense Base, demanded rifle and ammo, possible suicide plot; woman passenger feigned

DATE	NAME	AIRLINE	TYPE OF AIRCRAFT	FLIGHT PLAN	COMMENTS
					pregnancy pains and in confusion police boarded and overpowered hijacker who had only a toy pistol
‡ 8/19/70	3 men, 2 women	LOT(Polish)	IL-14	Gdansk/Warsaw (Domestic)	1 hijacker had grenade; landed Danish island of Bornholm, asked asylum
* 8/20/70	Gregory Graves (S)	Delta	DC-9	Atlanta/Savannah	AWOL Marine said he had bomb in lap but unseen
* 8/24/70	Robert Labadie (S)	TWA	B-727	Las Vegas/Philadelphia	Said he had bomb; landed Pittsburgh to refuel; first hijacker returned by Cuba directly to U.S. 9/24/70; committed
§ 8/27/70	Rudolf Olma	LOT(Polish)	AN-24	Katowice/Warsaw (Domestic)	Threatened crew with bomb which accidentally exploded injuring hijacker and 10 passengers;

DATE	NAME	AIRLINE	TYPE OF AIRCRAFT	FLIGHT PLAN	COMMENTS
‡ 8/31/70	3 men	Air Algerie (Algerian)	CV-640	Annaba/Algiers (Domestic)	landed safely at Katowice; wanted Vienna, sentenced 25 years prison
‡ 9/6/70	Group of guerrillas	TWA	B-707	Tel Aviv/New York	Palestine Liberation Front guerrillas took over after Frankfurt stop; land Dawson Field, Jordan, where blown up 9/12/70
‡ 9/6/70	Group of guerrillas	Swissair	DC-8	Zurich/New York	Palestine Liberation Front guerrillas took over near Paris; land Dawson Field, Jordan, where blown up 9/12/70
‡ 9/6/70	Group of guerrillas (3 men)	Pan Am	B-747	Amsterdam/London	Two Palestine Liberation Front guerrillas joined

DATE	NAME	AIRLINE	TYPE OF AIRCRAFT	FLIGHT PLAN	COMMENTS
					by 1 other after refuel in Beirut; taken to Cairo where blown up 9/7/70
§ 9/6/70	Leila Khaled Patrick Arguello	El Al (Israeli)	B-707	Tel Aviv/ New York	Armed steward killed male hijacker, female overpowered by passengers, landed London; female hijacker involved in previous incident 8/29/70; Miss Khaled released
‡ 9/9/70	Group of guerrillas	BOAC (British)	VC-10	Bombay/London	Palestine Liberation Front guerrillas forced plane refuel Beirut before go to Dawson Field, Jordan, where blown up 9/12/70
‡ 9/14/70	3 men	Tarom (Rumanian)	BAC-111	Bucharest/Prague	Landed Munich 3 men sentenced 2½ years in prison
§ 9/15/70	Donald Irwin	TWA	B-707	Los Angeles/ San Francisco	Wanted N.Korea; wounded by Brinks

DATE	NAME	AIRLINE	TYPE OF AIRCRAFT	FLIGHT PLAN	COMMENTS
					guard who was passenger when land at San Francisco to refuel; pending
§ 9/16/70	Sayed Seif el-Nasr	Egyptian Airlines	AN-24	Cairo/Luxor	Overpowered by security guard, 10 years prison
‡ 9/18/70	Bob Keesee	Bira Air Transport (Thai—Private)	Cessna	Domestic	Pretended to be movie scout; forced pilot to fly to N. Vietnam
* 9/19/70	Richard Witt	Allegheny	B-727	Pittsburgh/ Boston	Landed Philadelphia to refuel and deplane passengers; wanted Cairo but settled for Havana; had gun at throat of stewardess, which discouraged professional wrestler from trying to overpower hijacker
§ 9/27/70	Avraham Hershovitz Nancy Hershovitz	BOAC	VC-10	New York/ Tel Aviv	Arrested by security guards before boarding aircraft

DATE	NAME	AIRLINE	TYPE OF AIRCRAFT	FLIGHT PLAN	COMMENTS
‡ 10/10/70	Hassen Iahrani Ali Reza Mohammed Mahmoudi	Iran National	B-727	Tehran/Kuwait	Landed Baghdad; stewardess injured but hijackers apprehended
‡ 10/15/70	Brazinkas Koroyero Algedas Koroyero (J)	Aeroflot (USSR)	AN—24	Batumi/Sukhumi (Domestic)	Stewardess killed trying to block cockpit door; pilot, copilot, radio operator wounded; landed Trabzon, Turkey
* 10/21/70	7 men	LACSA (Costa Rican)	BAC-111	San Jose/	Refueled San Andres Island where 32 passengers deplane and 4 Americans held hostage in trade for release of 4 guerrillas held by Costa Rica
§ 10/27/70	Nikolai Ginlov Vitali Pozdeyev	Aeroflot (USSR)	AN-2	Kerch/Krasmodar (Domestic)	Landed Akliman, Turkey, site of U.S. radar monitoring station; ask asylum
* 10/30/70	L. Rosas	National	DC-8	Miami/Tampa/San Francisco	Had wife, 5 children with him

DATE	NAME	AIRLINE	TYPE OF AIRCRAFT	FLIGHT PLAN	COMMENTS
* 11/1/70	Felipe Larrazolo	United	B-727	San Diego/ Los Angeles/ Portland, Ore.	Refueled Tijuana, Mexico
‡ 11/9/70	6 petty criminals	Iran National	DC-3	Dubai/Bandar	Landed Baghdad
§ 11/9/70	Vitautas Simokaitis and wife, Grazina	Aeroflot	AN-2	Vilna/Palanga on Baltic Sea	Hoped to force plane to Sweden. Were overpowered and tried in Vilna. Man sentenced to death; wife, who was pregnant given 3-years. Husband commuted to 15 years in prison
‡ 11/10/70	1 man	Saudi Arabian	DC-3	Jordan/Saudi	Landed Damascus
* 11/13/70		Eastern	DC-9	Richmond, Va./ Raleigh, N.C.	
§ 12/21/70	Victor Lopez	Puerto Rican International	DeH Heron	San Juan/Ponce	Had bomb; was over-powered and landed safely at San Juan
* 1/3/71	2 gunmen	National	DC-8	Los Angeles/ Tampa/Miami	2 men, wives, children got off in Cuba

DATE	NAME	AIRLINE	TYPE OF AIRCRAFT	FLIGHT PLAN	COMMENTS
§ 1/10/71	Patrick E. Miranda	TWA	707	New York/Denver	Talked out of hijacking by crew; landed Denver; unclear where hijacker wanted to go. Sentenced to life in prison pending mental examination
‡ 1/22/71	Four Eritrean students	Ethiopian	DC-3	Bahr Dar/Gondar, Ethiopia	Landed in Libya
* 1/22/71	Gerald Grant	Northwest	B-727	Minneapolis/Washington	Hijacker originally wanted to go to Algeria. Armed with hatchet and bomb in briefcase
§ 1/23/71	Kim Sang-tae	Korean Air Lines	F-27	Kangnung/Seoul	Security guard shot hijacker; plane landed on beach; 2 hand grenades went off, killing co-pilot and wounding 13 passengers
† 1/26/71	Enrique Jimenez	Dominican Quisqueyana	L-49	Santo Domingo/San Juan	Hijacker overpowered when plane landed at Cabo Rojo

DATE	NAME	AIRLINE	TYPE OF AIRCRAFT	FLIGHT PLAN	COMMENTS
					for fuel. Hijacker reportedly used vial of colored water he said was nitro
‡ 1/30/71	2 Kashmiri men	Indian	F-27	Srinagar/Jammu	Landed Lahore, Pakistan; blew up aircraft 3 days later
* 2/4/71	1 Negro man	Delta	DC-9	Chicago/Nashville	
‡ 2/25/71	Chapin J. Paterson, 19-year-old draftee	Western	B-737	Ontario, Cal./ Seattle, Wash.	Reportedly wanted to go to Cuba; settled for Vancouver, B.C.
§ 3/8/71	Thomas K. Marston	National	B-727	Pensacola, Fla./ New Orleans	Youth boarded plane in Mobile, Ala.; pulled pistol; passengers allowed to leave aircraft; youth orders pilot to take off for Montreal. Pilot talks youth out of pistol; then, lands in Miami where youth surrendered to police

DATE	NAME	AIRLINE	TYPE OF AIRCRAFT	FLIGHT PLAN	COMMENTS
‡ 3/30/71	Six men	Philippine Air Lines	BAC-111	Manila/Davao City	Hijackers originally wanted to go to Peking; settled for Canton, China. Made refueling stop in Hong Kong. First recorded hijacking of plane to Red China
† 3/31/71	John Mathew (J)	Delta	DC-9	Birmingham, Ala./Chicago	Plane never left ground; youth talked into surrendering by ramp agent
* 3/31/71	Diego Ramirel Landeatta	Eastern	DC-8	New York/San Juan	
* 4/5/71	Carlos Hernandez	American Air Taxi	Cessna 402	Key West/Miami	
§ 4/13/71	3 youths	Midwest Airlines	Piper Navajo	Dauphin/Winnipeg	Youths wanted to go to Yorkton, Sask., but pilot landed at Winnipeg
§ 5/13/71	Eiki Kurosawa	All Nippon Airways	YS-11	Tokyo/Sendai	Wanted to go to North Korea. Threatened to blow up airplane. Pilot landed Tokyo with no incident

DATE	NAME	AIRLINE	TYPE OF AIRCRAFT	FLIGHT PLAN	COMMENTS
§ 5/17/71	1 man (S)	SAS	DC-9	Malmö/Stockholm	Threatened to kill girl friend; talked into giving up
§ 5/25/71	Steven M. Street	Air West	F-27	Redmond, Ore./Klamath Falls, Ore.	Demanded to be flown to Denver, Col.; arrested by police on trespass charge
§ 5/27/71	4 men, 1 woman	Tarom (Rumanian)	IL-14	Oradea, Rumania/Bucharest	Aircraft commandeered after takeoff from Orandea and flown to Vienna for fuel. Nose wheel damaged on landing at Vienna and hijackers finally surrendered to police
§ 5/28/71	James E. Bennett	Eastern	727	New York/Miami	Hijacked to Nassau after passengers let off at La-Guardia. Hijacker demands $500,000 ransom; upon landing at Nassau hi-

DATE	NAME	AIRLINE	TYPE OF AIRCRAFT	FLIGHT PLAN	COMMENTS
* 5/29/71	Ivan G. G. Landretta, 22	Pan Am	707	Caracas/Miami	jacker is over-powered and arrested. Aircraft, crew and passengers detained in Havana for nearly four days
§ 6/4/71	Glen Elmo Riggs	United	737	Charleston, W. Va./ Newark, N. J.	Wanted to go to Israel. Tried to get larger airplane upon landing at Dulles Airport in Washington, D.C. Overpowered by crew
§ 6/10/71	1 man (J)	Philippine Air Lines	BAC-111	Cebu City, Philippines/ Manila	Police, acting on tip, arrested youth at airport before he boarded aircraft
‡ 6/10/71	2 men (S)	Unknown	Unknown	Brazzaville/ unknown	Portuguese army deserters hijack plane at Brazzaville and order it flown to Pointe Noire, the Congo
§ 6/11/71	Gregory White, 23	TWA	727	Chicago/New York	First time passen-ger fatally shot

DATE	NAME	AIRLINE	TYPE OF AIRCRAFT	FLIGHT PLAN	COMMENTS
					on U. S. aircraft by hijacker. Hijacker wanted to go to North Vietnam. Passengers evacuated from aircraft O'Hare; plane then proceeded to JFK where hijacker was captured by FBI agents
† 6/18/71	Bobby White	Piedmont	737	Winston-Salem/ New York	Boarded aircraft parked at LaGuardia gate with only captain aboard and demanded to be flown to Cuba. Hijacker was overpowered by two skymarshals
† 6/29/71	1 woman	Finnair	DC-9	Helsinki/ Copenhagen	Woman with pistol wanted to go to Cuba; overpowered by crew
7/2/71	Robert L. Jackson Ligia L. S. Archilla	Braniff	707	Mexico City/ San Antonio, Tx.	44-hour, 7,500-mile hijack took aircraft to Monterrey,

DATE	NAME	AIRLINE	TYPE OF AIRCRAFT	FLIGHT PLAN	COMMENTS
					Lima, Rio de Janeiro and finally Buenos Aires where hijackers surrendered to police. Hijackers were given $100,000 ransom by Braniff officials in Monterrey. Couple to be prosecuted in LaPlata, Argentina
§ 7/11/71	Nelson A. Lopez Angel L. Rabi	Cubana	IL-14	Havana/ Cienfuegos	Two hijackers overpowered by crew; hand grenade goes off in scuffle, killing one passenger
§ 7/23/71	Richard A Obergfell, 26	TWA	B-727	New York/Chicago/ Los Angeles	Commandeered aircraft after takeoff from LaGuardia. Ordered plane return to LaGuardia; took stewardess hostage and drove to JFK in maintenance van. Was

DATE	NAME	AIRLINE	TYPE OF AIRCRAFT	FLIGHT PLAN	COMMENTS
					shot to death at JFK by FBI marksman while waiting for TWA 707 to be prepared to take hijacker to Milan, Italy. First time U. S. hijacker slain on ground during hijack attempt
* 7/24/71	1 man	National	DC-8	Miami/ Jacksonville	Stewardess and passenger sustained minor gunshot wounds

APPENDIX B

Antonov An-2	5
Antonov An-24	10
British Aircraft Corp. BAC-111	6
British Aircraft Corp. VC-10	2
Beech type	1
Boeing 707	24
Boeing 720	3
Boeing 727	46
Boeing 737	7
Boeing 747	2
Caravelle	5
Cessna type	9
Convair CV-440	3
Convair CV-600	1
Convair CV-640	1
Convair CV-880	5
Convair CV-990	1
Dakota type	1
Douglas C-46	2
Douglas C-47	3
Douglas DC-3	16
Douglas DC-4	12
Douglas DC-6 or -6B	8
Douglas DC-8 (includes Series "60")	27
Douglas DC-9	19
Fokker/Fairchild Hiller F-27	7
Fokker F-7	1
Hawker-Siddeley Comet IV	1
Hawker-Siddeley DH-ll4 Heron	1
Hawker-Siddeley HS-125	1
Hawker-Siddeley HS-748 (Includes Avro)	3
Hawker-Siddeley Trident 1C	1
Ilyushin Il-14	5
Ilyushin Il-18	3
Lockheed L-188 Electra	4
Lockheed L-49 Constellation	1
Nihon Aeroplane YS-11	4
Piper type	4
Vickers Viscount	5
Yakovlev YAK-13	1
Unknown	45

APPENDIX C

*Convention for the Suppression
of Unlawful Seizure of Aircraft*

PREAMBLE

THE STATES PARTIES TO THIS CONVENTION

CONSIDERING that unlawful acts of seizure or exercise of control of aircraft in flight jeopardize the safety of persons and property, seriously affect the operation of air services, and undermine the confidence of the peoples of the world in the safety of civil aviation;

CONSIDERING that the occurrence of such acts is a matter of grave concern;

CONSIDERING that, for the purpose of deterring such acts, there is an urgent need to provide appropriate measures for punishment of offenders;

HAVE AGREED AS FOLLOWS:

Article 1

Any person who on board an aircraft in flight:

(a) unlawfully, by force or threat thereof, or by any other form of intimidation, seizes, or exercises control of, that aircraft, or attempts to perform any such act, or

(b) is an accomplice of a person who performs or attempts to perform any such act

commits an offence (hereinafter referred to as "the offence").

Article 2

Each Contracting State undertakes to make the offence punishable by severe penalties.

Article 3

1. For the purposes of this Convention, an aircraft is considered to be in flight at any time from the moment when all its external doors are closed following embarkation until the moment when any such door is opened for disembarkation. In the case of forced landing, the flight shall be deemed to continue until the competent authorities take over the responsibility for the aircraft and for persons and property on board.

2. This Convention shall not apply to aircraft used in military, customs or police services.

3. This Convention shall apply only if the place of take-off or the place of actual landing of the aircraft on board which the offence is committed is situated outside the territory of the State of registration of that aircraft; it shall be immaterial whether the aircraft is engaged in an international or domestic flight.

4. In the cases mentioned in Article 5, this Convention shall not apply if the place of take-off and the place of actual landing of the aircraft on board which the offence is committed are situated within the territory of the same State where that State is one of those referred to in that Article.

5. Notwithstanding paragraphs 3 and 4 of this Article, Articles 6, 7, 8 and 10 shall apply whatever the place of take-off or the place of actual landing of the aircraft, if the

offender or the alleged offender is found in the territory of a State other than the State of registration of that aircraft.

Article 4

1. Each Contracting State shall take such measures as may be necessary to establish its jurisdiction over the offence and any other act of violence against passengers or crew committed by the alleged offender in connection with the offence, in the following cases:

(a) when the offence is committed on board an aircraft registered in that State;

(b) when the aircraft on board which the offence is committed lands in its territory with the alleged offender still on board;

(c) when the offence is committed on board an aircraft leased without crew to a lessee who has his principal place of business or, if the lessee has no such place of business, his permanent residence, in that State.

2. Each Contracting State shall likewise take such measures as may be necessary to establish its jurisdiction over the offence in the case where the alleged offender is present in its territory and it does not extradite him pursuant to Article 8 to any of the States mentioned in paragraph 1 of this Article.

3. This Convention does not exclude any criminal jurisdiction exercised in accordance with national law.

Article 5

The Contracting States which establish joint air transport operating organizations or international operating agencies, which operate aircraft which are subject to joint or international registration shall, by appropriate means, designate for each aircraft the State among them which shall exercise the jurisdiction and have the attributes of the State of registration for the purpose of this Convention and shall give notice thereof to the International Civil Aviation Organization which shall communicate the notice to all States Parties to this Convention.

Article 6

1. Upon being satisfied that the circumstances so warrant, any Contracting State in the territory of which the offender or the alleged offender is present, shall take him into custody or take other measures to ensure his presence. The custody and other measures shall be as provided in the law of that State but may only be continued for such time as is necessary to enable any criminal or extradition proceedings to be instituted.

2. Such State shall immediately make a preliminary enquiry into the facts.

3. Any person in custody pursuant to paragraph 1 of this Article shall be assisted in communicating immediately with the nearest appropriate representative of the State of which he is a national.

4. When a State, pursuant to this Article, has taken a person into custody, it shall immediately notify the State of registration of the aircraft, the State mentioned in Article 4, paragraph 1(c), the State of nationality of the detained person and, if it considers it advisable, any other interested States of the fact that such person is in custody and

of the circumstances which warrant his detention. The State which makes the preliminary enquiry contemplated in paragraph 2 of this Article shall promptly report its findings to the said States and shall indicate whether it intends to exercise jurisdiction.

Article 7

The Contracting State in the territory of which the alleged offender is found shall, if it does not extradite him, be obliged, without exception whatsoever and whether or not the offence was committed in its territory, to submit the case to its competent authorities for the purpose of prosecution.

Those authorities shall take their decision in the same manner as in the case of any ordinary offence of a serious nature under the law of that State.

Article 8

1. The offence shall be deemed to be included as an extraditable offence in any extradition treaty existing between Contracting States. Contracting States undertake to include the offence as an extraditable offence in every extradition treaty to be concluded between them.

2. If a Contracting State which makes extradition conditional on the existence of a treaty receives a request for extradition from another Contracting State with which it has no extradition treaty, it may at its option consider this Convention as the legal basis for extradition in respect of the offence. Extradition shall be subject to the other conditions provided by the law of the requested State.

3. Contracting States which do not make extradition conditional on the existence of a treaty shall recognize the offence as an extraditable offence between themselves subject to the conditions provided by the law of the requested State.

4. The offence shall be treated, for the purpose of extradition between Contracting States, as if it had been committed not only in the place in which it occurred but also in the territories of the States required to establish their jurisdiction in accordance with Article 4, paragraph 1.

Article 9

1. When any of the acts mentioned in Article 1(a) has occurred or is about to occur, Contracting States shall take all appropriate measures to restore control of the aircraft to its lawful commander or to preserve his control of the aircraft.

2. In the cases contemplated by the preceding paragraph, any Contracting State in which the aircraft or its passengers or crew are present shall facilitate the continuation of the journey of the passengers and crew as soon as practicable, and shall without delay return the aircraft and its cargo to the persons lawfully entitled to possession.

Article 10

1. Contracting States shall afford one another the greatest measure of assistance in connection with criminal proceedings brought in respect of the offence and other acts mentioned in Article 4. The law of the State requested shall apply in all cases.

2. The provisions of paragraph 1 of

this Article shall not affect obligations under any other treaty, bilateral or multilateral, which governs or will govern, in whole or in part, mutual assistance in criminal matters.

Article 11

Each Contracting State shall in accordance with its national law report to the Council of the International Civil Aviation Organization as promptly as possible any relevant information in its possession concerning:

(a) the circumstances of the offence;

(b) the action taken pursuant to Article 9;

(c) the measures taken in relation to the offender or the alleged offender, and, in particular, the results of any extradition proceedings or other legal proceedings.

Article 12

1. Any dispute between two or more Contracting States concerning the interpretation or application of this Convention which cannot be settled through negotiation, shall, at the request of one of them, be submitted to arbitration. If within six months from the date of the request for arbitration the Parties are unable to agree on the organization of the arbitration, any one of those Parties may refer the dispute to the International Court of Justice by request in conformity with the Statute of the Court.

2. Each State may at the time of signature or ratification of this Convention or accession thereto, declare that it does not consider itself bound by the preceding paragraph.

The other Contracting States shall not be bound by the preceding paragraph with respect to any Contracting State having made such a reservation.

3. Any Contracting State having made a reservation in accordance with the preceding paragraph may at any time withdraw this reservation by notification to the Depositary Governments.

Article 13

1. This Convention shall be open for signature at The Hague on 16 December 1970, by States participating in the International Conference on Air Law held at The Hague from 1 to 16 December 1970 (hereinafter referred to as The Hague Conference). After 31 December 1970, the Convention shall be open to all States for signature in Moscow, London and Washington. Any State which does not sign this Convention before its entry into force in accordance with paragraph 3 of this Article may accede to it at any time.

2. This Convention shall be subject to ratification by the signatory States. Instruments of ratification and instruments of accession shall be deposited with the Governments of the Union of Soviet Socialist Republics, the United Kingdom of Great Britain and Northern Ireland, and the United States of America, which are hereby designated the Depositary Governments.

3. This Convention shall enter into force thirty days following the date of the deposit of instruments of ratification by ten States signatory to this Convention which participated in The Hague Conference.

4. For other States, this Convention shall enter into force on the date of entry into force of this Convention in accordance with paragraph 3 of this Article, or thirty days following the date of deposit of their instruments of ratification or accession, whichever is later.

5. The Depositary Governments shall promptly inform all signatory and acceding States of the date of each signature, the date of deposit of each instrument of ratification or accession, the date of entry into force of this Convention, and other notices.

6. As soon as this Convention comes into force, it shall be registered by the Depositary Governments pursuant to Article 102 of the Charter of the United Nations and pursuant to Article 83 of the Convention on International Civil Aviation (Chicago, 1944).

Article 14

1. Any Contracting State may denounce this Convention by written notification to the Depositary Governments.

2. Denunciation shall take effect six months following the date on which notification is received by the Depositary Governments.

IN WITNESS WHEREOF the undersigned Plenipotentiaries, being duly authorised thereto by their Governments, have signed this Convention.

DONE at The Hague, this sixteenth day of December, one thousand nine hundred and seventy, in three originals, each being drawn up in four authentic texts in the English, French, Russian and Spanish languages.